THE MYTH OF THE SILENT WOMAN

SUELLEN DIACONOFF

The Myth of
the Silent Woman

Moroccan Women Writers

UNIVERSITY OF TORONTO PRESS
Toronto Buffalo London

©University of Toronto Press Incorporated 2009
Toronto Buffalo London
www.utppublishing.com
Printed in Canada

ISBN 978-1-4426-4005-4 (cloth)

Printed on acid-free, 100% post-consumer recycled paper with vegetable-based inks

---

Library and Archives Canada Cataloguing in Publication

Diaconoff, Suellen
  The myth of the silent woman: Moroccan women writers / Suellen Diaconoff.

Includes bibliographical references and index.
ISBN 978-1-4426-4005-4

1. Moroccan literature (French) – Women authors – History and criticism.
2. Moroccan literature (French) – 20th century – History and criticism.
3. Moroccan literature (French) – 21st century – History and criticism.
4. Literature and society – Morocco – History – 20th century.   5. Literature and society – Morocco – History – 21st century.   6. Women and literature – Morocco.   7. Feminism in literature.   8. Women in literature.   I. Title.

PQ3988.5.M6D52 2009   840.9'9287096409049   C2009-902571-X

University of Toronto Press acknowledges the financial assistance to its publishing program of the Canada Council for the Arts and the Ontario Arts Council.

University of Toronto Press acknowledges the financial support for its publishing activities of the Government of Canada through the Book Publishing Industry Development Program (BPIDP).

In friendship, I dedicate this book to Moroccan women

Contents

Acknowledgments ix

Introduction 3

1 Morocco's New Voices: Women Writers and the Socio-Political and Cultural Landscape 18

2 Mernissi and Scheherazade in Dialogue: Rereading and Acts of Subversion 37

3 The Myth of the Silent Woman 59

4 Transgressive Narratives 80

5 A Prison Narrative: Female Memory and a Woman Called 'Rachid' 105

6 The Female Body and the Body Politic: Harem and Hammam 125

7 Women and the City 150

8 Scheherazade's (Moroccan) Sisters: The Poetics of Identity and Democracy 169

Conclusion 194

Notes 199

Bibliography 241

Index 257

Acknowledgments

The genesis and elaboration of this book began when the US Department of Education Title VI program funded a two-and-a-half-year curriculum development project in international studies and the foreign languages at Colby College, entitled 'Focus on Fancophone Women in Africa and the Caribbean,' which I directed. Special thanks are due to Christine Corey of Title VI for her invaluable advice and encouragement.

Our Colby team was composed of colleagues from a half-dozen academic disciplines who had or developed teaching and research interests in either Africa or the Caribbean. I am particularly grateful to Guilain Denoeux, professor of government, for introducing me to Morocco and for proposing a student study abroad program focused on Morroccan NGO activists in support of women, and whose sites we visited in Rabat, Casablanca, Fez, and Marrakech.

It was this early exposure to the work of Moroccan women activists that spurred my pursuit of sabbatical funding from the US Fulbright-Hays Faculty Research Abroad program for in-country research. Bets Brown of the Colby Development Office provided me with much help and informed aid, plus a lot of laughs, in this respect.

My sabbatical months were spent largely in Rabat where I had close contact with the Center for Cross-Cultural Learning and its directors and staff members, including Abdelhay and Farah Moudden and their daughter Aya, my teachers of Arabic, Abdelilah and Bouchra, as well as Doha, Zhor, Larbi, Malika, and Samia.

Of course, I have been helped enormously by my husband Peter, who is always a great travel companion and who has been incredibly patient and supportive during the years it has taken to produce this book.

THE MYTH OF THE SILENT WOMAN

Introduction

Today the question of women in the Arab world is of particularly compelling interest in both the East and West, not only because woman has often been placed at the centre of the ideological conflict between the two poles, but also because, as Moroccan-American writer Laila Lalami has recently written, women are treated as pawns by both Islamist movements and Western governments, each seeking to actualize their own agendas. The result, she says, is that Muslim women have been saddled with the 'burden of pity,' by proponents on each side of the divide, with everyone wanting to speak on their behalf. [1] And yet, Arab women have their own voices, and have spoken out and challenged the notion of the silent and/or passive Arab woman for more than one hundred years, as Margot Badran and Myriam Cooke show in their collection *Opening the Gates: A Century of Arab Women's Writing*.[2] Now the latest group to take up the pen is Moroccan women, who, by implicitly or explicitly contesting hegemonic systems of thought in their writing, are engaging in a process of self-affirmation and cultural liberation, while demonstrating how the concept of decolonization may even be extended to the discursive practice of literature, formerly an all-male province.

Scarcely more than two decades old, this literature, whose existence has largely remained unexplored, is a remarkable presence in a deeply conservative country, which, for the last ten years, has embraced the rhetoric of democracy as part of its drive for modernization. In women's texts of fiction and non-fiction, these new writers seek to reshape society's expectations about gender identities, to reappraise traditional space and limits, and to deal openly with issues of sexuality, all in the name of democratic ideals. Such evidence suggests that they engage in literary writing so as to become protagonists *in* and not simply the spectators *of* history. And in so doing, they give the lie to the image of the silent woman.

To be sure, as Moroccan critic Abdallah Mdarhri Alaoui tells us, there is a long tradition of women's speech, beginning with the thousands of women poets from the Arabo-Andalusian Middle Ages, and continuing with successive generations of women, whose stories, proverbs, songs, and legends form a rich oral literature.[3] But it was not until the last decade of the twentieth century that a substantial number of Moroccan women writers began to publish novels and short stories, memoirs and semi-autobiographical texts, essays and criticism, books on history and Moroccan society, and thousands of journal articles in scholarly publications as well as in the popular press. Indeed, such literary output is substantial proof that the image of the silent woman is a myth.

Of course, a myth contains some element of truth. But it does not tell the whole story. Rather, it is the same story, told and retold, uncritically accepted, often despite evidence to the contrary. Which is why the aim of this book is to tell another story – that of Moroccan women writers who shatter taboos and transgress boundaries; who take issue with sexist assumptions and Orientalist stereotypes; who encourage women to make new roles for themselves in the body politic; and who remind their readers of women's courage and contributions during times of national political turmoil. In demonstration of Moroccan poet Abdellatif Laâbi's assertion that all writing is an act of resistance, these female writers expose the oppression of woman in society and boldly defend her right to individuality within the community.[4] At the same time that they write from within their *marocaineté* (Moroccan cultural heritage), they contest their social status quo and make what can be considered a feminist case for choice, which, in the Moroccan context, means their proposition that female identity is not a fixed essence but an individual realization of a self who will help create a new communal spirit. Indeed, the struggle toward, or, rather, to rewrite female identity has been central to Moroccan women's writing and corresponds not only to their typical Bildungsroman approach, but also to their drive for social justice and democratic ideals. Quite simply, they are persuaded that storytelling can initiate reform.

Though women's writing is often dismissed as telling only 'small stories' or being too autobiographical – typical accusations well known to scholars of European women's writing from earlier periods – in fact, neither charge accurately describes the work of Moroccan women writers, first, because the ostensibly 'small stories' of a single woman stand for many women negatively impacted by cultural or societal factors, and, second, because Moroccan women tend not to write autobiography as much as they write autobiographically, in the collective sense of women in the body politic. Therefore, if all writing is an act of resistance, such acts by women simultaneously bespeak a quality of resistance that is at once personal, political, and, dare I say, feminist.

Indeed, Moroccan women writers speak out on behalf of their sisters who represent the other face of women in Morocco, the more familiar image of the repressed and oppressed woman. In a nation of 30 million people, in which nearly a fifth of the population lives beneath the poverty line, and in which illiteracy continues to resist eradication, women, unsurprisingly, suffer disproportionately. Though there is widespread agreement among Moroccans that Morocco will achieve modernization only by integrating women more completely into the country's economic, social, and political fabric, a sizeable portion of women continue to be marginalized by patriarchal tradition and by rates of illiteracy that are 20 to 30 per cent higher than men's.[5] Women, who constitute 35 per cent of the work force, also suffer disproportionately from unemployment – a major problem, even for the well educated who are known as *les diplômés-chomeurs* (unemployed diploma-holders)[6] – and typically have a higher rate of unemployment than men, particularly in rural areas. A married woman can still be repudiated and cast aside by her husband, though with the revision of the Moudawana (Family Code) in 2004, the conditions under which a judge will sanction repudiation are more stringent. Women who are divorced or abandoned without the means to support themselves often find they have no choice but to roam city streets, with children in tow, begging in order to live. And in illustration of the devaluation of woman in society, a Moroccan mother could not, until spring 2006, pass her citizenship to her child if she had married a non-Moroccan. One of the worst abuses concerning women is the continuing practice of ignorant parents from rural areas who sell their daughters to become *petites bonnes* or indentured servants to bourgeois families in cities, a drama made worse if, through naivety or rape, the girl becomes a *mère célibataire* (single mother), often at the hands of an employer. It is estimated that over 100,000 women and girls from rural areas are employed as housemaids in urban areas.[7]

Yet at the same time, according to United Nations statistics, Moroccan women constitute some 50 per cent of university students and upwards of a quarter of university professors. Approximately 20 per cent of the nation's judges are female, women make up a third of all doctors, and a majority of Morocco's pharmacists are women. Women were granted the right to vote in the nation's first constitution of 1956, and in 2002 there were 34 women in parliament, Morocco being the only Arab nation to legislate that at least 10 per cent of its parliament be female. Since ascending the throne in 1999, Mohammed VI has appointed three women to senior positions in government, including a royal advisor. There are women filmmakers and CEOs, including the director of one of Morocco's major publishing houses, Le Fennec; women own and run businesses of all kinds – an article in the daily, *L'Opinion* for 6 March 2003 carried the headline 'Morocco counts 5000 women at the head of a business'; and every year, the woman's monthly periodical *Citadine* recognizes outstanding women in the areas of human rights, social action and development, the arts and culture, business, and media and communications. Nearly one quarter of Moroccan women are the primary wage earners in their homes. There are even female sports stars and a cab driver or two. And in terms of Islam, women have won new recognition, with the graduation in spring 2006 of the first class of *morchidates* – female religious guides.[8] While they will not serve in all the same ways as imams – leading prayers, for instance – they will be assigned tasks within the mosques, such as teaching the Qur'an or giving literacy lessons – a considerable break from the past.

Finally, there are hundreds if not thousands of women who actively participate in grass-roots democracy movements in the vast network of human rights and non-governmental organizations throughout the nation.[9] Their commitment to their sister citizens has led Moroccan journalist Aboubakr Jamaï, former editor-in-chief of the politically and socially liberal weekly *Le Journal hebdomadaire*, to call these women's work one of the best signs of 'hope for a genuine democracy' in Morocco.[10] Thus, while poor women and those in the lower middle classes enjoy neither power nor access to the powerful, and continue to occupy the ranks of the oppressed of society, there are scores of women who, by virtue of their education and relative privileges in society, are actively pursuing social justice and democratic reform.

Indeed, in the first decade of the twenty-first century, even some unexpected groups of Moroccan women are speaking up. Many in the West would be surprised to learn that in Morocco there are different kinds of feminism, from the liberal feminisms – in the plural – of most of the writers treated in this book, to the rise of Islamic feminisms – also in the plural. Indeed, one journalist has argued that Morocco has become within North Africa a veritable 'laboratory' of different kinds of

Islamic feminisms, ranging from the politically active, fundamentalist brand of Nadia Yassine, who leads demonstrations of proudly veiled women and who sometimes engages in street theatrics, such as when she marched with a bandage across her mouth in protest to feeling censored, to the kind of feminist 'jihadists' who argue that it is Islamic scriptural and legal scholars – all male – who used their religious and political authority to hand down laws that codified women's oppression and undermined the egalitarian reforms of the Prophet.[11] To trace in detail the variations of Moroccan feminism extends beyond the purview of this book, but it certainly does contribute to countering the myth of silent women.

It is therefore from within such dramatic contrasts and contradictions, as those described above, that Moroccan women's literature has taken shape during the last couple of decades. Writing in the 'house of the father,' so to speak – that is, from within the structures of patriarchy and in the shadow and memory of men's literary works – women writers have created a 'house of women' that has been opening new public spaces of discourse while contributing to the national debate on values and the future. They are proponents of women – feminists *à la marocaine*, or Moroccan-style feminists – seeking to produce opportunities for remaking female identity, while not denying their cultural heritage.

In this 'house of women,' I concentrate on the literary writing of a group of representative female writers, most of whom could be identified as cultural Muslims or secularist liberals and whose texts have been written in or translated into French or English. While reference will be made to dozens of texts and more than a dozen women writers, special attention is given to the writings of a handful of women, including Fatima Mernissi, Rajae Benchemsi, Siham Benchekroun, Leila Abouzeid, Nedjma, Yasmina Chami-Kettani, and Fatna El Bouih. Discussion of different aspects of their works may, therefore, appear in several chapters. For instance, chapter 2 is devoted to Mernissi and her 'dialogue' with Scheherazade, but there are also discussions of Mernissi's art and thinking in other chapters, placing her contributions alongside those of other Moroccan women writers. Specific examples include storytelling in chapter 3, her notion of the harem in chapter 5, and the role of Fez in *Dreams of Trespass* in chapter 7.

Furthermore, what is striking about this 'house of women' is that they have become 'un-silent' in what appears to be a foreign language. Because of this apparent peculiarity, I want to take the opportunity now to address the linguistic criteria of my selection. The question I hear from the reader is, 'Aren't you undermining the legitimacy of your project on Moroccan women's literary voices by studying only works in French, or sometimes English, when, after all, the official language of the country is Arabic?'

My answer is no, for the following reasons. The first, as stated by Moroccan literature professor Abdallah Mdarhri Alaoui, is that there is little difference of subject matter and approach between women writing in Arabic or in French, and both began publishing nearly at the same time.[12] My second reason is that by virtue of the fact that several languages of Morocco are oral, all Moroccan literature is written in a foreign language, either classical or modern Arabic or French.[13] A look at the linguistic map of the country reveals an uncommonly complicated situation since it shows languages that are spoken but not written, others that are written but not spoken, while still others, both spoken and written, are learned at school and adopted as the language of the writer's literature. Nearly half the population speaks one of the Berber languages at home, and the other half, Darija or Dialectical Moroccan Arabic, which is neither a written language nor a language readily understood by most of the world's Arabic speakers. At school, children study Modern Standard Arabic, much as they do French or Classical Arabic, though more intensively, to be sure. Newspapers are published in Modern Standard Arabic and television broadcasts in this language, but no one speaks *Fus'ha* at home. There are also newspapers and television stations in French, and of course the ubiquitous satellite dishes offer programming from both Europe (particularly France) and the greater Middle East. In other words, for nearly all of Morocco's citizens, there is no single mother tongue that is also written; the Dialectical Moroccan Arabic they speak is not (except for a few random attempts) written, and nearly the same is true for the Berber languages. As for the Arabic of the Arab world that Moroccans learn and read and understand from television or radio, it is not the common language of their daily communication. Therefore, it is not surprising that while Morocco is culturally and geopolitically affiliated with the Arab-Muslim context, the French language, a by-product of Morocco's colonial past as a French Protectorate from 1912 to 1956, continues to have a not insubstantial, even if somewhat reduced, role in the daily life of the country.[14] Whether or to what extent the French language endures in Morocco will be determined by history. Interestingly, the question does not arouse the same passions today as it did in the past, with the notable exception of writer Leila Abouzeid who accepts English more readily than French. In contrast to Abouzeid, a large majority of writers, in fact, applaud the plurilinguistic nature of the country, which, they believe, has given them access to greater riches and resources in their craft. In this respect, they adhere to the thinking of Abdelkébir Khatibi, one of Morocco's primary literary figures, who has often been quoted as saying that language belongs to no one and that, moreover, it is immaterial which language a writer uses, when the aim is to combat suffocating and alienating structures, whether their provenance is Western or Arab sources. The point is that to write in the language of the other does not ipso facto result in expressing the ideology of the other, nor in parroting the master, since it is always possible to subvert the language of the other and turn it against him.

Khatibi's views were strongly ratified at a 2007 book fair in Paris, devoted to books on and from the Maghreb, by the statements of writers and editors who all insisted that the old politically charged arguments about the colonizer's language and the guilt associated with using it are to a large extent dead.[15] At the fair, books in Arabic and French by writers from Morocco, Algeria, and Tunisia coexisted on an equal basis, and many of the writers lauded the benefits they had derived from a dual-language literary environment in the Maghreb. In an article by Professor Anne Roche of the University of Provence in support of an initiative taken by the French Ministry for Foreign Affairs to encourage all libraries associated with French cultural services in foreign countries to have a section devoted to francophone writers, she affirmed the aforementioned advantages, asserting that non-native French writers who have achieved high mastery of the language are actually enriching the language of France through an interactive play of images, metaphors, and syntactical expression from their own mother languages in contact with French.[16]

The enrichment Roche refers to can be seen in works by many of the writers featured in this book, and concerns what might be termed the *marocaineté* of their French – that is, specific lexical elements derived from the contact between languages and cultures and that form an important part of what makes reading a text in French by a Moroccan sometimes seem 'other.' What constitutes the 'different nature' of so-called Moroccan French in literary works pertains to the different nature of Moroccan culture and the necessity of the writer to convey that distinctiveness in a language – French – that does not provide easy and obvious equivalencies. Given the presence of several spoken languages native to Morocco – Dialectical Arabic (Darija) and three main Berber languages – plus of course the Modern Standard Arabic of the media and the Classical Arabic of the Qur'an, as well as the daily realities of an Arabo-Muslim culture, it is inevitable that a writer would simply be unable to find equivalents in the French language when dealing with such semantic fields as religion, popular culture, rural life and urban space, local commerce and education, and political life and law. This same writer could also be expected to draw upon the proverbs and sayings and images derived from a native culture with its own unique identity. Hence, a Moroccan writing in French about life in Morocco necessarily expands upon the resources of the language of Louis XIV, at times inventing expressions or new forms of words from French, at other times combining French and Arabic, or using words in new and novel ways.[17]

In *Etes-vous vacciné contre le harem?* Fatima Mernissi admits to taking liberties with the French language, arguing humorously that by writing 'une écrivaine' and 'une médecin' when referring to women and despite the fact that the gender of both words is masculine, she is doubtless angering 'le ministre Gaulois de la Francophonie.'[18] But then in one of her signature uses of humour combined with logic, she points out that the Minister would be wrong to feel that way, since the very spirit of internationalism implied by the concept of francophonie requires that others have the freedom to adapt and to modify and to recreate the French language.

Along this line it is apropos to note, as does Hervé Vernay, that of the more than two million people who speak French throughout the world, nearly two thirds are neither French nor Europeans.[19] Hence, as linguists have noted, the French language as it is lived and transformed on all five continents, is a living organism, evolving and expanding as it comes in contact with other cultures. Given this fact, it seems reasonable to state that Moroccans or other francophone authors do not write in a regional dialect of French, but, as Anne Roche said, they enrich the language by simultaneously proving that language, itself, is protean, at once multicultural and multiethnic.[20]

Why have Moroccan authors used another language besides their maternal tongue to write their texts? The question seems almost impertinent, given the number of obviously practical reasons. For example, Nadia Chafik, who writes in French and who was born in 1962, spoke Berber at home, and confesses that as a child she was unable to master Arabic because of the poor quality of teaching at her hometown school.²¹ Her father, therefore, taught her French, because he wanted her to attend a French mission school, whose quality of instruction he admired. Chafik subsequently received a doctorate in French studies at the University of Montreal, and returned to Morocco where she teaches and writes fiction in French. Similarly, Rajae Benchemsi, born in 1957, began learning French at age four, because it was the 'language of power,' and received a doctorate in literature from the Sorbonne. For her, French was never a foreign tongue 'unjustly imposed' on her, but rather a language that she feels 'inhabits' her, giving her full rein to express the poetry of her soul.²² Moreover, French, she has said, gives her the opportunity to 'reflect on [her] culture in a language that is not [her] mother language. It is an extraordinary liberation.'²³

If for Chafik and Benchemsi, French was a choice predicated on a father's decision about a daughter's education, for Fatima Mernissi, it is the second of two languages, the other being English, in which she always writes. Although Mernissi spent only a total of a half dozen years living abroad (in France, England, and the United States), returning permanently to Morocco some thirty years ago, she chooses to write in one of two non-native languages (depending upon an editor to make corrections), perhaps largely because the goal of much of her writing is intercultural exchange with a specific target audience.²⁴ Her best-known work, *Dreams of Trespass*, was originally written and published in English and later translated and published in French as *Rêves de femmes*. When she does write in Arabic, as with the original version of *Les Aït-Débrouille*, intended for a Moroccan audience, she has been quoted as saying that she wrote a kind of Arabic-French, using French words but incorporating the rhythm and structure of Arabic, in a reversal from her habit, when using English or French, of introducing Arabic words or expressions in italics, followed by a finely honed definition, intended to provide insight into Arab-Islamic culture.²⁵

On the other hand, another writer, Leila Abouzeid is adamant about not publishing in French given her accusation that it was French colonialism that put her father in jail where he was tortured, that the language of Napoleon was forced on her, and that, in her mind, French threatened to strip her of her native tongue.²⁶ Her disdain for French has perhaps lessened with the passage of years, but she continues to write in Arabic and to collaborate with translators so that her work can also appear in English.²⁷

So what about the future? Will French continue to be used by even a minority of writers in Morocco, or will it cede to the predominance of Arabic? The answer is not obvious. Young Maghrebian writers today are growing up in an era that not only prizes the intercultural but also sees it as a necessity. For many, French continues to be the language of success, a language whose acquisition is valued in that it permits them to look outward onto the greater world, and also equips them more practically in terms of employment – Morocco's primary trading partner being not another North African or Middle Eastern country, but France. Therefore, in the big cities of Morocco, French mission schools and degrees from France continue to carry substantial prestige; the French press and reading materials in French are readily available at French libraries and major urban newsstands in Rabat, Casablanca, and Marrakech. Opportunities for Moroccans to study at an English-language school are also available (though less numerous) with English-language high schools in Rabat and Tangier and the Saudi-financed university at Ifrane. Many well-to-do parents are said to want their children educated in French or English because of the greater economic opportunities they will have. In sum, Morocco's historical relationship to multilingualism perseveres and may even become stronger as the government seeks opportunities to strengthen ties with the economies of the West.

Aside from the aforementioned practical concerns that support the use of languages other than Arabic by Moroccans, there is the more 'philosophical' question as to whether an author can be 'authentic' if he or she writes in a language other than the mother tongue (presuming that it is also a written language). Today, the list of writers who were born in one language but choose to write in another is long, as Tahar Ben Jelloun both illustrates and declares, insisting that his Arab culture is no less strong simply because he lives in France and writes in French.[28] For a writer like Rajae Benchemsi, as well, the whole notion of being a Moroccan national but francophone writer is quite beside the point. In her view, the very idea of francophonie is a political concept, resulting from a major political failure to deal with French as a language rather than as a political tool.[29] Furthermore, for those who continue to live in Morocco but who seek to be read by the largest public, the choice between French and Arabic may well tip in favour of the former, because of a number of issues of literary sociology. These will be explored in chapter 1.

The bottom line, however, in response to why it is legitimate to write a book about Moroccan women's texts in French is that, quite simply, in the early years of women's literary production in Morocco, women did write in French. Whether or not French-language texts by women will continue to be produced in the future is not the point. The present reality is that there is a body of literature written in, or translated into, French for us to analyse, and that it completes and complements the discourses of other female authors writing in Arabic. What is of primary interest is what they are saying, not the language in which they say it.

So, why should we care about what the most recent group of Arab women writers have to say? The answer, obviously, is that if we are committed to a world of intercultural understanding and conversation, it behooves us to become good listeners and readers of Arab women's writing. Their texts will not only expand and nuance our understanding about who they are and how they experience their culture, but they will also challenge easy assumptions about Arab women's silence and passivity, and the quality of the information we receive in our media, whose underlying message of self-congratulation seems frequently to depend on over-sensationalizing Muslim women's repression. In addition, an acquaintance with Moroccan women's texts may help us to evaluate more judiciously the quality of Moroccan feminism, which partakes of certain qualities of Western feminism without remaining in thrall to it. Perhaps we might even be brought to deeper reflection on the problematic of assuming universal values with regard both to feminism and democracy. In the troubling and provocative politics of the early twenty-first century, these are surely compelling reasons.

In pursuit of the story of Moroccan women's writing, chapter 1, 'Morocco's New Voices: Women Writers and the Socio-Political and Cultural Landscape,' briefly reviews the literary history of men's writing in Morocco, which preceded women's writing by fifty years, and then describes the social and political factors that opened the door for women's writing, before discussing how key factors of literary sociology impact the chances of success for any writer in a developing country hampered by limited resources. In this respect, I take up the question of reading and readership in relationship to key issues of language, literacy, and the absence of a strong culture of reading both in the Moroccan educational system and the culture at large. I would argue that such issues of 'cultural geography' are in no way extrinsic, either to understanding the conditions in which Moroccan women write, or the challenges they confront, including the obstacles to publication. To map out the particular challenges facing the writer in a developing society is obviously of key importance. By exploring such factors from the outset, we will be free in subsequent chapters to study in greater detail both the formal aesthetics and ethical preoccupations of women writers.

Given that the preeminent woman writer in Morocco is Fatima Mernissi and that she has made the legendary storyteller, Scheherazade, a central figure in her writing, chapter 2 probes the parallel uses of subversiveness uncovered by rereading Mernissi and Scheherazade in dialogue. In this chapter, I examine the subversiveness of Mernissi's *Dreams of Trespass* in terms of two formal structures, genre and narrator, in order to underscore the basic hybridity of the text, a narrative non-fiction in the thin guise of fiction. In fact, this work is neither a memoir nor a novel, but rather a mosaic or montage that crosses borders, breaks rules, and not only narrates, but demonstrates the real poetics of trespass. For Mernissi, Scheherazade is the paradigmatic figure of the trapped woman, who by practising powerful speech saves her own life and changes the course of a nation, thereby becoming a model for Arab women in the contemporary world. That she succeeds by subversion is both a delicious irony and a lesson that Mernissi embraces in *Dreams of Trespass*.

Reprising the title of the book, chapter 3, 'The Myth of the Silent Woman,' seeks to 'prosecute' the myth and show how Moroccan women like filmmaker Farida Benlyazid, Yasmina Chami-Kettani, Touria Hadraoui, and Fatima Mernissi, have not only celebrated women's speech by giving an important role to women's stories and storytelling in their works, but have also, like the anonymous author of *L'Amande*, Nedjma, broken speech codes and violated sex taboos. As Nedjma says in her Prologue, she wrote her novel to make literature an arm of resistance, and 'to give back to ... women the power of speech confiscated by their fathers, brothers, and husbands.' Paradoxically, however, large numbers of Moroccans continue to repeat old shibboleths about women's silence and to lament their lack of speech, regardless of considerable evidence that women do speak and have spoken, even while risking the opprobrium of traditionalists in society. This chapter considers the many ways that women writers have recuperated women's speech within and by their texts through the art of storytelling.

In chapter 4, 'Transgressive Narratives,' I examine how, through the fictional mediation of eroticism and violence, whether sexual or intellectual, Moroccan women writers have defied taboos in order to give voice to silenced subjects and to assert a quality of freedom formerly thought to belong only to men. While looking at transgressions of flesh, gender, sex, and art that are inscribed in their fiction and that I study primarily in *L'Amande* and Benchemsi's collection of short stories,

Fracture du désir, I argue that these writers have produced works that not only incorporate unique voices, but also break barriers in terms of gender and genre. By using transgression in their writing, whether by subject matter or mode of writing, these women writers have profoundly challenged the stereotype of the silent woman as they have crossed the invisible lines of social and literary discourse and, in doing so, they mark the emergence of the female individual in the body politic as in literature.

Chapter 5, 'A Prison Narrative: Female Memory and a Woman Called "Rachid,"' deals with another form of transgression by a woman, Fatna El Bouih, who has written a memoir about her years as a political prisoner during the 'years of lead' under Hassan II in the 1970s, when dissidents were thrown into secret detention centres, where even women were tortured. In a compelling testimonial that describes scenes from her five years of incarceration and the miscarriages of Moroccan justice at the time, El Bouih tells a tale of suffering, yet also of triumph, to bear witness to the courage of women and to reinsert into the collective memory of the nation extraordinary examples of women's commitment to human rights. In the flood of prison literature written by former political prisoners since the late 1990s, El Bouih's memoir distinguishes itself by its powerful and poetic language, which simultaneously combines beauty and horror to serve as a memorial to the political convictions and ideals of another martyred woman, the young poet and political dissident Saïda Menebhi, who died as the result of a hunger strike undertaken in prison.

Moving from the body incarcerated in prison to two other iconic spaces associated with the female body in North Africa – the harem and hammam – chapter 6 uses the double prism, the female body and the body politic, to investigate how women writers exploit these spaces not only to deconstruct and reconstruct female identity, but also to delineate the very body politic itself. In both spaces, the female body is the site that women writers like Mernissi, Houria Boussejra, Rajae Benchemsi, and Siham Benchekroun use for exploring the cultural politics of gender and sexuality, and for developing their discourses on femininity and feminism. In revaluing the female body, these writers endeavour to lay the groundwork for reformulating female identity and individuality within the social body and prepare the way for introducing women into the spaces of the modern city.

Writing within, but also against, a literary tradition in which male writers in Morocco preceded them by nearly two generations, women writers tend to see space and place not as empty and gender-neutral concepts but rather as geographies permeated by relations of power. One of those geographies whose study has resulted in a wealth of interdisciplinary work is the city, which many scholars define as a field of experience that is different not only at different historical moments, but also for men and for women.[30] This being the case, the two sexes write the city differently in their texts, as Abdallah Mdarhri Alaoui has stated.[31] Through an inquiry into six texts and a half dozen different cities, chapter 7, 'Women and the City,' examines the ways in which the space of the city is a mediator of women's consciousness, or a physical location in which identity is shaped or contested. Through narrative use of the city, Mernissi communicates the theory and practices of colonial and gendered space (the Fez medina in *Dreams of Trespass*); Touria Oulehri reveals how the city becomes a parallel discourse of emotional turmoil and disruption (Agadir in *La Répudiée*); and Benchemsi uses the city as the palimpsest of cross-cultural identity (*Marrakech, lumière d'exil*). Two other writers incorporate the theme of travel to and from Casablanca to examine, through the poetic trope of the journey, the condition of women. In *Oser vivre*, Benchekroun uses the recurring motif of a train trip between two cities, to reveal a migration between places in the mind, as between places on the map, while Leila Abouzeid focuses on journeys of displacement and female identity in *Year of the Elephant*. I argue that through their geographies of gender, Moroccan women writers creatively contest the status quo and illustrate how space is not only an aesthetic tool but also a feminist one.

The final chapter, 'Scheherazade's (Moroccan) Sisters: The Poetics of Identity and Democracy,' analyses how two Moroccan women writers have used discursive practices in support of social reform, taking issue with the status quo and making a brief for a more equal society. They have conducted their polemic in large measure through the discourse of identity, endeavouring to show how female identity is neither fixed nor immutable, and, more broadly, pointing out that the way we talk about identity also reveals, as postpositive realists would say, a theory about the world. In consequence, issues of identity are concerned not just with definitions or redefinitions of the self, but of society. As a consequence, the challenge for the woman writer in an Islamic culture is often revealed as the need to carve out new ways for women to relate to the community while achieving a degree of individuality previously denied to them. In this respect, I study texts by Siham Benchekroun and Leila Abouzeid to scrutinize the ways that their female characters in fiction meet the challenge and, as a result, practise a unique form of feminism, at once consistent with, and in radical distinction from, their traditional culture.

Like Scheherazade, Moroccan women writers are storytellers with a purpose. While not all of them write for the same reasons – which accounts for the great variety of kinds of texts – most do, indeed, seek to tell stories to bring about results, that is, to advance the cause of women and to remake society. Writing within the structures of patriarchy and in the shadow and memory of men's literary works, Moroccan women writers are contributing to the national debate and to the creation of new public spaces of discourse in a demonstration of how literature can engage with a society under construction. A scant two decades old, their voices challenge simplistic conclusions about Arab women, feminism, and democracy, while they boldly lay assault to the myth of the silent woman.

1 Morocco's New Voices: Women Writers and the Socio-Political and Cultural Landscape

In 2006, when Morocco celebrated fifty years of independence from French colonial rule, Moroccan women had been publishing works of fiction for just over two decades. The first novel generally credited to a Moroccan woman, Halima Ben Haddou's *Aïcha la rebelle* – whose title may be an early augur of how women's writing would be seen – was published in 1982, whereas the first novel by a man, *Mosaïques ternies* by Abdelkader Chatt came out in 1932.[1] To explain that half-century lag between the initial forays into literary fiction by the two sexes, we need to consider not only the complex interplay of history, politics, and tradition that resulted in their different educational and social statuses, but also and especially a number of issues relative to the sociology of literature and the cultural landscape of Morocco. For our task is dual, both to understand the challenges of coming-to-writing in a country emerging from the long shadow of its colonial past, and to evaluate the early achievements of the first wave of women writers.

In pursuit of those two goals, this chapter will seek to uncover the conditions that have made it possible for women to come to writing, and to situate their creative output within the larger context of men's writing and the primary historical and political events characterizing the decades since independence in 1956. After this overview, the second half of the chapter will turn to the specific issues that had an impact on the sociology of the book in Morocco. This latter subject requires an investigation into what might be called the 'cultural geography' of literary production and consumption, involving issues of language and literacy, access to printed materials in bookstores and libraries, publishing, and literary criticism. In other words, a kind of 'mapping' of the culture of the book and of reading in a country that, according to one official at the Ministry of Culture, remains caught between a colonial past that it has not been able to leave behind and a technological future that it cannot afford.[2] Although such an inquiry into the realm of what in recent years has become known in academic circles as 'the history of the book' is always interesting – even if often ignored – when dealing with a country as culturally complex as Morocco, it becomes imperative. Only by understanding the network of the social, linguistic, and political factors that feed into the production of literature, I submit, can we attribute just value to the achievements of Morocco's newest voices – women writers.

Women's Writing and the Male Literary Corpus

Let us begin with a general assessment. Statistics reveal that a critical mass of female-authored works of fiction was finally achieved by the mid-1980s. Two decades later, in 2000, a team of researchers led by Moroccan professor Abdallah Mdarhri Alaoui catalogued more than 100 novels, stories, essays, autobiographical texts, and poems by more than sixty Moroccan women writers.[3] These figures are significant in view of the fact that in both the 1994 and 2000 editions of *Le Dictionnaire de littérature de langue arabe et maghrébine francophone* (Presses Universitaires de France) fewer than ten women of letters for the entire Arab world were mentioned, and not a single Moroccan woman, although the list included more than 400 men from the history of literature in Maghreb and the Machrek. At a time when women's voices had been validated in the West for several decades, the absence of Arab women in this French listing is puzzling. After all, as Mdarhri Alaoui points out, at the time, women were responsible for roughly 20 per cent of all the works published in French in Morocco, and 10 per cent of works published in Arabic.[4] Both feminists and conspiracy theorists might argue that women's work was being unconscionably ignored, especially in view of the fact that Margot Badran and Miriam Cooke's *Opening the Gates: An Anthology of Arab Feminist Writing* contains the names of nearly sixty female feminists from the Arab world, including three Moroccans – Farida Benlyazid, Fatima Mernissi, and Chaibia.[5]

As Mdarhri Alaoui also observes, whether Moroccan women wrote in Arabic or in French, they began publishing novels at about the same time and, furthermore, shared very similar themes and approaches. In other words, and the point is important, it is not the fact of one language versus another language that determines content but the quality of consciousness of the woman involved. It is not because she writes in French that the Moroccan writer finds it easier to take issue with her society; nor that she will be more 'conservative' when writing in Arabic. Both francophone and Arabophone women writers deal with the diminished role of women in their societies and both denounce the problems of women's condition in much more intensely personal ways than male writers, according to Professor Mdarhri Alaoui.[6] In this way, he further argues, women's writing differs from men's. While a woman may choose some of the same themes as males – the negative impact of repressive traditions on the social body, memories of the colonial past, critiques of abuses of power, personal aspirations for a modern life – women's writing is not a mere reproduction of men's, but carries a quality of emotional depth that he judges to be absent in male writing.

Still, since men's writing in Morocco has created many powerful voices, and because their names continue to be the ones cited when talking about Moroccan letters, it behooves us to recall both the figures and the key events of the postcolonial period that led to the development of a specifically Moroccan literature. At the same time, let us not forget the literal geographical and strategic location of Morocco and its role in both the history of the country and the making of the national character.

Located at the extreme western edge of the Arab world, as implied by the name *Al-Maghrib al-aqsa*, and at the literal and cultural crossroads between Europe and Sub-Saharan Africa, Morocco has been at the confluence of different civilizations, subjected to incursions by Phoenicians, Carthaginians, Romans, Vandals, Byzantinians, Arabs, Portuguese, French, and Spanish. As a result, it has been both the beneficiary and victim of all these cultures in contact and of influences from the outside, including various imperialist adventures, which together produced a complex sociolinguistic landscape and a wealth of cross-cultural legacies. If the original language of the country was Berber (which in one of its several forms is still spoken by some 40 per cent of the population), with Arabic being adopted only with the Arab conquest and implantation of Islam in the eighth century, Moroccan Arabic or Darija has shown an unusual openness to borrowings from other languages, particularly French, Spanish, and English, with which it has come in contact. It is for all these reasons that Morocco justly deserves its reputation as a 'plural personality,' and this helps to explain the diversity of the works and styles that characterize its literary corpus.

Those diverse voices can be traced from Morocco's first novel, Abdelkader Chatt's *Mosaïques ternies*, followed by Ahmed Sefrioui's *Le*

Chapelet d'ambre (1949) and *La Boîte à merveilles* appearing in 1954, and finally to the capital event in Moroccan letters, Driss Chraïbi's enormously influential *Passé simple*, also published in 1954.[7] This visionary novel marks a key rupture with the past and the entry of Maghrebian letters into modern consciousness. As its title implies, *Passé simple* is at once a novel that treats rebellion against the corrosive traditions of the past and anticipates the emergence of important social phenomena. In this sense, Chraïbi's novel is a precursor of the following two decades of intense effort by Moroccan male writers to renew literature and to create an authentic voice.

There are, thus, for many literary historians, two distinct periods in Moroccan literature, related to national history – the pre-Independence period that sought to affirm itself in reaction against the exoticism of French colonial literature, and the post-Independence period of innovation and engagement.[8] The long struggle for political independence and the triumphant return on 16 November 1955 of 'le sultan martyr,' the future Mohammed V, from his two-year, French-imposed exile in Corsica and Madagascar produced not only nationalist fervour and competition among rivals on the political scene, but also a renewed search for *marocaineté* or Moroccan identity in letters. What is particularly striking during this early literary period is the extent to which Moroccan letters were characterized by intense intellectual, political, and aesthetic interrogation, and the desire to create something new.

When Mohammed V died unexpectedly in February 1961, the young nation entered a difficult period of unrest and disillusionment, which would have a literary equivalent in the voices of a variety of male writers who sought to break from the past politically and aesthetically. In the 1960s, Morocco's writers issued literary manifestos, such as *Poésie toute* (1964) by Mohammed Khair-Eddine and Mostafa Nissaboury, and founded literary and culture journals, including the short-lived *Eaux-vives* in 1965. The key year, however, was 1966 when, in February, Abdellatif Laâbi, assisted by Mostafa Nissaboury, Khair-Eddine, Abdelkébir Khatibi, and Tahar Ben Jelloun, created *Souffles*, a left-leaning, bilingual cultural and literary periodical, which would have a far-reaching effect and also be banned in 1972. The years from the death of Mohammed V to the rise of the next king, who at age thirty-one became Hassan II, were particularly difficult, with a series of social, political, and economic crises in 1963 and 1965, attempts by political rivals on the left to gain power, the kidnapping and disappearance of Ben Barka in 1965, and attempts to overthrow the government by a military putsch in July 1971 and by General Oufkir in August 1972. Hassan II responded to these threats by increasingly repressive action, kidnappings and 'disappearances' of his opponents, who were sent to secret prisons and tortured, or even murdered,

Souffles was to have a profound influence not only on the literature of Morocco, but also on the evolution of literary production throughout the Maghreb. Its basic principles, as enunciated by its creators were, first, that literature was to be an arm in the struggle against reactionary structures, whether of Western or Arab provenance; and, second, that a new type of writing and aesthetic that abolished distinctions between genres and eschewed the reproduction of lived reality would distinguish these new works. The double engagement of content and form to achieve new aims is a classical expression of renewal in literature, particularly for those familiar with the literature of France. For the *Souffles* team, this artistic commitment would result in poems or novels whose meaning was derived not only from content but also from form expressed in structure and through linguistic means. Writers such as Laâbi, Ben Jelloun, Khair-Eddine, Khatibi, and later, Abdelfettah Kilito and Abdelhak Serhane put these principles to work to create rich and sometimes perplexing texts. As we shall subsequently see, nearly all early women writers would later embrace the principle of engaged writing, while later ones – such as Yasmine Chami-Kettani in *Cérémonie* (1999), whose aesthetics of poetic reenactment become as much the story as the slightly sketched narrative itself; or Rajae Benchemsi, whose short stories in *Fracture du désir* (1999) resemble multifaceted gems catching refractions of light – excel in renewing form through poetic imagery and imagination, combining both intellect and artistic sensitivity. For these latter two writers, politics takes a back seat to poetics.

In the 1970s, Moroccan literature, still the exclusive domain of men, reacted to the political turmoil of the period 1965–72, characterized by strikes, demonstrations, repressions and political trials, and the two attempts at a coup d'état in the 1970s, with a quality of engaged and powerful writing seeking to combat the political and social conformism of the times through texts of the avant-garde focused on exploring new ways of telling history as well as story. Abdellatif Laâbi and Mohammed Khair-Eddine were the soul of the movement. Their writing, exemplified by Laâbi's *L'Oeil et la nuit* (1969), became a veritable laboratory of experimentation, inventiveness, and creative abandon. Other writers such as Abdelkébir Khatibi and Tahar Ben Jelloun wrote with less overt political content but with a subversive poetics. The former produced

King Hassan II successfully asserted his hold on the throne through widespread repression and a secret police who arrested and jailed hundreds for political activities that ran counter to the king's autocratic rule (see chapter 5, 'A Prison Narrative' about Fatna El Bouih.) As a consequence, the 1970s were scarcely conducive to women seeking to empower themselves through writing, for, as Fatima Mernissi and other Arabist scholars tell us, every time an Arab political regime feels under pressure, there are negative consequences for Arab women.[12]

By the decade of the 1980s, however, there was a relative leavening in the politics of the nation, creating conditions more favourable to female self-expression. Some political scientists point to a successful restructuring of institutions by Hassan II after 1983, his growing commitment to allowing democratic change to take place, and the implementation of policies favouring economic liberalization, which resulted in the growth of an urban middle class.[13] Such liberalization was further advanced in the 1990s, which marks the real flowering of Moroccan women's voices. Joining with other Arab women writers, such as those anthologized in *Opening the Gates*, and their sisters in Algeria and Tunisia, Moroccan women began writing fiction dealing with themes of sexuality and the body, violence, unhappy relationships, and new formulations of female identity in the political community.[14] Since these are themes that contest the status quo, it is logical that without the liberalizations of the 1980s and especially the mid-1990s onward, it would have been largely impossible for them to mount even an implicit critique of society through writing.

A second factor that favoured the emergence of women's writing in Morocco, according to Mdarhri Alaoui, was the pressure applied by the international community, which linked funding of development projects to Morocco's progress in terms of human rights and the status of women. In 1995, the UN Conference on Women in Beijing adopted the slogan 'women's rights are human rights,' an unequivocal statement of international consensus that henceforth a nation would be judged according to the degree to which it included women in all aspects of life, from education, to politics, to cultural production. In Morocco, this has led some observers to feel that it became easier for women to publish because of governmental initiatives,[15] although that assessment was not ratified by others whom I interviewed at the Moroccan Ministry of Culture, or at the Service du Livre, the cultural arm of the French Embassy and an important partner in the publication of works in French in Morocco.[16]

On the whole, then, the cultural scene of Morocco in the 1980s and 1990s was a period in which traditional exclusions came under attack, particularly the long-entrenched one that denied women participation in the realm of the scriptural because it had always been linked to the sacred and hence to power.[17] Gradually more and more women began to challenge tradition through publication, and as they did so, it became increasingly apparent that the old image of the silent woman was fading. But were they being read? This is a question of an entirely different order, relating, on the one hand, to the status of the woman writer, and, on the other, to the status of fiction.

If, in the West, there is a gender gap in terms of reading, with women continuing to be the primary readers of the novel, as they have been since the origins of the genre, and if men seek out activities that confer status, which reading novels does not since it is considered a woman's genre, it is hardly surprising that in a country with a strong patriarchal tradition, like Morocco, women's works are neither widely read nor broadly recognized.[18] Indeed, I would argue that the diminished effect of Moroccan women's fiction on the wider public consciousness relates less to the quality of their texts than to the dual prejudice against both women and fiction. Indeed, as a new literature, Moroccan women's writing faces three specific challenges: misogynist prejudice against women as active producers of culture; disparagement of fiction as a genre; lack of substantial local readership because of high rates of illiteracy. Each of these points will be further addressed, in the pages ahead.

In sum, the relatively slow emergence of women writing for publication in Morocco can be explained by a large variety of reasons, from inadequate educational opportunities and low social expectations, to economic challenges and political dissuasion, to customary patriarchal attitudes. There are, of course, other factors that hindered the development of women's literature, and while many of them pertain equally to male writers, their impact on female writing is particularly strong, since women writers start from the traditional prejudice against female voices. In the next section, we shall look more closely at the factors that feed into the cultural landscape of books and reading and writing in Morocco.

Literary Sociology and the Culture of Reading in Morocco

I would like to begin looking at the question of the sociology of the book in Morocco with a personal experience. In spring 2003, when I was in Rabat on a Fulbright-Hays faculty research award to study women's writing, I conducted some informal research into issues of reading with the staff at the Center for Cross Cultural Learning where I was studying Arabic. My original objective had been to assess reader reaction to Moroccan women writers' fiction, but this goal had to be rethought when I was dismayed to learn that not a single one of my informants could give me the name of a Moroccan writer, aside from Fatima Mernissi, whom they knew largely because she was a colleague of one of the Center's directors and was frequently invited to lecture to American students who were studying for a semester in Rabat. Although the Moroccan staff members, young adults ranging in age from early twenties to mid-thirties, each had at least some university education, and one the equivalent of a doctorate, for the majority of them, reading – let alone reading fiction – was not an activity in which they engaged. The reasons they gave were instructive.

Aside from the universal lack-of-time excuse, many of my informants pointed to an educational system that they charged with turning students away from reading. Bouchra, then a twenty-eight-year old Arabic language teacher, who had four years of university education, told me, 'You have to understand that there is a problem with reading here,' to which I responded, 'Yes, I know, illiteracy.' But she shook her head and told me, 'No, that's not it. Most people don't want to read; they are not encouraged to read, and in fact our educational system turns us off reading. In school, we are so stuffed full of books that have to be memorized that we don't want to have anything more to do with books.' It was an explanation that I heard time and time again.

Still, Bouchra felt guilty about not having a positive feeling about reading and not doing more reading, because she indicated that reading was 'a moral good.' When I asked for specifics, she acknowledged that one of its benefits might be to teach her about her 'rights, specifically as a woman.' But two factors discouraged her: the cost of books (between three and five dollars, at the time), which she could not easily afford, and the lack of ready access to library books. At the Center, there was only a small library, and most of the books were in French or English, which meant that without sufficient skills in those languages, reading would be a chore. The concept of reading for pleasure did not seem to be a part of her thinking, but when I pursued this line of discussion and suggested different types of reading – for knowledge or for pleasure – she said that she thought an ideal arrangement would be 70 per cent for knowledge, and 30 per cent for pleasure.

When I queried her about how to categorize a work of fiction like Siham Benchekroun's *Oser vivre* that I described as chronicling the coming-to-feminist consciousness of a young Moroccan woman and her loss of romantic illusions, Bouchra agreed that fiction might, in fact, be seen as offering both knowledge and pleasure. But, she confessed, it was a new idea for her.

In fact, Bouchra had articulated for me the virtual double leitmotif in my discussions with others: reading was a good thing to do because it would improve their knowledge or because it was 'good for you,' but time spent reading books should be recompensed by enhancing their chances of finding a job or a better job, in an economy that has chronically been plagued by very high rates of unemployment.[19] Indeed, many felt that their society had 'let them down.' They had gone to university and had acquired book learning, but had had a very hard time finding a job. The result, Zhor said, was that she felt betrayed; her country had broken faith with her. Her disillusionment was particularly poignant because she described how her illiterate mother had encouraged her to do 'serious' reading (not reading for pleasure, which was dismissed as irresponsible daydreaming), and Zhor had, in fact, completed a university degree in the sciences, and then spent fruitless years looking for a job, preparing additional certificates, before finally securing a job having nothing to do with her education and obtained only through the intercession of a sympathetic relative.

By means of such informal interviews, and in conjunction with my attendance at meet-the-author talks at the bookstore, Kalila wa Dimna in Rabat, I came to understand the lack of existence of what I would call a 'reading culture,' coupled with the virtual absence of value attached to reading fiction – aside, of course, from a minority specialist elite, most of whom teach in universities.[20] I noted that general audiences at the bookstore talks were always more interested in historical or sociological or political issues than in the purely literary, even when well known literary personages such as Abdellatif Laâbi or Tahar Ben Jelloun were present. Perhaps this should not have been surprising, given the questions posed about the future of fiction, even in the West, and how much energy people in a developing country have to expend on 'the real and now,' which may explain why they seem to prefer non-fiction. Perhaps the woman writer, Rachida Yacoubi – author of the autobiographical work *Ma Vie, mon cri* (1998), and of *Mon Défi* (2003), the latter dealing with the Moroccan prison system and her twenty-two-day jail sentence for a crime she maintains was never identified by the authorities – best caught the sense of the literary versus the sociological/political in a developing country when she explained at her March 2003 talk at Kalila wa Dimna why she did not much like the word *liberté*, preferring instead *droits*, because, as she said, one can be free but have no rights. Could it be that for many members of the audience at those author talks, literary fiction was a 'decorative' way of dealing with *liberté*, while non-fiction carried the immediacy of real-life concerns with *droits*?

In light of this preliminary exposition on the challenges faced by fiction in search of readers and, more specifically, by Moroccan women writers seeking a toehold in the literary world, let us now turn to an examination of the all-important issues of literacy and language, access to book culture and libraries, publication realities, and the status of literary criticism in the Moroccan context. As we shall have opportunity to note, each of these factors plays a role in explaining why the literary texts of Morocco are often described as *orphelins de lecteurs* – bereft of readers.

Two issues are key: literacy and language. In spite of massive efforts on the parts of NGOs and the Moroccan government, Morocco continues to suffer from an alarmingly high rate of illiteracy, with some 40 per cent of the entire population in 2006 unable to meet even the minimum standard of literacy recognized by most education experts.[21] Not surprisingly, far more women than men are illiterate, with rates of illiteracy in rural areas sometimes reaching between 60 and 90 per cent.[22] To be sure, questions of determining and assessing literacy are complex. While the simple dictionary definition of literacy concerns the ability to read and write, many literacy advocates and international organizations like the World Bank and UNESCO postulate the primacy of practical, functional literacy, meaning the ability to read, write, speak, compute, and solve problems at levels of proficiency necessary to and concomitant with the specific needs of an individual to function at home, work, and in the community. Thus, functional literacy is a dynamic concept, subject to national cultural and individual contexts and changing over the course of a life.

Further complicating the issue of determining literacy is the fact that in practical application, literacy rates are whatever a country says they are, whether that be the per cent of the population having completed one or more years of schooling, or the score received on a nationally administered exam. Nonetheless, governments throughout the world and most international funding organizations continue to believe that basic literacy goals involving reading, writing, and elementary math skills are valuable not only for achieving more empowered individual lives, but also for the economic development of a nation as a whole, since it is generally assumed (though sometimes hotly debated) that rates of literacy are directly related to economic development as well as to issues of poverty and health, gender equality, human rights, and the very ideas of democratic political participation.[23]

Nonetheless, it would seem that everyone, including the Moroccan government, agrees with Ali Sedjari, professor of law at the universities of Rabat and Paris I, who writes that 'in a society in which illiteracy and ignorance dominate, development is merely wishful thinking.'[24] And most would have no quibble with writer, anthropologist, and psychiatrist, Ghita El Khayat, who calls the high rates of illiteracy in Morocco 'a national scandal.'[25] Perhaps fewer, aside from the intellectual elite, would also agree with cultural commentators like Daniel A. Wagner, Jack Goody, and Paulo Friere, who believe that the state of a society is revealed through its relationship to printed culture, that reading has the capacity to promote citizenry, and, as a consequence, that democracy and reading are mutually supportive.[26] But there is no doubt that basic literacy is clearly linked to the empowerment of the individual. We have only to think of the person who cannot read a street sign, a telephone book, or a simple letter, to understand how reading and self-empowerment are interrelated. Indeed, one of the cruellest scenes in Moroccan literature is of the illiterate woman in Houria Boussejra's short story, 'Saadia,' who receives a letter and must ask an outsider, the postman, to read it to her, an ultimately humiliating experience since it is a letter of repudiation from her husband.[27] That image of stark vulnerability because the woman cannot read constitutes one of the most affective and compelling arguments in favour of combating female illiteracy – and it appears in a piece of fiction.[28]

Adding to the daunting problem of literacy is the complexity of the sociolinguistic situation and the status of several different languages that characterize the Moroccan landscape. Arabic is the official language of the land, but the languages of the street are Darija, a Moroccan dialect of Arabic, or one of the dialects of Berber (some 60 per cent of the population claims Berber heritage). This is why sometimes Moroccan themselves underscore the issue of identity, asking just who *are* Moroccans, what is their cultural (historical, geographic, and linguistic) identity? Are they *one* people, or many people? If upwards of one half of the nation is illiterate, is it even possible to talk about reading and writing literature, they ask? Who, indeed, is a writer writing for when so many are unable to read in any language? And, furthermore, what does it mean for Moroccans to write in Modern Standard Arabic, which is not their spoken language? Similarly, what does it mean to read in a language you do not speak, and to speak in a language that is not written? Finally, is it true that Darija, the language of the domestic sphere but not of power, is looked upon as a devalued women's language in opposition to Modern Standard?[29] Educated Moroccan Muslims know the language of the Qur'an, which is Classical Arabic, somewhat Shakespearean in effect on the contemporary ear, and read newspapers in Modern Standard, but discuss their contents in whichever language they speak at home. Parliamentarians address their colleagues in Modern Standard, but as debate proceeds may revert to Darija.

And then there is French. For fifty years French was the language of the occupier, and then, following Independence, the primary language of the educated and professional classes. Even today when educational reforms have emphasized the use of Arabic in secondary schools, French continues to be considered by many to be the 'language of success,' since it is the language of international commerce with Morocco's largest trading partner, France, and the language that reaches outside the borders of Morocco.[30] A French education, either in a French mission school in Morocco or in France, and French certificates and diplomas are still highly valued. Doctors and lawyers and pharmacists and aestheticians proudly display their certifications from courses of study in France and French universities. French continues to be the language of instruction in the sciences, technology, and medicine in Moroccan universities. In the big cities, French is used on street signs, sometimes alongside Arabic, and, as the language of prestige, is featured on billboards and in much advertising. It is not surprising, therefore, that members of an educated urban elite will, in informal conversation, slide easily between Darija and French within the same sentence.[31] There are French libraries or cultural centres in the big cities with large collections of French-language books (and special sections for children and adults), reference materials, journals, and periodicals published in Morocco or in Europe. For a small annual fee, library patrons can check out books, videos, and CDs. Thus, Moroccans who know French and who live in the major cities have a wealth of cultural materials at their disposal in the well-stocked and open-access libraries that also sponsor lectures, art shows, films, and other cultural activities – all in French.[32]

Free public libraries for patrons of Arabic, on the other hand, do not exist with anything like the same richness of opportunity, and even most public schools do not have a school library. An article in the woman's magazine *Citadine* quotes Fadoua Maroub, president of a newly created Moroccan Association for the Support of School Libraries, who says that even when a school library does exist, it is often in 'disastrous condition' and does not encourage pleasure in reading.[33] And yet, Madame Maroub noted, schools can be 'agents of change,' whose mission is to contribute to the democratization of society – which, she suggests, is the proper role of books and reading and school libraries. Her concern with the status of school libraries is echoed throughout the Moroccan press in article after article outlining the crisis of reading and its close relative, the crisis in publishing, both of which negatively impact the present status and future prospects of the country. The lack of a reading culture is exposed by social critics and the daily and weekly press, analysed by scholars such as Abdelali El Yazami, lamented by book professionals like Souad Balafrej, owner of the bookstore Kalila wa Dimna in Rabat, deplored by Leila Chaouni, Director of Editions Le Fennec, and ascertained by observers of any Moroccan café where men wile away the hours over cups of coffee or tea, but rarely over a newspaper. El Yazami is one of the few who has conducted an analysis of reading in Morocco, and while his book deals primarily with readers of French, and very select ones at that, including teachers and librarians, that fact does not vitiate its usefulness, since the factors that he identifies as contributing to the absence of a strong culture of the printed word are ratified by more casual commentators, as well.[34] El Yazami's list of factors that make it difficult to become a reader in Morocco includes the cost of reading materials,[35] the scarcity of well-stocked public libraries, a lack of school libraries, inadequacies in the educational system that focuses on memorization or whose teachers may not know how to instil a love of reading, the paucity of attractive reading material for young children,[36] and the almost non-existent role of reading in the nation's cultural values. The publisher Leila Chaouni states the case succinctly, 'Reading is not a habit in Morocco. It isn't a part of our education. As long as reading is not taught as an integral part of daily life, the situation will remain unchanged.'[37]

To say that Morocco does not have a culture of reading is not, of course, tantamount to saying that it does not have culture, or for us to value only print culture over all other forms of cultural expression including oral culture.[38] But it is to say that without a developed print culture, it is not a fully developed modern culture. As Paulo Friere observes in *Pedagogy of the Oppressed*, a culture of silence can ensue in a society when people are without practice or training in critical awareness and when large numbers are incapable of looking critically at the world in dialogical encounters with others (13). His point, of course, is that those who learn to read and write come to a new awareness of selfhood, and may begin to look more critically at society and to become more interested in participating in or acting to transform that society. In that sense, education – in which reading is a key ingredient – can become a potentially subversive force, both in an individual life and in the life of a nation. In terms of gender, when a woman can read, she relates to public space differently: she is freer because she is no longer dependent on the intercession of others; she can travel because she is more confident about being able to read signs and find her way; she is more independent to make up her own mind.

And interestingly, she is also being a good Muslim. Tahar Ben Jelloun writes in *L'Islam expliqué aux enfants* that one of the *hadiths* of Mohamed enjoins Muslims to knowledge, 'From the cradle to the grave, seek knowledge, for whosoever aspires to knowledge truly loves God.'[39] Accordingly, Ben Jelloun says that the Prophet considered both the acquisition and teaching of knowledge as important as two of the Pillars of the Faith, fasting and daily prayer. The woman lawyer and author Fadela Sebti (*Moi, Mireille lorsque j'étais Yasmina*, 1995) likewise points out that the first five verses of chapter 96 of the Qur'an, which represent the first revelation that Mohamed received, sing the praises of learning as the instrument of civilization and culture. The sacred book enjoins all human beings, Sebti says, to learn all they can and contribute to the evolution of human civilization.[40] Moreover, *ijtihad*, or the struggle of the mind for the truth, requires reasoning, to which reading contributes significantly.

Such teaching about the value of reading is something that Moroccan women novelists sometimes include implicitly in their narratives, as when they incorporate the reading heroine. Novelists like Souad Bahéchar (*Ni Fleurs, ni couronnes*, 2000) and Touria Oulehri (*La Chambre des nuits blanches*, 2002) validate reading and the woman reader in their novels, showing that beauty in a woman – similar to how Fatima Mernissi describes Scheherazade – relates to the quality of her mind just as much as it does to her facial features. Of course, the portrait of the reading woman in the novel is like preaching to the choir, but her promotion is, nonetheless, important for the ideal of the validated, modern reading woman that the writer wants to convey.

At the national level, the issue of reading is deemed so serious that in spring 2003, the Moroccan Ministry of Culture announced a new government initiative to create 10 million readers by 2010, an endeavour that critics have likened to a similar one from the Ministry of Tourism, which also set a goal of attracting 10 million tourists by 2010. Some tongue-in-cheek observers suggested at the time that perhaps those same 10 million tourists might become Morocco's target 10 million readers.[41] According to a governmental plan spearheaded by the Ministry of Culture in spring 2003, 20 million *dirhams* had been allocated for promoting books and reading. Seventeen million were to be directed toward development of reading spaces, or libraries, while the sum of 3 million (roughly $300,000 at the time) was destined to help support publishing houses, which, like authors and bookstores, lament their inability to make a living when they are unable to count on being able to sell any more than 1000–2000 copies of a book. To be sure, announcements of 'major, new initiatives' are a constant of governmental ministries who wish to give the appearance of being active. The official at the Ministry of Culture, with whom I spoke, acknowledged that the creation of new readers consistent with the target figure would not only require massive social change, but also the participation of a large number of other ministries (of education and Islamic affairs, plus ministries responsible for construction), and that each would have its own different sense of national priorities.[42]

While the paucity of readers described above may suggest that Moroccan women would do well to write in Arabic because their books could be circulated in the Arab world, particularly in the greater Middle East, the fact is, as University of Rabat professor of law and political science Abdelhay Moudden told me, trade and financial relations with other countries in the Arab world are either so insufficient or non-existent that this is not really an option.[43] There is, therefore, no dissuasive reason for a writer who wishes to be read at home and abroad *not* to publish in French. Let us recall, once again, that given the orality of languages in Morocco, spoken but not written, the *whole* of Moroccan literature is written in a foreign language. Hence, the idea of producing a national literature in a foreign language is not as strange as it might first appear, in that *all* literary production in Morocco is written in a language that is foreign in some way. In other words, French is not for Moroccans as much of a foreign language as, say, for instance, it would be in Middle Eastern countries to the east. Given the complexity of the language problem and the small number of readers, some booksellers and publishers in Morocco think that their future viability depends upon translation, while others question whether this will significantly increase revenues without an equal increase in readers in Morocco.

While the primary purpose of creating more readers relates to the nation's need to combat illiteracy, it is also intended to have an economic benefit for publishers and for booksellers. And of course for authors, whose books need to be published and marketed. In this respect, new writers face a particularly difficult environment in which to make their voices heard and to find an audience.[44] One of Morocco's two largest publishing houses, Eddif, ceased publishing in the early 2000s, which left Le Fennec, headed by Leila Chaouni. Other publishers include Marsam, Tarik, Afrique-Orient, and some small, independent publishers including Aïni Bennaï, established by Ghita El Khayat, largely, it seems, to publish her own works. Most writers prefer, if at all possible, to publish in France (for instance, L'Harmattan, Actes Sud, Seuil) because their books will be better marketed and reach a potentially larger audience. However, if they wish to see their books sold in Moroccan bookstores at an affordable price, they must seek a publisher with a cooperative arrangement between France and Morocco, so that the books can be priced according to different market realities in each country. Some writers, perhaps those without contacts in the publishing world, decide to self-publish, and then distribute their book themselves to booksellers, returning periodically to see how many copies have sold. This was how the collected *Poèmes, écrits, lettres de prison* by the martyred Saïda Menebhi was published some years after her death by her family and a private press, Editions Feedback. In addition to being sold at bookstores and newsstands, books are also offered for sale by peddlers who spread out their wares, including magazines, on the sidewalk.

Both the Service du Livre associated with the cultural services of the French Embassy and the Moroccan Ministry of Culture offer competitive subventions to a handful of books each year. Typically, the book will already be in the hands of one of the publishers who represents it to a jury at the Embassy or Ministry of Culture. The subvention, made directly to the publisher, helps produce a book that may have only a few hundred readers, at best. When a book, like Fatna El Bouih's *Une Femme nommée Rachid*, receives a subvention from the Service du Livre, it carries the inscription 'Publié avec le concours du Service de Coopération et d'Action Culturelle de l'Ambassade de France au Maroc' on its title page, along with the name of the publisher, in this case Editions Le Fennec. When I spoke with the director of the Service du Livre in 2003, French writer and playwright Marie Redonnet, she indicated that no particular preference is given to women's titles, and that in her estimate it does not appear that women have any more difficulty in getting published than their male texts of great culture and intellectual power that have been said to resemble an exotic dance (*La Mémoire tatouée*, 1971, and *Le Livre du sang*, 1979), while Ben Jelloun cultivated mystery, legend, and 'the strange' in works like *Harrouda* (1973), *La Prière de l'absent* (1981), *L'Enfant de sable* (1985), and *La Nuit sacrée* (1987), for which he won the coveted Goncourt literary award.

As the decade of the 1980s opened, the function of the writer was being redefined, from the collective voice in search of utopia to the individual voice of the author face to face with his society. Abdelhak Serhane, for instance, wrote scathing texts of disillusionment about a society ravaged by moral, sexual, and material misery and corruption. He denounced in the most virulent of tones the abuses of a patriarchal system in *Messaouda* (1983) and *Les Enfants des rues étroites* (1986), and later in 1995 with the short stories of *Les Prolétaires de la haine*. It was also in this decade and in this literary climate that women began writing and that Halima Ben Haddou published *Aïcha la rebelle* in 1982.

If it had taken several decades more than their male counterparts for women to find voice, the reasons can be found not only in gender oppression but also in colonialism. In 1950, six years before Independence, there were a mere forty Moroccan university graduates – all men – and just a handful of six girls who had graduated from secondary school.[9] Fatima Mernissi remembers that when she enrolled at the University of Rabat in 1960, four years after Independence, she was one of only twenty-seven females among the 1000 students.[10] (Some forty-seven years later, there would be 250,000 students in thirteen universities.) Obviously, then, a primary reason for the absence of females among the nation's early published writers is that few had the necessary education and exposure to writing and literature.

For those few like Mernissi who did get to attend the university, it was an exciting opportunity. Christine Daure-Serfaty recalls their enthusiasm for knowledge and eagerness to find their place in the new nation.[11] Interestingly, magazine photographs from that period show smiling university students milling on campus, the young Moroccan women resembling their chic counterparts in France, with bouffant hairdos, wearing high heels and skirts that fall just to the knee, without any form of headdress or even the Islamic head scarf, in stark contrast to female attire some fifty years after Independence,

This vanguard of young female students would, however, in the following decade of the 1970s face major obstacles, particularly in the politically repressive period known as 'the years of lead,' during which counterparts. The challenge, instead, comes in the considerable problem of finding a substantial audience of readers. Unlike in Tunisia where a literary prize, the Prix Didon (named for the founder of Carthage), was established for women's writing, there are no national literary prizes for women in Morocco.[45]

A typical press-run for books published in Morocco is between 1000 and 3000 copies, and a book that sells as many as 5000 copies – perhaps even much less – is considered a best-seller.[46] Ahmed Marzouki's *Tazmamart: Cellule 10*, copublished by Tarik and Paris Méditerranée in 2000, was a huge best-seller, going into multiple editions, On the other hand, Malika Oufkir's *La Prisonnière* (Grasset, 1999), recounting her family's twenty-year incarceration following an attempted coup d'état by her father, General Oufkir, in 1972, never appeared on bookshelves in Morocco, though it was available on the clandestine circuit. For Ghita El Khayat, the fact of small press-runs in a country of nearly 30 million people in which roughly half *are* literate, portends ill, not only for the future of the nation, but also for the quality of work that writers, themselves, will produce.[47] She asserts, 'By jumping with our feet tied into the realm of knowledge and sensibility, we remain in the superficial, the imitative, and mediocrity.' In other words, the benefits of reading and seeing how other authors have framed their narratives and developed their art would aid would-be writers who otherwise stay enclosed in their own insular circles, repeating themselves. It is a warning also issued by writer Nadia Chafik, who enjoins women, in particular, to avoid repeating clichés about women's conditions in their writing.[48]

Once the book is published, unless it is by one of the well-known male writers, it has to struggle for recognition. In Morocco, women's works are often dismissed by erstwhile critics on the street as being excessively self-referential or propagating a negative view of Morocco because of the implicit criticisms of society and the presentation of female protagonists who suffer from social injustice. Many, even those sympathetic to women's writing, might agree with Marie Redonnet that Moroccan women writers have yet to produce their first chef-d'oeuvre. But others, including Tahar Ben Jelloun, who often reviews women's writing from his home in France, admire specific works. In Morocco, various *littérateurs* like Abdellatif Laâbi speak respectfully and encouragingly of women's works, while university professor and critic Abdallah Mdarhri Alaoui is a sympathetic reader who fairly judges the value of women's works, justifying their consideration apart from men's literary production, because otherwise they would be 'overwhelmed' in terms of sheer numbers.[49] Other literary notables, such as Abdelkebir Khatibi and Abdelfettah Kilito, have not addressed women's writing in a critical fashion, while writer, critic, and journalist Fouad Laroui believes that some of the most interesting intellectual production today is being produced by women from the Maghreb.[50] Women's writing, both fiction and non-fiction, is often the subject of university conferences and round tables, and of course many professors of literature publish articles in university publications that result from these conferences. A prestigious, large format periodical, *Prologues: Revue maghrébine du livre*, is published four times a year, with articles in French and Arabic, and synopses in the other language.

In terms of serving the non-specialist university public, book reviews rarely appear in the daily press, but figure in the weekly or monthly press, including *Tel Quel* and *Le Journal hebdomadaire*, and women's magazines such as *Femmes du Maroc* or *Citadine*. Scarcely, however, is there any developed analysis, just a brief descriptive paragraph, accompanied by line or two of personal evaluation in a column like 'Culture livres' or 'C à lire,' since editorial policy aims to keep the reader up to date without information overload. Not surprisingly, there are no book discussion shows on television, though occasionally a writer who has also been active in other respects, such as Leila Abouzeid, may be profiled.

In sum, then, the problems regarding literary culture are circular, involving for Morocco particularly thorny issues of language and literacy that, together with the lack of adequate financial resources, impact every aspect of book culture, from print production to consumption, and that have made it particularly challenging for women writers to have an impact on the Moroccan literary landscape. It is not politics or history or gender, alone, that have made it difficult for Moroccan women to get a toehold in the literary world, but also, the very sociology of reading and the absence of a robust culture of reading. And yet one female writer, Fatima Mernissi, is internationally known and has played a key role for all subsequent women writers in Morocco. It is therefore fitting to begin our investigation of Morocco's new voices by looking at how she brings together the issues of woman's voice and reading.

2 Mernissi and Scheherazade in Dialogue: Rereading and Acts of Subversion

Scheherazade is a great reader, a fact directly, if surprisingly, related to her survival. If she had not had in her possession such a great storehouse of tales and wisdom acquired from years of reading, she would not have been able to seduce the bloodthirsty king into sparing her life, allowing her to live for yet one more day so that she would be able to finish each story and begin a new tale, also left in suspense, night after night after night. Indeed, by her sagacious choice of story and her creative use of narrative postponement, Scheherazade subverts the king's murderous compulsion for revenge against women, ultimately curing him through story and restoring order to the kingdom.

Because Scheherazade had read not only literature, philosophy, and medicine, but also poetry and history and was well acquainted with the sayings of men and the maxims of sages and kings, according to Husain Haddawy, she was, as Fedwa Malti-Douglas writes, an *adîba*, a woman well versed in the arts of literature and society.[1] With knowledge so vast and wisdom so deep, she possessed 'the credentials of a perfectly accomplished Faquih, a Muslim religious authority,' according to Moroccan historian Abdesslam Cheddadi, whose view is seconded by Fatima Mernissi when she lauds Scheherazade's 'encyclopedic erudition' and her impressive mastery of sacred literature, the Qur'an, Shari'a, and texts from various schools of religious interpretations.[2]

As unexpected as this reading motif may be for the general public who typically think of Scheherazade as a sexy, seductive beauty, literary critics find in *The Thousand and One Nights* evidence that her power in fact comes not from her physical attributes or sexual appeal, but from her mind and intelligence, cultivated through books and reading, since it is thanks to them that she becomes the consummate storyteller.[3]

Furthermore, some critics, such as Mernissi, extend the reading metaphor by casting Scheherazade as a gifted reader of the figurative or psychological, recalling that for the first six months she tells her stories, the king does not utter a word, thereby leaving Scheherazade in suspension, much as she does with her own stories. She can only guess at the workings of his mind by observing exterior signs, and endeavouring to control both her fear and his actions by choosing and shaping her next story in ways that protract his pleasure and her life. Thus she tells her stories, perhaps modifying or editing them in relationship to her auditor, but always spinning them out to fill the hours until, in the words of the refrain, 'And as dawn chased off the night, Sheherazade interrupted her story.' In delaying the ending until the next evening, at which point she immediately begins a new, even more amazing story, she so bedazzles and entraps the monarch that he repeatedly postpones and even forgets his plan to have her killed. As Abdelfattah Kilito defines her strategy, Scheherazade appears to give freely, while hiding her intentions, always promising exquisite pleasure, while holding it back.[4] Hence, it is not by sex, but by story and subversive narrative technique that Scheherazade survives.

The textual nature of the relationship between Scheherazade and Shahriyar is underscored by Eva Sallis, who proposes that not only does Shahriyar have a double role as listener and protagonist, but that since Scheherazade simultaneously tells and experiences a tale, each of the two, alternatively, inhabits an ambiguous realm between reader and text.[5] Another critic who uses the reading metaphor in analysing *The Thousand and One Nights*, Georges May, argues that the relationship of power between Scheherazade and Shahriyar is reversed, with the king being the silent, receptive reader of Scheherazade's texts.[6] Outwardly passive, but in fact susceptible to the power of narrative, in which, as Kilito says, the marvellous (*'ajîba*) and the strange (*gharîba*) commingle,[7] the king is quite literally entranced by the adventures Scheherazade narrates. Many would argue that his consciousness is altered and, ultimately his distrust, cynicism, and mad need for revenge are purged.[8] What Scheherazade has cannily manipulated is his response, soliciting from him an affective, ethical reading that will lead him to make the experience of the text both touchstone and springboard for personal reform. By means of words and subversive narrative technique, she outmanoeuvres the king and counters imminent violence with non-violent means, taming – indeed, conquering – her opponent who, as an engaged 'reader,' is transformed by the stories and the ceremony of storytelling.

One twentieth-century critic, who made an early case for Scheherazade's feminism, even argues that Scheherazade was responsible for turning Shahriyar into a man of cultivation, a lover, a feminist, a wise man and a philosopher – 'in sum, truly a man.'[9]

In a variation on the idea expressed by Robert Scholes that the human condition can be seen as one of textuality and its component parts,[10] one might also suggest that the 'narrative cure' pertains not only to the king, but to the woman, as well. Just as it can be argued that Scheherazade's stories are key to the king's recuperation of health, so are they equally key to her, since it is through speech that she survives. For this reason, a feminist interpretation will recall the reciprocity of textuality in that Scheherazade, as an example to other women, enacts her own survival/cure from the illness of female passivity and resignation when she lays claim to speech. Hence, she uses reading and narrative technique not only to subvert the relationship with Shahriyar and reverse the balance of power, but also to 'model' a cure for women.

It is within this dynamic interplay of reading and speaking, and the potential for creative, subversive readings and rereadings, that I shall locate the thrust of this chapter. My argument is that Mernissi's fascination with the Scheherazade figure can be analysed in relationship both to Proust's notion that 'every reader, while he is reading is a reader of himself,' and to Matei Calinescu's theories on rereading, and particularly on the potential for the ludic that lies within the act of rereading.[11] Putting Mernissi and Scheherazade in dialogue will provide the opportunity to examine the dynamic of subversion inherent in both reading and narrative.

Calinescu's ideas about rereading may even explain the many conflicting interpretations of Scheherazade, since all rereadings have the potential to become acts of subversion, not so much in the sense of falsification, but in the sense of creative interpretation. As the power broker of narrative, the reader seeks to make logic or a story of the text. According to Calinescu, an experienced reader will engage simultaneously in a diachronic reading (a kind of innocent, curious, engrossing reading of the unfolding story) and a synchronic *re*reading, in the attempt to construct the text or to perceive it as a construction. Hence, there is a double reading. Furthermore, since rereading implies a sharpened structural attention, the reader will be looking for elements that might easily be overlooked but actually play a huge structural role in the text. In the case of *The Thousand and One Nights*, this element may well be Scheherazade's original subversion through postponing the ending of her stories, which might on a first reading be forgotten or overwhelmed by the accumulation of so many stories themselves, but which a reader, like Mernissi, retains as the key structural and narrative device assuring Scheherazade's success. Subversion is, then, both the key personal strategy of Scheherazade and the key narrative strategy of the text as a whole, and Mernissi's attraction to the figure of Scheherazade is deeply embedded in a reading that privileges feminist subversiveness.

Scheherazade, the reader, is read/reread by Mernissi who makes of her a feminist narrative. She is the woman of intelligence, erudition, and resolve, who uses speech to win freedom, both for herself and for her people. Indeed, Scheherazade is the founding myth of Mernissi's own career, a fact that is important, since Mernissi is a pivotal figure in Moroccan letters, the best-known Moroccan woman, and a pioneering feminist in North Africa. It is from her reading of Scheherazade that Mernissi derives both her feminist principles and the ludic subversiveness that describes her own writing, which I shall subsequently examine in *Dreams of Trespass*. It is through her reading of Scheherazade that Mernissi taps into the power of narrative, the savvy praxis of prose, and accesses lessons about how the politically or socially weaker can prevail through the art of language and narrative. Additionally, the story of the Scheherazade and Shahriyar couple ratifies Mernissi in her basic optimism and belief in the ability of men to change, and of women to surmount difficulties. In the narrative relationship between the two, I see Mernissi reading important truths about the dynamics between author and reader, including how to engage her reader, to make use of the dimension of the ludic, and ultimately to make story a tool with the power to bring about change. In her reading of Scheherazade, Mernissi perceives a woman who couples frankness with ruse, and who recognizes the subversive potential of narrative. It is therefore not only what Scheherazade symbolizes for Mernissi in terms of the power and agency of female speech that underlies a double-identification between the woman of legend and the contemporary writer, but the art, psychology, and narrative intentions demonstrated in Scheherazade and reprised by Mernissi, which in turn are illuminated by rereading.

To explore this idea, I begin by recalling several principles that Calinescu sets forth that apply to the notion of reading and particularly to the rereading of Scheherazade vis-à-vis notions of subversive narrative techniques and feminism. The second half of this chapter will consider the ways that Mernissi weaves the art of subversion into the very core of her *Dreams of Trespass*, not only in terms of the subversiveness inherent in women's dreams of trespass onto men's freedoms, but also in terms of a text that breaks with cunning skill from the rules of genre and unitary narrative voice, and that uses aspects of game theory ('work for play and play for work') to prompt from the reader the kind of reading to which she aspires. Calinescu describes this kind of reading with reference to Roland Barthes's characterization of the 'work' of reading as 'work from which labor has evaporated,' with further reference to Witold Gombrowicz concerning 'the art of discussion.'[12] In his *Diary*, Gombrowicz underscores that 'people who forget about other people and concentrate exclusively on striving for Truth speak heavily and falsely ... But those who know how to liberate pleasure, who treat discussion as both work and play, play for work and work for play ... will not ... be crushed and ... will sprout wings, flash grace, passion, poetry.'[13] This is the perfect description of Mernissi's text. In the genial subversiveness that is the hallmark of *Dreams of Trespass* and in which pleasure is liberated, we access both the originality and the persuasive power of her unique voice.

Reading and Rereading

All reading, according to Matei Calinescu, implies rereading, which means reading with an effort toward interpretation. He compares reading and rereading through use of the language of the visual arts, speaking of the first reading as being of a linear-temporal nature, and of the second as a 'landscape' reading, in which the reader endeavours to see how everything fits together. Yet, as Calinescu also observes, there is no such thing as a 'pure' first-time reading, and certainly not for literature-trained readers. Indeed, he suggests that even alongside a first reading there can exist a retrospective logic of rereading or the reader's attempt to 'construct' the text under perusal, or to perceive it as a construction.[14] Naturally, as in the case of reading Scheherazade, the issue of 'reading' in the sense of interpretation becomes that much more complicated because of the 'modifications' or misreadings of translators and adapters, to say nothing of the ideologically driven readings of those who impose certain kinds of interpretations on the text.[15] For instance, in *Sheherazade Through the Looking Glass*, Sallis emphasizes the persistence of misreadings, not always conditioned, she maintains, on various textual variants. To prove her point, she does a cross-section of some eighteen different translations of the frame stories to show how 'elastic,' inaccurate, and subjective the versions are, and how details and action have been changed depending on the translator.[16] Even in terms of the texts in Arabic, she says, the editions by both Macnaghten and Bulaq reveal, for instance, that Scheherazade is prepared to kill Shahriyar should she not succeed in changing him. This is a variation of considerable consequence, because it opens the possibility that the king's life may be in as much danger as Scheherazade's, and that Scheherazade may intentionally be using the stories that contain motifs of infidelity, especially with black slaves, to goad the king or test his limits.[17] Such a variation clearly supports a strong feminist message absent from other versions. Obviously, then, the interpretive reading of a piece of world literature that exists in multiple versions is dependent upon the version used, which makes reading a very 'slippery' process, indeed.

But in addition, as Calinescu writes, the reader rarely comes to a text tabula rasa. Therefore, in forming a 'landscape' interpretation of a text, the reader will focus on structural elements, real or embryonic, of the text that conform either to a preconceived idea or to a tendency to unearth certain kinds of 'evidence.' This does not always mean that the reader dishonestly expropriates the text to impose his or her own meanings on it, but rather that material within a narrative lends itself to creative 'extensions' in conjunction with the individual's own ideological or analytical propensities. Thus, the text is subject to the creative processes of the reader, and rereading has the potential to become a subversive and procreative act, not in the sense so much of misreading, but rather, as Calinescu says, in the sense of making larger and more pervasive an element or structure that underlies a text.[18]

In this respect, we might briefly consider how the notion of rereading functions with regard both to the conundrum that the figure of Scheherazade presents for many modern literary critics, and to the fruitful exploitation that Mernissi has made of her as the model of feminist agency and an ingenious strategist who brilliantly disproves all the old adages about the lack of value or seriousness of women's speech. Others who agree with Mernissi include M. Lahy-Hollebecque, who in 1927 wrote an entire book, *Le Féminisme de Schéhérazade*, based on a reading of the 'feminist denouements' within the tales themselves; and more recently, Eva Sallis, who focuses on Scheherazade's proactive role and transforming power through word and psychology, has concluded that she is a powerful feminist force. On the other hand, Daniel Beaumont, in *Slave of Desire*, argues that Scheherazade is not 'a triumphant counter example to the cultural idea of a submissive woman,' that she is not a feminist, and that the *Nights* is no postmodern tract, despite some 'transgressive moments.'[19] Largely agreeing with him, Robert Irwin opts to balance out the extremes, by saying that neither feminism nor misogyny dominates the *Nights*; rather, the extremes in female characters are largely intended to reveal stereotypes, typical in the oral tradition.[20]

Perhaps the reading that has received the most attention in recent years is that of Malti-Douglas, who deals with Scheherazade in the context of *écriture féminine*. In her book *Woman's Body, Woman's World*, in a chapter entitled 'Narration and Desire: Shahrazad,' she effectively argues that Scheherazade controls the relation between desire and text, using narrative to redirect desire and hence sexuality.[21] This would appear to be a strong argument for feminism, but Malti-Douglas ultimately opts for the contrary by reading the epilogue or closure of the frame story as the reintegration of Scheherazade into the patriarchal system. Rather than acceding to the view that the female protagonist has cured the king, she suggests that Scheherazade, in essence, allows herself to be co-opted by a sovereign who finds he cannot do without her. At the end, Malti-Douglas argues, by accepting marriage and motherhood, Scheherazade consents to the reestablishment of male preeminence, and, furthermore, no longer produces or controls literary discourse, since it is the king who has the stories written down. Interestingly, this view has received wide support among feminist scholars, including Moroccan professor Hasna Lebbady, who studies a folktale, 'Aïcha Bent Ennejar,' based on a Scheherazade-type heroine, and who dismisses any notion of feminism, judging that, on the contrary, the conclusion sustains the hierarchical structure of power that keeps women in an inferior position.[22]

For many, the crux of the problem of Scheherazade's so-called feminism is that she does not appear to be sufficiently militant and ends by negotiating with the system. Surprisingly, however, such a view seems to overlook the fact that while Scheherazade and Shahriyar are each powerful individuals, their practice of power is entirely different: where his is destructive, hers is transforming, non-aggressive, and civilized. In other words, by concentrating on 'outcomes,' according to a fairly absolutist scale, these critics make their case by focusing on specific elements and disregarding others.

They may also do a kind of 'foreshortened reading' of the writing of other critics. For instance, Malti-Davis makes a slighting comment about Mernissi's interpretation of Scheherazade, curiously drawing only upon *Chahrazad n'est pas marocaine*, and accusing Mernissi of casting Scheherazade as an innocent girl, led to Shahriyar's bed by a fatal destiny and managing to triumph only through her innocence.[23] As a result, Malti-Douglas charges Mernissi with belittling Scheherazade's wisdom and cleverness, her initiative and mastery, a most puzzling conclusion, which she bases on a single paragraph in *Chahrazad n'est pas marocaine*, when, in fact, the whole thrust of what Mernissi says in that book is just the opposite.[24] In the section, 'La Bibliothèque de Chahrazad' (15–22), Mernissi underscores Scheherazade's erudition, which is vital to her thesis concerning 'the relationship of women to knowledge. And necessarily to power' (7). In support of her view of an educated and insightful heroine, Mernissi quotes approvingly the Mardrus 1980 edition of *Les Mille et une nuits*, which presents Scheherazade as having read books, chronicles, and legends of every kind, of possessing a thousand books about the peoples, kings, and poets of antiquity.[25] Indeed, Mernissi's entire point is that it was because of the woman's vast storehouse of knowledge, a sign of class privilege in *The Thousand and One Nights*, that Scheherazade was able to survive, and that modern Moroccan women should use her example as their own strategy in a world in which the levers of power are in the hands of men.

To argue that Mernissi undervalues Scheherazade's intellect is all the more rash, because Mernissi's reading of Scheherazade functions as a veritable double reading – of herself and of the woman in legend, as though twin images of the same woman. Indeed, the parallels between her reading of Scheherazade and herself cannot be missed. Constantly referenced throughout her works, Scheherazade is, in effect, Mernissi's virtual soul mate, featured in the titles of two books, *Chahrazad n'est pas marocaine* and *Scheherazade Goes West*, and serving as the empowering symbolic mother figure of the art show Mernissi organized in 2003, 'Fantaisies au harem, nouvelles Shéhérazades.' In an article for the show's catalogue, Mernissi extends the reach of the Scheherazade type into the modern, technological age of digital Islam. Arguing that television has created 'a golden opportunity' for women 'to enter the power game in the Middle East,' Mernissi asserts that 'the Sheherazade profile' of 'the brainy, self-confident storyteller,' is in big demand by the Arab network, Al Jazeera, 'winning crowds every night' through the eloquence of its female news anchors such as Jumana Nammour and Kaduja Bin Guna, and economics expert Farah al-Baraqaui.[26] To equate these contemporary practitioners of the word with the storyteller from *The Thousand and One Nights* is not only a colourful way to suggest the enduring relevance of the speaking woman in Arab society, but also revealing evidence of the priority that Scheherazade enjoys in Mernissi's thinking.

In addition, Scheherazade is an ideal vector for Mernissi, since the legendary storyteller occupies a place in the popular thinking of both East and West, and since Mernissi, the student of societies, is interested in being a bilateral 'reader' or explicator of cultures. Certainly that is the premise of *Scheherazade Goes West*, which addresses misconceptions Mernissi believes reign in the West concerning the nature of Scheherazade. The task, as she conceives it, requires her to present the 'real' Scheherazade, together with 'Eastern' ideals of female energy and activity, healthy and passionate sexuality, while at the same time, critiquing Western feminism, as she perceives it, in which women are less free than they maintain, particularly in terms of body image and an ostensible ideal 'size six' into which they must struggle to fit.[27] The point, according to Mernissi, is that because the West has generally misconstrued Scheherazade (*Dreams of Trespass*, chapter 2, note 2), it is equally probable that it has misconstrued Arab women, ignoring successful, if exceptional, women, like the announcers on Al Jazeera, who emulate the values of the woman in legend. At the same time, Mernissi's reading of Scheherazade is equally intended for her own countrywomen who are encouraged to be inspired by the model of female strength and self-empowerment from Middle Eastern culture. As she writes in the aforementioned note, 'Like Saladin and Sindbad, Scheherazade makes us more audacious and more sure of ourselves and our capacity to analyze difficult situations, and to elaborate strategies that multiply our chances of happiness.' Hence Mernissi's reading of Scheherazade further functions as a two-sided mirror, one side speaking out to the West, the other to Middle Eastern women themselves.

Scheherazade is, therefore, not only the figure in the background hovering over Western readings of Middle Eastern women's works, but she is also for Mernissi, the inspirational and mythic figure of Near Eastern tradition, at once courageous, talented, and insightful, a confirmed reader in every field of intellectual inquiry, a storyteller to the powerful, a female who despite her vulnerability ultimately changes the balance of power by means of language. In *Dreams of Trespass*, Mernissi speaks admiringly of Scheherazade, describing her as 'one of our rare female figures of myth who has the power to change people and the world. An astute strategist and extraordinarily intelligent, she succeeds in reversing the balance of power thanks to her knowledge of psychology and human nature.'[28] She might have been speaking of herself.

In the view of Maggie Huff-Rousselle, Mernissi is, in fact, the new Scheherazade because, like her predecessor, she is an artist of the intellect, working with ideas and telling stories.[29] Moreover, she is the model of the Eastern woman who rebels with intelligence and charm, engaging the reader with her warmth and humour, and at the same time she remains wholly committed to improving the world and to showing Arab women, in particular, the ways of breaking down barriers and emulating the female models of freedom from their own culture. Hence, Mernissi follows in the steps of Scheherazade, outwitting authority and conventional power by uniting knowledge, insight, wit, and the imagination to create an often subversive and always unique voice.

At the heart of Mernissi's enterprise in *Dreams of Trespass* lies reading. She rereads the Scheherazade myth, as well as stories from *The Thousand and One Nights*, and others from Moroccan history, along with Middle Eastern and Islamic customs. She pretends to tell one story – the story of her childhood – but in fact tells a much broader story, derived from sources other than her own life, and she wins over her readers in much the same way as Scheherazade does and with the same purposes. It is in our rereading of Mernissi's art of subversion that we will best be able to attest to the lineage between two extraordinary women, one a Moroccan with an international reputation, and the other, a figure of legend and the world's first female storyteller, who, as Mernissi says, 'has nothing at all to do with Morocco!' since 'Scheherazade is 100% Asiatic,' born in the imaginaries of some far off lands – yet one who represents for the author the symbol of affirmative subversion and female empowerment.[30]

Dreams of Trespass and Subversiveness

Indeed, I would argue that Mernissi took from her reading of Scheherazade three important values, each of which carries a considerable potential for subversiveness. The first is the power of freedom as an ideal, which corresponds to the overarching thrust of Mernissi's entire oeuvre; the second is the subversive potential of storytelling, which can inspire dreams and change the course of affairs; and the third is the empowering and often subversive value of women's speech. While it may be arguable whether *Dreams of Trespass* can be called a patently subversive work in the usual sense of the word, it is nonetheless true that a kind of genial subversiveness runs throughout the text, from its conception as a hybrid, composite genre –sometimes inaccurately called an autobiography or a memoir – to its choice of a child-narrator as a narrative ploy, to the principle of the ludic, functioning as a deceit or strategy for the pleasure of the reader. In point of fact, *Dreams of Trespass* is a text of heterogeneity, at once comic in its false *naïveté* and engaging in its fairy tale aspects, owing much to the genre of the *conte philosophique*, yet also scholarly in its ethnographic presentation of Moroccan and Middle Eastern traditions and culture, sociology, history, religion, politics, literature, and fashion. Because this latter material is largely presented as footnotes at the end of the book, there are two authorial perspectives in the text, that of a child whose identity with Mernissi is denied (although she carries the same first name) and that of the teaching scholar. As if this were not enough, the actual form of the text is protean, depending on the edition, the language, and the audience addressed.[31] Indeed, this very heterogeneity suggests something dynamically organic about Mernissi's conception of narrative, consistent with the themes of freedom that she posits in the text.

In comparison, Scheherazade's own subversion is more focused. She has come to the palace to break the cycle of violence, and does so by outwitting and outmanoeuvring the king, telling stories intended to entertain but also to buy herself time and ultimately to change both the king's mind and his actions. It is her qualities as a strategist who plots her personal and narrative moves to affect and move her reader that Mernissi applauds and incorporates in her own writing. Mernissi, too, always has her reader in mind, and like Scheherazade, she is acutely conscious that the relationship with this person is key to her ultimate success. Therefore, she knows how to make her readers listen, drawing them in by humour, feigned innocence, impertinence, genial deceptions, and subversive distortions so that they, like Shahriyar, become absorbed in the games of subversion.

Crossing the Lines of Genre, or Subverting Genre

First published in English in 1994, then translated and adapted into French and published by Michel Albin in 1996, *Rêves de femmes* was reissued in 1997 by Fennec in an edition that includes twenty-two evocative photographs – one for each chapter – of Moroccan doorways, windows, stairways, grilled gateways, architectural columns, and women in profile, or from behind, or partially concealed. The photos are the work of Mernissi's long-time collaborator on visual issues, Ruth V. Ward.[32] The narrative text itself is a collage of episodes, presented in the twenty-two chapters that feature members of the narrator's extended family (mothers, grandmothers, cousins, playmates, aunts, beloved female domestics), as well as princesses, either real – like the Lebanese princess Asmahan, who was a singer and actress and who died a mysterious death at age thirty-two – or make-believe (such as Princess Budur from *The Thousand and One Nights*), fictional heroines from Moroccan history (Tamou), and real women from other Arab lands, including early Egyptian feminists (Aisha Taymour, Zaynab Fawwaz, and Huda Sha'raoui). There is no plot, per se, but rather snapshots of life in a great-house of Fez in the years during and shortly after the Second World War. The real nucleus of the text, however, coalesces around a narrative presentation of themes and ideas central to Mernissi's thinking concerning freedom and the barriers to its realization, the conflicts of tradition and modernity, and the new and sometimes inchoate dreams of women who would be modern. And it is all told in the fresh voice of the lively, young girl, who bears the name of the author, while the eighteen pages of notes with explanations and bibliographical references are presented in the authoritative voice of the author-scholar, Fatima Mernissi.

Despite this obvious hybridity, the text has variously been described as an autobiography, a memoir, a fictional memoir, a novel, a primer for Westerners to the Arab world, and even a fairy tale. But there are good reasons why it cannot be identified exclusively by any of these categories (as I discuss below), though it shares elements of each, which is why I suggest that it subverts the very notion of fixed genre, just as, thematically, the text subverts space, borders, and boundaries. Indeed, the subversion of all such *hudad* is wholly consistent with one of the most insistent themes in the book: boundaries are unnatural separations that *should* be crossed. Crossing the boundaries of genre, then, becomes a part of the larger 'poetics of trespass' suggested by the title in English, *Dreams of Trespass*.

In arguing that this work by Mernissi is autobiographical, critics often cite the first chapter in Philippe Lejeune's *Le Pacte autobiographique* in which he discusses the standards by which a text can be determined as autobiographical.[33] What people mostly remember is his sentence saying that to be autobiographical, a text must formally present itself as autobiography and be recounted in the first person. By that single criterion, Mernissi's text counts as autobiography since her first sentence reads, 'I was born in a harem in Fez in 1940.' But that is not all that Lejeune had in mind. Moreover, it completely ignores Mernissi's own words in note 2 of chapter 3, which specifically say that the mother is 'a fictional person, as is moreover the child who speaks and who is assumed to be me.' Further, she adds, 'This book is not an autobiography, but a fiction presented through the form of tales told by a seven-year old child' (302). Rather than personal testimony about her own life, the book contains the kind of collected testimony gathered from interviewing Moroccan women for *Le Maroc raconté par ses femmes* (1984), including one Batul Binjalluna, interviewed in 1974, who was the child of a female slave from a prosperous harem in Fez in the 1930s.[34]

Furthermore, neither true autobiography nor fictional autobiography uses the text as a pretext to provide substantive footnotes, which in *Rêves* constitute a sometimes competing, often corrective perspective, penned by the author, who elaborates on the story or elements of it presented by the child-narrator. For instance, consider the very interesting discourse on the 'politics of the sartorial' in note 1 to chapter 4, or the discussion of different kinds of harems in note 4 of chapter 4. Both examples come from the chapter entitled 'La Rivale de Yasmina,' which recounts in a humorous vein the child-narrator's visit to the farm where her beloved and liberated grandmother lives as the preferred wife of her polygamous, kindly grandfather. In fact, the chapter serves as a pretext for Mernissi's discussion in note 3, arguing that women's liberation does not have to be imported from Paris or New York, because it is 'an idea endogenous to the Arab and Muslim spirit and which developed in the great centers of Muslim thinking at universities like Al-Azhar in Egypt, Zitouna in Tunisia, and Qaraouiyine in Morocco.' Further, she adds, 'A woman like me could never have gotten to the university if the leaders of the nationalist movement, with the *ulémas* of Qaraouiyine at their head, had not created in 1948 a section for females in the university.'

Even if we agree with Nancy K. Miller that both biography and autobiography in the postmodern world are, in fact, constructions, whether of the other or of oneself, and that autobiography as a genre has come to be understood as a fiction of self-invention,[35] *Rêves de femmes*, by its very title and by the multiple references to other women in Middle Eastern and North African history throughout the text, is telling us that Mernissi's subject is women and not one woman. Her role, as she states further in note 2 of chapter 3, is as the scribe of recollections of others: 'Memories of what those illiterate women in the courtyard and on the terrace recounted' about the insolence of a French Résident Général and the noble mission of Mohammed V, backed by nationalists throughout Morocco, in January 1944.[36] At that time, of course, Fatima Mernissi would have been only four years old; she is not claiming to be resurrecting a direct personal memory, but rather the memories *du peuple marocain* that were to take on mythical importance in the national psyche.

So, if *Dreams of Trespass* is neither autobiography nor memoir, is it a novel? According to Mernissi's own words, the work is a fiction. But does that mean it is a novel, or is she using the word 'fiction' to mean 'untrue' or 'made-up,' to convey the opposite sense of 'true' autobiography? To be sure, it does have many of the elements of the novel: narrative, setting, description, figurative language, action, conflict, dialogue, point of view. But it also has explanation and exposition, short essays, standard rhetorical patterns, and researched facts that characterize non-fiction. Nor is it, in my estimate, even possible to call the text a fictional memoir told in the words of a child, laid in an earlier time in Morocco's history. Although it is loosely about the socialization of a young girl in the 1940s and 1950s, it does not focus primarily on the child's life, since most of the episodes do not place her, but rather other members of the extended family, at the centre. Moreover, if it is a fiction, why are there eighteen pages of notes that are the product of the teacher-ethnographer? Their inclusion, commenting and embroidering upon elements of the story, is atypical of fiction of any kind, since any auxiliary comments by an author, when they occur (which is rare), are affixed in a preface or afterword to a text, devices more common in non-fiction. And if it is a fictional memoir, why incorporate stories, such as that of the Princess Budor, from an earlier literary work, *The Thousand and One Nights*? Finally, why, in one edition, are there photographs that include streets and buildings and architectural detail, as well as the faceless forms of women? While the photographs leave the reader with a powerful but illusive visual imprint that complements without over-determining the text, their presence is idiosyncratic in an ostensibly fictional memoir.

There are certain fairy tale aspects to the work, as well, particularly in that the main subject is a child and the moral didacticism of the text concerns lessons of fearlessness, courage, industriousness, kindness, loyalty, and other desirable traits. But Mernissi's main theme, that of freedom, is not exactly a typical theme in the fairy tale. Moreover, unlike the fairy tale, which is about or intended for a child, though not told by the child, in Mernissi's text, it is the child herself who speaks, describes, compares, and sometimes even analyses – at times from an exceedingly mature standpoint and with a quality of knowledge that defies her age. This fact, in addition to Mernissi's well-known desire to communicate cross-culturally, has led to the suggestion that the text is intended as a primer for Westerners on the Arab world, in which the child becomes the ambassador of Arab culture. Young Fatima, in fact, reveals such sophisticated and keen sensitivity to cultural differences, knowing just what to explain and when, that the reader both laughs and learns simultaneously. However, the child-narrator is not a consistently reliable guide, so the reader must still be wary about distinguishing between her childish exaggerations and precipitous judgments. Clearly, then, while there are elements of the text that suggest the fairy tale or the primer, neither classification describes the text overall.

Finally, in terms of identifying genre, *Dreams of Trespass* is also not creative non-fiction (sometimes called the fourth genre, after poetry, fiction, and drama), which is a branch of writing that employs literary techniques and artistic vision to report on actual persons or events.[37] To be sure, the text does have elements of the three main forms of creative non-fiction – the literary memoir, the personal essay, and literary journalism – but there is also frequently distortion of the truth (precisely because Mernissi narrates through the eyes of a child), and truthfulness is a requirement of creative non-fiction. Moreover, one needs to account for the presence of a second, sometimes correcting narrator, plus characters who are composite types (the aunts and uncles, for instance), and the emphasis on imagination and certain fairy-tale aspects, none of which is permitted according to the rules of creative non-fiction. So, despite the fact that *Dreams of Trespass* is built like creative non-fiction with vignettes, episodes, slices of reality, and 'scenes' that trigger and develop the text, such an identification is countermanded by the presence of doubled narrating voices and the lack of distinction at times between them when, for instance, the child 'educates' rather than simply recounts.

In the final analysis, I suggest that *Dreams of Trespass* can best be described as narrative non-fiction done with the flair and licence of fiction – but it is still, in my estimate, a new kind of literary form, without precedent or subsequent example, proof of Mernissi's originality and uniqueness – a creative subversion. Along this line, it may be helpful to recall that what fascinates Mernissi about *The Thousand and One Nights* is that the work begins as a tragedy of betrayal and revenge and ends as a fairy tale, thereby passing from one genre to another.[38] Given her own commitment both to crossing borders and to changing minds through narrative, it is not surprising that *Dreams of Trespass* retains its right to be protean and refuses fixed boundaries, choosing instead to mix genres. For Mernissi, as for Scheherazade, the purpose of narrative is to engage the reader's interest so that he or she can engage with others and society in beneficial ways. By incorporating the resources of several genres and disciplines in unusual ways, Mernissi breaks with the rules of traditional narrative discourse to enhance her objective. It is the same message taught by the progressive women of *Dreams of Trespass*, from Fatima's mother and her grandmother Yasmina, to Princess Budor of *The Nights*, who even crosses the line between the sexes when she disguises herself as a man and marries a woman, to Mina, the beloved domestic from Sub-Sahara, who had been dropped into a well by her kidnappers but who used that well as a trampoline from which to jump to the heavens. Given that the primary lesson these women teach, by speech or example, is to value and practise freedom, it is perfectly logical that Mernissi, too, would eschew strict lines between genres, opting instead for porous borders and a hybrid form of narrative. To make such a choice reveals a modern mentality and a modern, open concept of literature – the readiness of the author to subvert traditions of more than one kind.

The Ludic: Subverting the Narrator/The Subversive Narrator

In another example of the quality of genial subversiveness that characterizes *Dreams of Trespass*, Mernissi both subverts her child-narrator and turns her into a subversive narrator. Indeed, I would argue that her use of a child-narrator is at once a narrative ploy and a rhetorical device, linked to her conception of reading relations between writer and reader, as well as to the principle of the ludic that informs not only this text, but often her very theory and practice of influence and argumentation. In my reading, Mernissi's embrace of the notions of game theory – 'play for work' and 'work for play' – reveals in her writing the fine art of subversion and opens the secret to the pleasure of the text. Outwardly lightweight and playful, *Dreams of Trespass* in fact deals with serious issues concerning feminism, philosophy, and politics, but in a playful, amiable, and accessible manner.

In studying the emotional effects that a creative writer can arouse in the reader, Calinescu points to the key mediator of a special kind of play, called artistic play, by which an author turns to games in order to produce a certain kind of receptivity in the reader.[39] He further distinguishes between two types of games. The first, from the Greek, *paida*, pertains to games that are joyful, turbulent, improvised, potentially chaotic, and fantasy-oriented, while the second, from the Latin *ludus*, describes games in which calculation, contrivance, and ingenuity are the main qualities of the play.[40] Roger Caillois has said that *paida* can be disciplined or 'domesticated' by *ludus*, the game with rules, or, as I would say, the game with a purpose.[41] In *Dreams of Trespass*, in which play and playfulness abound – the 'practice play' of the theatrical performances of cousin Chama, for instance, or the 'symbolic play' of the women's dreams – there are elements of both *paida* and of *ludus*, but it is clearly the latter, requiring a clever and ingenious mind, that describes Mernissi's artistic approach. Her intention is not only to seduce the reader through charm, but also to divert, in the double sense of the verb: to deflect and to entertain.

Hence, the many paradoxes associated with the child-narrator. To begin with, although the child bears the same first name as the author, Mernissi tells us in an early chapter (chapter 3, note 3) that it would be a mistake to believe that narrator and author are the same person. But if that is so, why give the child-narrator her own first and last names? This merely invites the reader's assumption that the author is describing her own life and results in the mistaken assessment of critics that her text is an autobiography or at least semi-autobiographical. Second, the child-narrator is so simultaneously sophisticated and gullible that she requires the reader's willing suspension of disbelief. How are we to rationalize her fears, caused by over-credulity, with her very developed understanding of exactly what an adult Westerner would not understand about Arab culture? Indeed, how would a seven-year-old have the mature sensitivity to abstract concepts specific to Arab culture – *haram*, *hal*, *hem*, *hanan*, *qu'ida*, *tashif*, *mhyuza* – and turn them into a veritable dictionary? And, how is this naive child who has travelled very little, just out to see grandmother Yasmina on her farm, able to compare the life styles of Fez with Marrakech?

Of course, a real child cannot, but this particular child, like so many other naive narrators in fiction is, in fact, a kind of 'ruse' on the part of the writer, who with a subversive wink toward the reader invites him or her to share the deception and to read between the lines. The feint of the child's 'naive' response to her world is, in fact, a rhetorical tool for Mernissi and part of the pleasure of the reader who recognizes that the child, shadowed by authorial intent and knowledge, understands more than she should if she were truly naive.

The ruse that is associated with Scheherazade, who has been described as both the 'mistress of the word' and the 'mistress of the ruse,'[42] is both different and the same. Scheherazade is definitely not naive, but rather, like Mernissi, she is the storyteller who seeks to affect her 'reader.' Her stories are intended to do more than merely entertain the king since she came to Shahriyar's palace not resigned to lose her life, but to save it and, ultimately, the kingdom. Therefore, she needs to exercise upon the king a kind of invisible influence, to engage his interest and to create a bond with him. She does this not by being like any other woman, not by appealing to him directly, but through the indirect means of narrative art, using techniques intended to seduce or entrap: a surfeit of action, oppositional characters, stories within stories, suspense and suspended narration. Similarly, Mernissi adopts some of the same techniques, including the ruse of the naive narrator, who, like Scheherazade, is something other than what she appears.

As we know, in folklore the notion of the 'ruse' is most often associated with animals and simple people, though often, too, with the wily woman – hence, Farida Benlyazid's fairy tale film of the Andalusian tale based on a Scheherazade-like figure is entitled in French *Ruses de femmes*, and in English *Women's Wiles*. Typically the tool of the weak, the ruse is directed against the powers that be or against authority in general, and is an old device of the storyteller or fabulist, who, for example in American tradition, delights the audience with tales in which Bre'r Rabbit or the wily fox outwits convention or overturns the usual rules of the game. As a result, the very promise of the ruse is inherently pleasurable to the reader, the tip-off that the tables are about to be turned. In *Rêves de femmes*, it is not the child-narrator who is wily, but the author herself, and it is a narrative technique she often employs.

The adoption of a naive perspective and persona is a typical technique and rhetorical device that Mernissi adopts in other texts, even when she speaks on her own behalf. In part, it is a psychological ploy, because by appearing naive or helpless in the face of bigotry or blind authority, Mernissi gets the reader on her side, establishes a complicity of sympathy, and readies the reader to rally to her. Both *The Veil and the Male Elite* and *Scheherazade Goes West* offer examples of this approach. In the first, at the beginning of her text, Mernissi 'naively' asks her grocer whether a woman could be the leader of Muslims and uses the ensuing scene, in which the grocer and his male customers loudly object, citing a Hadith to disparage women, to launch her own investigation into how this Hadith had taken on such 'extraordinary power over the ordinary citizens of a modern state' (Introduction, 2; see also chapter 6, page 129). In another example of her own ostensible *naïveté*, in *Scheherazade Goes West*, she says that when travelling in a foreign country, she is likely seen by others as exuding self-confidence, but in fact is very frightened because she is 'afraid of failing to understand strangers' ('The Tale of the Lady with the Feather Dress,' 1). For an internationalist and world traveller, who is in her sixth decade at the time she writes these words, it hardly seems a frank statement. But by adopting the stance of the easily rattled woman, whose anxiety is hidden from her audience only because she is armed with a 'huge Berber silver bracelet' and her 'red Chanel lipstick' – comic additions which make us smile – she establishes an immediate and intimate relationship with her reader through a declaration of vulnerability.[43] The same mechanism operates with young Fatima, the narrator, who, as Gauch perceptively writes, 'depicts her task [to present the Mernissi family] as terribly daunting and herself as a bit of an unworthy blunderer,' but then displays consummate skill in her storytelling.[44]

In another example, Mernissi demonstrates upfront awareness of her reader, in a 'confidence' on the first page of *Chahrazad n'est pas marocaine; autrement, elle serait salariée!* when she writes, 'Making confidences in guise of an introduction is the best way to establish an intimacy between myself and the reader.' Similarly, in *Dreams of Trespass*, she speaks of the necessity of seducing her reader. In the note following her avowal that the text is neither an autobiography, nor a memoir, she says, 'Do not forget that the version I presented coincides with the literary packaging that I needed to seduce my reader' (chapter 3, note 3). In other words, the adoption of the perspective of a naive narrator, or expressions of self-assigned inferiority, is instrumental in helping her to create a relationship of intimacy with the reader.[45] While Mernissi seeks in the footnote to explain the slant given in *Dreams of Trespass* to a historical event, in terms of 'how people in fiction experienced the reality of it,' what is most striking, I believe, is her acknowledgement of, and intention to appeal to, her reader. What she is emphasizing is the importance of a likeable narrator, and if that means speaking in the first person while playing a role and feigning *naïveté* to win over the reader, then she will do so.

Accordingly, her typical mode of self-presentation is as a somewhat foolish woman who takes the world literally – which is, of course, an effective way to reveal its illogic. Similar to little Fatima's wide-eyed innocence in *Dreams of Trespass*, the adult Fatima Mernissi becomes an innocent when she speaks as the literal-minded woman or as the figure of straw whose views run entirely counter to the prevailing winds or 'received truths' of her society. Assuming a veil of innocence, Mernissi asks impertinent questions or makes impudent declarations, alleges incomprehension of officialdom and its rules, finds herself in the midst of disputes she caused but pretends not to understand. These are all the devices of the false-naive that permit her to engage her narrative in such clearly non-fiction works as *The Veil and the Male Elite*, *Etes-vous vacciné contre le harem*, and *Scheherazade Goes West*.[46] What she does in these works is initially to subvert one kind of authority – authorial – for the immediate goal of drawing in the reader, for that will better ensure her long-range goal of being 'heard' more completely.

Could one not say that Scheherazade's subversive narrative technique has similar goals? For though Scheherazade comes to the king's palace of her own free will, she arrives with a premeditated plan. Her intention is to survive not by striking at the life of the king, but by luring him into an enthralment with the magic of narrative. She is the ingenious narrator, the master tactician. Accordingly, the king is duped, not just once but one thousand and one times, consistently falling for her promise that if he found the present tale extraordinary, the next one would be even more so. Her ability to refashion sexual desire into narrative desire depends on the success of her initial subversion. It also points to the fact that she is no ordinary woman, but rather one who understands that to be 'heard,' she will need to be an engaging and shrewd narrator.

Mernissi's seven-year-old child-narrator would hardly seem comparable to Scheherazade, let alone capable of shrewdness. But in fact, her effect on her reader, like Scheherazade's on Shahriyar, is such that we are beguiled. Neither he nor we were expecting to be so cleverly entertained by a woman of the realm or a child of Fez. But young Fatima is a delightful observer who makes us smile. She is curious and intelligent, a child and yet knowledgeable beyond her years, Her wide-eyed innocence becomes a genial 'front' for revealing truths about the quaint customs and injustices of the great-house of Fez as of the cultural practices of the time. She is, of course, the spokesperson of the author, but her very conception is based on a cheerful 'deception,' a playful subversion of the so-called pact of transparency between writer and reader. And in subverting her narrator at the same time that she makes her speak subversive truths, the author cleverly combines *paida* and *ludus* for the pleasure of the reader.

In this section, I have proposed a reading of *Dreams of Trespass* that focuses not on content but on form, or perhaps, I might say, on the technique of creating narrative pleasure. What Mernissi admires in Scheherazade is not only her ability to harness the unseen power of words, formed into stories, to produce a new narrative of survival, but also the storyteller's subversive ingenuity in making narrative technique serve her purposes. Accordingly, in my reading, Fatima Mernissi reframes Scheherazade's subversive strategies, in pursuit of survival through narrative, into a kind of genial subversiveness that gets at the heart of the pleasure of the text, combining both the writerly and the readerly. Narrative technique in Mernissi is, I submit, fundamentally strategic, potentially radical, and always pleasing, all lessons learned from a storyteller par excellence, Scheherazade.

Conclusion

Mernissi's obsession/fascination with the Scheherazade figure is linked to her reading of the woman in legend, a reading that turns out to be a projected self-reading, since she attributes to Scheherazade all the characteristics that she herself demonstrates. In this sense, she exemplifies what Proust had said about every reader being the reader of his or her own self. Thus, when Mernissi interprets Scheherazade as a political hero, a liberator in the Muslim world, who articulated key philosophical and political questions, she is, in fact, doing a self-reading.

For Mernissi and many others, Scheherazade is the paradigmatic figure of the trapped woman who, by practising powerful speech, saves her own life and changes the course of a nation, thereby becoming a model for Arab women in the contemporary world.[47] Like many of her counterparts of today, Scheherazade is disadvantaged by cultural prejudice and male privilege, and is, moreover, the virtual captive of a political tyrant who destroys life with impunity. But she becomes ultimately both standard-bearer and symbol of female courage and speech, when, by means of savvy storytelling and persistence, she succeeds in breaking the cycle of violence perpetrated against women by a vengeful king, and in the process remakes both her life and his. By reading Scheherazade in this light, Mernissi makes the point that today's women, no less than Scheherazade, possess the arms of resistance. While women may be 'trapped' according to conventional logic, they are also endowed with the ingenuity, insight, and intelligence to resist or to subvert the system, and to make crucial questions about freedom and power part of the larger debate.

Hence, just as the original Scheherazade stories offered key teachings to young Fatima's grandmother Yasmina who passes them on to her granddaughter, and just as the figure of Scheherazade represents for

Mernissi the womanly model of shrewd intellect and creative talents, so does Mernissi become the role model and teacher for the generation of Scheherazades who succeed her – the Moroccan women writers featured in this book. The dialogue created between Scheherazade and Mernissi, through the latter's reading of the legendary figure, has produced nearly all the dominant discourses of subsequent women's works, whether the specific themes concern female freedom and resistance, tradition versus modernity, or initiating reform through storytelling. Simply stated, Mernissi is the pioneering female figure in Morocco who disproves the myth of the silent woman. She breaks the ground that others will continue to cultivate.

3 The Myth of the Silent Woman

Into a closed mouth no flies can enter.

Moroccan proverb

One of the most striking images in Fatna El Bouih's prison memoir, *Une Femme nommée Rachid*, describes how lying side by side on the cold cement floor, blindfolded and gagged, she and the other female political prisoners were able to communicate by using their fingers like pens to trace letters on the 'pages' of the palm or the flank of the woman next to her, transmitting messages of hope and encouragement. Despite the rule of silence, enforced by their jailors, these young women telegraphed with deft fingers, letter by letter, 'des contes du merveilleux, des récits et des blagues' (tales of the marvellous, short stories, and even jokes) on the hand of another, who 'read' these Braille-like traceries and found in them courage and solidarity.[1] In this extraordinary calligraphy of silent speech by prisoners, the power of women's 'voice,' as of story and storytelling, could hardly be more profound, or stand in starker contrast to the culture of silence that is too often said to define women's lives and has even been called one of the bases of Moroccan civilization.[2]

Later, El Bouih would recall that like all girls of her generation, she had, indeed, been marked by *le silence féminin*, taught that the model of propriety was to lower her eyes, never to raise her voice, to keep her mouth closed so that 'no flies can enter,' as the Moroccan proverb instructs.[3] But, at home, she also learned other values – those of justice, truth, and human rights – from an extraordinary father who believed in the emancipation of women for his daughter's generation (if not that of his wife), and from an illiterate mother who taught her daughter strength and counselled her to keep her word.[4] In part because of their teaching and confidence in her, as we shall see in chapter 5, El Bouih was led to practise a form of radical political speech in the public sphere. Even as a teenager in the 1970s, boarding as a scholarship student at a high school in Casablanca and then continuing for university studies, she engaged in the most forbidden of speech for women – political protest – and later, during the five years of her incarceration as a political prisoner, the speech of self-preservation and human rights. She and her sister detainees were not silent or paralyzed by fear of the power of the state. Rather, they were assertive, reclaiming speech by every act, issuing statements, demands, and declarations, and insisting on their right to negotiate with prison officials for better conditions and recognition as political prisoners.

In this respect, El Bouih and her cohorts trod in the footsteps of strong women before their time, going back generations to Fatima El-Fihri, who in the ninth century founded the University of Qarawiyyn in Fez; Zineb Nafzaoui, wife of king Youssef Ben Tachfine, who played an important role in establishing and cultivating the Almoravid empire in the twelfth century; Seyyda El-Horra, who governed the entire north of Morocco and led the *jihad* against the Spanish and Portuguese; and others evoked by Ghita El Khayat to counter the view that Moroccan women's history is one of submission and silence.[5] Fatima Mernissi wrote an entire book about the powerful but forgotten queens of Islam, *Les Sultanes oubliées*, and celebrates early Arab women feminists – Aisha Taymour, 1840–1906; Zaynab Fawwaz (1860–1914); and Huda Sha'raoui (1879–1947) – in chapter 14 of *Dreams of Trespass*.[6] Closer to home, El Bouih and her friends also inherited the examples of courage and speech from all those women who had aided in the struggle for independence, from Malika al-Fassi (a relative of the independence struggle leader Allal al-Fassi), who was one of the signers of the Manifeste de l'Indépendance and the author of essays on female education in the 1930s, to *résistantes* like those interviewed by Alison Baker for her 1998 film, 'Still Ready' – Ghalia Moujahide, Saadia Bouhaddou, and Rabiaa Taibi – who, seemingly unlikely partisans of political action, were committed to the nationalist cause, carrying guns and supplies to the Resistance and risking torture, just like men, if they were caught.

In the early, heady days of Independence, the best and brightest of Moroccan women joined men at the university, while later in the 1970s they sought to link the cause of women's rights to a Marxist-based class struggle. In the 1980s sociologist and feminist, Latifa Ajbabdi, along with members of the New Left, founded an Arabic language monthly newsletter, called *Le 8 Mars* in honour of International Women's Day. The publication included a page on legal issues and a discussion of women and the Moudawana (family code), as well as a page devoted to illiterate women whose views and concerns the editors solicited. In the 1990s the development of women's non-governmental organizations exploded in number, including the Association Démocratique des Femmes du Maroc and Union Nationale des Femmes Marocaines, whose commitment is to women's needs, particularly literacy programs and other services.[7] In the 1980s and early 1990s, numerous research projects were undertaken from a woman's standpoint, resulting in published series such as 'Femmes Maghreb' (*La Femme et la loi au Maroc, Femmes et éducation*, etc.) under the direction of Fatima Mernissi and Omar Azziman; 'Approches,' under the direction of sociologist Aïcha Belarbi; 'Collection Visibilité des Femmes' (for instance, *Marocaines & médias* by Fatima Boutarkha and published with the help of the National Endowment for Democracy in 1995). The female CEO of Le Fennec, Leila Chaouni, published most of these volumes.

So, we have to ask, silent women? Passive women? Repressed women? Given the foregoing, that is a very incomplete picture.[8] Indeed, regardless of various laments, Moroccan women have neither been silenced, nor are they totally silent about their 'I.' It is important to declare this, because so many contemporary Moroccan women repeat the mantra that, given the kind of instruction in the non-'I' they receive as girls, women either cannot speak, or that if they do, they can only tell stories of their own subjugation.[9] The consequence of such lamentations about women's lack of voice, or lack of effective voice, despite evidence to the contrary, is 'the myth of the silent woman.'

It is important to note that I am using 'myth' as does a Princeton University historian, who writes that a myth is 'not a false story, but one that, for all its richness, remains radically incomplete and therefore misleading.'[10] This is precisely what I mean: to speak of the silent woman, the woman silenced, or to recall the moral injunctions about closed lips taught to little girls is not tantamount to telling a lie, but rather to presenting only an incomplete image of truthfulness. And this incomplete image is misleading and ultimately both treacherous and collusive in the insidious effect that it produces. The woman who continues to repeat the line about the silent woman, even if true for herself or in the broader society, has failed to recognize all the ways in which the story is not true – that is, for all the women who have spoken and written and stood up for themselves not only in the last few years, but going back decades and generations and indeed even centuries. To speak exclusively of women's verbal mutilation and/or linguistic violation, when there is substantial confirmation of the contrary, is to reiterate the myth, and, for the women who do so, equivalent to re-inscription and denial of a part of women's collective history.

Moroccan literary historian, Abdallah Mdarhri Alaoui, reminds us that there were literally thousands of women poets in Andalusia during the Middle Ages, proof that when Arab society was at the height of power, women's voices flourished. Furthermore, he asserts, even during times of repression, Arab women expressed themselves by the bias of oral literature, in stories, proverbs, songs, legends, nursery rhymes, and comic anecdotes.[11] Recently, a British scholar has chronicled the existence of some 8000 female Hadith scholars who taught, debated, and issued fatwas.[12] And Moroccan-American writer, Laila Lalami, declares, 'Muslim women are not, nor have they ever been silent,' observing that 'a significant portion of *hadith*, the Prophet's sayings that form the basis of the Sunna, are attributed to his wife, Aisha.'[13]

As for Moroccan women, they, too, have a tradition of speech and engagement, whether in speech acts – dances, trances, protest marches, embroidery, painting – or through storytelling and the development of a rich oral literature with its abundance of memorable characters, marvellous adventures, and pithy sayings.[14] Indeed, as demonstrated in so many women's works, stories and storytelling have played key roles in women's daily lives, not only because of high rates of illiteracy especially among women and/or the absence of a reading culture, but also because storytelling functions to ratify community and connectivity, to reaffirm and preserve culture, to build dreams. Every culture has its stories and legends, just as every culture has its storytellers, often revered figures who transfer cultural values and morals and accumulated wisdom. But there are also the simple storytellers, the ones who reside in family groups, who do not perform in the village square but from a cushion in a quiet corner on the terrace of a great-house (like Mernissi's Aunt Habiba) or in a darkened room (like Touria Hadraoui's Grandmother Jedda), and whose tales of the extraordinary produce a sense of wonder in the children at their feet. They are the tellers of stories that resource past, present, and future, that tap the collective memory of a family, that connect the listener to her essential humanness. More than any other form of communication, the telling of stories is an integral and essential part of the human experience, a legacy of incommensurable value, an invisible gift. And, interestingly, as sociologists tell us, it is women who are thought to be the most active gift-givers.

It is precisely this fact of women's stories and women storytellers that will form the basis for this chapter, as we chart a path from speech, to story, to the violation of speech codes, in pursuit of the goal of showing how the silent woman is a myth – too often a reflexive, self-fulfilling prophecy or reiteration of a partial social reality, ignoring the thousands, indeed, millions of real storytelling grandmothers, aunts, mothers, daughters, and cousins who are celebrated in women's works of fiction and non-fiction. In this endeavour to recuperate them, I shall first consider the clever intelligence of woman's speech in Farida Benlyazid's film, 'Women's Wiles,' then the role of storytelling and storytellers in Mernissi's *Dreams of Trespass*, Hadraoui's *Une Enfance marocaine*, Yasmina Chami-Kettani's *Cérémonie*, and Malika Oufkir's *La Prisonnière*, before concluding with a brief discussion of the combat waged by Nedjma against *hchouma* and speech taboos in *L'Amande*, which will be further addressed in chapter 4.

In Celebration of Women's Speech and Storytelling

Farida Benlyazid's feminist fairy tale 'Women's Wiles' (Ruses de femmes) is a charming confection about the war of the sexes, which sets Aïcha, who bears the name of the Prophet's favourite wife and is one of the most popular names for women in Morocco, against the Sultan's son, Sidi Mohammed.[15] As Hasna Lebbady correctly observes, their conflict begins on the level of language and is primarily carried out through language.[16] Through a series of encounters, the prince becomes smitten with Aïcha, attracted by her beauty but also, though he does not recognize it, by her deftness with words, but as a man and a prince (meaning, who expects to dominate), he repeatedly attempts to assert superiority over her. In their various conversations, whether concerning quantification (often considered a 'male' discourse), or morality and manners, they spar in lively exchanges. She responds to his blandishments and then pranks with her own taunts and tricks and ultimately escapades, as Benlyazid reveals how hidden in linguistic playfulness is a play for power. Indeed, by showing her heroine outwitting the prince in terms of language and boldness of act, by demonstrating that Aïcha can slip out of the underground prison in which the prince had locked her, then precede him in his *nzahat* or pleasure excursions, and seduce him while disguising her real identity, Benlyazid invites the spectator to applaud the mental and physical agility of her female character. When Aïcha surpasses the prince in terms of language and creativity, she proves her superiority and gains for women just revenge – made all the more sweet because in fact she really loves him. Hence, like Scheherazade, Aïcha is the mistress of both the word and the ruse.

For most viewers, this would be a Moroccan feminist fable told against an *Arabian Nights* backdrop, but Hasna Lebbady reads it differently. The folktale, on which Benlyazid bases her film, has done nothing to challenge sexist, patriarchal assumptions, according to Lebbady, who, in a Foucauldian reading, proposes that woman is shaped by and according to the interests of those in power. Hence, while Aïcha is not silenced, she is, in effect, reduced to telling the story of her own subjection and victimization, since in the end, and after the birth of several children, she marries the prince. In the final analysis, according to this argument, though Aïcha had not been forbidden access to language, she is ultimately entrapped in the male's narrative, kept at the margins of power, which, in effect, is what makes it possible for men to retain the centre of power. For Lebbady, the role of the tale is to 'enable women to submit to their confinement' (187), and narrativity, itself, has been used to confine yet another woman.

This is a rather damning indictment of a simple fairy tale, similar to the charges commonly raised by some feminist critics in the West against the genre.[17] The problem, it seems to me, is that while the argument is provocative, it misconstrues this literary genre, trying to make it an arm in the arsenal of gender wars. To be sure, as Fatima Mernissi has pointed out, there is an ancient Islamic tradition of oral storytelling in which women are the clever ones, in contrast to Muslim law in which men are given the right to dominate,[18] but that statement does not seem to imply to me that every tale with a clever woman will ultimately find herself appropriated by a dominant male counterpart. One could just as likely conclude that in proving her mettle and demonstrating grace and intellect through her speech, Aïcha is a particularly validated feminist heroine. She is imprisoned, but stages her own escapes, at will; she loves, but is not servile; she is charming, but will not be charmed or cajoled into submission. In the course of the tale, she plays many roles and adopts many costumes, but will not play the role of the fragile, witless, silent female. As one specialist on the fairy tale, Marina Warner, has suggested, when a woman bears witness to the wit and verbal cleverness of another woman, it sends a message of pride and identity, with its own rewards.[19] Aïcha never stops speaking her mind, or using her tongue and intelligence. Indeed, if anything, her story is a testament to the woman who is not silent, who adroitly exploits her talent with words, and who achieves a relationship, on her own terms, with a man she loves. In the end, she prevails, and he has to raise her up and through her, all women. Hence, the two have achieved an essential equality, a most fitting conclusion for the 'optative' fairy tale, brought about in a deft display of the magic that lies within 'this formidable female art,' to borrow Touria Hadraoui's phrase, of women's speech.

The Storyteller

In homage to so many other women who also were not silent and who told stories whether in legends, proverbs, or sayings, Moroccan women writers today incorporate myriad female storytellers in their texts, simultaneously underscoring the ways women have spoken and the power of their speech on listeners and in memory. These are not the professional storytellers – all male, moreover – of the public place, like Jemaa el-Fna, but the women who hand down family legends or who tell their own stories of the imagination, those moving stories of heroines, real or imagined. These are the women in possession of magical voices and narrative skills, who speak sometimes as though in a trance, certain about neither where their stories come from, nor how they will end; or who fall comfortably in the well-oiled grooves of a favourite story already recounted numerous times. They are women who command the art of storytelling through which they empower their listeners.

In *Dreams of Trespass*, Aunt Habiba, who was repudiated by her husband and is living *mhyuza*, or literally 'added on' to the extended family in Fez, is one of those memorable storytellers who, while no longer having a place in society, finds a new place for herself in words. She has at her disposal an endless storehouse of tales, and much to the pleasure of the youngsters who are her audience, is ready to tell of marvellous encounters and thrilling adventures far into the night. The contrast between Habiba's own existence and the stories she tells reveals the dual purpose of storytelling and the conjunctive and intimate relationship between storyteller and listener. For while Habiba cannot act directly upon her society on her own behalf, she does have the capacity to create in the little girls who sit, enraptured, at her feet, the desire for wings and independence. Indeed, Aunt Habiba's stories are instrumental in their dreams. Like so many storytellers both before and after her, Aunt Habiba draws on *The Thousand and One Nights*, never failing to delight young Fatima with stories that include a heroine who triumphs over her enemies, or who, like Princess Budor, adopts the disguise of her husband who mysteriously disappeared and subsequently marries a woman, in order to survive, while at the same time winning this woman's support (chapter 15, 'Le Destin de la princesse Budor').

There are other female storytellers in *Dreams of Trespass*, notably Mina, the black slave from Sudan, whose terrible tale of slavery and the black pit of the well into which she is dropped (chapter 17, 'Mina la déracinée') make a huge impact on young Fatima, the narrator. In fact, this story gives Mernissi the opportunity to demonstrate, both through Mina's story and Mernissi's own, key functions of storytelling – to entertain, to instruct, to inspire, and finally to cure. In telling her story and putting to it a narrative framework, with lessons and inner logic, Mina makes sense of her experience. Repeatedly, little Fatima asks her to retell the story, not only because children enjoy the ritual of repetition of the familiar, but because, as she says, she has a powerful need for the message within: 'I needed to hear it again and again so that I, too, became capable of crossing the desert and arriving on the terrace' (214). Stories in which the heroine meets adversity and triumphs are lessons in life for the child, who needs to learn all the details, 'especially, how to escape from the well.' It is in the double demonstration of how story serves the needs of both Mina and Fatima – both storyteller and listener – and creates a bond between them that Mernissi taps into the power of oral transmission and pays homage to the capacity to create links between people.

It matters little that these stories are told by illiterate women, since their effect on little girls inspires them first to imagine and then to construct their own dreams of freedom. On the wings of words – from the lips of storytellers telling of women's ordeals and triumphs – they will build their futures. Having grown up listening to stories, having served a kind of apprenticeship to the adult women storytellers in her entourage, little Fatima is eager to practise her own 'talents as a storyteller' (27). Like Aunt Habiba and Mina, she will embrace stories and not silence, and declares, 'I will cherish words. I will cultivate them so as to illuminate the night, pull down walls, and destroy all barriers' (148). She confides to her beloved aunt that like her, she will become a magician of words, shaping them to share dreams of trespass with other women. The voice that speaks is not only that of the little girl, but also Mernissi's own, whose message within the story is about the remarkable role of women's stories told for all women.

Likewise, Touria Hadraoui, in her semi-autobiographical *Une Enfance marocaine* (1998), valorizes women's speech, first, in the portrait and role of storytellers, so key to the young girl growing up, and the examples of forceful and creative female speech within the extended family; and, second, by the quality of the voice the author herself practises. Similar to Mernissi's *Dreams of Trespass*, Hadraoui's text, identified as a novel on the title page, is a collection of first-person anecdotes about the life of a young girl in Morocco in the decade after Independence. As the narrator, Touria (who carries the same first name as the author) recalls her childhood, from age five to about twelve, the reader learns that storytelling was a fundamental part of her growing up, involving both the stories she herself invents and those she hears. The first were the stories that she and her little friends invented in that privileged space, 'that place of perpetual enchantment,' according to Hadraoui, on the terrace. Located on the roof of a house, under the open sky, high above the bustle of daily activities on the floors below, the terrace is where Hadraoui's little girls come to lose themselves in a world of make-believe, recreating with their dolls adult relationships of courtship and marriage and the family, which they have observed from life below. These are the earliest stories they tell themselves and act out.

Later there will be the wonderful stories from Ramadan days, told by older boys from the neighbourhood who have heard them from their grandparents and now repeat the tales of the trials and tribulations of figures from Islamic history and legend. As young Touria says, 'What fascinated us wasn't so much their moral,' for they were too young to understand such teaching, but rather how the images and the sequence of events unfolded on an impressive rhythm, and the way the boys embraced the manner of the narrator, like professional storytellers from the ancient past (27). In other words, the children were especially receptive to the techniques of storytelling – such as the handkerchief to muffle a voice, the use of varying diction, gestures and mimicry, comical grimaces, pantomime, and animated dialogue – the tricks of the trade of ancient storytellers in the cafes of Tangier or the streets of Marrakech or the coffee houses of Cairo or Damascus.[20]

The purpose of the boys' storytelling during Ramadan in *Une Enfance marocaine* is, of course, the transfer of culture, for the holy month is also a time of evening entertainments and performances in which the stories of Islamic history are told. These are the evenings when the storyteller ignites the imagination of the listener, eager to be awed and inspired both by the *samar* ('things of the evening' or wonder stories) and by the storyteller himself, brandishing his gifts of language and drama. This is storytelling in which the play between the audience and storyteller, listener and narrator, has been enacted for generation upon generation, in many different parts of the world and at different historical moments, all with the same purpose. In the role of listener, young Touria recalls, 'We travelled on the mysterious paths of an imaginary or real past, thanks to the power of the narration and the magic of the words. The most banal reality became fantastic. The most insignificant anecdotes with regard to the Prophet Mohamed or his daughter Fatéma Ezahra, or his cousin Ali, took on extraordinary dimensions!' (27). On this page, she re-accesses these memories, with an abundance of exclamation points, underscoring the wonder and excitement of the child under the spell of storytelling.

But the most important storyteller, by far, in young Touria's life is her Grandmother Jedda to whom she devotes all of chapter 5. Jedda is a master weaver of text and of textiles, a storyteller who during the day works the great quantities of wool she keeps in her room, while in the evenings she excites the children's imagination with tales of terror and escape. Unlike the stories of the grandfather or the boys in the neighbourhood who recounted the heroic exploits of prophets or saints, Jedda's stories are thinly veiled tales from her own life, always featuring a heroine who is beautiful, delicate, and obliged to wage battle on her own against an evil force. Jedda's favourite story, 'Heina and the Ogre,' features a female protagonist kidnapped by an ogre from whom she tries repeatedly to escape. Touria adores this story because of its drama and ritual reenactment of terror and deliverance, and only inchoately understands that the story is based on the life of her grandmother, who in her early life had suffered greatly. Still, like Mernissi's Mina, Grandmother Jedda makes this story magical for the child. Sitting in the dark shadows of her grandmother's room, Touria recalls that the only light 'came from the images created by words,' and as Jedda tells her story, almost as though in a trance, the children see and feel every episode, shed tears of sympathy, hear their own hearts thump in fear as the ogre approaches and often catches Heina. Hadraoui's description captures the dynamic of storytelling, in which there is a kind of reciprocal process of creation taking place between the storyteller and her audience. It is the storyteller who carries the story in her mind's eye and reaches into her great trunk of phrases and narrative devices, crafting the images so powerfully that the pictures in her mind become the experience that her audience feels and sees. For Jedda, as for Mina, storytelling is a way of negotiating a route through the sadness that shows in her face and body, a way of releasing the words that otherwise throughout the day remain locked up, while she silently works the wool to create exquisite textiles. In this sense, Hadraoui evokes a creative tension between the dual processes of women's weaving and storytelling, simultaneously reminding the reader of the grandmother's role in the family and in the community. As historians of textiles and costumes are wont to recall, all languages are rich in textile metaphors. We speak of the 'fabric of life,' and of 'weaving together community,' and of 'the thread of the narrative.' And this is precisely the role enacted by the woman storyteller in these texts who passes down to her granddaughter a legacy of feminine wealth in story and beautiful hand-loomed fabrics.

Jedda had one prized possession – a great, painted wooden trunk, inherited from her own mother, who had died in giving birth to her. In it, Jedda stores a fine collection of fabrics, to whose touch and sight she is exquisitely – artistically – drawn. When a new fabric falls into her hands, she grazes it with nose and hand, caressing and admiring it, before adding it to the trunk. This exquisite sensitivity to the details of fabric, as to words and wool and weaving, is all part of the impact of her storytelling on her granddaughter, who, like young Fatima, grew up on an older woman's stories that would later help her shape her own.

Indeed, Touria makes a story of everything: of her budding breasts and other promising and exciting signs of approaching adult female maturity and hence of social worth; of girls and boys playing games of 'house'; of Driss, her first pubescent love and his gifts of money (a custom common to children and adults at the time); of a great-uncle who once climbed into her bed and placed her hand over his sex organ; of the clandestine rendezvous between unmarried women and men; of how she learns the vital importance of keeping her virginity despite the models of non-virgins she has in her aunt and cousin – her Aunt Keltoum, for instance, would envelope herself in a *haïk* and slip out, incognito, to meet a lover, while her father was at his prayers (chapter 7); of her first skirmishes with sensual pleasure, rather than shame or fear, when her cousin Kemal, seated next to her while watching men at a wedding ceremony get inebriated and act lustfully toward the women dancers, plants a kiss upon her cheek (87–8); of her presence outside the wedding bedroom of Omar and Mina, while the women of the two families anxiously await the bloody cloth, proving both the consummation of the marriage and that Mina is still a virgin; and, of course, of all the other powerful events of family life – relations between her parents, her father's disloyalty, her mother's sense of humiliation at being well educated but having married an illiterate man on whom she is totally dependent.

The young narrator tells stories about many subjects that a reader might think would be taboo, particularly in portraying childhood in a Muslim country: sexuality, promiscuity, physical violence within the extended family. But the author implies that while society may consider such events taboo, they happen and are part of every child's coming-of-age, and hence there is no shame in giving voice to them. The implicit message is that childhood, like storytelling, is not just about pleasure and innocence, but also about life like it is. Indeed, what makes *Une Enfance marocaine* such an empowering and delightful text is that Hadraoui paints childhood as a period of multiple realities, some magical, others rudely un-ideal, but none of such effect that the young girl, raised on storytelling, is incapable of dealing with them. When at the end, the young *narratrice* is thrashed by an angry father and dismissed by a cold and heartless mother after being falsely accused of having engaged in sexual play with a classmate, her response to this injustice is to pack her suitcase and leave the village for Casablanca where she will stay with relatives – and make her own future. Grandmother Jedda's stories of Heina and the ogre have fortified Touria against injustice and betrayal, and encouraged her in the belief that she will prevail. In emulation of her grandmother, and like Mina and Aunt Habiba, she rejects silence in favour of voice and memory, to make stories that will, in turn, become her legacies to other girls and women.

Both Hadraoui's and Mernissi's texts are identified on their title page as fiction. Both are narrated by a child who bears the same name as the author. Both narrators are curious and delightful children who observe the conflicts and semi-truths of adult life and comment 'naively' upon them. Both treat the period around Independence, and both succeed in presenting a fuller and more nuanced story of childhood than a reader from the West might expect to find. To some extent, both are the story of a young girl's coming-to-age, although each text is organized by episodes, recalling colourful family members and events and the lessons of childhood, rather than a formal plot. Jean Déjeux has said that it is often difficult to find a clear line of demarcation between autobiography and the autobiographical novel and the novel per se.[21] He believes that many Maghrebian women writers adopt the autobiographical 'I' both for the immediacy of its impact on the reader and because recourse to fiction makes it more acceptable to say 'I.' Something similar might be said about the women storytellers from Aunt Habiba to Mina to Grandmother Jedda, who through the processes of storytelling both avoid the 'I' forbidden in direct discourse and continue to speak it.

The Power of Storytelling

Stories keep us alive, says Moroccan critic Abdelfettah Kilito in an interview about the enduring relevance of *The Thousand and One Nights*.[22] Nowhere is this clearer than in Malika Oufkir's *La Prisonnière*, entitled in English, *Stolen Lives: Twenty Years in a Desert Jail*, in which, like Fatna El Bouih but in greater development, she shows how stories literally function to keep a prisoner sane, attached to her humanness, alive. Of course, politically, as well as socio-economically, there is little that brings these two writers together, since Malika was a privileged member of the upper class, while El Bouih was a Marxist-Leninist activist. My point, however, is that while everything seems to separate them, each pays special tribute to storytelling in her text.

In her memoir, Oufkir, the daughter of General Mohamed Oufkir, who was assassinated as a result of an unsuccessful coup d'état to overturn Hassan II in 1972, gives a dramatic account of her family's twenty-year imprisonment, enforced upon them because in the skewed logic of an oppressive and fearful political regime, innocent family members were required to pay for the sins of the father. Buried in a crumbling palace prison, replete with scorpions, cockroaches, and snakes, physically separated from one another in their dark cells, each family member depends on Malika's previously unknown talent for storytelling. Night after night, she tells, in serial form, stories she is scarcely aware of inventing and that quickly become the family's sole reason for living, their single defence against insanity and alienation, perhaps even the crucial motivator in their decision to dig an escape tunnel, with only the meagre tools they possess: a spoon, a can top, and a broken knife.

That at age nineteen Malika would become a storyteller capable of saving her family hardly seemed foreordained, despite her name, which in Arabic means 'queen.' In fact, she was almost a princess, having been adopted in 1958, at age five, by Mohammed V, to live at court and become a playmate for his own little daughter. As she recalls in her memoir, life at the royal palace exposed her to scenes that seemed to come from *The Thousand and One Nights*, in which, 'concubines were beaten, repudiated, banished, and disappeared for ever in the depths of the prison-palaces'

(59). In December 1972, after her father's probable assassination, the same fate befell the Oufkir family – mother, four daughters, and two sons, accompanied by her mother's cousin. They were sent first to a remote area in the desert near Algeria, where they occupied an antiquated barracks in abysmal condition, and later to Tamattaght, a disintegrating palace that had belonged to pasha El Glaoui of Marrakech. In February 1977, they were moved to the Bir Jdid Prison, isolated from one another in separate cells, forbidden to exercise, and kept malnourished. For the ten years they spent in this dungeon, they were able to communicate only because of their ingenuity and the use of hidden amplifiers and electrical wire strung between the cells, providing the means by which Malika was to become 'like Scheherazade ... the family's nightly storyteller.'[23]

In a section of *Stolen Lives* entitled 'Scheherazade' (154–9), Oufkir describes the vital role that her stories were to play for the family during their imprisonment. Once she begins telling the Story, she quickly realizes the extent of her power over the family members, and, equally, her responsibility toward them, for it is by the magic of the Story – always capitalized – that they survive. She writes, 'The Story was so real to them that I could manipulate and influence them at will. When I sensed they were unhappy, I would restore things with a few phrases' (156). The Story, involving some hundred and fifty characters, was set in nineteenth-century Russia, making it a place so far away and far removed from the present that the family was able to escape in time and space. As they followed Malika's characters through courtship and marriage, the birth of children, illnesses, and death, they entered, without knowing it, her 'emotions, fantasies, desires, and nightmares,' which she, as 'novelist, screenwriter, director, and actress,' explored 'to the full.' The Story was a lifeboat, it 'saved us all,' Malika writes. 'It helped give a pattern to our lives ... Thanks to the Story ... we didn't succumb to madness.' When she describes 'the ball gowns in intricate detail, the beaded dresses, the lace, taffeta, and jewellry, the carriages, the dashing officers and the beautiful countesses waltzing to the strains of the Tsar's orchestras,' each unhappy member of the family 'forgot the fleas, the sanitary towels, the cold, hunger, filth, the salty water, typhoid and dysentery' (159).

Such is the magic and power of story.

The Ceremony of Storytelling

In an eloquent yet elusive novel that does not really tell a story but is actually about the art of storytelling, Yasmina Chami-Kettani explores how stories with their liberating and healing powers function in our life. When her novel was published in 1999, it was widely praised by critics who could not, however, agree on what it is 'about.' One says it is an identity quest or interrogation (Michèle Bacholle); a second online source states that it shows how the cultural and social environment impacts women's affective lives (*Marrakech Info*); another proposes that the novel reveals how death launches fiction, even as it gives birth to two family legends (Isabelle Larrivée); another, still, calls it a clash between Morocco of the past and Morocco of today, and judges the character of Aunt Aïcha (who in the end becomes a bird who sings, outside her parents' home) to be one of literature's most 'irresistible heroines' (Mehdi de Graincourt); while Tahar Ben Jelloun deems *Cérémonie* primarily the story of disillusionment.[24] In truth, the novel is all this and more.

At the superficial level, the novel is the story of the cousins Khadija and Malika who come together in the Khadija's father's house for the marriage of her brother, Saïd. An architect by profession and the mother of two young daughters, Khadija has recently been rejected by her husband, not for another woman, but just because he no longer wants to be married. Her brother's wedding comes, therefore, at a moment of extreme vulnerability for her, and she is depressed and tentative, yet simultaneously agitated, at this time of another's joy. Malika, who suffers her own lack (she is sterile though happily married), tries to reach through the despondency of her cousin by recalling the stories and legends that have become legacies of family history, including, especially, those that both girls had heard at the knee of their beloved maiden Aunt Aïcha who died, in her forties, of breast cancer.

Written in a language that is evocative and poetic, the novel, as we just saw, is 'about' very little other than loss and disillusionment, the workings of memory, and the lines and planes that may or may not coincide, invoked through the notion of ceremony. It is a particularly rich and evocative concept for a writer like Chami-Kettani, trained in anthropology, since anthropologists are interested in the ceremonies of different cultures and how they accompany all the key moments of life, from birth to marriage to death. Specific ceremonies mark the passages of a life, such as birthdays, and other important events, a circumcision, for instance, or high holidays. They are key events in an individual life, just as they are in society, as a whole, or in a community. Through formal and repeated gestures and words of an incantatory quality, some ceremonies connote solemnity and commemoration; others aim to create sociability, a sense of community and associated joys. They are the rites of life, and from that standpoint, resemble storytelling and literature itself.

But ceremonies, which are thought to deal with hidden essences or 'truths,' and which couch themselves in such language, seeking to inscribe the individual in the social fabric or to create and renew bonds, do not always achieve their ends in the most direct way. Sometimes they promise much, but do not deliver. Or, as Khadija puts it, 'What good are ceremonies when everything is ephemeral?' But like the family legends of this novel, through which a narrator (Malika) seeks to reaffirm the knots of connectivity with her listener (Khadija), and to evoke the power of the past to act upon the present, ceremonies may elude simple understanding while nonetheless having a powerful effect. And ceremonies, like the ceremony of literature, not only celebrate tradition and continuity, but may also offer the possibility of tapping deep personal resources, for as Malika tells Khadija, 'life is like a ceremony in slow motion in which all the moments are strung [like beads] together ... What is magic in the ceremony is the exquisite feeling of discovering all we've always known' (11). That is a description of the very power that a legend or a family story has on a listener or reader, bearing on the familiar, embracing a truth, reiterating shared values, opening symbolic doors.

In this novel that takes place in the house of the father, where the family has gathered to celebrate a son's marriage, the first line reads, 'It was for her the only house possible.' Khadija is in the house of her father, the house of her childhood, yet as a woman who had had her own house, her own family, she is now a supplicant with three children in tow, a failure as a wife, a woman who had been left like 'a box abandoned in an empty house after a move' (79). She, an architect who built houses for other people, cannot keep her own house from being destroyed ('I can do nothing to keep it standing; its very walls are falling down around me' [73]), and has now returned, in the middle of the night, to the house of her father, her point of origin and first refuge, in a kind of life journey in reverse: 'And today, her superb body now a shell of itself, at the marriage of her brother, in the house of her father, where she has returned as though on a trip going backward' (101).

Believing in the power of story to heal, Malika reaches back in memory to retap the stories of their past, the legends that had grown up around the family, and seeks to 'restring the pearls of the necklace' for her cousin. In a new kind of ceremony, that of storytelling, she endeavours to elicit from her cousin a change of heart, a liberation from her depression. Through the rituals of storytelling and the ceremony within legends, Malika acts to re-access the power of family legends, to put the listener back in touch with 'all we've always known.'

The two legends in this novel, the story of the white mule and the story of the young girl raised by an eagle, relate to and complement one another, in conjunction with the story of Aunt Aïcha. The legend of the white mule and the magnificent saddle owned by the great-great grandfather of Malika and Khadija's tells of his inordinate pride in the saddle, and of his wife Lalla Zohra's sense of foreboding that such vainglory will visit upon the family some horrible misfortune. So when this happens and their beloved grandson drowns in the river, she quietly takes matters into her own hands one night to prevent any further evil from befalling her family by slitting the mule's throat. Just how the mule died would remain a family mystery, of great sorrow and consternation to its formerly proud owner, and a secret that Lalla Zohra shares only with her servant, who had lent her aid. What the story shows is not so much the woman's superstition, as her resolve and ability to act without a man's permission, and indeed even against what would be his own desires, and to lock within herself a secret in order to keep her family safe.

The second legend is told by Aunt Aïcha. It begins with a woman who had been unable to conceive and consults a witch who gives her a magic apple.[25] By mistake, the husband eats it and subsequently gives birth through his foot to a baby girl. An eagle comes and takes the misbegotten infant to its nest where the years pass and she grows into a beautiful woman with an enchanting voice. One day a prince hears her sing and falls in love, but she will not descend from the tree because the eagle has forbidden it. When the prince realizes that he cannot have her, he becomes heartsick and offers a reward to anyone who can bring her down, and death to whoever tries but does not succeed. Many fail, until one day an old woman comes to the foot of the tree where she tries to build a fire to make her dinner. Repeatedly foiled in her attempts, she calls upon the young girl for help, and finally, out of pity, the girl decides to disobey the eagle and descends in a show of sisterly support. Of course, she subsequently marries the prince and becomes his queen. Thus her action, like Scheherazade's, brings to an end the unjust murders perpetrated by an arbitrary prince, a common theme in *Les Mille et une nuits*.[26]

The meaning of Chami-Kettani's two stories derives from women's agency, or internal resourcefulness or power, meaning that 'magic' can be found within, or as Malika tells Khadija somewhat more prosaically, 'le placard [est] en toi' (the cupboard is within yourself), rather than in the house of either the father or the husband. Human existence necessarily implies loss and sacrifice, but also recovery and liberation. In the legends, Lalla Zohra loses a grandson, and the beautiful young woman has lost her original human family, whereas in the novel, Aïcha loses a breast, Khadija a marriage, Malika the hope for motherhood. But against those losses are the women in the two legends who find ways of meeting a challenge, disposing of that which risks destroying them, finding ways to free themselves. Aïcha's relationship to the female protagonists of the legends and her pleasure in recounting their stories derives from the woman's power to affect her surroundings. Indeed, the final image of Aïcha, metamorphosed after death into a turtledove who sings on a branch outside her parents' new home, shows that the voice of the storyteller will still be heard. In the ceremony of retelling, in the family circle, as in the house of literature, deep roots are rediscovered, and through the reenactment of memory and the language of poetry, potentially curative powers are released. Hence, family legends have the power not only to reaffirm the ties of blood, but also to point the way toward healing, through words and stories.

In this sense, then, the most important ceremony in *Cérémonie* is not the brother's wedding, which does not occur before the novel concludes, but rather the acts of storytelling that take place. It is in the celebration of story, the techniques of the storyteller, the play between the teller and listener, the transaction of the pleasure and emotion of the story, the impact of narrative on life, that Chami-Kettani has created the most important ceremony. It is in this sense of the ceremony of literature that *Cérémonie* is both a meta-literary text and a liberating one. In the recuperation of women's speech and stories, the author gives wings to her heroine and points the way toward recovery.

Violating Speech Codes

In another register, altogether, *The Almond* is an audacious, boundary-breaking work of semi-autobiographical erotica by an anonymous author who calls herself Nedjma and who claims to be an observant Muslim. In her work, she shatters taboos in terms of the depiction of male-female relationships, woman's speech, and the female's participation in the genre of what some would call pornography. To a considerable extent, however, her story is about language – saying everything, speaking 'like a seasoned whore' (195) – because, as with the Marquis de Sade, language is a good part of the breaking of taboos. In a culture in which so many feel that silence reigns, it is crucial, Nedjma asserts, to mount an assault on Arab society and the kind of social dysfunction that perpetuates male dominance over women. By destroying limits on speech, by breaking taboos on what women can say, by flourishing an erotically charged female pen, Nedjma takes a political stand. She will make literature, she says, a 'lethal weapon,' in an effort to give back to women the power of speech. By writing an erotic story, the genre dominated by men, and by outdoing the male writer in terms of boldness of description, explosive imagery, and striking originality, she will move dramatically beyond Farida Benlyazid's Aïcha, both to assert women's talent for words and writing, and their talent for and pleasure in sex, and to strike a well-aimed blow at cultural paralysis. In the prologue to her work, she says that she sees speech – specifically, women's speech – and the appropriation of 'the confiscated mention of the body' as advancing the larger quest of healing society. Hence, she lays claim to a social purpose: to cure men of an unspoken and metaphoric illness, and to liberate women. In defiantly choosing the bluntest of language, she intends to reclaim for women their right to speak about sexual pleasure and pride.

Because readers in the West as in the East are unaccustomed to women writing stories of flesh and soul in such explicit language, the sceptical reader is at first suspicious that the writer may be a man writing as a woman, since as literary scholars know, the phenomenon of men imitating women's voices is not unknown in the world of letters, and the purposes are often unhelpful to women. But Alan Riding, who interviewed Nedjma in Paris in summer 2005, definitely met a woman, a 'feisty 40-something North African,' intent upon writing a 'cry of protest' against the self-serving pieties of hate and hypocrisy in both East and West.[27] Of course it is possible that the woman he met might have been impersonating the actual author as part of an extended hoax. But even if that were the case, there is no getting around the point that the book represents the ultimate claim to free speech on behalf of women. Writing for *Le Journal hebdomadaire*, Najat Chatr, the woman who manages the Bookstore Chatr in Marrakech, strongly recommends the book to readers, precisely because she believes that it calls into question so-called truths about what women can and cannot do.[28] Expressing no reservations about the sex of the author, Chatr finds it natural that the writer of such an 'extreme story' of raw and daring eroticism, written in such scorching and fierce prose, would prefer to be anonymous. In the final analysis, we might conclude, what matters is that a writer called Nedjma has not just written courageously, but also fearlessly, using textual images both vividly and lyrically to speak the unspoken, to articulate extreme pride and pleasure and power in woman's sexuality and her speech. This writer is a storyteller whose language is at once crude and elegant, obscene and sensual, exalted and stunningly rich – and definitely not silent.

Conclusion

The myth of silence is deeply engrained in this Arab land. Yet, in fact, as this chapter has endeavoured to show, women have a long history of speaking, particularly all those aunts and grandmothers and female cousins and sisters who are such celebrated storytellers. And for the last three decades, despite the daunting challenges, political and personal, that face the writer of either sex in Morocco, women novelists and essayists have published scores of works, as we saw in chapter 1. Thus, while the psychology that prompts the complaint of being rendered into silent women is understandable, it is difficult to accept the charge unconditionally, let alone join with those who dramatize women's sense of impotence by speaking of 'female verbal mutilation.'[29] What the former are talking about, of course, is the inferior status of women in society, while those in the second group are concerned with the disrespect shown to women's words in a patriarchal tradition that, in emulation of autocratic rule, reifies and depends on the silence of women and/or the silent woman. In this respect, we recall the traditional charge that the undervaluation of women's speech derives from the Qur'anic verse (2:282), where it says that it takes two female witnesses to equal one male witness.[30] But we should equally recall that women's speech in Morocco has neither been publicly forbidden nor censored, even if culturally discouraged, while the same cannot be said for other forms of speech in the public sphere – for example, those of satirists and human rights activists and of Berber heritage, whose pronouncements have been severely sanctioned and forcibly silenced, at times.

Paradoxically, while women writers lament women's silence, they themselves exercise a liberated tongue to deplore the cult of female silence. In the double tension of the contradiction, they risk a further and more injurious paradox whereby by reiterating so endlessly the tale of women's silence, the statement takes on the value of a self-fulfilling prophecy. To be sure, the quality of female imagination and speech have often been diminished and discredited in the West, as in the East, and scorn can be a strategy to silence women. But that tactic is successful only when a population takes refuge in the pernicious myth of the silent woman, and refuses, despite the evidence, to see or to hear all those many women who have spoken out.

Edward Said is credited with the phrase 'the silence of the native,' by which is meant that certain people – Muslim women, we might suggest – somehow cannot speak for themselves. But as this chapter demonstrates, Moroccan women writers give ample evidence that no one needs to be called on to speak on their behalf. They are fully capable of doing this themselves, as writer after writer has so powerfully illustrated. By refusing silence, the Moroccan woman writer may be transgressing upon earlier expectations of her culture, but by contesting the barriers, she is also changing that culture.

4 Transgressive Narratives

Transgress, v.t.**1**. to pass over or go beyond (a limit, boundary, etc.): to transgress the bounds of prudence. **2**. to go beyond the limits imposed by (a law, command, etc.); violate; infringe; break: *those who transgress the will of God.* – v.i. **3**. to break or violate a law, command, moral code, etc.; offend; sin.
Random House Dictionary

Women's writing emerges not only as a transgression against the norm, but also as a sign of the emergence of the individual.
Abdellatif Felk, Tel Quel, 15–21 mars 2003, 45.

[Transgressive fiction is] a literary genre that graphically explores such topics as incest and other aberrant sexual practices, mutilation ... urban violence and violence against women ... and that is based on the premise that knowledge is to be found at the edge of experience and that the body is the site for gaining knowledge.
Anne H. Soukhanov, The Atlantic Monthly, December 1996, 128.

To utter the words 'transgression,' 'violence,' and 'eroticism' in the same breath as Moroccan women writers appears, in itself, to violate everything that we think we know about North Africa. Both we and they have bought the notion that Arab Muslim women are highly conservative, if not actually repressed, about sex, that Islamic culture commands silence and modesty of women, and that no member of the female sex, as opposed to a man, writes openly about the body, sexual desire, and practices.[1] It would be *hchouma* (inappropriate or shameful behaviour) to do so, a grave crime against *hichma* (modesty), a transgression of *qa'ida* (norms), a perilous foray into the forbidden or *haram*.² And yet Moroccan women have written about sex and sexual perversion and every sexual issue from deflowering and premarital sex, to the wedding night, to rape, including marital rape, to the rape-mutilation of a young girl by a group of crones; to bisexuality and homosexual attraction, boredom in the conjugal bed, lesbianism, masturbation, childhood sex games, and even female paedophilia. In addition they have used themes of prostitution, repudiation, adultery, polygamy, domestic abuse, and sexual violence perpetrated not just by men but also by women on other women, plus explicit and imaginative sexual imagery to convey the sensual body responding to sexual stimuli, or the nightmare of patriarchal society as a figurative city of 'sexes en érection.'³ In fact, there is very little that they have not said. And yet, typically, even educated Moroccans would claim that while men like Mohamed Choukri (1935–2003) can write about sex of the rawest kind and in the most graphic and vulgar of detail, a woman neither can, nor would, write about sex, let alone cruelty, violence, and violation.⁴

The fact of the matter is quite different, as evidenced in works written in French by Houria Boussejra, Souad Bahéchar, Bahaa Trabelsi, Rajae Benchemsi, and especially the anonymous Nedjma, while in Arabic Sanaa Elaji has published a sexy novel about adultery, passion, and hypocrisy.⁵ By including in their works such controversial subject matter as paedophilia, necrophilia, dismemberment, and genital mutilation, or even, for that matter, sexual passion, such female writers give voice to silenced subjects marginalized by common taboos, and challenge the phallocentric power structure of society, and of language. Their writing often shocks and disturbs, yet by ignoring taboos, these female authors not only break new ground and 'see' differently, they also assert a quality of freedom heretofore unclaimed by women. By making transgression and violence a part of their writing – as they are of a woman's life – their creative works stand in diametrical opposition to public expectation that women's literature will be delicate, sensitive, decorative, and distracting. As a result, conventional notions about what women can write and how they will write are wholly confuted.

In this chapter, I will treat two primary kinds of transgressive fiction. The first concerns social, sexual, and moral transgression, and will focus on the body, sex, and woman in Nedjma's *L'Amande* (*The Almond*), a form of literary pornography with Sadean elements.⁶ The second, which can be called literary transgression, involving intellectualized and aestheticized violence and eroticism, coupled with mysticism and obsession, and influenced by the ideas of Georges Bataille and Maurice Blanchot, will be studied in the short *récits* of Rajae Benchemsi, collected under the title of *Fracture du désir*. As I examine the role and function of transgression in these two works, supported by references to other women writing in a similar vein, my objective is to understand how Moroccan women writers have striven to arrive at new forms of knowledge by pushing the envelope and using the transgressions of flesh, gender, sex, and art in fictions that are at once original and highly literate, and that expand the normal boundaries of genre.

Eroticism, Violence, and Violation

> In essence, the domain of eroticism is the domain of violence, of violation.
>
> Georges Bataille

Transgression is at the very centre of Nedjma's enterprise in *The Almond*, which has been described by a Moroccan critic as 'a cry of protest,' and by Nedjma, herself, as being against ideologies of violence concerning the body in both East and West.[7] She explains that in the former, the body represents the 'last taboo ... where all the political and religious prohibitions are concentrated,' particularly for women, whereas in the West, and despite official rhetoric, the body is undervalued, witnessed by the prevalence of retaliatory wars and ideologies. Nedjma told Alan Riding that she sees her book as a means by which to conduct a battle for democracy on the very field that no one seemed to care about – the human body – an argument that the Marquis de Sade or D.H. Lawrence or Henry Miller might have made. And like them, she tells her 'story of soul and of flesh' (as she describes in the prologue) in the most transgressive way possible, uniting eroticism with crude sex, violent desire with taboo practices, unburdened 'by any moral standards other than those of the heart.' And all in a language that knows no boundaries, that breaks every rule of decorum, and yet is also both powerfully lyrical and powerfully vulgar. Political, feminist, pornographic, and blasphemous, Nedjma's novel transgresses conventions of gender and genre, 'to break down the walls that now separate the celestial from the terrestrial, body from soul, the mystical from the erotic' (prologue).[8]

Her first-person narrator, Badra, is approaching age fifty and retraces her life through its sexual history. She has returned from Tangier and decades of sensual exploration to her native village of Imchouck where she has just buried the only man she ever loved, Driss. Boastfully crude and dismissive of everything but herself and her own body, Badra takes her pen to write 'in response to' Cheikh Nefzaoui, who had composed one of the pillars of Arabic erotic literature from the sixteenth-century, *The Perfumed Garden*. Her intent is to surpass Nefzaoui, who had celebrated the male sexual organ, 'straight as a lance so it may wage war inside the vagina,' by glorifying her own peerless sex organ. The story, told in the first person, is developed through chapters written either in plain text or italics, non-chronologically, and through memories of childhood and adult experiences in which sexuality and culture are intermingled. Married against her will at age seventeen, raped by her husband with the help of his mother and her own sister on her wedding night, Badra escapes to Tangier to live with Aunt Selma whose liberal mores suit the younger woman's own inclinations. She soon meets Driss, a wealthy and famous cardiologist, who gives her 'time to fantasize about his voice, his hands, and his smell,' to 'ripen quietly during long pomegranate-filled afternoon naps' (96) before, in an extended and exquisitely erotic scene (99–105), he 'opens the almond' to its full potential.[9]

Nedjma's technique is to juxtapose scenes, not consecutively or chronologically, but logically, between socially sanctioned but repugnant sex and unsanctioned erotic passion. Thus, the chapter, 'Badra's Marriage' (29–34), is followed by her depiction of the ugliness of sex with the forty-year-old, twice-married husband (37–8), his family's surveillance of her belly to see if progeny is forthcoming ('Your vagina must be like a sieve. It can't hold on to any semen!' [43]), and finally 'The Night of Deflowering' (109–15) telling about when the despised husband tries repeatedly to penetrate her 'padlocked hymen,' until, with the aid of women who tie her down, he at last rips through her (109–15). Those segments stand in contrast to the early scenes with Driss (99–105), a riff on happiness ('Happiness is making love because of love' [107]) and on cunnilingus and masturbation and contraceptive and sexual beauty rites (117–26), in addition to those scenes involving sexual memories from her childhood. Badra recalls, for instance, her first experience of sexual feeling as a child, near a bridge over the Harrath Wadi ('Badra's Childhood,' 77–8), in which a figure (real or unreal) accosted her in such a pleasurable way that she was to say, 'A second heart had been born between my legs' (78). In another scene from childhood ('Badra at the School of Men' [127–36]), she recalls at age ten engaging in sex games with other girls under the bed ('hands were playing a delirious score on consenting bodies' [133]), and later exhibiting herself without panties to boys who paid a coin to her cousin, Saïd, who organized the peep show in order to buy a ball with the financial proceeds ('My pussy for a ball!' exclaims Badra in a comically pornographic turn on Richard III's exclamation, 'My kingdom for a horse' [136]).

Eventually there will be a downward spiral to the affair, as Driss, the cardiologist ironically demonstrates that he knows little of the heart, and is incapable of making Badra his exclusive partner. Now, sex with Driss includes mental cruelty (149–53) and discussions on God ('He claimed to be an atheist. I claimed I was a believer. Such crap! Out of love for Driss, I accepted playing chess with God' [152]); he insists on group sex and episodes involving the lesbians Najat and Saloua (155–9, 168–70, 179–83). There is his infatuation with Hamid, a married man who is 'a professor of medieval history and [who] knows more about Pepin the Short and Bertha with the Big Feet than anyone else. More important, he has an ass like a queen' [192]), and with gay sex in general (189–96). And then there is his violence toward Badra, bondage and physical pain (he makes her swallow burning coals, to which she does not object, but only says, 'He always went further than I could imagine, always surpassed my fantasies and nightmares' [209]). Against these scenes, Nedjma intersperses a chapter, 'Naïma, the Overjoyed' (161–6), on Badra's sister, whose midnight coupling with her fiance, like a 'battle above the head of a sleeping Ali' (the eleven-year-old brother who was supposed to be chaperoning the engaged pair), inflamed the twelve-year-old voyeur, Badra, causing her to vow that one day she, too, 'would make beds creak, beds as enormous as the fields of Imchouck,' her 'husband [would] shout with pleasure,' because her 'cunt would be that ardent, biting like the burning waves of the Chergui, tight as a rosebud' (166). At another point, she recalls her experience at boarding school, 'a purring brothel' ('Hazima, the Roommate,' 171–4), and 'fiddling around with someone of the same sex,' an ostensibly innocent activity, 'merely preparing ourselves to receive the male' (173) until, she says, her 'cunt put an end to [her] studies, as Hmed the notary was drooling with impatience to possess it' (174). But these are only momentary diversions in the narrative headed for break-up between the two principals, after which Badra continues her 'career' as a sex-obsessed protagonist, consumed with the 'desire to play, kill, die, betray, spew out, and curse … To screw while not giving a royal fuck for the container' (213–14), to be 'a slit,' imperious and increasingly cruel, to men but especially to a woman, Wafa, who had fallen in love with her (219–24).

In 1991, fourteen years after leaving Driss, she sees him again, and he informs her that he has cancer: 'He told me about the metastasis, the morphine, and the final stage' (227). He asks her to marry him, and she refuses, but she does agree that he can accompany her back to Imchouck where she cares for him physically and emotionally until his death. She refuses only his entreaties to make love, not because of distaste for having sex with a dying man, but fearful that he 'would suddenly grow slack when faced with the body' – hers, no longer as firm – he 'had celebrated so much' (232). He lives long enough to regret his earlier spurning of her, and at the end says, 'Merciful God, make Badra know that I have loved only her,' just as she has loved only him. Ultimately, then, the novel can be read as a story of a great love that ends tragically.

However, in a comic coda, on the last couple of pages, Badra feels a 'presence' in the room where she has been writing the very book we are reading, describing him as a visitor, an angel, who leans down to read, over her shoulder, the history she has traced of herself, from 'the mischievous child' to 'the Arab geisha,' from 'the incantations of faith and the obscene words' that fill the pages of her text, to her love for Driss (236). As the angel reads aloud, she feels 'something hardened' against her back. 'An angel's sex organ?' she queries herself, at the same time that he objects, 'Aren't you ashamed of what you've just written?' And then he berates her, 'Not a single one of God's creatures would tolerate hearing so many obscenities out of the mouth of a woman' (237). When she turns to confront him, she sees only 'gigantic balls hanging down and a penis jutting out that resembled Chouikh's donkey's in every detail,' while Driss's voice chides her, 'Oh, my almond! ... When faced with the sins of a woman, angels are men like all the others.'

In that final scene, combining the comic and the sexual, Nedjma foresees the hypocrisy that will greet publication of a novel that transgresses so many boundaries, laws, and commandments. And that also transgresses on the rules of literary genre and gender. Is her novel straight-out pornography or literary pornography? Is it feminist pornography? A tragic love story done up in pornographic language? A mixture of comedic vulgarity and despicable cruelty? A critique of the sexual mores and dissimulations of Moroccan culture? A pagan and blasphemous text or a song of praise in the manner of early Arabic erotic literature?

To address those questions, we must recall that, while Islam is widely thought in the West to be a conservative and perhaps even sexually repressive religion, paradoxically, ancient Arab civilization is responsible for having produced one of the richest and most abundant literatures of eroticism. There are literally hundreds of treatises, penned by men, on love, desire, and the passions inspired by women. The nature of many of these treatises, detailing the quality of sexual foreplay and the kinds of caresses to be bestowed on various parts of the body, advice as to the signs of female sexual arousal and the degree and angle of penetration, is joyously explicit.[10] Thus, in Franco-Algerian Yasmina Benguigui's documentary film, *The Perfumed Garden*, anthropologist Mohamed Lasly observes that love and sex were considered by men of religion during the period of 'permissive Islam,' from the ninth to the sixteenth centuries, in a very scientific way, precisely because the notion of pleasure constituted an important pole of the sacred.[11] During this period of openness, corresponding to the flowering of Arab civilization before the imposed retreat of Islam from Andalusia, carnal pleasure was recognized as having a genuine role in the life of the believer. Some declared that such pleasure was a part of God's plan not only for procreation, but also for bringing the individual closer to God. As Fatima Mernissi observes, one of Islam's greatest theologians, Abu Hamid al-Ghazali (d. 1111), wrote in his *Revivification of the Religious Sciences*, 'Sexual desire as a manifestation of God's wisdom has, independently of its manifest function, another one: when the individual yields to it and satisfies it, he experiences a delight which would be without match if it were lasting.'[12] The sex act, he continues, is 'a foretaste of the delights for *men* in Paradise, because to make a promise to *men* of delights they have not tasted would be ineffective ... This earthly delight, imperfect because limited in time, is a powerful motivation to incite *men* to try and attain the perfect delights, the eternal delight ... [of] heaven' (emphasis mine). A valid question is whether Ghazali's text applies only to *men* or to *mankind* in the sense of *humankind*, which would include women in the equation.

In view of the preceding paragraph, it is quite possible that Nedjma writes as the first Arab woman to wage fierce competition with those powerful and erotic pens of the male writers from ancient Arab civilization. However, her text also raises questions about the apposition of sex and religion. Erotic sex is a new religion for Badra, but her relationship to God continues to be present in her thoughts, and hence her sense of sin, when she directs her 'supplications to God in the middle of screwing'

(186) and implores him to avert her gaze when she makes love with Driss during Ramadan. 'Don't look at me now,' she beseeches him. 'Look elsewhere until I am done' (187). Badra has blind faith in God (150), she believes she has a soul (ibid.), but at the same time she also admits to Driss 'Sometimes I tell myself you and God are the same. Too much power! Too seductive! I love you so much that making love seems to me to be the only prayer capable of rising to heaven and being written down in the register of all my actions that are worthy and justified in the eyes of the Eternal' (151). One might say that she utters these words in memory of the writings of all those early theologians, imams, philosophers, and poets who had argued that God created sexual love and pleasure as the greatest happiness and that both receiving and giving pleasure are duties of the believer. But Badra may also know that this is only true for *nikah*, the 'legitimate act of love,' declared by El Bokhari, the famous compiler of hadith (the words and deeds of the Prophet) to be a veritable 'act of faith,' a kind of charitable 'giving' when authorized by marriage, but sinful, otherwise.[13] And Badra is nothing if not keenly conscious of which side of permission she occupies. Indeed, she confesses to knowing that she 'had crossed a divine line after crossing a social line,' that she is living in 'pagan territory,' that her 'faith had disappeared between [her] legs,' but she prays to God to let Driss make love to her again (152). She appears torn between knowing that she sins but that God still loves her (153), and claiming that her conscience is clear because she gives alms to the sick and poor, and also because it is God who has made sexual pleasure so possible. 'Welcome to God, to wheat and to olive trees!' she exults, 'Welcome to hearts pierced by love and behinds blessed by the holy water of the stars' (122). By combining especially sinful sex, in both the religious and the conventional senses, with religious expression, Nedjma mixes tones, uniting the sacred with the base, yet she also illustrates the sinner's true anguish. Hence, during a particularly graphic scene with Driss and the lesbians, the author has Badra say, 'I was getting so wet that even Judgment Day was forgotten. I was getting wet and praying to the Lord, "Please, do not watch! Please, forgive me! Please, don't forbid me to walk into Your Kingdom and pray there again! Please, deliver me from Driss! Please, tell me that You are my only God who will never abandon me! I beg You, Lord help me leave this hell!"' (181–2).

What this discussion reveals is the multiplicity of Nedjma's motives: to glorify the sex act, as pornographers often do, raising it to a kind of religious ecstasy; to be simultaneously angry, serious, and irreverent, combining parody and paradox in her choice of libertine conventions, striking a blow against the centuries-old repression of Muslim women, and at the same time showing the conflicted nature of Badra's freedom. Certainly the novel can be read as mordant social criticism, a judgment that does not put it at odds with a reading of feminist pornography or perhaps even a tragic pornographic love story – something of a transgression in itself. But the novel may just as likely be termed non-feminist, not only because Badra lets herself be victimized and ultimately abused by Driss, but also because the portrait of a liberated Badra after she leaves him is of such an angry woman. Georges Bataille has defined eroticism as a movement toward the limits of the individual's subjectivity, and the phrase seems particularly apt with regard to Badra. But in the end, the reader has to ask, does Nedjma really succeed in reversing typical sexual domination of women, or does her use of violent, sexual imagery and coupling continue the demeaning objectification of women? In what way does this text heal or liberate women – her ostensible purpose announced on the first page of the prologue – aside from proving the equally capacious nature of the female sex drive compared with man's, or in terms of exploding the notion that women cannot write about sex as powerfully as men. The novel is a love story, to be sure, but thoroughly suffused with the pulsating beat of violation.

Indeed, it is through violation and art that Nedjma seeks to have an effect. Like the writers to whom I compared her earlier, Sade, Lawrence, and Miller, Nedjma brings to bear considerable literary and aesthetic qualities to her enterprise. She is cultivated and well versed in Arabic, European, and American culture and history. She knows the conventions of pornographic literature; she has isolated its structures, themes, and motifs, and uses them effectively. She knows how to travel in the text between temporalities, to keep the reader in suspense, to renew again and again the language of desire, of coupling and orgasm. She uses striking visual images, at times uniting the dissimilar and unexpected, as, for instance, when she has Driss describe men at a funeral wearing 'silk djellabas, shining like bidets' (193); or when, to evoke the feeling of sexual bliss, she has Badra say, 'The world had suddenly become a caress. The world had become a kiss. And I was nothing but a floating lotus flower' (105). There can be no dispute that her language is powerfully evocative, lyrically or pungently, as the case may be.

Still, like most writers who write in the pornographic mode, Nedjma has been criticized for a lack of effective characterization, accused of bringing forth protagonists that are not much more than stick figures.[14] On the contrary, I would argue that both Badra and Driss are richly endowed and original 'types' for this kind of writing, memorable characters in their own right. They are, of course, student and master, acolyte and priest, as befits the erotic convention, but they are also more than that. Badra is not the classic naive who discovers in spite of herself her sensuality. Rather, the author is at pains to establish her character's basic, natural sexual nature from childhood to maturity. Badra is, in fact, a new version of the modern Moroccan woman in that she is intelligent, discerning, and active in securing her own liberation from a despised husband. She is a non-conforming female, rejecting traditional notions of shame and guilt to assert freedom; she violates social norms to affirm herself. Indeed, the author, by narrating the 'natural' female body (the *Harrath Wadi*, the childhood sex games, the unharnessed sexual passion of the unmarried woman) against the policing of the woman's body ('I held it against Imchouk that it had connected my genitals with evil, had forbidden me to run, to climb trees, or to sit with my legs spread' [81]), and the socially sanctioned prodding of the female body (to determine whether the bride-to-be is still 'intact' [34]), and women's own role in constraining the female body (Badra is literally tied down by her sister and mother-in-law on her wedding night [115]) – by narrating all that, the author is making a powerful case for Badra's subsequent actions. By giving her a culturally based past, Nedjma motivates her protagonist's future actions, an atypical choice for straight pornography. Moreover, Badra is an emotionally multidimensional character, intensely capable of love, but not ultimately so blinded by her emotions and her body's desires that she accepts a thoroughly compromised relationship with Driss. To be sure, her subsequent debauchery denies her any standing as a model heroine for the reader, but it is equally true that she is a free woman who retains the right to be and to do as she wishes – even to love Driss to the very end and ultimately to triumph. In fact, just before his death, Driss makes a final prayer-lament-confession to God that he has sinned, been 'blind, leprous, paralytic, and deaf' (232) to the song of love and to this woman's love. In the sense that reciprocal love marks the last pages, Badra is avenged, perhaps somewhat conventionally, but in that she is an intelligent, independent woman, fully responsible for her own actions and who deals with loss from a position of strength, she is emblematic of a new kind of feminism.

Nedjma has written Driss as the figure of the aesthete-sensualist, the man of broad culture and expertise, a brilliant physician known throughout Tangier but also widely travelled, a lover of books who reads Simone de Beauvoir, Boris Vian, Louis Aragon, Lamartine, Racine, and who adores Oum Koulthoum and Abou Nawas. He is a type not unknown in nineteenth-century European letters. But through his egotism, tempered in the beginning of his affair with Badra by his tenderness, the author uses her pen to skewer the prerogatives of males, even intelligent, cultured, professional men like Driss. He is the high priest of sex, the teacher and educator not only of sensualism, but also of literature and music, politics and wine, and the great capitals of the world. But he knows too much, he has done too much. Even at the end, he can only partially redeem himself with the reader when, consumed by cancer and hence physically vulnerable, he admits his emotional vulnerability, lamenting that he had spat upon Badra's love when in fact he had loved only her. So, unlike Sade's Dolmancé, he seeks forgiveness and receives it from her, not so much a hero as a man like others, weak in the flesh.

In the final analysis, *L'Amande* is a text of multiple intentions that arguably succeeds as literature at the same time as it acts less nobly. Doubtless, Nedjma writes scenes of erotic pornography, but she also goes beyond pornography, often lampooning its pretensions, undermining them through comedic intrusions. She uses pseudo-scientific language to present the body's longings, writing, when Badra prepares to break with Driss, 'The body is always a session behind. I hate the memory of the cells for its canine devotion that taunts the neurons and merrily scorns the cortex and its wild fantasies' (197–8). By violating expectations about women's writing, as well as literary conventions about the tones and levels of language, and by veering toward blasphemy or profanation in the union of religion and sex, Nedjma creates a powerful example of transgressive fiction and claims a new place for the woman writer in Moroccan letters. Through the portrayal of forbidden behaviours, Nedjma shocks her reader, but also authorizes her protagonists's pursuit of personal freedom. She is not the first Moroccan woman to write about sex, but she is surely the most explosively graphic.

From Sex to Sexual Violence

Indeed prior to Nedjma, but in a much less erotic way, Touria Hadraoui writes about the child's awakening to sex in *Une Enfance marocaine*, recalling the child's eagerness for breasts and pubic hair as signs of impending womanhood and of her early experience with adult sexuality through exposure to older girls in her family. She recalls the exploits of her aunts Keltoum and Zina: the former had sneaked off to visit her lover while her father was preoccupied with his prayers (chapter 7), while the latter, even more cunning and eager for erotic adventures, had used young Touria as an alibi for visiting a lover and then making love with him while the child waited in a nearby room (chapter 8). Young Touria also remembers prostitutes (chapter 9), and childhood games of 'grown-up' that hinted at play-sex (chapter 10), and a molestation by an uncle (chapter 10). But obviously, Hadraoui's text of coming-to-age – a small jewel of considerable charm – is hardly shocking, though it does deal with subjects that a conservative application of *hchouma* would have found unacceptable.

The author of *L'Amande* is also not the first to write of lesbian attraction or homosexuality (see Bahéchar's *Ni Fleurs, ni couronnes* and Trabelsi's *Une Vie à trois*); or of strong sexual desire (Trabelsi, *Une Femme tout simplement* and Benchekroun, *Oser vivre*); or of an abusive love relationship (Trabelsi, Benchekroun); or of physical violence of women on women (Boussejra, Bahéchar); of fleshly pleasures or the thrill of discovering sexual feelings (Trabelsi, Benchekroun); of the relationship between alienated sex and murder (Benchemsi, 'Kira et Slima'). But it is true that no other writer before Nedjma had done so with such a mixture of aesthetics and vulgarity, such crudeness and poetry, such powerful and fierce prose, in a conscious drive to scandalize and to make a searing impression on the reader.

We might speculate that the Moroccan woman writer is often drawn to portray violence both for sociocultural reasons (because in Moroccan society women often feel victimized) and because she seeks to shock the reader out of complacency and to break down the barriers of *hchouma* by the inclusion of violation in her narratives.[15] In part, the violence she narrates is predicated on conventions of the novel which privilege the dramatic; in part, it tells the story of her female character's victimization by family, lover, or husband; but even more so, the violence directed at or through her character represents a critique of the social body. It is by means of the rape or the repudiation or the punishment or marginalization of her main character that the writer tells not just an individual woman's story, but also the broader story of society.[16] As an anthropologist who studies violence as a cultural phenomenon explains, 'Violent actions are deeply infused with cultural meaning and are the moment for individual agency within historically embedded patterns of behavior.'[17] And it is also by writing the violation that the writer, herself, ostensibly 'violates' the norms of language, gender, and culture, which is an ironic commentary on the gendered politics of writing.

Moroccan women's writing frequently contains themes of violence against women, including rape. There are, in fact, several kinds of rape in women's texts, from the rape of a servant girl by a master, sometimes as mere background without either it or her being the main story, or at other times involving a main character (such as Hafsa, one of the principal females in Damia Oumassine's *L'Arganier des femmes égarées*); there are legalized rapes, as in the deflowering of the unwilling bride (*L'Amande*), and what amounts to marital rape (described in detail by Benchekroun, *Oser vivre*); there is the rape of a child by a woman (Boussejra's 'Tamou'); rape as the motivating factor for an adolescent's descent into mental exile (Benchemsi, *Marrakech lumière d'exil*); and a rape-mutilation in Souad Bahéchar's *Ni Fleurs ni couronnes*.

Interestingly, both Bahéchar's and Boussejra's rapes are perpetrated by women as acts of revenge. In fact, in Bahéchar's Bildungsroman, *Ni Fleurs, ni couronnes*, a rape-mutilation becomes the key violent and expulsive factor that leads the main character, Chou, to set out, like a female Don Quixote, on a quest for her own identity. The unusual quality of Bahéchar's novel comes from its hybrid nature, which unites both the hyper-real and the unreal. It is part savage fairy tale (the first chapter, especially, dealing with the greedy, dumb, and violent people called Mramda), part Harlequin romance, part social criticism. And because of the number of adventures, it is also part Moroccan picaresque. Mostly, though, it is a woman's story of victimization, but more of survival, of realism as well as magic realism, of romance and rejection, even if, ultimately, romance is rejected.

Like Boussejra's character, Tamou, who is the product of disenfranchisement in a society of extreme class divisions, Bahéchar's Chou is the victim of the greed and meanness of a father and a village – a kind of divesture of the female by the patriarch and by the community. At birth, the father had named his child Chouhayra, after a rich foreigner and property holder who was envied and hated by the jealous and vengeful Mramda peasants vying to inherit her lands upon her death. By giving his daughter the woman's name, the father intended to win the old woman's favour, and when that does not happen, the child is turned into a proxy who inspires fear and repulsion in the village. Rather than defend his daughter, the father does nothing to protect her. In fact, because of her superior intelligence, recognized only by the village schoolmaster, Chou is increasingly ostracized and then banished to the outskirts of town. One day she meets a young man, an errant shepherd with whom she, as a child of nature, engages in sexual relations. When the townswomen learn of her violation of their law, they turn into a furious mob and capture the girl, taking her to a forest where they conduct a cruel and twisted rite of punishment (ostensibly, purification), by burning her at the site of her sin, on the genitals. The young shepherd, however, is merely made to submit to the gentle ritual of being cleansed with a woman's milk mixed with water, because, 'For us, when a man sins, it's because a woman has tempted him' (49). The violence perpetrated on the young girl marks her for life, physically and psychically, although it will not destroy her – which is the point of the whole novel, a kind of allegory of the female's drama of 'disinheritance.' Made into a scapegoat, literally branded as a sinner, Chou had been disinherited from birth, and her non-conformity to society's expectations only further underscores her outsider status. But she survives because of her energetic resourcefulness and courage, and in the end becomes a genuinely independent female heroine.

Throughout her peregrinations in search of a place to belong, Chou continues to encounter violence and violent individuals. She meets a series of exploitative men (notably, Ansar) and a paedophile (Doulabi) before coming to know Najib, a photographer who makes images of abused women, because he wants his art to bear witness to their victimization, and, ultimately, Luigi, an Italian restaurant owner who becomes a kind of cantankerous protector for her. What Bahéchar chronicles in the life of her heroine is the cultural violence that women face, their sexual vulnerability, and at the same time the survival skills they acquire in the face of moral and social challenges. Thus, where Boussejra gives an image of cynical violence because of radical social exclusion in her portrait of the debased maid, Tamou (see the discussion in chapter 6, 132–5), Bahéchar offers an opposing image of a woman who is not degraded by the repeated assaults of the forces of evil, who heroically resists, and who eventually prevails. This latter theme has enjoyed a privileged place in women's writing: female protagonist confronts the violence and conformist values of the community, and, in the end, emerges stronger.

Another writer who has creatively incorporated violence in narrative – albeit primarily literary rather than sexual violence, is Rajae Benchemsi, one of Morocco's most lyrical and interesting, if often difficult, female writers, and whose collection of short stories, *Fracture du désir*, merits a section of its own, precisely because of its transgressive nature.

The Poetics of Violence

> Poetry leads to the same place as all forms of eroticism – to the blending and fusion of separate objects. It leads us to eternity, it leads us to death, and through death to continuity. Poetry is eternity ...
>
> Georges Bataille

In her collection of short stories, *Fracture du désir*, Benchemsi deals with transgression and violence in very different ways than we have heretofore seen. While there is prostitution and murder in one story ('Kira et Slima'), a severed head and a headless body in another ('Foire des Zaërs'), a voice without a body in yet another ('La Boutique russe'), and a body without a voice ('L'Homme qui ne mourut pas'), Benchemsi's primary focus is on exploring notions of loss, absence, death, and separation/separateness through narrative. In order to do so, she intellectualizes violence, while at the same time destabilizing the foundations of reality, disrupting the opposition of 'high' and 'low,' and abandoning causality and actuality in favour of limitless possibility. The *récits* she creates are simultaneously rich and opaque, in the domain of transgressive poetry.

As a student in Paris, Benchemsi wrote a doctoral dissertation on Maurice Blanchot, and like him, in *Fracture du désir*, practises an aesthetics that links the literary to the experience of absence and death. Thus her short stories are all investigations into the realm of the mind and the erotics of ideas. As we shall see, her texts have less to do with sexuality than with a poetic philosophy that seeks to explode normal categories of thought and reality and to break down barriers between the real and unreal. While the body is very much the vehicle through which her stories pass, and while sexual relationships may figure in the narrative (though usually only secondarily), Benchemsi's real interest is in the non-corporal and in making experimental, poetic journeys into a world beyond everyday reality. That is the sense in which the title of her collection should be understood: as the analysis of desire in all its permutations. It is as though the author slices Desire into thin crosssections, *fractures*, to study its composition and decomposition. In that sense, it is the problematic of desire, sexual and erotic, violent or philosophical, destructive or sacrificial that focuses Benchemsi's lyrical explorations into transgression.

The first story, 'Kira et Slima,' is the most accessible of the six *récits* in terms of character and plot. There is a daughter, Slima, who is intent upon revenge against her father, who has repudiated her mother, leaving her seriously ill and destitute, while he takes up with a young woman half her age. Formerly a university student with literary aspirations, indicated by the green notebook that she treasures, Slima manages to feed her mother and herself by becoming a woman of the streets. Still, the prostitution that she practises is less forced upon her than consciously chosen in retaliation against her father. By embracing the ignoble (as she indicts him for doing), her acts of sex will sully his honour every time she 'services' a man who may, she grimly reflects, be one of his friends. By debasing herself physically, Slima engages in figurative self-immolation, and her degradation and hate for herself are only further emphasized when she is invited by Kira Mayer, the madame of Meknes's most famous brothel, to work for her. Almost immediately after this interview, Slima begins to stalk her father, spying on his movements, observing how each morning, dressed in white and driving a white car, he drives to the town hall where he is president of the municipal council. In a text of strong, dominant colours – black, red, and green – the insistent use of white here underscores the difference between the exterior appearance of the father and quality of his 'crime' against her and her mother, in Slima's mind. Her conscious intention is to confront him with the ravages his actions have wrought in order to 'paralyze the happiness of a father who knows no shame' (27), though subconsciously, another objective has been formed and will be acted upon, almost as though she were sleepwalking, when she finds him sitting in his office of power and honour, and fatally shoots him. As Slima is driven away in the police car bound for prison, her mind sinks into 'a white cottony haze of suffering,' 'thicker than death.' She is only hazily aware that her act of violence has freed her from 'all those male sex organs in erection,' standing like barricades that permit no glimmer of hope or even any future. At the same time, however, she begrudges her father's freedom in death, and solicits for herself a descent into 'the torments of madness' (29–30).

The story is unremittingly bleak, yet stylistically powerful for the harshness of its vision, the quality of its chiaroscuro effects, and its sexual imagery. Slima's nights are spent in a world of 'penises in erection,' 'her legs wide open,' as each 'successive violation' sends her deeper and deeper into 'the abyss,' each 'penetration hollowing out her being' (9–10). When the madame offers a contract for Slima's exclusive services, for which in turn she will have benefits for life, Slima sees it as a form of 'carnal slavery with a life sentence,' reducing her to an 'open vagina for eternity,' equivalent to 'swapping her soul for sperm that has a cash worth' (22). It is the patriarchal principle of male organs in tumescence and the feminine exploitation through the 'gaping vagina' that focus a reading of social criticism. In presenting society as an endless parade of sex organs, but making the female the perpetrator of violence, Benchemsi's text, however, rewrites the gender dynamics of the crime of passion, pitting daughter against father, making her murder of him equivalent to an honour killing in reverse. In the violent economy of sexuality in this story, Slima's act of violence is both an expression of despair and loss (of her past and of her future) and an emphatic indictment of the vulnerability of the female condition in this society.

The physical violence of the text is further situated within the theme of silence, which permeates the text. There is the silence between daughter and father following his abandonment of the mother; the mother's own resigned silence in her refusal to pursue legal recourse against her husband; the affectionate silence between mother and daughter ('A series of rituals had replaced words' [12]); the alienated silence that reigns between Slima and her customers ('she screamed, but from the inside, without making a sound: I will have my revenge, Father. I will avenge myself' [13]); the stolid silence of Slima during the madame's monologue and offer of employment; the disappointing silence of the lawyer-lover whom Slima had counted on to help her ('He listened to her without saying a word and didn't appear in the least outraged' [20]); the empty silence of the medina in early morning ('the single most austere thing in the world, because there is no living movement' [23]); the morgue-like silence of the town hall as Slima approaches her father's office; the white silence of death and the tormented silence of madness, at the end. Ultimately it is the sum total of all the silences of her life that separates Slima from herself and from everyone else. She has become a mere phantom, existing 'in the shadow of the dreams of others' (23). When she moves to break the silence between daughter and father, it will not be by speaking, but by acting, and her act will lead both of them into 'a vertiginous delirium of terror. Together' (28).

For a writer who loves language and words, the silence that reigns throughout so many of her texts seems oddly perverse, but we must recall that as a poet of prose, Benchemsi is more interested in *what is not* than in what is, and that the challenge she sets herself is to narrate the missing, the transient or ineffable, the thing that exists but has no physical presence. It is for that reason that she is attracted to the various manifestations of desire, which is intangible, felt or imagined, but never seen, and which vanishes into the air when satisfied. Significantly, for Benchemsi, desire is about ideas and obsessions related to objects and even loss, rather than merely about sex. What she probes in narrative is primarily, then, the philosophic dimensions of desire.

Thus, desire for the severed head in 'Foire des Zaërs' is not the manifestation of necrophilia, but the woman's search for understanding of the nature of things and the author's exploration of the quality of reality. Benchemsi sets the scene not far from Rabat, at a fair, a key choice of locale for an investigation into the occult. In the first sentence of the story, the narrating woman describes the severed head sitting on a garden table outside one of the tents of the fairground. Fascinated, she enters the pavilion, described as the 'antichambre du désir' (35) and sees a mirror in which is reflected a body with an attached head. In the tent, there is also a body without a head, which powerfully attracts her, but when she goes to touch the headless body, to check its temperature, the magician prevents her from doing so, saying that she can only touch the body in the mirror. The head is first described by the narrator as 'cheerful,' perhaps even a 'laughing head,' with dark eyes and a 'provocative look.' It is a striking break from reality to attribute to a severed head a living personality, so to deal with that infraction, the narrator becomes analytical. 'Separation of body and of spirit,' she assesses, followed by a self-correction, 'No. Separation of the head from the body.' She observes that the headless body, 'which sits in all its 'single' (*célibat*) glory on a red chair,' still seems to contain a soul, and she notes that it had been carefully decapitated at the neck, around which a thick cord now hangs – a sign of violence, but with an unreal quality since there is no blood, and, moreover, 'The decapitated body presages nothing of a cadaver' (34). It is a mystery, for how is it possible to relate the separated body and head that are, curiously, reunited in the mirror? What the woman sees resists all explanation, and because it does, she becomes more and more drawn to the surreal aspect in which 'life and death are nothing more than a mockery. In which nothingness and existence are both destroyed, leaving nothing more than the excess of illusion' (35). She is, after all, at a fair, the site of the *carnavalesque* but also of optical illusions and phantasmagoric deception.

In subsequent scenes, the narrator recalls a trip to Père Lachaise ('the cemetery of dead poets' in Paris), and makes a visit to her friend Hannae who is conducting research on the foundations of Roman sexuality, and has just been left by her lover, Anselm, whose letter announcing his departure and the end of their affair is cruelly direct, 'All attraction for you has ceased in me' (43). Both trips, to or away from, represent endings – rupture, disruption, absence, loss.

When the narrator, who is totally obsessed by the image of the decapitated body, returns to the fair the next day, intent on solving 'the absurd swindling of reality' (44–5) that she had witnessed, neither the head nor the body is there. The mirror is at the same place, but contains another image, and the magician, now dressed as a storyteller from *Les Mille et une nuits*, is regaling a crowd with a tale of adventure. Thoroughly perplexed, the woman wonders what is real and what is not? Is everything 'perversion or illusion,' or 'transgression of time and its woefully impoverished linearity' (45)? The narrator feels that her sense of utter emptiness brings her closer to her friend Hannae: 'As though the primary effect of the loneliness felt after losing forever an object is not only to foreshorten time and space, but to make that absence, now physical and material, the very object of desire.' And she adds, 'We were now terribly bound by desire left suspended' (46). What this means is that absence not only motivates desire, it becomes the very thing that exists as a desire in limbo. Hence, the experience of unrequited ardour for what is lost brings together individuals for whom the desired object is entirely different. None of this has any basis in material reality, though that fact does not makes the effects any less powerful.

Such evidence reveals that the 'sense' of the story comes not in plot or character, but through the accumulation of signifiers indicating separation, absence, termination, death, loss, and the ways in which elements of the story complement one another to make the same point. The fair is an outdoor stage situated in an in-between world, where sleights of hand and feats of the unreal are expected, though that fact does not deter the rational being who tries to explain them. Mentally and spiritually, the fair is a space located midway between the cemetery (Père Lachaise), signifying finality, and the almost banal reality of Hannae's apartment and her sorrow in her terminated relationship. All three places are associated with 'transgressions' of time and space, and emotions that defy rational understanding. The exercise that Benchemsi sets for herself is to give material narrativity to absence and to call into question our notion of the real and reality itself.

In the next story, 'La Boutique russe,' the distinction between the immaterial and material is likewise thrown into dramatic opposition. In this story, a woman finds herself drawn into what appears to be a tiny, dark boutique on a street in the Marais, 'a real Russian bazaar,' stocked with lacy dresses, rich embroideries, heavy velvet draperies, porcelain objects, exquisite copies of icons – once again, an environment in which the foreign and mysterious reign. And then she hears a voice, seemingly emanating from the cellar, chanting a kind of 'song in Arabic from Syria.' She is entranced, totally captivated, instantly and euphorically in love – with a voice. The narrator, like all female protagonists in Benchemsi, is a highly educated and cultivated woman, who lives substantially in her mind with writers like Baudelaire, Erasmus, Hallâj, Malcolm Lowry, Henry Miller, Dostoyevsky, and composers and conductors, Handel and John Eliot Gardiner and Alfred Deller. References to both high and popular culture abound in the story – a man reminds her of characters from Beckett, a photograph of Antonin Artaud seems to stop the flow of time; she feels as though she were in a Edgar Allen Poe story, that a couple looks as though they came straight out of *Playboy* magazine, that she is participating in the joy of post–Second World War personified by Edith Piaf. Later, after a trip to Rome (Benchemsi's characters are always very mobile), she hears a radio report that Marguerite Duras has died.

As the foregoing demonstrates, the *récit* is peopled by a veritable bazaar of figures indicative of the breadth and eclectic cultural tastes of the woman narrating, as well as her attraction to those who tested the limits either in their art or in their lives. Earlier she had attended a gallery opening for a young Moroccan artist, unexpectedly meeting again the Russian woman from the boutique. She had sipped absinthe with a woman friend while reading aloud from Roger Caillois's *La Chute des corps*, and listened to recordings by Milva, all the while obsessed with the Voice, feeling as though her body were 'dilating' and that 'all notion of limits [had become] so blurred as to cease to exist completely' (62). There are evocations of being outside time and space, but especially of death, foreshadowing what will happen when, finally, she meets the man who possesses 'the voice from the Russian shop.'

Nate, the proprietress of the boutique, has offered to serve as intermediary, and the two attend a concert at the Cité Universitaire by the young man, Saâd. His wholly common name is a presage of what is to occur; the narrator knows that she is in the grip of an erotic obsession of the mind; she knows that her true longing is for the same ecstasy felt that day in the boutique – to hear that voice again. At the concert, she awaits breathlessly to be transported, to reexperience the singular and ethereal thrill of hearing the voice from the Russian boutique. But, alas, it is an experience that cannot be repeated; the voice is not the same, or, rather, the effect is not the same. She understands that her experience of the voice from the Russian boutique had been only for her, that she alone heard it like a communication from one soul to another, rising up out of chance and the unknown (71–2). Still, ardently enamoured of the voice, she engages in an act of sex with the man. But his physical body is not what she desires. What she wanted was that wonderful thing she had experienced once and that was now inaccessible. For any other kind of pleasure of a merely physical nature she is 'as dead' (75).

What is striking about the story is precisely the obsession with and search for the immaterial, the perfect moment, the ineffable thing that cannot be repeated, that necessarily, even, must remain inaccessible, an ideal beyond reach. The attempt to mediate absence and presence is doomed. The narrator would, if she could, tear apart the body in order to have the voice, but in the end she must make do with a mere body.

One can say that just as the text treats art – literature, music, and painting – as expressions of our desires, so does it reveal how desire is born in the mind and how the mind will continue to seek the intensity of the feeling, less than the realness of the other person. At the same time, what Benchemsi deals with in both 'Foire des Zaërs' and 'La Boutique russe' is the body/mind and spirit contrast. In the first, there is the head separated from the body, a head that lives independently and remains animated with life even when severed; in the second, there is the voice, separate from the body, immaterial but emanating a kind of soul, which holds the real power. Is the author saying that the body is inferior to the mind/spirit? That the intellect/spirit is more important than the flesh, and that the spirit triumphs and survives even when separated from the body? Or that the spirit is the source of all corporal power, and that once separated from the intellect, the physical body is unable to survive independently and vigorously? The possibilities are multiple, each involved with pushing the limits of what we consider normal reality. Indeed, Benchemsi's mission is to lead the reader out of the quotidian and into poetic journeys of the mind, and in that sense, her art reflects the influence of Blanchot who draws upon the work of Stéphane Mallarmé in formulating a conception of literary language as antirealist and distinct from everyday experience. For Benchemsi, literary writing offers the opportunity to engage with abstract notions that are more in the realm of the philosophical than so-called realistic fiction. By creating an atmosphere of violation ('Kira et Slima'), destabilization ('Foire des Zaërs'), and displaced eroticism ('La Boutique russe'), she lays the groundwork for the narrative encounter with the abstract.

Similarly, the remaining three short stories of the collection investigate absence in its multiple manifestations. First, through the loss of speech in 'L'Homme qui ne mourut pas' by means of a character who believes he must be dead, reasoning that the gravediggers had forgotten to remove his soul, whereas, in fact, he had had a tumour on the brain and a surgical operation had destroyed his ability to speak. Second, in 'Elle,' through a nebulously defined character who might be inspiration, creativity, death, obsession, writing, life, literature, memory, muse, imagination (all of which, in French, are feminine nouns) and, hence, whose very essence remains ambiguous. Finally, in 'Au Bord de la mémoire,' Benchemsi focuses on memory in which a woman 're-accesses' an uncle who had been absent from her mind until she revisited the farm where he had lived and read a book he had cherished about a saint. It is clear, then, that for this writer, as for Chami-Kettani (see chapter 3), the art of literature is conceived as a poetic investigation into philosophic and aesthetic concepts. Benchemsi is less involved with storytelling than with using literary means to inquire into ideas, conditions, immanence. Her engagement is with that intermediate world, partaking of the real and the unreal, transgressing on the reader's expectations, but also making reading a creative if sometimes perplexing act of the intellect.

Indeed, Moroccan literature has a considerable tradition of delving into transgressive realities and emotions, perhaps influenced by Sufi mysticism, perhaps by the unnamed storytellers of the Place Jemma al-Fna who combine the bizarre with the ordinary. Benchemsi represents the aesthetic, intellectual current in this kind of writing, while an example of folkloric, non-realistic transgressive writing is seen in a short story, 'Le Tatouage bleu,' by Nadia Chakik.[18]

This eight-page story is told by a woman, desperate to deal with a drunkard husband, who travels to a carnival in another town in search of the performer-storyteller, Aouïcha, reputed to sell unconventional but efficacious advice. Aouïcha is, in fact, the real protagonist of the tale, ostensibly a woman, though of indeterminate sexuality, built like a man, with tobacco-stained teeth and hairy limbs. She is a veritable hag, strangely mixing sexuality and vulgarity along with feminine wiles and her trademark mantra, 'La caravane passe et le chien aboie' (the caravan passes and the dog howls). But if the carnival audience mocks her effrontery, they also submit to the spell she casts and become easy prey to her accomplice, a young lad, who circulates in the crowd to pick their pockets while Aouïcha bewitches them into awed contemplation of the sky during an ordinary sunset. At the end of the performance, the woman seeking aid is invited to Aouïcha's hovel in order to explain her problem in private. There she discovers that Aouïcha has a blue tattoo on her arm, much like the tattoo of her own wayward husband, and that, moreover, Aouïcha, who grunts and burps and who is motivated by money, seems to have unusual knowledge of him: 'It seems I know this man ... I believe I have already met him in another life, centuries ago, in my dreams ...' (23). The advice the *halqa* performer sells is at once ludicrous though practical – learn karate in order to beat up your husband – and cunningly naive: scare him into obedience by disguising yourself as a disgusting creature, arrange spiders and cockroach shells in your hair, along with a rat, wear clothes that smell of animals, garbage, and excrement. When the woman returns home, she learns that her husband has disappeared with a young lad from a nearby village. She returns to the carnival, but there is no Aouïcha; indeed, the other performers have never heard of her. The monkey trainer seems oddly familiar, however, and his actions are suspicious, for he seems to be hiding a *djellaba* (a hooded robe) and a piece of a *bendir* (drum) that belonged to Aouïcha. Bewildered, the woman client finds her way back to Aouïcha's hut, now smoldering in embers. There is no sign of Aouïcha, just a pack of dogs snarling over a tattooed arm.

Clearly, the story has a pattern of indecipherable coincidences: Homane (the husband) and Aouïcha are related through the shared tattoo, Homane and Aouïcha both have a sidekick who is a young boy; both Homane and Aouïcha disappear at the end. Only the blue tattooed arm remains. What Chafik recreates is the carnival of the subconscious in order to traffic in the disturbing and repulsive, yet also oddly magnetic. She conjures up feelings of apprehension, uncertainty, and insecurity, at the same time as she produces an unforgettable story that defies rational deliberation. By the indiscriminate mix of the strange with the familiar, by choosing a locale that fuses the marvellous with the exploitative, and by introducing a protagonist who is not only of indeterminate gender but also lewd, grotesque, and even odious, she creates a story composed of a veritable texture of transgressions that fascinate and repel almost simultaneously. And finally, with the portable symbol of the blue tattoo, Chafik reminds us not only of the violations of the text, as within narrative itself, but also of the indelible power of storytelling.

Conclusion

In this chapter, we have looked at how transgression is used by Moroccan women writers, whether it is motivated by the design to disrupt social and gender expectations as with Nedjma, or is used to reveal the violence that accompanies a woman's life as in Bahéchar, or to convey aesthetic and philosophical principles, as with Benchemsi. Critic Fouzia Rhissassi has suggested that while Moroccan women have not been physically maimed or mutilated, as they have in certain other societies, they have been psychically damaged, and that writing is their way of re-becoming whole.[19] According to this argument, women's writing would be an affirmative transgression against the status quo, an act of self-affirmation against powerful forces in culture. When, furthermore, the woman writer chooses violent subject matter for her text, or writes in a way that violates cultural norms, she is in essence forcing recognition of her separate existence. For her, art becomes the way of engaging intellectually with a culture of violence that permeates modern society.[20]

While it is certainly true that in Morocco, as elsewhere in the world, violence against women is a fact of life, and while there is much interesting work to be done on the relationship between the issue of women and violence in society, and the violence they write in their texts, my primary focus in this chapter has been on the role of transgression in women's literature.[21] I have argued that by incorporating transgression in their texts, whether through theme or mode of writing, these women challenge the stereotype of the reticent, uninvolved, silent woman. By talking about what we (and many in their own society) thought was forbidden, by using text and sex in ways that violate expectations, by bringing violence into their narratives, and even by exploding notions about the nature of the world and reality, these women writers have transgressed the invisible lines of social and literary discourse to signal the real emergence of the female individual in the body politic as in letters. Explorations of gender, genre, and the limits of language have been at the heart of their enterprise, whether they have been engaged with problems within their society or with the poetics of literary inquiry. Either by writing transgressively, or writing about transgression, these writers demonstrate a fundamental concern with liberation – of women and readers, alike.

In this respect, Moroccan women writers have conducted an intense assault on *hchouma*, refusing, as in the case of Nedjma, to let it silence her, though it did make her take a pseudonym and perhaps to write in French.[22] *Hchouma* did not prevent Bahéchar from writing a scene in which her character was burned at the very 'site' of her sin for having had premarital intercourse. Nor would *hchouma* thwart Benchekroun from cataloguing the disgust and humiliation Nadia feels in submitting to what she calls 'the absurdly legal rape of her body' in the marriage bed (*Oser vivre*, 132), or prevent Trabelsi from dealing with the issue of homosexuality in Casablanca (*Une Vie à trois*). Indeed, they reject *hchouma* in terms of speech, theme, and subject matter, precisely in order to reveal the public hypocrisy and conformity that permit its existence. And yet, despite their boldness, despite the transgressiveness of their writing, the general public in Morocco, both male and female, still maintains that women could not possibly write as women have already done. Despite the complaints of a husband in a letter to a sex columnist for the daily newspaper, *L'Opinion*, about his wife's disinterest in fellatio and cunnilingus, and an article about erectile dysfunction, by a sexologist in the same news source;[23] despite the feminist editorials and sexual advice and information in women's magazines, *Citadine* or *Femmes du Maroc* or *Ousra*; despite widespread access to European television by the ubiquitous satellite dish; and despite Naamane-Guessous's sociological research, to the contrary, people will still say, almost reflexively, that Morocco is a very conservative country and that its traditions do not permit much openness about sexuality. It is as though in the realm of the rhetorical, it is a matter of both good manners and good upbringing to present a particular image. Of course, this *is* the reality for many people. But it is not the whole truth, as this chapter has shown. One is led, therefore, to conclude that even in speech, there are mores of public decorum founded on history, tradition, and religious strictures that demand that the interlocutor present a conservative face, regardless of what social realities might demonstrate. As a consequence, for most of the public, *hchouma* extends even to descriptive speech about cultural norms, and determines public *rhetorical* conventions about sexuality, including conformity to shibboleths, which, inevitably and in circular fashion, are reinforced by their very utterance. Ironically, of course, as long as the general public refuses women equal rights as writers, it also ensures that women will continue to write transgressively.

Ultimately, we must acknowledge that when women use the poetics of transgression, they are engaging in one of the great traditions of artistic creation. In combating cultural taboos and offering alternative visions of reality, their writing gathers creative force and promotes sometimes shocking and often original and insightful ways of seeing and understanding the world around us. In this sense, transgressive fiction simultaneously reminds us of the power of the literary arts, and of women's speech.

In the next chapter, we shall see how woman's transgression can carry into yet another domain – the political.

5 A Prison Narrative: Female Memory and a Woman Called 'Rachid'

> At that point I remembered what my father used to say when I was little and awoke from some nightmare based on his storytelling from *The Thousand and One Nights* ... tales of kidnappings and abductions of women and girls. Papa would say, 'Those are just stories from long ago.' It never occurred to him ... that it could happen in our lives.
>
> Fatna El Bouih, Une Femme nommée Rachid, 12

On a spring day in May 1977, Fatna El Bouih and a male classmate from the university arrive at a friend's apartment in the Océan quarter of Rabat, with the intention of spending the afternoon studying for their upcoming exams. When Fatna knocks at the door, it flies open and she is yanked inside. Instinctively, her companion bolts, but is quickly halted by a warning bullet that barely misses his leg. In the apartment, men brandishing firearms slap the students and unleash a flood of insults, questions, and accusations. Dazed by this startling rupture from the mundane, Fatna feels as though she has been swept into a film ... A car screeches to a stop on the street, the students are hustled out and driven to another location, where they spend the night being roughly interrogated. The next morning, they are blindfolded, shoved into a van, and ordered to lie on the floor of the vehicle. Then it takes off at high speed, careening around corners, throwing the occupants into one another. After several hours, the van pulls up to another locale, where there are more angry interrogators, insults, and accusations. This time there are threats and pistols held to their heads. This time, the breaking of the prisoner begins in earnest.

According to a conventional script of torture, the barrage of verbal insults, physical intimidations, and psychological humiliations leads, ineluctably, to physical torture. But first the prisoner is stripped of her identity, her sex, her very name. Henceforth, Fatna will be known as 'Rachid, numéro 45.' Not Rachida, in the feminine. But Rachid, the male form. Simply because, as one of the jailors in a subsequent prison sneered, a woman who practised politics, as Fatna had done, was the same thing as a man.[1] Renaming the prisoner is a part of the psychological attack on a prisoner. By erasing sexual distinction, by attributing a man's identity to a woman, the torturer destabilizes and destroys the prisoner's bearings, softening her up for the physical and mental torture that ensues. It is also an expedient for prison officials who seek both to camouflage the existence of women in a prison for men, and to make the fact of men torturing women more opaque.[2]

In the secret torture centre outside Casablanca, known as Derb Moulay Cherif, Fatna is joined by six other young women, also political activists and members of the outlawed student union, UNEM (Union Nationale des Etudiants Marocains). They, too, had been abducted by the secret police in a roundup of more than 100 antigovernment protesters. For the next seven months, the blindfolded female detainees are held in a room where they are forced to remain lying on a cold cement floor, prohibited from speaking to one another, and even from dislodging the fleas and lice that feast upon them. Under 24-hour floodlights and the constant surveillance by guards equipped with machine guns and bullwhips, the women are permitted to arise only for an occasional trip to the toilet, or, when compelled, to the nearby chamber where the *hâjs* interrogate and torture them.

In riveting prose, Fatna tells about the terrible virtuosity of the *hâjs*, the name by which their jailor/torturers wanted to be known.[3] Having been 'made into men,' the women are subjected to the same tortures as men: the *falaqa*, the 'airplane ride' or cruxifixion '*à la sauce marocaine*,' electric shocks, whippings, hangings by arms or feet during interrogation, threats of rape – the latter, ironically, despite their male names – until, mercifully, they lose consciousness. Her friend, Latifa Ajbabdi, remembers that each torturer had a specialty, like one who gave cuffs to the head that caused days of deafness, another who administered blows that made her think her ribs had been shattered like crusts of dry bread.[4] She recalls being threatened by the *hâjs* with group rape, or rape by a dog. One torturer, known as the Camel, was a specialist of the various degrees of the 'airplane ride' in which the prisoner is lashed to a bar by joining hands and feet behind the body, then, head hanging down, eyes blindfolded, is raised into the air, turned like a chicken on a roasting skewer, and beaten and whipped, before being turned over to another torturer known as the Chacal. Because of the blindfolds, the victims never saw the faces of their torturers, but Fatna writes that she 'recognized' them by way of her other senses: from their odours, the smell of their cigarettes, their footsteps, glimpses from under her blindfold of their shoes, the marks left upon her body by their hands and blows.

Remarkably, despite the prohibition against speaking, the women develop an extraordinary means of communication. In a striking image of how women use their bodies to produce silent speech, El Bouih evokes the artfulness of women's communication. Lying side by side on the jail floor, their bodies often wracked in pain, the women use their fingers to trace letters on the hands or flanks of a comrade, spelling out messages of hopefulness and solidarity. Similarly, in another prison, each woman, isolated in her individual cell, senses, without being told, that one of her comrades had been raped during her interrogation. Then, overwhelmed with sorrow for the victim and outrage against the agents of injustice, one woman, then another raises her voice in lamentation until the entire cellblock reverberates with a chorus of wails and protests.[5] On this 'memorable night,' writes Fatna, 'the walls of the prison heard for the first time cries of protest, and what's more, those cries came from women' (20). Which leads the reader to protest in turn: silent women? How incomplete that story!

By publishing her memoir, first in Arabic and then translated into French in 2001, Fatna El Bouih not only broke a taboo against women's public speech, but also challenged official silence about Morocco's 'years of lead,' during which political dissent had been crushed by the brutal and repressive measures of the government under Hassan II. In the decade of the 1970s, hundreds if not thousands of political dissenters had been imprisoned and tortured, often for weeks or months, without being formally charged, while hundreds of others 'disappeared' and were never heard from again. Political trials were a sham, with groups of detainees being tried en masse and sentences of five to twenty years or even life, handed out with impunity.[6] Hence, when Fatna took up the pen, her mission was first, to contribute to her country's need for transparency and truthfulness about its past, and second, to reveal how women, so invisible in the official version of the nation's history, had played roles as courageous as men's. By dedicating her work to other female political prisoners who suffered the same fate and sometimes shared her cell; to the soul of the martyred Saïda Menebhi, the twenty-five-year-old poet, teacher of English, and Marxist-Leninist arrested for political activity, who died during her imprisonment on a hunger strike; and to Fatna's own young daughters, Najwa and Lina, in the hope 'that their innocent eyes would never have to see the scenes of horror witnessed by their mother,' El Bouih bears eloquent witness to her commitment to Moroccan women and to the struggle for human rights in her country. Because *Une Femme nommée Rachid* is at once a memoir, a memorial, and a call to conscience, no chronicle of women's writing, or of women's history in Morocco, would be complete without examining its narrative and its contribution to collective memory.

Breaking Silence: Prison Literature and Collective Memory in Morocco

El Bouih's prison narrative is not, of course, the only memoir bearing on 'the years of lead.' Indeed, this most somber period in national history has produced an extraordinarily rich literature of both personal testimonial and fictional re-creation, making it, today, one of the most compelling genres in Moroccan letters. Books in French by Ahmed Marzouki (*Tazmamart: Cellule 10*), Ali Bourequat (*Tazmamart: Dix-huit ans de solitude*), and Mohammed Raiss (*De Skhirat à Tazmamart; Retour du bout de l'enfer*) recount the horrors of Tazmamart, that secret prison known as a 'house of death' (*mouroir*) where more than half the prisoners died and the other half were barely kept alive on a daily ration of three peas, some watery soup, and a hunk of bread.[7] Abdelaziz Mouride shows the cruel, inhumane, and degrading treatment of prisoners in an illustrated book, *On affame bien les rats*, published in Morocco in 2000, while Jaouad Mdidech, who was incarcerated in Derb Moulay Cherif at the same time as Mouride, tells his story in *La Chambre noire* (2000). The highly respected poet, novelist, playwright, essayist, and human rights activist Abdellatif Laâbi served eight years in prison for his dissident activities, and based his *Chroniques de la citadelle d'exil: Lettres de prison (1972–1980)* on that experience. Recalling how political idealism and literary art have functioned in his life, he asserts that the essence of literature is both freedom and resistance, dual themes that surely characterize all prison narratives.[8] More recently, Mehdi Bennouna's *Heures sans gloire, échec d'une révolution* was a huge success.

As for fiction writers, both Tahar Ben Jelloun and Abdelhak Serhane fashioned the tragic plight of the prisoners at Tazmamart into novels, which, in the case of Ben Jelloun's *Cette Aveuglante Absence de lumière* (2001), led to widespread criticism in Morocco, first because of a disagreement between the author and a survivor of Tazmamart, Aziz Binebine, who had wanted him to tell the story, and then because many in the country felt that it was too soon to turn such an event into fiction. Mostly, however, it was because many Moroccans were scandalized and resentful that Ben Jelloun had not used his fame and reputation much sooner to expose the repression and abuses of the Hassan II regime.[9] For his part, Ben Jelloun objected that he, like others, did not know what was happening, particularly given that since the early 1970s he lived only part-time in Morocco and mostly in Paris.[10] Serhane's *Kabazal* was written and published in 2004 without similar furor.

As for women writers and the prison genre, it is noteworthy that in addition to newspaper articles recounting their experience as political prisoners, four women produced non-fiction texts. Besides Fatna El Bouih's memoir, there are the collected writings of the martyr Saïda Menebhi, *Poèmes, écrits, lettres de prison*, published by her family following her death in 1977. In 1999 Malika Oufkir, the eldest daughter of General Oufkir, who was accused of a failed coup against Hassan II in 1974, wrote *La Prisonnière* in which she chronicles her family's twenty years of incarceration determined by Hassan II, who forced her, her mother, and her siblings to pay for the crimes of the father and husband.[11] Rabea Bennouna wrote *Tazmamart: Côté femme*, in which she relates her own story as a young wife whose husband was swept up in the roundup of those charged with the assassination attempt on Hassan II at the Skhirat ocean-side compound on 10 July 1971. She presents the problems she faced as a dependent wife without a husband in the face of government stonewalling.[12]

In addition to these texts, either written in or translated into French – the testimonials of El Bouih, Latifa Ajbabdi, Mohamed Raiss, and Abdellaziz Mouride were first written in Arabic, while those of Marzouki, Bourequat, Laâbi, and the Serfatys were composed in French – others have been published in Arabic by former political prisoners and still await translation into a Western language.

Clearly, then, there has been an enormous outpouring of written words since the late 1990s concerning Hassan II's prisons, secret detention and torture centres, and the brutalities and sexual humiliations endured by political prisoners during a particularly dark chapter of Moroccan history.[13] Though in the latter years of his reign, the king took a number of initial steps toward a process of democratization, it was not until late 2003 and early 2004, under Mohammed VI, that the official silence concerning secret prisons and torture was publicly ended. With the establishment of a truth commission (Instance Equité et Réconciliation, IER), headed by Driss Benzekri who, himself, had served seventeen years in prison for political activities abhorrent to Hassan II, ordinary Moroccans could, for the first time, hear the testimony of some 200 former prisoners on the airwaves of national radio and television. It was a momentous and risky venture, intended to lead to reconciliation and a reformulation of national identity, consistent with the reminder by the French historian Ernest Renan who said that nations are defined as much by what they collectively forget as by what they collectively remember. By telling their stories before the nation, the victims of abuse were seeking not revenge so much as recognition of the injustices both they and the nation had suffered under a brutal regime. It was a risk for the country to allow them a platform, but as El Bouih has said, 'no society can do without its memory.'[14]

To break silence at the national level required the acquiescence if not the initiative of the regime. To break silence as a woman – and to do so several years prior to the establishment of the truth commission – meant that El Bouih had not only to counter the traditional stricture against women's speech in the public domain, but also to remember and relive the horrors she had experienced in prison. Yet, following a televised interview, which released in her a flow of memories, she realized that not only were women prisoners the great forgotten in society,[15] but that women as a group were absent from the pages of Moroccan history and the consciousness of most citizens. Her countrymen and women, she concluded, were ignorant not only of great swaths of their own history, but especially of women's participation in the nation's history. The factors responsible for their lack of knowledge included not just widespread illiteracy, but also the absence of written accounts concerning the darker side of the nation's history. In consequence, she designed her memoir to be more than a personal cathartic journey. It would be a 'work of memory,' whose intention was to denounce tyranny and to speak out on behalf of its victims, while promoting humanistic values, but also and importantly, to reinsert women into the history of Morocco and thus into the collective memory of the country. Her memoir was intended to expand the role and impact of female memory beyond its traditional value in Morocco as an inexhaustible source of stories and tales, to one capable of transmitting history and politics – a potentially subversive gesture.

What made it possible for Fatna El Bouih to challenge the place granted to women both in official discourse and in reality and to break ground in order to cultivate a new field of female memory through writing?

Background

To answer the question and appreciate El Bouih's achievement, we need to look at her own life. Born on 10 July 1955, eight months before Morocco gained independence from France, she was one of ten children, and grew up with six sisters and three brothers in the village of Ben Ahmed in the area of Settat. Her mother was illiterate, but having observed, during the Protectorate, the freedoms that European women enjoyed, she was eager for her daughters to have a life different from her own. Later, Fatna would say that it was on behalf of her mother and all the women like her who had had so few opportunities in society that she chose political action as a way of changing society.[16] She was equally inspired by her father, whom she describes as traditional, but who from her early childhood spoke to her about the abuses of colonialism, while extolling the beauties of Arabic literature. Since he supported the idea of education for a girl who showed capability, when Fatna won a scholarship to attend the Lycée Chawqi in Casablanca, he quickly consented for her to leave home to pursue higher studies, something of a first for her village where, typically, girls quit school after five years of instruction.

Fatna's arrival in Casablanca in 1970 coincided with the mid-point of opposition to the government, begun in 1967, when politically active students and professors organized strikes and protests. Their early platform demanded that education be the right of all Moroccans and not just the elite; they demonstrated for better student stipends and scholarships, improved housing in the *cités universitaires*, and an end to the discriminatory practices that favoured French degrees over Moroccan degrees. In that respect, El Bouih remembers having to read in her high school French class one of France's great classics, Stendhal's *Le Rouge et le noir*, to which she objected on the grounds that if the pedagogical objective was to access first-rate literature in French, the professor should ask the class to read *Nedjma*, by Algerian writer Kateb Yacine, from their own North African tradition.[17] In the mid to late sixties, left-wing opposition to the government on university campuses was spurred on by three important events that had radicalized opposition politics throughout the country: March 1965 and the insurrection of Casablanca with its bloody repression by government forces that killed hundreds of union demonstrators and supporters;[18] June 1967 and the humiliating Arab defeat in the Middle East Six-Days War; May 1968 in France, plus, in the international context, growing student protests on U.S. campuses against the war in Vietnam. For many activists, disillusioned by the lack of republican values in post-independent Morocco, the opening years of the 1970s and a period of Arab nationalism led to questioning the path that the young Moroccan nation should take. Should Morocco become a socialist republic like its neighbour Algeria? Should the monarchy be retained or discarded?[19] For many, a more just society seemed attainable only through the tenets of Marxism-Leninism, which, in essence, meant what the French historian and specialist on Morocco, Pierre Vermeren, has called 'a frontal attack' on Makhzen, the name given to entrenched power coupled with absolute authority.[20]

Dissidents in the military sought to overthrow Hassan II on two occasions. Two plots, in 1971 and 1972, against the regime were foiled, but not before many in the political opposition were murdered and many more were jailed.[21] New intelligence and counterintelligence bodies with far-ranging powers were created; restrictions were placed on public freedoms; mass trials became the rule. Members of the opposition party, Union Nationale des Forces Populaires (UNFP), created by Mehdi Ben Barka in 1959, were brought before the military tribunal of Kénitra and charges were made against 157 people in the Plot of 3 mars; in July, the trial of Casablanca began in which eighty leftists, including Abdellatif Laâbi, Abraham Serfaty, and Anis Balafrej were found guilty; and in the summer of 1971, fifty-eight officers and *sous-officiers* were transferred from the prison of Kenitra to the secret prison of Tazmamart.

At the university, Fatna engaged in impassioned discussions with fellow students, champions of egalitarian ideas of democracy and human rights. In 1973 the UNEM (Union Nationale des Etudiants, the major student union) was declared illegal, its president and *adjoint* arrested. In 1974 Fatna was arrested for the first time for belonging to a banned group, and spent a day in prison. After that wave of arrests, the student dissidents retreated briefly until 1976 when they once again began meeting to discuss how to redress the ills that beset Moroccan society. In May of 1977, Fatna was kidnapped and kept in secret detention at Derb Moulay Cherif where she was tortured for seven months, and then transferred to the Ghbila prison in Casablanca. Nearly three years later, in December 1980, her case was finally brought to court, and she was charged with conspiring against the security of the state, membership in an illegal group, and distributing political tracts and posters. In a trial whose conclusion was determined before any defence was heard, she was sentenced to five years in prison, counting time already served. Ultimately, El Bouih served her sentence in five different prisons in four different cities: Derb Moulay Cherif and Ghbila in Casablanca, Sidi Saïd in Meknes, El Alou in Rabat, and, finally, Kenitra – all, because, as she said, she had had the audacity 'to have imagined a better tomorrow, and a world in which the rights of all would be respected, and in which women would no longer be considered inferior' (51).

In 1990 the French writer Gilles Perrault published an ironically entitled book, *Notre Ami le roi*, in which he chronicled how the reign of Hassan II, beginning in 1961, devolved into a long period of serious miscarriages of justice.[22] Describing Hassan II's personal reign as 'l'horreur hassanienne' (334), Perrault repeatedly expressed outrage that France, the former colonial power who maintained close ties with Morocco, mostly kept its eyes closed during the period. In an afterword to the 1992 edition of his book, at which point political prisoners, including the Oufkir family, Abraham Serfaty, and the twenty-eight survivors of Tazmamart had been freed, Perrault remained unconvinced that the king was truly committed to a better, freer Morocco in which citizens could both debate and share in power; instead, he continued to judge, as he had earlier, that Hassan's idea of democracy was a mere pantomime, resting on a tripod of repression, fraud, and fear (355–6).

El Bouih shared Perrault's scepticism and has said that only with the king's death in 1999 did she really begin to breathe more freely. In a 2001 interview with American professor Susan Slyomovics, she declared, 'As a former political prisoner, I feel this enormous psychological relief and unburdening since the death of King Hassan II and note the [positive] changes in me and in Morocco.'[23] Her statement helps to explain why it was nearly a decade after her release from prison in 1982 before she spoke out and became active in politics. Her first order of business, after five years of incarceration and at age twenty-seven, was to readjust to society, which she confesses to finding more difficult than adapting to prison. Ultimately, she married, became a high school teacher of Arabic, and had two daughters. When she did reengage in the human rights struggle, she focused her energies on behalf of women prisoners and female victims of violence in society. But over time and in conjunction with her work, she came increasingly to believe that historical memory was crucial to changing society, and that, furthermore, as a woman, she had a special responsibility to bear witness to women's courage and actions in the struggle for human rights. By writing a memoir, which required remembering the past, she would in effect be contributing to the new future so ardently needed.

Memory and Art in *Une Femme nommée Rachid*

El Bouih has said that writing is for her a way to investigate memory in its multiple manifestations – official memory, collective memory, personal memory, and woman's memory.[24] And that statement, I submit, is key to understanding her memoir.

From the opening pages of this text of fewer than 100 pages, its literary nature is clear. Memory and art interact in a text composed of fragments and flashes designed to evoke the physical impact and psychic landscape of her five years of incarceration. Incorporating stylistic techniques such as shifting perspective, aesthetic detachment, and surreal imagery, El Bouih does not seek to give a complete account of her years in prison, but rather glimpses of its emotional essences. This is, of course, the way memory works, not as a strict chronology of the passage of days and years, not as a single, direct route through the thicket, but as a labyrinth of possibilities, some inviting lingering, others quickly dispatched. Hence, the varying length of the fourteen chapters, from slightly over a page ('Une Visite Exceptionnelle') to almost thirteen pages ('Le Minaret s'est écroulé'), and hence, too, their sometimes playful chapter titles: 'Le Minaret s'est écroulé: pendez le barbier,' or the telegraphic, 'Flashes d'une vie de détenue,' or more poetic, 'Automne d'une vie sans printemps,' or more foreboding, 'Journal d'une grêviste de la faim,' or the oxymoron, 'En Prison naît un homme libre.'[25] Each chapter represents a memory that is at once seared in the author's mind and processed by time. Unlike the prison narrative written from prison that carries a pressing immediacy, hers – written close to two decades later – is characterized by a different quality of reflection and a more conscious choice of narrative devices, in an interweaving of art and memory. Because of the way in which she merges poetic evocation and realistic description, because she has personal sensitivities grounded in the study of classical Arabic literature, but especially because her text has a triple purpose as memoir, memorial, and call to conscience, El Bouih's work stands apart from all other prison narratives by Moroccan writers of the period, however much they have in common.

To explore in greater detail how memory and art function in *Une Femme nommée Rachid*, the following discussion will be divided into three parts: a focus on time, space, and perspective; style and imagery;

and the body and the senses. In the aggregate, these elements reveal the originality of El Bouih's text, which is both artful and artless, poetic and political, suffused with an 'I' that remains unwilling to speak exclusively in terms of personal experience and that seeks to activate the 'we' of the nation.

Time, Space, and Perspective

All prison writing is concerned with Time, which is both a thematic and narrative element in any memoir, but especially in the prison memoir in which the prisoner is 'doing time' and real time is counted not on the 24-hour watch, but in the prisoner's consciousness. The reader wonders how the prison memoirist will write (or remember) the hours and days, the months and years, without saying the obvious – that time is endless and weighs heavily – or without taking recourse to simple diary-like entries, which with a retrospective memoir would be difficult to reconstruct. As El Bouih and her friends learn, time has another clock in prison and any request – to confer with lawyers, to receive permission for needed medical attention, to have their status as 'prisoners of opinion' recognized – entails endless waits, because prison is not a place of order and precision, but often of disorder and anarchy. Hence, in writing, El Bouih typically reconstitutes the time of prison as distorted, arbitrary, and unnatural, an endless cycle without beginning or end, often with scant relationship to the clock, as, for instance, during periods of torture when the mind shuts down, or during the hunger strike when time is contorted into a kind of faceless grimace. In other words, El Bouih seeks to write time in the same way she experienced it in prison, as simultaneously arbitrary and chaotic, eccentric and hallucinatory.

On the pages devoted to the hunger strike (35–41), time takes on nightmarish shapes and proportions. It is not so much the torments of hunger the women fear, but time itself. Their most fervent desire is not for food, but for the hours to pass, for sleep to transport them. But sleep is like a 'mirage' in the desert, El Bouih writes (37), constantly beyond reach, while time expands into 'centuries,' 'all eternity,' virtual timelessness. As one day succeeds another and their bodies begin to fail, El Bouih speaks of time as the 'black pit' of 'interminable nights' and 'the sea of shadows' (39). When the second week succeeds the first, each day assumes an inimitable flavour: Monday is bitterness; Tuesday, bone-chilling cold; Wednesday, expectation; Thursday, foreboding; Friday, certainty; Saturday, suspense; and Sunday, long silence (38). The passage of time is rendered by an ever-renewed and exhausting round of emotions, physical and mental, moments of crazy hopefulness followed by utter alienation, trailing off into uncertainty even as to whether her body still holds a living being. Fatna recalls fixating on her inability to verify her existence by a photograph or a mirror (39), her mind constantly asking for physical proof that she lives in a body, rather than only as a spirit, unanchored and floating. Thus, in sum, El Bouih uses Time poetically and idiosyncratically primarily to reconstitute the physical and emotional experience of prison, not to mark the passage of days on the calendar.

A second narrative element that contributes to writing the 'feeling' of prison is the treatment of space. Almost all prison narratives talk about prison walls, those spatial signifiers denoting separation and the loss of freedom. Prison walls not only press in upon the prisoner, sometimes almost literally entombing her, but they also carry the spectre of former prisoners whose tears are imagined as running down the rough stone surfaces, broken and cleft like a human heart. The walls of a prison cell can also tell the tales of former prisoners, or even, as in the case of Abdelaziz Mouride who drew, hide in their crevices the visual story of torture and abuse.[26] In El Bouih, prison walls 'speak' in another way. On the night at the Ghbila prison when she and her co-detainees learn that Saïda Menebhi had died as a result of her hunger strike (roughly two years prior to their own), the garrison walls become like virtual loudspeakers, broadcasting the sad news. The report of Saïda's death passes not through the conventional means of spoken words, because no official would speak directly to the prisoners of such things, but through the sound, first, of one woman's wailed lamentation echoing down the corridor, and then, as woman after woman joined in, a massive outpouring of grief, magnified by the craggy, hard surfaces of the stone walls. Devastated by the death of a comrade whose demise makes their own deaths a more tangible potentiality, the women stifle their fears, and through unified voice and shared vision, simultaneously honour Saïda and reaffirm their commitment to justice and their faith in their cause. As El Bouih writes, 'Despite the high ramparts and terrifying silences, the prison walls now become like loudspeakers. We raise our voices and salute Saïda's death with a song that bonds us together' (29). Paradoxically, the actual walls of the prison become their allies against the impassive, figurative wall of silence maintained by the authorities aimed at destroying them. The women's song of resistance and solidarity ends with the triumphal phrase, 'Friends, tomorrow we shall gather together, it is certain. The crowds are with us, the streets themselves will open to us.' Theirs is a song that reasserts their ultimate victory over space as much as in the political domain.

In her article affixed to El Bouih's memoir, Latifa Ajbabdi calls prison a non-space, by which she means a space so removed from normal reality that the prisoner, deprived of the benchmarks of normalcy, feels adrift. As a result, in prison, the women prisoners struggle to organize their space and time in ways that permit them to retain a sense of themselves. Survival is a daily challenge, one, as Fatna and her friends learn, that depends upon finding techniques and strategies to protect themselves. Interestingly, El Bouih adopts some of those same strategies in her writing, in order to defend herself against the pain caused by memory.

One of those techniques is the stance of aesthetic distancing. While she usually frames her presentation through the first-person pronoun, at times she adopts the distancing device of the third-person, as for instance in two chapters, 'Une Nuit à El Alou,' which she calls 'Acte I,' followed by another, 'Le Jugement,' which is 'Acte II.' By such a 'theatrical' division of memories into the 'acts' of a play, the writer takes the vantage point of the spectator. The chapter begins with a comment by a prison matron revealing distaste for the female prisoners whose cells she locks each evening and whose 'filth' she cannot seem to wash from her hands, and then flows into the prisoner's repeated and ritual recall of times past, set in counterpoint to the present. The ritual is induced almost reflexively each evening when the cell is locked for the evening, the prisoner left in the solitude of her memories. The hour on the clock reminds Fatna of what that time had formerly meant, the walk through the fragrant olive grove, the after-school rite of a snack shared with a beloved father who wants to know about her lessons and asks her to examine her conscience regarding her moral behaviour that day. That same hour of the day in prison has another taste, and as the writer evokes in memory its routine, she adopts a third-person perspective, *elle*, and 'sees' herself in the present tense, to denote the habitual nature of the event. 'She runs her gaze over her cage-like cell, with fissures in its walls, like the fissures in her heart,' and expresses disbelief: 'She had never imagined it possible that anyone could reduce the life of a human being to these few square metres.' This realization produces a physical reaction: 'She closes her eyes, gripped by nausea. She sinks into the dark solitary reaches of her mind, moving away from the present walls that conserve so many thousand stories of tears' (44).

This third-person distancing from her self in prison continues through the next chapter in which some two and a half years after her abduction she is at last brought to court and sees in her mind's eye the lawyer, brandishing her frail arm before the judge, demanding to know what was so fear-inspiring about it. 'Could this arm bring down a government?' he asks rhetorically. 'It is so little,' and 'the accusation made against it so great' (51). Nor did his client even have in her possession anything very dangerous, he insists, arguing, 'the evidence against her is only whatever is found on the shelves of bookstores, and in ideas and dreams.' By stepping outside her skin, in a manner of speaking, Fatna narrates the scene in which she is the principal, as though writer and subject are not the same person. This separation from her self is not merely the result of the passage of time, between living the event and writing it, but of the same strategy of distancing she adopted as a prisoner.[27] By writing episodes of her prison narrative in this way, or by looking at herself through the lens, so to speak, she succeeds in capturing both the unreal, cinematic quality of what she had felt and the degree of alienation purposefully wrought by the penal system's campaign to depersonalize and disavow the prisoner's individuality. In unflinching terms, she indicts those at the highest levels, 'My God, to whom have we confided power in this country!' (16), and bitterly declares, 'In our "dear country," I have never seen anything as efficient [as the power of the state and its police]. They are super-rapid, even supersonic in kidnapping and interrogating. The cries and moans of the tortured fill the space with terror. Death is all around me, front and back' (19).

At other times, distance is achieved when El Bouih narrates by means of the 'floating pronoun' perspective. Occasionally in a single scene she alternates between 'I' and 'she,' 'we' and 'they,' to create an unstable perspective. This occurs in the chapter evocatively entitled 'Le Minaret s'est écroulé: pendez le barbier' (The Minaret has fallen: Hang the Barber) in which she describes the chaos of authoritarianism when a high-level commission of inspectors pays a visit to the Meknes prison, causing panic and fear among both local prison officials and the prisoners. What El Bouih emphasizes with the title of her chapter is a kind of 'kill-the-messenger' logic, or utter illogic of a prison system in which there are always consequences, but where the relationship between cause and effect is either absent or wholly disproportionate. To communicate this idea of disorganization and the anarchy of misrule, she intersperses changes in narrative point of view, switching between 'we' and 'they.' She underscores her point by ending the chapter with prison officials pummelling and abusing another woman inmate who had dared to raise her voice against the head matron, 'the high and mighty suzerain' of the cellblock. They call the prisoner 'crazy' and send her to spend the night in solitary confinement, naked and without food. The fate of that woman (not one of the political prisoners) who had been dispossessed of everything but her tongue (69), as the memoirist observes, prompts Fatna's sympathy and an incisively bitter comment concerning the quality of the irrational that obtains in a society driven by a mentality of incarceration. 'Life in prison,' she says, 'resembles life on the outside; it's just more concentrated' (70). Furthermore, triumphs are never final, she presciently judges. 'In Morocco, nothing is ever acquired once and for all, especially when it comes to human rights,' a phrase she had written in French (Au Maroc, rien n'est jamais définitivement acquis, surtout lorsqu'il s'agit des droits de la personne) even in the original Arabic text. What has just been described – the ironic chapter title, the presentation of a scene, the sardonic criticism – shows how El Bouih joins the three goals of her narrative: to write of her experience, to speak on behalf of those who are victimized by the system, and to make a ringing indictment of both the penal and social systems of Morocco.

In tapping her memories of prison, El Bouih used the narrative tools of time, space, and perspective to recreate the sensate essence of that experience. Clearly, then, it is the emotional landscape – the way the entire experience felt and still feels in her mind when she re-members the past – that the poet of memory wishes to convey.

Style and Imagery

If El Bouih chooses to evoke fragmented acts and state of mind, rather than an account of discrete events in a linear chronicle, it is because of the way that memory works, and also because she seeks to convey the anguish of imprisonment whose impact remains in the subconscious long after liberation. It is for this reason that her memoir moves primarily by imagery and stylistic effects intended not to tell a story from beginning to end, not to answer the reader's desire for contextualization and personal family background, not to reconstitute prison in its entirety, but in ways that focus on the emotional truth of what she strongly believes was a collective experience. She does not 'remember' in her name alone, but on behalf of all the women with whom she experienced the abuses of a barbaric penal system and a brutal political regime, both of which condoned torture and inhumane treatment. What she does is to process memory through the imagination, something she likewise did while in prison when she began working on the literary legend in pursuit of a master's degree. Fertile ground for the prisoner, the imagination now permits her to travel through memory and to tell a political legend – her own – in the language of literature.

As described at the beginning of this chapter, the opening pages of her memoir are highly effective in setting the stage for the drama of her abduction. Without offering any historical or political contextualization, El Bouih propels the reader through a dreamy, first-person reverie in which water dominates, to a surreal world of terror and torture. The writer's decision not to provide the political context of her abduction may surprise readers accustomed to a detailed background of the narrating subject and the exact nature of events leading up to abduction.[28] It could be argued that the absence of such contextualization is the result of a cultural disinclination, particularly on the part of a woman, to make personal revelations. Or, it could be that El Bouih assumes that most readers will already know the facts, or agree with her that no context could possibly justify what happens to her. But more pertinent, I believe, on the narrative level, El Bouih is seeking to convey to the reader the same brutal shock that she felt when she was torn from the mundane and cast into the unreal. This rupture is prepared within the narrative by first evoking the ways in which flowing water had created in her mind that day a kind of gauzy reverie, begun with a morning trip to the steamy vapours of the hammam, and continuing on the placid waters of the Bou Regreg, as she is rowed across the river on a spring day. The only suspicion of what lay ahead comes in the midst of her dreamlike trance, brought on by the movement of the boat and the view of a limitless horizon leading out to sea, when she feels a shiver of apprehension: what if the oarsman were suddenly to veer from his course and she were carried out to open sea? It is a premonition of startling acuity, for, indeed, that is what happens when she is yanked into the apartment by a plain-clothes agent, later that day.

Just as El Bouih returns repeatedly to evocations of water imagery, the sea and river, which figure so strongly in her memory, so does she frequently evoke journeys, both real and figurative, that mark her five years in prison. Such images speak a language of poetry in the most unpoetic of places, and in juxtaposition with the realistic descriptions of the physical and mental cruelties, contribute to the ongoing tension between dream and reality, as between beauty and horror, sustained throughout the narrative. She writes of literal journeys between prisons and from prison to court, the long journeys of parents from other cities in hope of gaining entry to the visitors parlour to see their daughter, the journeys to freedom of released prisoners who worry about whether they can make their way on the outside. And there are those other journeys into the bowels of hell when she or her sister prisoners are closed in the torture chamber with the *hâjs* or *tortionnaires* (torturers). In fact, El Bouih refers to the seven months at Derb Moulay Cherif as a kind of extended journey – a veritable, if perverted, pilgrimage, thereby evoking an ironic contrast between those who journey to Mecca and prisoners, pilgrims of another kind, whose journey would be neither 'blessed nor fruitful' (27), leaving them haggard and emaciated (26), beaten but definitely not broken.

When El Bouih describes the promiscuity of communal life in the spaces of the prison, the dank and airless cells, the underground caverns through which the blindfolded prisoner is led, the tortures and insults and vulgarity of the guards, she might be writing like any other prison memoirist. But when she remembers the prison as 'that infernal harem' (56) or likens the women's block to the souk in the medina, except without the colours and sounds of joyous life (47), her touchstones are all North African. And when she describes the jailer's/torturer's hands that probe and search and leave their imprint on her body, she writes as a woman – more specifically, as a North African woman, violated. As she said, 'Those hands that go everywhere, that enter and search the body, do not leave the same imprint on a man as on the body of a woman.'[29] And this point is important. To write as a woman, and to return to a past she can neither forget nor recover without pain, El Bouih employs images and stylistic devices, or the art of prose, both to help her access memory and to make it more bearable.[30]

Body Memories

In the logic of imprisonment, as presented by Foucault, the confined body will be disciplined and learn submission, so as to emerge chastened and rehabilitated, ready to be incorporated into the larger body of society. In reality, far from reeducating that body, the prison experience, or 'crucifixion,' as Fatna describes it (45), endeavours to destroy human dignity physically and psychologically. In the house of correction – a term Fatna derides – the prisoners live with fear as their constant companion and in 'an atmosphere of terror' (59), characterized by sudden prohibitions, broken or false promises, arbitrary punishments, and silent cruelties on the part of the matrons.[31] In such an emotionally charged atmosphere, the senses are on alert, the body braced for the worst. It is reasonable, then, that when a writer endeavours to re-access the mental/emotional texture of her prison experience through memory, her attention will be strongly focused on the physical body and the senses, and how they were both assaulted and reshaped. As those who study how memory functions tell us, memory is highly attuned to emotion, which in turn is dependent on the senses.[32] Because of this and other more philosophical reasons, it is hardly surprising that so many prison memoirs are narrated through the physical body or what might be called body memories.

For Fatna, body memories take many forms and have many purposes. In the surreal world of prison, disarticulated body parts – hands, heads, faces, eyes, feet, fingers – populate both her daily life and her dreams. Sometimes floating faces track her in her cell, to support her, as when family members appear in her half-awake dreams, while at other times, she confronts faces convulsed in anger or disgust against her, like the matron who could never seem to get her hands clean after dealing with the prisoners (43). She recalls the odours and the breath of her torturers, whose faces she never saw, but whose hands leave their marks upon her body. She rehears the sound of her torturers' voices dissociated from human bodies – vulgar, rough, and shouting, now threatening, now boasting of the damage they inflicted on their victims. And she recalls the hated matrons, who with icy fingers probe her body cavities during humiliating searches.

There are also, of course, the body memories of the hunger strike, when the prisoner ironically becomes, as El Bouih writes, 'her own torturer' (35), metaphorically cannibalizing herself to protest her lack of human rights. Since the physical body is the prisoner's sole resource through which to assert will and power, her body becomes, in a tragic irony, simultaneously the agent and victim of the attack directed against the state. On the pages devoted to the strike, Hunger is personified as the inevitable and unwanted visitor who attaches to the prisoner, accompanies the migraine that fogs her vision and hounds her even during attacks of colic, chases away sleep, possesses the insidious power to undermine health and to play for keeps. Yet, curiously, starvation is also a visitor who makes things clearer for the prisoner, intensifying resolve and commitment to her cause.

Complementing body memories are other physical details that loom large in the writer's memory and whose presence creates a lasting impression on the reader's mind. There is, for instance, the matron at Sidi

Saïd waving in her hand a huge pair of rusted scissors to be used to cut the prisoners' fingernails (26), which, bizarrely, had grown 'spectacularly' during the months of torture and near-starvation at Derb Moulay Cherif, and now resemble the claws of raptors. And there are the shackles the women political detainees must wear each time they leave their cell for the outside world, such as when they are transferred from one prison to another. Given both their sex and the political nature of their 'crime,' it was an absurdity, but as a policeman sarcastically reminded her, 'For us, you are a man and will be treated as such. It's true that we don't handcuff women prisoners, but the likes of you have nothing to do with real women' (50).[33]

Life in prison, El Bouih underscores repeatedly, is a distortion not only of normality, but of logic and sanity. In prison, the physical senses, like the body, are alienated, distorted, deprived, and assaulted. Remarkably, however, she finds that when one sense is disabled, another takes its place. Having grown accustomed to the loss of vision at Derb Moulay Cherif, she discovers that when her blindfold is removed seven months later at Sidi Saïd, she initially feels confused and suffers from sensory overload. In order to hear well, she says, her eyes need to be covered ('Pour bien entendre, il faudrait que j'aie les yeux bandés' [25]). At the same time, having so long been forbidden to communicate through speech, she initially feels incapable of speaking coherently when she receives a visit from the renowned professor, Fatima Mernissi, who has come to discuss the subject of Fatna's masters thesis.[34] Not only is verbal language a habit she fears she has lost, but her sense is that she no longer speaks the language of the outside, having replaced it by that strangely coded language of incarceration, in which words are used by the jailors to command attitudes and denote moments and movements within the prison. By recalling the two ruling exhortations of authorities at Sidi Saïd, 'Respect!' and 'Obedience!' Fatna simultaneously re-accesses the alienating shorthand of prison speech and invokes its military-like call to attention and reminder of subservience. Language communication as practised by the jailors flows in a single direction and is intended to produce both a sensory and physical reaction on the part of the prisoner. In recalling this, Fatna demonstrates her conviction that since prison is a distortion of logic and sanity and normality, its language, too, will reflect this perversion.

By writing through the body and the senses recalled, El Bouih communicates powerfully to the imagination of her readers, who leave the text *feeling* the experience of prison even more than knowing it.

Conclusion

If it is true that conscience and collective memory are key to a modern nation, then memoirs by former political prisoners play a crucial role in reminding Moroccans that it is not just colonialism that silenced voice and sought to destroy memory, but a repressive political regime of their own. As the nation strives to remake its political culture, these prison memoirs from the 'years of lead' serve not only as that conscience and critical memory of the past, but also as evidence of recent democratic progress. It is highly salient that among these works, figures one by a remarkable woman.

Indeed, in paying tribute to all those who resisted and paid heavily for their opposition, Abderrahmin Berrada recalls in the preface to Mouride's *On affame bien les rats!* that Moroccan women did not wait for the year 2000 to take to the streets in support of political change, pointing to all those who had 'long since boarded the train,' including such notables as Evelyne Serfaty, Rabia Fettouh, Fatima Oukacha, Saïda Menebhi, Latifa Ajbabdi, and of course Fatna El Bouih.[35] This is a chapter of Moroccan women's history that demands recognition, both by their fellow citizens and by the West, for, clearly, submissiveness and ineffectiveness, silence and resignation have been neither the lot, nor description of all Muslim women.

By giving powerful testimony of female memory and of women's role in the struggle for human rights in Morocco, Fatna El Bouih demonstrates that while she may have carried a man's name in prison, she now resolutely writes her work in her own name and in the name of all Moroccan women.

6 The Female Body and the Body Politic: Harem and Hammam

In the textual and visual depictions of North Africa and the greater Middle East, two iconic spaces traditionally associated with Orientalism and issues of power and powerlessness are the customary site for investigating the cultural politics of gender and sexuality: harem and hammam. Conventionally, the harem is that part of the Oriental house reserved for women, while the hammam or baths are located outside the home in establishments with abundant water and heating capacity to produce steam. Gender-specific spaces of intimacy, closed off from the outside world and ruled by precise laws regulating inclusion and exclusion, these spaces of the body, according to certain currents of Western thought, confine women both literally and figuratively through the projection of male fantasy or desire. In the somber or steamy dream spaces of a Delacroix or Ingres painting, female figures, lost in silent dream or erotic reverie, docilely and compliantly offer themselves to the viewer, who, in turn, determines female identity and significance through the body.

In contrast, a contemporary oil painting entitled 'Le Harem' by Moroccan artist Rachid Sebti and shown on the cover of Houria Boussejra's *Femmes inachevées* marries harem and hammam, along with both traditional ideas and a modern socio-psychological approach. He shows a group of five women, robed but unveiled, in various states of awareness, from self-absorption to apparent trance, disarray or possibly madness, ambiguous friendship or lesbianism. More pointedly, while he paints them as confined in a blurred, watery kind of space, behind a massive, windowed wall, grilled or barred, he also shows, in the far distance, blue sky and mountain tops, of which the women appear unaware. In this way he juxtaposes both the inside and the outside worlds, presenting the harem/hammam in a modern North African context, while at the same time retaining traditional essences, and inviting the viewer to expand the discourse on women in the body politic. This chapter will seek to do likewise.

Though in the twenty-first century, only one of the spaces under study – the hammam – is an actual reality, since the harem exists primarily as a cultural, social, and psychological concept without a literal architecture, both spaces are centrally concerned with circumscribing and signifying female identity through the body.[1] Despite earlier references to male painters, the use of the harem or hammam is not, in fact, the sole province of men. Indeed, both are strongly in evidence in the writing of Moroccan women, who, while demonstrating ties to the tradition, nonetheless differ fundamentally from their male counterparts in their presentation of the two sites. Far from reenacting male conventions of observation through the gaze of desire or the gauze of steamy vapours, women writers reconceptualize the two spaces in order to reassess the female condition and to reclaim the discourse of the body. Indeed, Fedwa Malti-Douglas argues that woman's voice in Arabo-Islamic discourse, classical or modern, is 'indissolubly tied to sexuality and the body,' whether the woman speaks through her body or in reaction to it.[2] In reformulating the language of the body, Moroccan women challenge and sometimes reverse sexual politics, while addressing issues of freedom and control from a decidedly female standpoint. By reappraising the politics of women's bodies, their texts open a new dialogue about women's marginality in society and lay the groundwork for rethinking women's roles in the body politic.

In the discussion ahead, we shall analyse how women writers challenge both Orientalist and sexist thinking about the female body, and, more specifically, how they exploit these spaces to deconstruct and reconstruct not only female identity, but also the very social body, itself. In that respect, it is logical to begin with Morocco's pioneering feminist, Fatima Mernissi, who made the harem the key to her system of thinking about women.

The Harem

Published in 1987, *Le Harem politique* propelled Mernissi onto the intellectual scene in both East and West.[3] Initially censored in Morocco, a fact that insured high readership, the book was first published in Egypt, and subsequently received both extravagant praise and sharp criticism.[4] One of nearly two dozen works by Mernissi, it posits the harem at the centre of her thinking on society, politics, and sexual relations. Most of her subsequent works reformulate its premises, whether in the narrative non-fiction, *Dreams of Trespass*, or in her many non-fiction works, such as *Etes-vous vacciné contre le harem?* (1998), or *Scheherazade Goes West* (2001), or the international art show that she curated in 2003, 'Fantaisies du harem et nouvelles Schéhérazade.' For the latter, Mernissi selected 150 visual representations of the harem, from both classic and contemporary traditions, including paintings by European masters (Ingres, Delacroix, Matisse, and Picasso), plus miniatures, engravings, and books by Persian masters, Turks, and Indian Moghols, in addition to recent works by North African and Middle Eastern women artists. Setting these various pieces in dialogue by means of their very placement on the museum wall, she sought to open a discussion on the different ways that women have conducted their struggle for freedom from within the constraints of the social and political harem.[5]

Coming from the Arabic word *haram*, meaning the forbidden and the sacred space, where access is controlled by precise and strict laws, 'harem' is the veritable lynchpin of Mernissi's thinking on the individual, the woman, and the social body. For her, the harem can be a real space, as in the imperial harem of the Ottoman Empire or, more likely, an abstract idea of separation, exclusion, confinement, and invisible lines. While she begins *Dreams of Trespass* with the famous phrase, 'Je suis née en 1940 dans un harem à Fès' (I was born in a harem in Fez in 1940), that harem is the antipode of an imperial harem in which there is a sultan who reigns over many wives or female servants. Instead, her harem in the Fez medina is a domestic harem, which, in essence, means the extended family of brothers and their wives and children, a grandparent, servants, and the occasional divorced aunt who has no other place to live. Nevertheless, while it is not the relationship between one man and the many women of his entourage that focuses the author's interest in *Dreams of Trespass*, in point of fact, the principle of 'harem' obtains there as much as it does in *Le Harem politique*. As Grandmother Yasmina explains to young Fatima, the family harem is 'a protected space, organized by a precise code. No man can penetrate the harem without the permission of its owners ... A harem is defined by the idea of private property' (chapter 7). Additionally, the child learns, the 'harem' may be carried within the self, the result of cultural and gender socialization. This is the 'invisible harem,' *qu'ida*, customs and traditions. In the 'domestic harem' of *Dreams*, created by the linkages of blood or the alliances contracted through marriage, the strongest female characters push against the strictures, real and psychological – the *huda* – that confine them. Taken together, *qu'ida* and *hudud* bedevil little Fatima, who fears she will inadvertently transgress upon them without even knowing they exist. Trying to figure out these limits becomes a full-time occupation, and she confesses to feeling great anxiety each time she is unable to fix the often invisible lines of what she deems her powerlessness.

Indeed, from the very first pages of the text, Mernissi sets out the geometrics of life in the domestic harem, concentrating on spatial indicators, such as doors, thresholds, borders, stairways, courtyards, and terraces, but also the lines of demarcation between the Medina and the Ville Nouvelle, Christians and Muslims, occupiers and occupants. The point is that harem-like relations exist wherever there are relationships of power, whether the divisions and partitions are political, sexual, or geographic. Furthermore, since the very notion of the harem implies an interior and an exterior, or an 'us' and 'them,' the point of separation between the two is often described as the border or the frontier or perhaps even the 'gulf' or chasm dividing the two. Borders are conceived to separate the powerless from the powerful, but are also subject to changing conditions. Thus, while at home and in the labyrinthine streets of the Medina, the Moroccan husbands and fathers carry authority, in the greater city, under French colonial command, they are subservient to the occupiers, obliged to request permission to travel from one city to another. In the harem metaphor applied to social relations, borders are often artificial and arbitrary, existing only, as little Fatima observes, 'in the head of those who have power' (9), but they can still subject certain individuals to confinement and require others to protect the fortress of their own making.

In view of the above, it is obvious that for Mernissi 'harem' is a multivalent concept. Whether it is the sociologist or feminist in her speaking, the harem principle is like a metaphorical 'architecture,' adopted to explain the exercise of power and the mechanics of exclusion. In the actual imperial harem, woman occupies a hidden interior space, forbidden to all men with the exception of the master, while man moves freely in the *polis*, open to all with the exception of women. Hence, the distinction not only denotes two spheres of private and public, but, through the bias of excluding one sex from both realms, inequality. This is Mernissi's real interest, whose origins she intends to trace.

In *Le Harem politique*, Mernissi returns to the source, the Qur'an, to determine whether sexism and antiwoman sentiment are firmly established in the holy book of Islam. With her trademark light and personal touch, she describes the genesis of her project by an anecdote in which, playing the sociologist par excellence, she asks her local grocer, 'Can a woman be a leader of Muslims?' an idea that shocks him to the tip of his toes, while another customer replies in the negative, backing up his point of view with the following Hadith: 'Those who entrust their affairs to a woman will never know prosperity!' Now it is Mernissi's turn to be shocked. Momentarily silenced, but 'furious,' she writes, she retreated from the grocer's determined to 'inform' herself about this 'sledgehammer argument used by those who want to exclude women from politics' (4). The result is *Le Harem politique*.

Although Mernissi was one of the first women to argue that it is Islamic scriptural and legal scholars – all male – who used their religious and political authority to hand down laws and to make translations that undermine the early egalitarian reforms of the Prophet Mohammed, other scholars, including Leila Ahmed, Amina Wadud, and Asma Barlas, Carolyn Moxley Rouse, Kecia Ali, and Ingrid Mattson, to mention only females, argue that when Islam returns to its roots, societies that base themselves on the Qur'an will no longer be able to oppress women freely.[6] In formulating a new exegesis on women in Islam, these scholars have embarked on an important enterprise substantially more liberal and progressive than centuries of traditional scholarship and, as a result, seek to renew the debate about women, evident in the very titles of their books – Ahmed, *Women and Gender in Islam: Historical Roots of a Modern Debate*, Wadud, *Qur'an and Woman; Rereading the Sacred Text from a Woman's Perspective*, and *Inside the Gender Jihad: Women's Reform in Islam*, and Barlas, *'Believing Women' in Islam: Unreading Patriarchal Interpretations of the Qur'an*.[7] Inevitably in this pursuit, they have raised the hackles of traditional Muslims who condemn their efforts toward the very process of *ijtihad* (informed inquiry) enjoined to the faithful in the Qur'an itself, which recognizes that Islam is a living faith.

Mernissi's feminist interpretation of women's rights in Islam is argued through her concept of the 'harem' in the French title, *Le Harem politique*, or the 'veil' in the title translated into English, *The Veil and the Male Elite*. Whether 'harem' or 'veil' (*hijab*), both have been used to split Muslim space, in Mernissi's argument, and the result is separate and unequal relations between the sexes. In the broadest sense, however, the concept, as she describes it in chapter 5, 'The *Hijab*, The Veil,' carries triple significance, having visual, spatial, and ethical components.

> The concept of the word *hijab* is three-dimensional, and the three dimensions often blend into one another. The first dimension is a visual one: to hide something from sight. The root of the verb *hajaba* means 'to hide.' The second dimension is spatial: to separate, to mark a border, to establish a threshold. And, finally, the third dimension is ethical: it belongs to the realm of the forbidden. So we have not just tangible categories that exist in the reality of the senses – the visual, the spatial – but also an abstract reality in the realm of ideas. (93)

In that last sentence, Mernissi demonstrates how embracing for her the concept of *hijab*, veil, 'harem' is and, hence, its suitability as the veritable backbone of her master narrative of social, political, and gender relations.

To explain how *hijab* became so determinative in Muslim cultures, Mernissi describes what for her is a critical moment in Islam, presented in the Qur'anic verse (33:53), called the 'descent of the *hijab*,' in which space is divided into two realms, the public and the private. Indeed, for her, the descent of the *hijab*, together with the linguistic, social, historical, and religious aspects of *hijab*, is as key to Muslim civilization 'as sin is in the Christian context, or credit is in American capitalist society' (95). In her discussion of the verse, Mernissi turns to earlier scholars, notably al-Tabari (839–923), one of the guardians of the sacred text, who explains and situates the Qur'an in events from the life of the Prophet.[8] This verse, al-Tabari had written, was received in relationship to the Prophet's marriage with Zaynab Bint Jahsh. Following the ceremony, several guests seemed impervious to the fact that it was time to take their leave, and continued trying to engage Mohamed in conversation, even as he tried to withdraw to the conjugal bedroom, until at last Mohamed had to lower a curtain to separate his private space from that of the community. Mernissi maintains, therefore, that this first descent of the *hijab* is an act of visual, spatial, and ethical significance, which, in its origins, carried no gender dimension, let alone gender discrimination. Those aspects, she asserts, were added in subsequent generations after the Prophet's time. Since she reads the descent of the *hijab* as the original division of human space into two realms, she declares that its subsequent application to women, through the command to wear a piece of cloth – the *hijab* – whose sole purpose is to hide the face or body, is tantamount to deforming and dramatically diminishing the principle of *hijab*, as well as making woman's body into the symbolic representation of the Islamic community. This is a serious misinterpretation, according to Mernissi, perpetrated by generations of male interpreters who have got it badly wrong.

Her interpretation of verse 33:53 as a key division of space, subsequently to be used against one sex, and the founding principle on which is established a theory about society, politics, and the sexes, makes it an edifice of both substantial importance and considerable fragility. To be sure, her reading of the verse is not widely shared, even by liberal interpreters of the Qur'an. Anouar Majid, for instance, declares that while her argument is brilliant, it 'desacralizes the Qur'an' by reducing it to a 'mere historical document,' suggesting that it was produced in a series of human negotiations in which God always intervened – rather diplomatically – on behalf of the Prophet.'[9] For Mernissi, however, it is important for understanding how generations of Muslims reached the conclusion that the Qur'an disenfranchised women. Like other feminist scholars of Islam who seek to read the sacred text with new eyes, and therefore to discern how earlier readings might be misreadings, Mernissi brings to her task extensive scholarship and a probing intellect. She understands how subversive new readings can be, but she also believes that rereadings can become a source of hopefulness for Muslim women. Beginning with *Beyond the Veil: Male/Female Dynamics in Modern Muslim Society* (1975), based on her doctoral dissertation in sociology at Brandeis University in Massachusetts, and continuing with *Le Harem politique*, which Mernissi considers her most important book,[10] she has, indeed, courted controversy, but consistently sought to understand the dynamics of exclusion in society.

Her broad reading of the metaphor of the harem is, as shown above, located in the politics of space and the maintenance of male power, both of which are present throughout her writings. In fact, the actual word, 'harem,' occurs in the title or subtitle of five of her works – *Le Harem politique: Le Prophète et ses femmes*; *Rêves de femmes: Contes d'enfance au harem*; *Scheherazade Goes West: Different Cultures, Different Harems*; *Etes-vous vacciné contre le harem?*' and *Le Harem européen*. Similarly, the word 'harem' occurs in four of the twenty-two chapter titles of *Dreams of Trespass* (chapters 1, 3, 7, 13), plus figuring substantially in others, such as, for instance, 'le harem de la ferme' in chapter 5. The reason is clear: for Mernissi, the harem is a spatial concept and a power structure that defines the mechanics of women's oppression, whether in the East or the West. The application of her notion of the socio-political-cultural harem goes beyond feminism to become the bedrock of her overarching theory on the practice of exclusion in society.

Given how the word 'harem' carries associations in the history of the region, there can be little doubt that any North African woman writer uses it innocently. And yet the harem is a frequent metaphor on the pages of their texts, as when Siham Benchekroun refers lightly to 'the resurgence of some harem from legend, peopled by exquisitely pleasing and irresistibly inconstant beings' (*Oser vivre*, 63), or when Fatna El Bouih speaks of the women's prison as an 'infernal harem' in *Une Femme nommée Rachid* (56). This latter example is not simply a casual and colourful reference to an all-woman environment, but conveys, instead, an intentionally retrograde essence, belonging more to a dark underworld, recalling the author's several references in her memoir to *The Thousand and One Nights*. To speak of the 'infernal harem' is to invoke the worst kind of separation, to underscore the nightmare quality of power in the hands of monsters. Given what the preceding pages revealed about the harem as a system of exclusion, it is no accident that El Bouih would describe prison in such terms, or that she would further suggest its malevolent, diabolical, demonic nature in the word 'infernal.'

In the pages ahead, let us examine how two other Moroccan women writers incorporate the notion of the harem as a space, or a linguistic or political concept, denoting a relationship of power, in their works of fiction. As we shall see, Houria Boussejra builds on Mernissi's notion of the harem in the body politic in terms of class warfare, while Rajae Benchemsi departs from more traditional approaches to offer a rewriting of the harem from a pro-woman standpoint.

Houria Boussejra

As we just saw, Fatima Mernissi has articulated the theory of power and exclusion through the harem. She has also said that in any society in which the principle of the harem reigns, there will be permanent revolt.[11] That statement will be illustrated in Houria Boussejra's 'Tamou,' the opening story of her *Femmes inachevées*, whose first line, pronounced by the title character, reads, 'I was not born in a harem,' an obvious refashioning of Fatima Mernissi's first sentence from *Dreams of Trespass*. Tamou recalls that harems are structures from the past, with their cloistered women, at once dreamy and Machiavellian, residing in the 'closed and inaccessible world of masculine desires' (9). Yet at the same time she insists on the similarity between past and present, asserting that 'the harem still exists' and 'in every woman there lurks a harem' (33). How, then, are we to understand Boussejra's harem, and in what way might it be said to build on Mernissi's notion?

Tamou is the first-person narrator and servant in the home of a well-to-do couple whose young children she cares for, in addition to providing other domestic services. Though she gives every appearance of being devoted to the family, in fact, she is seething with rage. Her bitter resentment of the undeserved good fortune of the family is directed particularly against the wife, whom she is slowly poisoning, but also the daughter, whom she drugs into passivity, and the young son whom she assaults sexually. Tamou's plan is to seduce the husband and to replace the wife, thereby avenging the injustice of her social position as a subservient. Like a true Machiavellian, she bides her time, adopting a demeanour of calm acceptance. But as the story develops and her vengeful intentions become dreadful acts, Tamou reveals herself as a totally immoral protagonist, whose misdeeds are never fully understood by her employers. In the end, her evil plan fails in a surprise denouement (that could, however, be foreseen) when the young son reverses the teacups that hold the final fatal dose by which Tamou intends to kill the mistress, and it is Tamou, herself, who consumes the deadly potion.

Melodramatic and shocking – though it does go far in proving that no subject is really off-limits for the Moroccan woman writer – the story can be read simply as Tamou, evil incarnate, or as the tragic consequences brought about through class envy. The latter interpretation is supported in the author's development, which describes how Tamou was abandoned by her mother who ran off with a lover, then was ignored by a father who soon remarried, and then found herself bounced from neighbour woman to woman, who provided her with minimum care. Thus, Tamou grew up emotionally and socially scarred, as is each of the other five female characters, all *femmes inachevées* ('unfinished women,' or women lacking in some necessary quality) in Boussejra's collection. Despite her considerable physical and intellectual attributes, Tamou has been sentenced to a life of service to others. In a world that privileges some through no merit but that of their birth, the struggle is not simply between the sexes, but between the haves and the have-nots. In consequence, says the writer, Tamou 'dreamed of exacting her revenge on society' (16).

This will be class warfare, and to succeed, Tamou must displace the weaker members of the ruling class, and appropriate their position: she sees herself as part of a higher race that nothing could defeat or bring down. To achieve her ends, she uses the weapons of both sexes – seizing the reins of power, as might a man, or being tender or sexually provocative, as a woman – and if that is not sufficient, she is ready to commit acts of depravity that belong to neither sex ('She became male or female, according to need. And sometimes neither one nor the other' [33]). As a domestic servant, deprived of the material advantages of her bourgeois employers, Tamou determines to change the very grounds on which the middle class is constructed, disposing of three members of the family, while claiming the husband for herself, because through him she will gain access to the social and class standing to which she aspires ('Only a man could save her from the hate and solitude that suffocated her' [17]). She strikes out against her employers as though they were directly responsible for the social system that has excluded her from the goods and emotional benefits enjoyed by other women in the privileged classes. As the mistress of the house, Ghita, says, 'Tamou is a marginal in the community because of her status. A maid in our society counts for less than nothing' (26), a theme reiterated in other stories in Boussejra's collection.[12] But Ghita's sympathy for Tamou is not recognized by the servant, who considers herself the woman's slave. Consumed with hatred and jealousy, perverse, rapacious, and driven by the desire to be simultaneously adulated and feared, the treacherous Tamou becomes the essence of destructiveness, usurping the very principles on which the harem had classically been based – arrogant self-interest and cruel power – making them her own. She appears as the essence of *jahiliyya*, unbridled, egotistic, cruel and immoral.

The troubling view of sexual and social relations in this short story makes two points. First, as the story's narrator says, the harem principle in society – here, the extreme separation of the classes – 'splits our very being into an unrecognizable duality' (33). The result is that the weaker members of society, in this case, the woman, will use whatever means they have at their disposal to reverse the tables of power. To be sure, the textual development lacks sophistication, and the author may unwittingly be taking up the conservative notion that female sexuality is dangerous and potentially destructive of the social order (which had earlier been the justification for the seclusion of women). But the story is also about violence and oppression, violence from oppression, and violence as a response to oppression. The author implies that female sexuality is a power that potentially can destroy the social order, but that its exercise for ill results from the reigning social order and its fundamental injustices.

In this way, Boussejra's reading of 'harem' focuses on class divisions and the inevitability of corroding jealousies within the oppressed class, ultimately transmogrifying into cunning acts of cruelty, perversion, and criminality. But while the author condemns the ruthless acts and criminal intentions of Tamou, she also implicitly accuses the naivety of the mistress of the house, whose blindness to the corrupt nature of her domestic makes her an easy target for Tamou. In a real sense, both the master and mistress are essentially unequipped to live in the harem of society – the master is weak, incapable of resisting the temptation offered by Tamou; the wife believes she is showing solidarity with her domestic when she refuses to fire Tamou despite her husband's anguished fear of repeating his infidelity with the maid. Yet, in another sense, they, too, are caught up in the vise of the harem in which the principles of dominance and submission play out cataclysmically in the body politic. By repeated use of the concept of harem, Boussejra underscores the point that society is immorally and unhealthily divided by class as much in the modern world as it was in the age of imperial harems. Female perversion is merely the mirror image of the perversion that occurs in a society operating from a basis of arbitrary and radical exclusion.

Rajae Benchemsi

If harem essentially equals class warfare in Boussejra another woman rewrites the harem in both a positive and feminist way. There are, in fact, two kinds of harems in Benchemsi's novel entitled *Marrakech, lumière d'exil*, one a vestige of an earlier time, involving the *narratrice's* relative, Bradia, and the other, a virtual harem, never identified as such but in essence constituted by several women who work for a common goal. In both, the women defy the normal rules of containment in ways that are positive for their gender and that lead the reader to rethink easy assumptions about the harem and freedom.

One harem represents a story-within-a-story, and the second is the story of the novel itself. The first is a circa 1940s harem, or great-house, in which Bradia, a free spirit and the great-aunt of the *narratrice*, lives, along with her husband, Hammad, who is deeply in love with her and denies her nothing. The story of that harem is told by Bahia's mother, Lalla Tata, who had been a domestic servant in the harem, following the death of her husband. The second harem is a revalourized version of the harem as a community of women who join forces to cure an adolescent suffering from trauma-induced autism. In bringing together the two harems in its text, the novel not only creates bridges between tradition, culture, and modernity, but also argues for a more nuanced view of the past and against absolutist definitions of freedom and the kind of feminism that privileges abstract law over direct and immediate aid to those in need.

In that sense, *Marrakech, lumière d'exil* is very much a continuation of Benchemsi's use of the literary to inquire into ideas and states of being, as she did in her collection of short stories or *récits*, *Fracture du désir*. On the one hand, *Marrakech* is a profoundly 'Moroccan' novel, set in the cosmopolitan ancient city, '*l'incommensurable matrice*' (the infinite womb), at the crossroads between the Sahara and the door to the West (see also chapter 7, 'Women and the City'), and, on the other hand, it is a novel that seeks to reinterpret cultural tradition while critiquing modernity, ultimately to reconcile the two through a new brand of female community.

The text is narrated by a woman who remains nameless and who, after a long stay in France for educational and professional reasons, returns to Morocco. Her return has been precipitated by learning that the illegitimate daughter (Zahia) of a former domestic servant (Bahia, now a tattoo artist on the Place Jemaa-el-Fna) has fallen ill and is being treated at a hospital for a form of autism resulting in aphasia (speechlessness) and a loss of all emotion. The narrator's mission is multiple: to offer succour to Bahia and Zahia, whom she had adored as a baby, to 're-situate' herself in the world through a better understanding of her family's past, and ultimately to reconcile the modern, perhaps too Europeanized, woman she has become with her familial and cultural roots. She is thus involved in a spiritual quest for knowledge and understanding, which is narrativized through two kinds of 'harems' and a broad swath of other themes involving female memory, female speech and speechlessness, the clash of the modern and traditional, and the theme of 'the return.' Indeed, the latter is a favoured structure in North African literature, first, because the route between France and North Africa is so well-travelled by Moroccans, Algerians, and Tunisians, and, second, because it deals with fundamental problems of existence and exile, related to problems of cultural and personal identity. Interestingly, however, because the female narrator of *Marrakech* never tells her own story in any direct way, but is much more the literary medium through which the stories of other women (notably those of Bradia and Zahia) are told, the novel lends itself also to being read as a political or existential allegory of the Moroccan nation itself, caught between a traditional and conservative past and a clash with the modernity of the West.[13] Hence, the multiple levels on which to read the novel make it not always easily transparent, but constantly poetically provocative.

On the level of feminine quest and memory, the *narratrice* repeatedly asks Lalla Tata, who had been a domestic in the great-house of the harem, for stories about Bradia, whose life fascinates her, not least because it offers access to her own cultural roots. What the narrator admires about her legendary female relative is how even from within the harem – the family into which Bradia had married and for whom tradition reigned supreme – Bradia was able, along with her servant, Dada M'Barka, to transgress the morals and manners of the age. Remarkably, despite the difference in class, these two women shared both friendship and boldness, living freely within the 'harem,' drinking and smoking, in complete complicity. It is Dada M'Barka who teaches Bradia about female sensuality and how to make sexuality a power for her own pleasure – but importantly, within the union with her husband. What Bradia and Dada M'Barka represent is freedom within the constraints of the harem, and their stories in turn function as lessons for the narrator, teaching her that freedom is multifaceted, rather than a mere 'expression of the law' (29), which, in her view, robs women of the rich and complex nature of their femininity.

For the *narratrice*, the magic of the past is recaptured in the voice of Lalla Tata, whose words and memories evoke the very texture of her origins (27). All those many far-off figures are resuscitated in the very fullness of their being, their presence at times physically palpable to the *narratrice* whose mind is 'awash with the mysterious power of illusion' (28). She never tires of hearing their story, which, she says, her imagination had 'managed to make her very own.' And what is it that she finds so delectable in that story? It is Bradia's and Dada M'Barka's transgressions of the strict customs of their time, for these two women 'had assumed the mantle of audacity that other women of their times had not experienced. They became the very sign of freedom in the bosom of the harem' (29), a phrase potent with meaning. It is their exercise of freedom within constraints but consistent with 'the Moroccan feminine' that the *narratrice* lauds and finds exhilarating. The example of the two women, she writes, is 'at the origin of my profound disdain for feminism such as it has been circumscribed by the twentieth century,' ignoring as it does 'the true nature of the Moroccan woman' (29). Her opposition to modern feminism derives from her judgment that it demonstrates no nuance and is seemingly content to reduce woman to her status in law, thus denying the wholeness of her feminine nature and potential. In such a feminism, there is no tension, no soul. In counterdistinction, Bradia and the beautiful black slave, Dada M'Barka, 'had entered into freedom as one enters an order, powerfully armed with the very essence of their femininity' (29–30). In other words, Benchemsi's narrator does not assent to the view expressed in *Dreams of Trespass* about how women can find only diminished forms of liberation from within the constraints imposed on them.[14] For Benchemsi's narrator, instead, the beauty of Bradia and M'Barka's freedom is that it is neither diminished, nor granted by impersonal law, but rather achieved through the women's own acts and consistent with their own culture.

Assuming that Western feminism is the probable point of reference about law and freedom, the narrator's critique of it is important both in terms of what the novel is about and in staking out a different position on feminism in the Moroccan context. Linking past and present through feminine memory, the narrator's quest is to find a counterweight to the soullessness of modernity epitomized by the psychiatric hospital where Zahia resides as a patient. Juxtaposing the harem against the hospital, so to speak – the past against modernity – Benchemsi reevaluates what is possible in the two structures, one of cultural tradition and the other of cultural anonymity in which medical and psychiatric techniques prevail. What she finds in the first harem is love and human feeling, which make even moderated freedom a daily joy, whereas the hospital, though run by competent individuals, is not a place either of joyful complicity or of curing powers. It is for this reason that the *narratrice*, with the aid of Lalla Tata and her sister, Lalti Taja, and her servant, Dada Johra, and Bahia remove Zahia from the hospital to care for her within what might be considered a reconstituted 'harem,' a community of females, at home. The hope of these women is to embrace Zahia with the power of curative love and to bring her back to health, an aspiration that is partially fulfilled when, toward the end of the novel, they take her to a saint's sanctuary where other mental patients are brought and observe how Zahia, for the first time, breaks out of her expressionlessness and laughs, even while still inhabiting 'her own world.' The triumph is small and impermanent; there will be no miracle. After meeting a mother who has four daughters, all of whom suffer severe mental alienation and live fulltime at the sanctuary, the *narratrice* realizes that though she will continue to proffer aid to Zahia and to give her everything, she will not be able to give her 'this inaccessible part of my existence, which makes it possible for me to say "I" and impossible for her to utter that "I"' (189).

Narrative resolution in this novel of memory and ideas will be as frangible as Zahia's mental condition. In the epilogue, which comes full circle to close at the Place Jemaa-el-Fna with a favoured storyteller who recalls past exploits in history, and at the Sidi Abu L-Abbas al-Sabti Mausoleum, where the *narratrice* is greeted by the master who invites her to enter the *qobba* normally reserved for men, she is transfixed by the architectural beauty of the place and the voices of the singers, who fill her soul as though it were a 'receptacle' (195). Earlier she had said that she had learned to calm her own internal conflicts between past and present and to accept that events and the course of affairs often transpire according to rules that are indecipherable. But by retouching the bases of her culture and Soufism, she refers on the last page to a kind of mystical illumination: 'I had the feeling that each thing in the universe had at last found its place' (197). In the end, she seems to accept reconciliation with what is, as well as what cannot be.

In the two 'harems' of her novel, Benchemsi has taken three generations of women, from Bradia to Lalla Tata to Zahia, to rewrite the harem and the issues of freedom, power, and powerlessness. Within constraints, Bradia was free, but while she could conduct her personal behaviour however she wished, she could not leave the confines set for her by society; perhaps she was not even particularly aware that she was constrained. Zahia, on the other hand, is unfree despite her physical freedom, inhabited by a total alienation of the spirit. With Bradia, Benchemsi gives back to woman pleasure in her body and pride in her resolve and intelligence. And with the second 'harem' focused on freeing Zahia from her illness, the author celebrates women's solidarity and their commitment to a cause even if it ultimately defies resolution. In the two harems, the narrator had sought to integrate the magic of past family history, revolving around Bradia's sense of personal liberation, with the present of unified female action. What she learns is that there are limits to each endeavour, but that the value is in the effort, not the literal result. By reworking the motif of the harem, by reinvesting it with nuance and shared emotion, and by modernizing the harem in terms of a community of females working for an end, Benchemsi acknowledges tradition and revitalizes its role in women's writing.

Moroccan women's continued use of the concept of the harem as a way of visualizing society and social groupings in society shows that Orientalist depictions are only one of the many ways in which the notion of harem functions. In reworking the topos, they are able to reassert a relationship between the past and the present and at the same time to 'modernize' it. Will that other space of Orientalism, the hammam, work similarly in women's works?

The Hammam

As the fully 'undressed harem,' the hammam scene is the almost obligatory tableau in North African texts, the site of refuge or restoration at the same time as it is a sexually segregated space, in which no member of the opposite sex, past childhood, is allowed to enter. Hence, the affirmation of the line of demarcation between the sexes, as in Mernissi's *Dreams of Trespass*, when young Samir is expelled from the women's hammam 'for having looked at the women as would a man' (chapter 22, 'Un Homme dans le hammam!'). Her scene is highly reminiscent of Férid Boughédir's 1990 film, 'Halfaouine,' in which the boy, Noura, wanders through the steamy haze of the women's hammam in search of the forbidden fruit of sexual knowledge, and is ultimately also chased out for the same reasons.[15] Filmed as a scene denoting the passage from innocence to the erotic, an event that is reenacted in real life as much as in art, Boughédir's film is premised on the psychic/physical aspects of coming-to-age, whereas Mernissi's hammam, in the last chapter of *Dreams of Trespass*, is the concluding demonstration in her theory of separation as the key principle of both gender and social organization.

Although writers from North Africa, male or female, rarely fail to include a scene in the hamman in their fiction, they do so with different purposes and results. This is true not only because, as Marta Segarra says, women view the hammam as 'a woman's space par excellence,'[16] but also because in the woman's hammam, both the perspective on the female body and basic attitudes about the control and ownership of her body are different. This change of perspective is of capital importance in liberating the female subject from her socially determined corporality. In the female-written hammam, women are freed from the social policing of their bodies and from the limiting sexual roles set by society for them. They are no longer objects of desire, but the acting subjects of the text. By reclaiming the female body through writing, the woman author seeks both to revalue the devalued female body, in Fedwa Malti-Douglas's formulation,[17] and to re-conceptualize women's roles in society. By challenging Orientalist stereotypes and dismantling sexual and gender politics, the woman writer makes the hammam a privileged place not only of personal renewal and figurative rebirth through the physical ritual of cleansing, and, more abstractly, the regeneration of the spirit, but also the place of her reeducation.[18] In this hammam, the woman finds a refuge from the corrosive prejudices of society and from the threats posed to her in the body politic. She learns to look upon her body not as 'shameful, defective, imperfect,' something to be covered, but as resplendent in its diversity. In the hammam, with its absence of masks and pretences, she finds a place of sociability, shared intimacy, quiet contemplation. And while the hammam is not a female utopia or privileged community of perfect equality and solidarity, it is most assuredly a place of female legitimacy.

Because, according to feminist scholars like Leila Ahmed and Fedwa Malti-Douglas, woman's body has become a battlefield on which issues of sexuality and narration are debated, the study of the female body presented by women writers offers the potential for a revealing discourse on the language of the body and, by extension, that body in the body politic. These ideas will be explored in the pages ahead, through an examination of the hammam in Siham Benchekroun's *Oser vivre*, Rajae Benchemsi's *Marrakech, lumière d'exil*, and Yasmina Chami-Kettani's *Cérémonie*, with brief references to the work of sociologist Soumaya Naamane-Guessous. The focus will be on how the woman writer reclaims the female body in the hammam while contravening Orientalist and sexist myths, how she deconstructs the sexual politics implicit in conventional scenes in the hammam, and, ultimately, how she endeavours to prepare the way for a new role for women in the body politic. Thus, the so-called gynaeceum no longer harbours the sense of 'the secret and the private,' and does not focus on desire or the eroticized eye, but, rather, merely establishes and proposes a set of values based on individual identities that can be brought into the community as a whole. In these hammams, women writers demonstrate values that are to be the foundation of a new order.

Rewriting the Body in the Body Politic

Siham Benchekroun's novel, evocatively entitled *Oser vivre* (*Dare to Live*), follows a young woman's trajectory from romantic rebellion against a conventional family, to courtship and marriage to an equally conventional husband, and finally to the painful realization that she has reached early middle-age having lived according to everyone else's expectations. The female protagonist, Nadia, left her university studies to marry Ali, and to become a mother of two children and a very competent homemaker, but over time realizes that she lives in a society in which the roles of the sexes have been ossified by tradition and resistance against the status quo is unthinkable. If the plot line seems to the Western reader to hark back to early feminist literary texts from the

1960s and 1970s, the observation is accurate, but also reminds us that while feminist consciousness throughout the world may travel by similar pathways, it does so on its own clock. In constructing her story of one woman's evolution to consciousness, Benchekroun turns her novel into a psychological drama, which takes place primarily within the head of the female protagonist. Her path to awakening – a veritable *prise de conscience* – is slow and often torturous, as Nadia comes to understand that she and all women have been defined exclusively through their biology and are expected to follow a single pattern in their lives.

Key to her changing perspective is the scene in the hamman (63–7), set in apposition to a nearby feminist discourse (69–71), which leads the reader to contemplate the relationship between the author's validation of individual female identity in the hammam and woman's collective identity in Moroccan culture. The hammam scene transpires in Nadia's memory, representing a glorious image from her childhood, prior to her 'bourgeoisization,' she says, when visits to the hammam are no longer required because she has adequate bathing facilities at home. It is a scene engraved on her mind, joyous and exalted, in which the principle of female multiplicity is celebrated in Nadia's description of all those different-sized breasts and bottoms, hips and thighs and stomachs:

> Flat bottoms. Pear-shaped bottoms. Sagging bottoms ... breasts that are proud or timid, exalted or tired, slack ... or budding ... flattish or full, or pouty, receding, well separated, snow-white or ebony ... Stomachs that are sunken, narrow, puckered, naughty/saucy, coquettishly rounded, modestly promising ... amazing ... gigantic, flabby, spacious, rippled. Fat-bellied. (65)

By emphasizing the wide disparity between women in their physical attributes, a kind of 'Dantesque dream' (65), Nadia calls it, the author is proposing not the stages of a woman's physical life, but the very idea that female identity is not single, but multiple, and that while they are all members of the same sex, they are not all the same. Moreover, she has changed the language of the female body, detaching it from an exclusive obsession with the sensual or the erotic. Flaccid breasts and pot-bellied stomachs are shown along with proud bosoms and shapely bottoms. This is the female corporeal in all its nonconformity and dissimilarity.

It is a key message, since traditional female socialization that Benchekroun negatively presents throughout the novel had taught the essential, unequivocal, so-called natural sameness of women, while casting any notion of difference as applicable only in the opposition of the two sexes. 'Year after year, I absorbed that fear of living, fear of my body. The shame attached to loving,' Nadia declares, 'Against my will I accepted the various roles that others expected of me' (73), the rule of conformity, whereby women are to be whatever traditional culture stipulates, resulting in iron-clad gender roles and expectations in bourgeois society. Hence, Nadia expresses the feminist idea, well known for decades in the West, that anatomy is not destiny. 'What connection can you see between my anatomy and my role in society?' she asks her mother, who, for the daughter, incarnates all the prejudices and retrograde stereotypes she despises. 'Exactly how does my body predestine me to dust and cook? Have you never suspected that the truths we're taught serve only men? Have you never considered that we are the consenting victims of male egotism?' (69). The division of labour in the family should not be determined by a woman's body, which does not make her more naturally skilled for housework. While the argument may seem a relic of the past for many readers, it is evidence that all feminist struggles go through stages of development, an obvious fact that does not diminish its importance for Moroccan women.

Nadia gives further expression to her feminist convictions, objecting to the cruel inheritance passed from generation to generation of women who teach 'the cult of man the master,' and the female's unquestioning submission and acceptance that virtue be imposed rather than chosen, She laments the admonitions to girls that they show no anger, curiosity, or self-concern, the prudish prohibition of physical pleasure, the foolish resignation to endless patience (70–1). In this 'terrible brainwashing,' a woman's socialization is all negative: 'Don't bother yourself with ambitions ... you're only a woman. No studies? No work? Not understood? What's the difference, you're only a woman. No memory, no words, no confidence: a woman.' Bitterly, Nadia assesses her life:

> Ever since my birth condemned me to being female, I have had to swallow the indigestible carpings of all those shut-down women. *Assbar*. The patience of the resigned. Being a woman is like serving a life sentence, integrating failure, learning that winning is never an option, resigning yourself. You learn that if you accept being 'just a woman,' you spare yourself so many humiliations. Nothing to prove. Nothing to lose. Nothing to give a damn about. (71)

Looking back, she is disgusted with herself because she hadn't dared to choose personal freedom over social acceptance. Instead, she says, 'I consented to do violence to my own self' (73).

Given this context, Nadia's celebration of the diversity of the feminine in the hammam, which proposes that women have many individual identities, rather than a single undifferentiated identity, is a foundational argument in her critique of society and a key to the quality of imagery structuring the text. Nadia had learned from her mother, her relatives, and her husband that all women are the same, that they have a single destiny and must be self-abnegating, acting in accord with society's traditions, or risk shaming themselves and their family. To break free from the fetters of tradition that determine her life as woman, daughter, wife, and mother, and the constant and endless repetition of the same gestures, words, and even thoughts – that 'absurd destiny of women' (62) – Benchekroun wants her protagonist to 'dare to live,' to be an individual within the collective, not a collective identity. Through Nadia's memory of women in the hammam, which throws into high relief the rich and complex diversity of woman in her natural state, with no one woman the exact model of the other, Benchekroun endeavours to set out a new position on women's role in the body politic. In essence agreeing that women have a biological role in society, but insisting that such a role does not imply total sameness, or a single function in society, she uses the exuberant nature of female diversity on display in the hammam to suggest that, similarly, women are individually unique in terms of personality, talents, and identity. Through the scene of the hamman, Benchekroun contests the limiting sexual role set for women by society. By setting in dialogue Nadia's feminist discourse with the positively encoded scene in the woman's hammam, the author provides women with the rationale to enact in their own lives the injunction that resides in the title, *Dare to Live*.

Challenges to Orientalism: Yasmina Chami-Kettani and Rajae Benchemsi

As Moroccan sociologist Soumaya Naamane-Guessous tells us, for centuries *le bain maure* or Moorish bath has been both a kind *of institut de beauté* (beauty spa) and the site of female sociability.[19] While men could gather in the souk or in cafés or at the mosque, women in towns developed their sociability in the hammam, or if they lived in the countryside, at the fountain. Hence, the veritable giddiness of Mernissi's cast of veiled women in *Rêves de femmes* when they prepare for their weekly excursion to the bathhouse (chapter 21, 'Peau fine,' and chaper 22, 'Un Homme dans le hammam!'), for there, they will have access to information, gossip about the latest fashions and what is going on in the neighbourhood. There, and there alone, will they be able to exercise a kind of power of association, by brokering connections with other families, as they size up the worthiness and naked charms of young, unmarried girls. In *Cérémonie*, for instance, Chami-Kettani writes, 'At times a young woman ... would traverse the room ... She would be followed by the practised eyes of older women who were evaluating her prospective fecundity by the suppleness of her hips, a rounded bosom, and strong limbs' (86).

That female eye, while judgmental, does not, however, carry the same aggressive erotic desire of the male eye, which assaults the woman in a painting or on the street. This is why Samir and Noura must be expelled from the hammam. It is essential that the hammam remain the one place where women can escape from the corporal enslavement they feel on the outside and society's policing of their bodies. As Marta Segarra observes, the theme of *le regard subi*, or being subjected to the gaze of others, is a commonplace in women's texts, implying an infringement of her rights and the attempt to dispossess her of her own body.[20] The curious boys may not yet command the power of violation of adult males, whose 'gaze' is variously experienced by women as 'eager,' 'consuming,' or 'devouring,' a veritable 'fantasmatic rape,' but women in the hammam are adamant about not having the sanctity of their site as a retreat compromised in any way. If, as Malek Chebel says in *Le Corps dans la tradition au Maghreb*, society gives complete freedom of expression to the male while defining the girl by a repertory of prohibitions and what she cannot do, then it is all the more important for women to assert the hammam as a space of inviolate female borders.[21]

For the woman writer who aims to control the discourse over the female body, it is equally important to retain the freedom and emotional solidarity of a single-sex refuge. For instance, in the all-woman environment of *Cérémonie*, Yasmina Chami-Kettani needs to create a space of intimacy and confidence in order not only to liberate women's language, but also because she is going to tell women's stories in part through the vulnerable and unsensual female body. The hammam therefore becomes the place not of the fairy tale, or of the sensualized female body of the Orientalist text, but the locale in which not only the generosity of the female form, but the susceptibility of the human body to emotional deprivation is put on display.

In her slight text of little more than 100 pages, Chami-Kettani uses the occasion of a family gathering for the marriage of a son as the pretext for evoking the feelings, emotions, and lives of three women in the extended family: Aunt Aïcha, who will die of cancer, and her nieces, Khadija and Malika, now adult women who remember their aunt with great fondness. As the text meanders through the filter of the past and reaccesses female memories of family members, Chami-Kettani makes two forays into the hamman, bringing together Aïcha and young Malika in one scene (84–8), and Khadija and Malika in another (94, 99–100, 103–6). What the author underscores is the vulnerability of the human body, first with the prepubescent Malika, who shyly tries to cover herself, and her Aunt's joking reproach, 'What do you think you have that I don't?' (84), and then with an evocation of the silent cancer ('a voracious djin whose sharp teeth tear into innocent flesh' [88]) that first attacks one breast of Aunt Aïcha, and then consumes the whole body while she is still in her forties. In the bathroom, Aïcha raises her tunic to reveal 'the gaping emptiness next to the single remaining breast, the flesh mutilated by the still rosy stitches of the wound' (90). The shock of her missing part causes a moment of incredulity, 'Where did the other one go,' she silently asks, as her hand grazes the space on the empty left side. And then concludes (as would not an Orientalist), 'Well, a single breast is surely good enough for a single woman; what would she do with a second one?'

In the second hammam, Chami-Kettani reveals two other female bodies, the vibrant if sterile body of Malika, happily married but incomplete in a culture that declares a wife without children an oxymoron, and the shrivelled, forsaken body of her cousin, Khadija, the mother of two, but abandoned by her husband of seven years who has left her like a 'package abandoned in an empty house after a move' (79), thereby robbing her of confidence in her femininity and disabling her assurance about the future. Khadija experiences her husband's rejection through the body, an observation Malika makes when she compares Khadija past and present, asking, 'Where is the Khadija of full breasts and sexy, sleek legs?' (88). The image Malika now sees is of 'a pitiful and sad woman with square shoulders, flat breasts surrounded by blunt, brown hairs, and whose figure is as shapeless as the skin is full; only her beautiful small feet remain the same, but even they have tufts of coarse hair sprouting from the big toes' (88–9). The woman's physical body not only reflects the devastation in her emotional life, but her defeminization into an asexual, perhaps even masculinized being.

Stripped of her identity as a married woman, rejected not only by the husband, but also by a society that does not know what to do with a divorced woman with two children, even if she is a professional woman, Khadija is physically transmogrifying, much as the material body does before death. This becomes even more apparent when Malika observes, as the room fills with steam, that her cousin seems to disappear 'in the bathtub, narrow as a tomb' (89).

Chami-Kettani writes the body in the hammam not with regard to any theory of *écriture féminine*, not to evoke the lascivious eye, but to illustrate how the female body becomes a text. In a novel that explores loss, absence, and sadness, the language of the body speaks more powerfully and eloquently than any declarations of fact, which, moreover, would be out of place in such a poetic work. What interests this author in the hammam, is the 'ceremony' of life, accompanied, inevitably, by the presaging of death. In the rituals of the hammam, from the beauty rites indicated by Aunt Aïcha's great satchel of beauty products, to the ritual of visits determined by moments in a woman's life – marriage, pregnancy, childbirth, the end of widowhood – the hammam covers a lifetime.[22] In the hammam, the bodies of three women tell each individual's story, from health to sickness, pride to sorrow, and joy alongside incompleteness. Thus the hammam becomes the site for storytelling and story-making, the steamy mirror of history, writ both large and small.

Another woman writer who also challenges stereotypical depictions of the hammam is Rajae Benchemsi, who writes the scene as producing a poetic fusion of body and soul. Indeed, the extended hammam scene in *Marrakech, lumière d'exil* (169–75) functions importantly within the overall thematics of the novel to help the *narratrice* renegotiate her personal divide between Europe and Morocco, as between modernity and tradition, and to re-tap the fountain of Arabo-Muslim culture, its spiritual and cultural essence. It is in the 'divine mysteries' of the hammam, always the scene of the senses rather than of speech, that through touch and smell, and in the steamy, humid heat ('one of the most powerful sensations of my life') that the protagonist is reborn, renewed and freed of the 'tenacious aggressions of modernity' (169), represented by the harshness of the language of materiality, a kind of linguistic yoke, she says, shorn of poetic sonorities.

A teacher of literature, the *narratrice* has just come from giving a course on French poetry, whose unsatisfactory outcome left her concluding that literature should be read rather than taught. Ready to resign from her job, 'beset by feelings of indescribable anguish' (167), and still under the spell of Lautréamont's Maldoror, she seeks to escape the torments of the intellectual through a visit to the hammam, to be 'reinvented' and revivified by going back to the original source of life, water (169). Through the rituals of the hammam and the perfumed essences of her culture, fragrant with olive oil, amber, and musk, rose petals, cloves and almonds, and in the heat and humidity of the place, she enters a state of plentitude, a harmony of deep pleasure and happiness. Recalling a line by Eluard, 'Comme aux temps anciens, tu pourrais dormir dans la mer' (170), she says, 'I descended deep within myself, at last reconciled with life' (170). Through the fragrances of Morocco, a kind of olfactory variation on Proust and his madeleine, she not only transcends the sexual body, but embarks on an interior monologue on language and culture, the old world and new, conducted through the senses.

What Benchemsi's text suggests is that culture speaks through the evocation and memory of smell, every bit as much as it does through words, images, sounds, or music. In evoking the aroma of water mixed with the waft of orange in *rassoul* and of henna, the protagonist experiences 'an enormous sense of fusion' with her people, asserting that this is 'a perfumed essence profoundly linked to [her] culture' (173).[23] Hence, in the curative atmosphere of the hammam, the woman returns to a personal peace, as she does to the very foundations of her culture. By re-tapping cultural resources, she reclaims her roots and refinds her way.

In Benchemsi's hammam, the female body is presented as a vessel not of sexuality but of physical sensibility and receptiveness to cultural radiance. In the hammam, where the fusion of body, soul, and culture produces a new esthetic, Benchemsi's poetry reaccesses the light of the past to unite it with the alchemy of intellect to create a corporal and psychological pleasure akin to sex that is not, however, sex. As she has said, 'There is no greater pleasure than the pleasure of the mind.'[24] Her realm of interest is intellectual sensualism, her intentions are philosophic, her mode is poetic. She has stated that her aesthetics lead her not to writing essays, but to analysing the nature of life's mysteries through literary writing. In the poetry of the hammam, Benchemsi goes beyond the body to explore those mysteries.

Conclusion

In a culture in which women often feel both demolished and highly valued, since as Lahcen Haddad has said, 'in patriarchy, woman is seen as the purveyor and source of values, transmitted by her behavior, her body, and her words,'[25] the hammam and the harem offer ideal theatres in which to narrate culture, gender, and sex relations in North African society. By incorporating these locales and their essences in their works, Moroccan women writers demonstrate their ties with the literary convention of North African literature, while at the same time imprinting them with their own stamp. Much more than indicators of local colour, their harems and hammams become ways both to explore women's roles in the body politic and to lay the groundwork for rewriting those roles.

The symbolics of the harem, for instance, propose a mechanism by which to represent woman's condition in space, suggesting the constraints either exacted upon her or that she imposes on herself, and throwing into question the nature and limits of freedom. Since the harem is about division and power, whether it is Mernissi's theory of the *harem politique*, or Boussejra's class warfare, or Benchemsi's dual proposition, the device of the harem provides a structure for studying social and sexual behaviours, for organizing those observations into an explanatory theory, and for mounting either a broad critique or a commentary on society. What is fascinating, of course, is how this space has been recovered and reenvisioned by these Moroccan women writers in their contemporary texts.[26]

Similarly, in the microcommunity of the hammam, women's bodies are revalorized, their identities as individuals legitimized, the poetics of inquiry into female existence fully engaged. In this gynaeceum, woman is not 'other' in the sense of the non-essential, but the subject herself, and it is on the grounds of her very 'otherness' that the writer might lay claim to a new place for women in the body politic. Playing off Plato's *Laws* and *Republic*, Monique Canto has said that women in their otherness are essential to the city, yet they are also responsible for rendering that otherness political.[27] While I would not claim that Moroccan women's hammams carry the full sense of the political, and while it is true that outside the hammam, women's social marginality may be reinscribed, I would still submit that their hammams are quiet manifestoes for a different kind of female presence in the body politic.

In the de-Orientalization of two iconic spaces of North African literature, Moroccan women writers challenge old stereotypes and reformulate issues of female power and individuality, as they prepare the way for a parallel decolonization of another important space – this time, of the city.

7 Women and the City

The great dramas of recent centuries – the triumph of industrialization and capitalism, the erection of powerful state apparatuses and the outbreaks of political insurrections, the exercise of colonial control and eruptions of anticolonial movements – were enacted on the stage of modern cities. These urban spaces have shaped, and were shaped by race, class, and gender relations and exclusions.

          Gyan Prakash, *The Spaces of the Modern City*

To investigate the issue of women and the city is to become a cultural geographer and to incorporate the principles of feminist geography, focusing on the intersections of gender, identity, and place. It is to understand that the city as a field of experience is different not only at different historical moments, but also for men and women, who may construct, negotiate, and contest its boundaries in disparate ways. It is to see how the city can become a kind of cartography of connections and disconnections, a network of possibilities and of dichotomies.

When literary critics become cultural geographers, they open doors onto rich interdisciplinary collaboration with sociologists, psychologists, political scientists, and urbanologists, all of whom conceive of space not as empty or mute, but rather as a symbolic geography capable of telling stories. In the spatial dynamics of gender in the city, the literary imagination finds provocative metaphors in streets and buildings, maps and borders, movement and travel, which become potent signifiers of theoretical, psychological, and political import. Moreover, to write women and the city, or, even more so, to write women into the city, is to break with earlier narratives about 'where women belong' and how women conceive of the future and of modernity itself.[1]

It is also to advance the discussion of space and women beyond the now somewhat tired binary of public versus private. Scholar Nicole Jouve Ward declares that woman's space is far more complex than a simple distinction between private and public, or between the interior and exterior, observing that woman's space changes from era to era, culture to culture, group to group, and class to class.[2] Ward argues that we need to move away from easy polarizations and bifurcated analysis, suggesting that while the examination of women's space within the field of cultural geography represents a fresh approach to the study of women's status, the critic should use it as an interpretive tool that seeks not to simplify, but to reveal the complexity of lived reality.[3] Another scholar, Janet Levarie Smarr, proposes that the study of urban space has often fallen back on the private-public binary because that is the most obvious example of a constructed correspondence between gender and spatial coding, whereas, in fact, notions of the centre and the margins could be far more useful.[4] Hence she and others support the kind of feminist scholarship that argues for a deconstruction of the binaries as essential to women, in recognition of the fact that boundaries can be dynamic, negotiable, and permeable under certain circumstances. Such thinking is echoed by social scientists Alev Çinar and Thomas Bender in *Urban Imaginaries*, who emphasize 'the city as a field of experience' and by Kevin Lynch who speaks of the 'cognitive map,' which often deviates from the cartographer's map of solidity and boundedness.[5]

When a text moves woman to the city, it not only openly contests the borderlands of female experience and exclusion, but also makes the city the site for negotiation of what is to be included in the making of national community and what is to be excluded. As Çinar and Bender write, 'Narratives of the city serve to construct, negotiate, and contest boundaries' (xvi), which is, I submit, also what women's writing does. Moroccan women novelists may not begin by saying 'I am going to look at women and the city,' or how the city impacts woman, but by emphatically moving the woman to a city – whether it be Casablanca, Fez, or Marrakech – they invite our speculations as to the dynamics of this relationship.

With all this in mind, my focus in this chapter, located in the broad domain of cultural geography, will be the discursive practices that six Moroccan women authors adopt in presenting women and the city. I focus on the city particularly because I have been struck by the fact that when contemporary Moroccan women tell women's stories, they almost always locate them in the city, perhaps because the city in its physical reality and cultural construct represents not only the most realistic locale (where more than half the country's population lives, in fact), but also the place whose identity, like Moroccan women's, is in transition.[6] While the major cities of Morocco are traditionally attributed a specific identity in the national consciousness, their identity is constantly being reshaped as more and more people leave the rural areas for the city, and as the city spaces push further and further out into surrounding areas. Still, broadly speaking, Fez is known as the city of tradition and the spiritual centre of the country; Casablanca is a great port city and the financial heart; Rabat the administrative nucleus; Marrakech the soul of the cosmopolitan south and gateway to Sub-Sahara Africa; Tangier, the ancient seaport city of unsavoury reputation and colourful characters from its days as an international zone (1923–56). To place the woman in fiction in these cities, or to have her move between them, or to create a parallel discourse between the protagonist and the city is a revealing choice on the part of the woman writer, who, in adopting strategies of cultural geography, gives her work both substance and specific Moroccan identity.

We can speculate that when Moroccan females incorporate the city in their stories of women, it is not only to lay claim to a space that formerly was not theirs, or to embrace for their female character either the paradoxes or the modernity offered by the city, but also because by writing women into the city, or vis-à-vis the city, the writer may be engaging in an act of figurative decolonization. Samia Mehrez writes that, 'decolonization is not just the physical ousting of colonial administrators' and occupying armies; it is also the liberation from and 'confrontation with' all kinds of 'hegemonic systems of thought,' including those that seek to rule over a sex.[7] Since the city in Morocco has by and large been the construction of men (despite the mythical female who has sometimes given her name to a metropolis) and represents the structures of power and hegemonic thinking that have restricted women to the margins, the woman writer who brings her female protagonist to the city, or shows the city as the mediator of women's consciousness, or how the woman and city can interact positively, or where she can contest traditional identity and sometimes achieve liberation is offering a model of decolonization through discourse.

Not all stories of woman and the city are the same, of course. For some women writers, the city becomes a refuge in the central clash between notions of tradition and modernity, while for others it represents an escape from both the village and the patriarchal family, typified, according to two cultural historians of Moroccan architecture, by the private, familial space of the traditional Moroccan house, based on the principle of inversion.[8] In contrast to the traditional houses of the countryside, urban architecture is both more anonymous in its large apartment buildings and more outwardly focused in its monuments and public buildings, train stations, major post offices, commercial centres, and its planned parks and gardens, walls, and wide avenues. The newcomer is likely to be impacted by this new environment of different sights and shapes and colours, in ways that make the city an inevitable locale for personal change. For most protagonists, the move to the city is motivated in terms of the story/narrative, but it may also be designed by the woman writer to produce her protagonist's emancipation. Ironically, rather than feeling alienated, or dislocated, or lost in the metropolis, a female heroine like Nadia (Benchekroun), Zahra (Abouzeid), Niran (Oulehri), and Badra (Nedjma) is much more apt, ultimately, to 'find' herself in the city.[9] Perhaps this is due to the fact that cities have historically been the driving forces in the growth and development of the nation, cauldrons for channelling human energy and creativity, theatres for the rising bourgeoisie.[10] To be sure, the city also has its slums, its despair, and certainly its dangers, especially for women. But for the female protagonist in fiction who migrates to the urban area, the city typically represents the potentiality of more dynamic boundaries, negotiable and/or permeable.[11] At other times, of course, the city can be used to underscore malaise and ambivalence, or even the woman's marginality, undermining any ostensible myth of national unity and harmony.

In sum, we might hypothesize that the city in Moroccan women's fiction is a creative mediator of the female psyche and of woman's condition. Reading the woman in, or into, the city is, moreover, both a way to tell a collective narrative and to mount a critique of society through gender. In the pages ahead, I shall look at the multiple ways in which gender and geography interrelate in the works of half a dozen different writers and five different Moroccan cities. Through narrative, one writer explores how the city is denied to woman, thereby proposing a relationship between the theory and practices of colonial space and gendered space (Fez in Mernissi's *Rêves*); another reveals how the city becomes a parallel discourse of emotional turmoil and disruption (Agadir in Oulehri's *La Répudiée*; while another uses Marrakech as the palimpsest of cross-cultural identity (Benchemsi, *Marrakech, lumière d'exil*), and yet another suggests how the city and the woman represent mirrored geographies of morals (Tangier in *L'Amande*). The fiction of two other writers incorporates the discourses of travel, migration, and journey (Benchekroun, *Oser vivre*, and Leila Abouzeid, *Year of the Elephant*) in a demonstration of how feminist geography uses the metaphors of itinerancy to reinterpret the politics of identity into a politics of location, in the formulation of Momsen and Kinnaird.[12]

Fez and the Colonial Space of the Medina

Linda McDowell points out that a feminist geography starts from the basis that since men and women are positioned differently in the world, their relationship to the places in which they live is also likely to be different.[13] Because women experience the city in ways that are unlike those of men, they will, of necessity, write it differently. According to Moroccan critic, Abdallah Mdarhri Alaoui, the Fez of Tahar Ben Jelloun – and I would add the Fez of Abdellatif Laâbi – is totally at odds with the Fez of Fatima Mernissi.[14] Unlike her male contemporary, Mernissi describes not so much a city, as a feminine universe; a daughter-mother complicity; a female community within the interior of the great-house, standing in opposition to the streets outside on which men walk freely or gather in cafes and mosques in easy sociability as they create bonds outside the family. In contrast, poet and essayist Abdellatif Laâbi has said that his autobiographical novel, *Le Fond de la jarre*, was written specifically to capture the soul of Fez and to pay homage to the city.[15] Set during the late colonial period of the French Protectorate, from 1948 to 1953, his memoir deals with a pivotal period of transition between the traditional world and the new one opening up, as one Morocco disappears and another one begins to take its place. Fatima Mernissi's *Dreams of Trespass* covers roughly the same period, and her narrator is about the same age as Laâbi's. Yet the experience of the two young children in terms of place consciousness is in stark opposition. Mernissi's young narrator could not possibly have written in homage to a city she hardly knew. What she did know was the interior of the great-house and a mere handful of pedestrian streets in the medina, when the entire female entourage of the Mernissi household would be shepherded by a designated male to the hammam or movie house. Even then, what the medina connotes for her is narrow passageways, walls, an absence of windows facing outward, heavy portals that are always closed, presided over by a 'warden,' like Hmed, the porter of the Mernissi house.

Later, in a non-fiction work, in speaking of her childhood in Fez, Mernissi still recalls the city as 'stuffy, narrow and judgmental.'[16] It is a personal experience of the city that Laâbi does not share, for he had spent a liberated boyhood roaming about in the city.

For her part, young Fatima calls Fez 'a town of anguished souls,' and compares it unfavourably to Marrakech, 'the city of ochre-coloured walls,' which she characterizes as more authentic because it is 'in utter harmony with the essences of Africa,' warmer and more connected to the outside and hence more human than Fez, which is 'swept by the cold winds of winter' (*Dreams*, 207). As a child who has never visited Marrakech, young Fatima is in no position to make this comparison (another example of the false-naivety of the character; see chapter 2). But it hardly matters, since the author draws on oppositional imaginaries of each city to convey her idea of a narrow-minded Fez, closed off and insular, just as life is for the women who live in the great-house. Marrakech, on the other hand, represents all that Fez is not, for it stands at the crossroads between Sub-Sahara Africa and Europe, on the fabled caravan route with camel trains and merchants from many lands. It is the cosmopolitan, exotic other, the locus of activity and free movement, the meeting place for whites and blacks, where languages interlace, and different nationalities commingle and must find creative ways of communication. In her imagination, young Fatima sees Marrakech as an engaging and lively city where travellers speak through body language when their different tongues make conversation impossible.

Fez, on the other hand, despite its reputation as the cultural and spiritual centre of the country, is constricted, offering the young girl only enclosed spaces, closed doors. It is not that her life is joyless – far from it, for there is much tenderness among the various members of the family. But for the female members of the great-house, daily life takes place on the inside, in a 'harem' of visible and invisible lines and rules of decorum. The young girl dreams of Marrakech, because it represents freedom, but she lives in Fez, where gendered space resembles colonial space – the same prohibitions, lack of freedom, exercise of power by the stronger and attempts to subvert that power by the weaker. Colonial space is defined by division, into the Old City and the New City, just as gendered space is divided into areas for men and for women. Colonial space asserts its dominance by what and how it builds.[17] In the New City, inhabited by the French occupiers, streets are laid out in a logical pattern, while the Old City of the medina is composed of a labyrinth of alleys and passageways that defy logic and make egress a challenge to all but the initiated – in *Dreams of Trespass*, the initiated are Moroccan men but not women.[18] Colonial space is further regulated by a system of borders, checkpoints, controls, and permits. Gendered space is controlled by its own system of 'forbiddens,' as well as by male chaperones, like the porter, Hmed, who stands sentinel at the front door of the great-house, preventing the departure of those without formal permission to leave.

To further underscore the lack of freedom in spatial terms, Mernissi draws a stark contrast between the absence of real nature in the harem and the strictly enforced artistic motifs that women are expected to follow when embroidering. Indeed, Mernissi emphasizes just how unnatural the harem is when she says that the only flowers that survive in the harem are those of the coloured brocades of the upholstery on the sofa or of the embroidered silk draping windows and doors. Captured in thread, they are immobile, static, lifeless.

Mernissi's city – or more precisely, the great-house of the Fez medina – is a geography that illustrates precisely her thinking about 'harem' and the structures of visible and invisible power that affect women's lives. Hence, she creates a veritable 'cartography of power and power relations' between men and women that resembles that of colonialism. To reveal, as Mernissi does, the double impact of patriarchal *and* colonial space on the women in the great-house of Fez is to explore the personal and political simultaneously. In revealing the great-house as the site of continuous negotiations by some of the women for greater freedoms, the text models the drama taking place on the outside. And by juxtaposing the real and imagined spatial boundaries of Fez and Marrakech, and showing how both pre- and post-Independence Fez offers only an atrophied experience of life for women, she puts into play two competing ideals for the nation as for women, while implicitly asking questions about a freedom that is based on exclusions.

Agadir: Parallel Discourses of Disruption

While Mernissi's work dealt with political geographies of gendered and colonial space in relationship in the city, Touria Oulehri will focus on the emotional complementarities between woman and the city in *La Répudiée*. The narrative is divided into two parts, the first called Fez (9–103) and the second, Casablanca (107–75), but the city that has the largest presence is Agadir, situated on the Atlantic ocean, in west-central Morocco, site of a disastrous earthquake, in 1960, which destroyed 80 per cent of the city and killed 15,000 people, a third of its population at the time.[19] Simultaneously developing both the central story – a wife whose sterility has resulted in her repudiation by a husband who still loves her but whose need for progeny is stronger – and the account of events leading up to and including the earthquake in Agadir some thirty-five years earlier, Oulehri juxtaposes the emotional seismic event with a cataclysmic geologic faulting of the earth, drawing parallels between the two. In the sense that her heroine's individual tragedy is paralleled by the city's much larger one, and that one year after the disaster, Agadir gives some positive signs of a comeback in the midst of the continuing rubble, the novel presents a narrative of encouragement to women about recovery after personal calamity. In the final line of the novel, 'Agadir survives. Which is far more than one might have hoped the day following the quake ...' (175), the woman within the text, as outside it, is invited to see a favourable omen, regardless of whether she has been repudiated, divorced, or betrayed.

Against the story of her protagonist, Niran, who constantly recycles the past in memory, while trying to cope with a personal disaster, Oulehri interpolates accounts of events in Agadir, as they are experienced by a small cast of characters from Casablanca who are passing through the sea resort. These passages are set in italics, beginning on the fifth page of the novel with a short paragraph, as though extracted from a newspaper report, telling of two pre-shocks on 23 and 29 February 1960, producing concern among the population but no physical damage. In the next passage on Agadir, the town is presented as the sunny, smiling city of the future, but then, in stark opposition, the third and longest entry describes the actual earthquake. At 11:47 pm on 1 March 1960, Agadir is wracked by a devastating three-second quake that will change everything, just as repudiation does for Niran. The city is turned into a castle of cards, buildings crumble and collapse. Like Niran herself. What remains in the ruined wasteland of the city are only a few 'islands of houses,' like strange, uncertain phantoms – similar to the memories of better times that haunt Niran. But she, like the chance visitors to Agadir, Anas and Ali, cannot escape the realization that an apocalypse has occurred. The world as each had known it has ended; the city has been martyred and so has the woman. In a mere three seconds, the city that had existed for centuries and whose very name means 'a fortified granary or village' was reduced to rubble. Similarly, the few words of the official letter announcing the repudiation destroy Niran's life. She feels that she is falling into a black hole. According to newspaper accounts that describe the nightmare of destruction and blazing fires throughout the night, rescuers worked frantically in response to the cries of the trapped, fearing that daybreak would reveal even more massive destruction. A correspondent for *Le Petit Marocain* speaks of his own survival as a 'return from another world,' to face a vision of the Apocalypse; the spectacle of destruction touches the hallucinatory. Yet with the birth of a new day, strangely splendid and sunny, and in the middle of the wasted town, are small signs that miracles did occur – a baby in a crib, for instance, suspended in air outside his missing nursery – unharmed, indeed, even, sleeping.

The new day finds Niran pacing the deserted conjugal bedroom. She drives to a park, but cannot find the force to venture far within, in part because she feels fearful of having become 'yet another unhappy woman,' one for whom 'the private has been transferred into the public sphere.' She supposes that the fact of repudiation 'legitimizes the scornful look of others who see a female who is no longer desired by a male' (58). Like the survivors of the earthquake in a perpetual state of nerves, futilely grasping for what no longer exists, Niran has the feeling that all time has stopped (42). She is described as constantly on the verge of the same crisis of tears as the young girls in Agadir who were awakened out of a sound sleep, to be thrown on the floor or tossed out the window, as they saw their parents' bedroom disappear, their baby sister's cradle empty, fireplaces flying in the air, cars disappearing into gaping crevasses that opened in the streets as people tried to flee.

A massive international rescue and evacuation operation is undertaken, bodies recovered, victims transported to hospitals in Rabat, Casablanca, and Marrakech. Everyone's thoughts are with them. Meantime, decades later, for another victim, Niran, there is no outside intervention, no rescuers, although a part of her survival will depend on an evacuation of her own: 'I decided to move to another town' (101), she says. She will 'emigrate' to Casablanca, in order to make a new life.[20]

The second half of the novel, corresponding to the post-quake period and Niran's journey toward recovery on 'the path of revolt and of liberty,' marks the end of her most intense self-absorption, and is recounted in the third-person, unlike the first-person narration of part one. In Casablanca, Niran finds a job, which gives her financial independence (115), travels on business to Marrakech, where she has a brief romantic encounter (not a relationship) like something out of *The Arabian Nights*, throws out the false wedding ring she had bought to prevent unwanted advances from men, and takes stock of her life.

In the last pages of the novel, the one-year anniversary of the end of her marriage is marked against the same point in time for Agadir. Both the city and the woman have survived, if not fully recovered. Neither is perhaps what she had been or what she will become; both are still works-in-progress, following the cataclysm of earthquake and repudiation. For both, there are many questions about the future and how to rebuild. How does one make the structures of the future city more resilient and able to withstand the furies of nature or man? As engineers and town fathers pour over their blueprints, so Niran assesses her past, asking herself what kind of woman she had been and wants to be, and whether she, an intellectual who loves books and art, should ever again lose herself in love so much that she loses her own identity.[21] At this point, the novel seems to risk going astray, but on the last page Oulehri returns to the story of Agadir to imprint on the reader's mind the last image of the city's unexpected survival, which seems to point to the same for the female protagonist.

In drawing parallels between a natural disaster and an emotional upheaval, Oulehri makes geography and the story of a geologic eruption a predictive metaphor of double value: destruction and recovery. By choosing to tell a woman's story of emotional cataclysm and recovery in juxtaposition with the Agadir earthquake, the author conveys a far more expressive story than had she merely told the woman's story without the city. In Oulehri's novel, the city is not only the backdrop, but a precursory model of regeneration for women.

Tangier: Aging Libertines

In *The Almond*, the city and the woman do not just parallel one another; they appear to reinforce and nourish one another. Given Tangier's reputation in guidebooks and in popular understanding, it seems appropriate that *The Almond* be set in the rough and steamy port city in northern Morocco, home to legendary hustlers and today resembling, as one guide says, 'an aging libertine, propped up languidly at a bar.'[22] The reference to a woman is historically founded, because Tangier is named after Tingis, the mythical wife of the giant Antaeus and later Hercules.[23] In terms of its early history, Tangier was successively captured and lost by various European powers from the fifteenth to the seventeenth centuries, first Portuguese, then Spaniards, and finally British. Only under Moulay Ismail did Muslims finally take control in 1684. However, when Morocco became a French protectorate in 1912, the future of Tangier was a matter of controversy involving France, Spain, and England. Finally on 18 December 1923, the city was declared an international zone, controlled by eight countries. It was to be a city in which political and military neutrality was compulsory and would enjoy complete economic freedom. Because of free trade and the abolition of taxes, foreign capital flooded into the city, as well as smugglers and spies, gunrunners and money launderers, pimps and prostitutes, along with criminals on the lam. In the 1940s, artists and writers also came, including Jacques Majorelle, Kees Van Dongen, Tennessee Williams, Paul Bowles, Jean Genet, Henri Matisse, and Paul Morand, as well as Morocco's own Mohamed Choukri, with whom Tangier is most associated, and all of them contributed to the city's reputation for artistic freedom.[24] Later, they were joined by hippies and drug dealers.

With *The Almond*, Nedjma becomes the female equivalent of Mohamed Choukri, speaking without shame or euphemism, though she, unlike Choukri, also tells a tale of love, for until the point when it becomes clear that Driss is unable to accept the uniqueness of his relationship with Badra, and she orchestrates the final breakup by inviting his male sex partner, Hmed, to join them in a sexual threesome, it is clear that Badra has loved Driss intensely, even to the point of submitting to the basest of his desires. Indeed, when she is totally possessed by her love, she says, 'I wasn't in Tangiers. I wasn't anywhere. I was inside an incredible and total love ... a love that knew nothing but how to love' (125). The extreme of Badra's love is matched by the extremes found in Nedjma's expression. Like Choukri, Nedjma puts no restraints on her language, precisely because the liberated tongue is crucial to her claim of equality and to the broader feminist project of her writing – to say everything that a man has said and thereby to reclaim women's rights to speech when it comes to sex. Hence, her scenes of coupling are alternately lushly carnal, or, like those of Choukri, raw and violent.

Against the lustful excesses of the characters, Tangier is not just a backdrop, but a virtual force. It is the fulcrum of non-conformist behaviour and hence the ideal theatre in which to stage the depiction of a woman's absolute physical, social, sexual, and ontological liberation. No timid, hesitant, or flirtatious mistress, Tangier seethes with animal appetites and physical drama. It is not so much that Badra 'finds herself' in the city or that it finds her, but that they are in a reciprocal relationship, a congruence between its rhythms and hers. Badra anthropomorphizes the city, calling it a 'wanton libertine,' 'half Arab and half European, sly and calculating, singsong and God-fearing'

(57), and describes the effect that Tangier produces in her, inculcating her with a 'delicious poison' (59). She is literally intoxicated by the city, which is imbued with an essence like an overripe fruit, oozing fermented juices. She describes Tangier as a 'lazy slut with wide-open legs, half Turkish delight, half dirty pig' (124), and feels the pulse of the city in tune with her body. She says, 'What had Tangiers made me into? A whore. A whore similar in every way to its Medina' (185). And just as Tangier is often base and cruel (51), so Badra at times is crude and just as cruel.

The Tangier of Nedjma's novel is like the Paris of Henry Miller in *Tropic of Cancer*. There is, of course, another Tangier and another Paris, but this is the one the author needs in order to communicate fever and reckless, hot-blooded intensity. It is not coincidental that both Nedjma and Miller are engaged in a process of breaking down barriers through their stories of 'soul and of flesh.' What each writer found in a city that exists in the imagination as much as on a map is a locale that meshes with their project to take on the critics and 'to break down the walls that now separate the celestial from the terrestrial, body from soul, the mystical from the erotic,' as Nedjma said.

Marrakech: The Palimpsest of History

If moral consanguinity shared by women and city characterizes *The Almond*, it is the rich fabric of history that signifies in *Marrakech, lumière d'exil*. For Rajae Benchemsi's female protagonist, Marrakech is 'one of the most complex and pleasant of palimpsests,' an evocative and key image linked to the poetics of her text and the nature of the protagonist-narrator's quest.[25] On the one hand, the city of ochre walls and roses, a flowering oasis of gardens and verdure set against the perennially snow-capped Atlas mountains, stands as a welcoming host, while, on the other hand, it is the gateway to the great unknown of empty, endless desert, leading to black Africa. Now a cosmopolitan hub of three quarters of a million inhabitants, Marrakech has for centuries been both an ancient and contemporary crossroads for caravans and tradesmen moving between north and south, a true nexus of exchange for ideas, goods, and culture, whether of Arab, Berber, Sub-Saharan African, or European origin. Because of its position, the city has become like a 'parchment paper' on which various groups have left their imprint, and though their marks may subsequently be washed or rubbed out, or covered by a new 'text,' the many layers of invisible text continue to have a kind of 'virtual' existence. Hence, the city is enveloped in an atmosphere of timeless confluence and of intertexuality.

McDowell has said that place is a sort of spatial text that can be interpreted differently according to gender, class, ethnicity, age, and life experience.[26] For Benchemsi, place, as in the city of Marrakech, is a text of rich cultural and universal meanings. Her protagonist comes to this city to reaccess her cultural roots, to discover how to integrate the transitory and the modern with the eternal, and, in so doing, to understand better her own place in the wider universe. She has come to the right place in Benchemsi's poetics, for in a highly feminized image, Marrakech is described as the 'cosmic vagina where all of humanity comes to draw on the feminine and maternal energy so indispensable to creation and to one's own renewal' (le vagin cosmique où l'humanité tout entière peut puiser l'énergie féminine et maternelle indispensable à la création et au ressourcement essentiel [18]): Marrakech is the source, the matrix, the womb, the bountiful and nourishing mother.

In the opening chapter and again in the epilogue, Benchemsi's narrator goes to the famous square, Jemma-el-Fna, through which some 10,000 people pass on a typical day – spectators, residents of the medina, buyers and sellers, storytellers and acrobats, snake charmers, healers, and purveyors of both the practical and the magical.[27] At the intersection of Arab and Berber culture, embodying centuries-old traditions, the square is quintessentially Moroccan. There, Benchemsi's *narratrice* finds the soul of her country, the mystical beginning of life, the invitation into the unknown: 'The desert is there. On the square. The illustrious Jemaa-el-Fna. Mosque of Nothingness. Beginning of life. Threshold of mediation. Of communion with the unknown' (14–15). Time is suspended in this timeless place; there is a communion between the supernatural and the world of mankind. She will also find her friend, the tattoo artist Bahia, who practises through her art a mystical connection to the past, in the ancient 'graphismes de l'Islam,' the geometrical forms and arabesques, the spiral – her favourite form, denoting both the beginning of life and its end – rather than the insipid designs (hearts, for instance) that so many of her customers request. As the narrator waits for Bahia to finish her day's work, she finds that she becomes at one with the square, this moving landscape of people, sounds, and the smells of her culture. Here, she experiences a foretaste of the reunification that she seeks and finds in Marrakech. Islamic architecture and poetry provide the light that brings her out of the exile of the modern world. Marrakech represents a harmony of many voices into a single voice, an ecstasy of union. All voices – those of Bradia, Zania, Lalla Tata, the Place Jemaa-el-Fna, the East, and the West – become a single one (196). As the character says on the last page, 'Everything in the universe had at last found its place' (197).

Place for Benchemsi's character is not about the politics of individual identity, but the poetics of belonging, of finding one's specific place and linking it with the larger universe. Through the poetics of geography, Benchemsi explores the processes of freedom and reunification of past and present by means of the city, which represents both a timeless essence and a constantly renewed resource.

Journeys of Displacement: Casablanca

It has been observed that travel as a category of analysis has become for cultural geographers one of the key terms and metaphors in writing influenced by postmodern ideas.[28] Similarly, for feminist geographers, travel in the broadest sense of movement, displacement, migration, and nomadism is uniquely qualified to reveal insights about women's conditions and identity. It is through this lens, specifically the notion of journey, that I shall study two other Moroccan writers, Siham Benchekroun and Leila Abouzeid, to analyse how travel to and from Casablanca signifies in their narrative.

The French-born journalist Zakya Daoud, who has lived in Morocco for many years, has called Casablanca a city of contradictions on a huge scale, a cosmopolitan centre of tremendous energy and dynamism, vitality, and generosity, but also of violence, misery, pollution, and noise.[29] A veritable cauldron of opposites, Casablanca is a city of paradoxes, at once modern and conservative, Westernized and impoverished. Modern villas, hidden behind walls covered with hibiscus and bougainvillea, contrast with seamy popular quarters and the sooty industrial suburbs, while the central part of the city owes much to General Lyautey, who played a role similar to that of Baron Haussman in Paris in designing the town and calling upon urban planners and architects to build apartments and villas in art-deco, modern, or neo-Moorish style. Fiction writer and journalist, Bahaa Trabelsi, loves Casablanca for its vibrant, ceaseless activity, its cafes and parks, its diversity, calling it a 'city of power and opposition to power, a city of love and of hate, proud and insolent, a city of flesh and blood.'[30]

For her part, Siham Benchekroun's Nadia in *Oser vivre*, who has moved from Fez to Casablanca soon after her marriage with Ali, a banker, experiences the city negatively, for there, her dreams of personal freedom meet the pinched realities of life as a female, not only because of Ali's narrow ideas, but also because, she laments, neither the street nor the night belongs to woman (197-9), an observation familiar to urban dwellers throughout the world. Nadia is suffocating in her marriage and the four walls of her apartment. But when she ventures to go out, everything on the outside throws her back to the inside and to the constricted bourgeois life style she had been trying to escape. For unaccompanied women, even the cultural amenities of a big city like Casa are relative, first, because a woman does not go to nightclubs or the neighbourhood restaurants or even to the theatre or the cinema. Moreover, none of the cultural locales sounds very appealing: public places are littered with cigarette butts, public parks are ill-kempt, restaurants are too expensive, and cafes are populated only by men. Feeling trapped in a marriage and society that seem to offer no room for the individual woman, who, moreover, is a mother and a wife without a profession, Nadia struggles with the knowledge that she, unlike her friend Leila, who went to France in search of personal liberation, must begin by freeing herself of a way of thinking that has colluded against her. Caught in the conservative notions of propriety, Nadia needs to liberate her body and to remap her mind.

Toward that end, Benchekroun chooses the motif of travel, or more specifically, a train trip between two cities (Fez and Casablanca) that represent two symbolic ways of being an unhappy female. What Nadia needs is a third way, and so Benchekroun uses the actual physical movement between cities – a kind of migration between places in the mind, as between places on the map – in an essentially metaphoric way to capture the route toward and processes of female individuation. It is not accidental that the 'real' locale of most of the novel is on a train moving between Fez and Casablanca. This is so because Nadia is neither a gypsy nor a nomad, but a proper bourgeois woman, and her trip is less about arriving in another city than it is about a journey into herself. Born and raised in Fez, she feels constrained and even persecuted by its traditions, but when she moves with her husband to Casablanca, she finds another kind of bourgeois constriction. During the long hours of the trip between the two cities, and in sections of the novel written from the pronominal perspective 'I' or 'she,' depending on whether she feels in command of herself or subjected to others, Nadia recalls, through non-linear memory, key events in her life. Seated in a moving train – that is, in a space between two places – and lulled by the measured, methodical forward motion of the train, she begins, haltingly, and never radically, to forge a new consciousness.

Through the trope of travel and the moving train, Benchekroun focuses on the idea that female identity is not fixed, but rather 'a fluid amalgam of memories of places and origins, constructed by and through fragments and nuances, journeys and rests, of movements between.'[31] At one point, Nadia muses, 'What long and obstinate work it is, this path to identity' (17). Ironically, it is through her frequent displacements that Nadia finds her place. As she moves between two cities and spends idle but liberating hours on the train meditating about her life, Nadia both discovers and moves toward a new self. In the ambiguous space between urban spaces, Nadia finds the certainty to define herself.

Like Benchekroun, for Leila Abouzeid the notion of 'journey' is a poetic trope. Figuring in the subtitle of her novella, *Year of the Elephant: A Moroccan Woman's Journey toward Independence*, her reference is to a nascent feminist consciousness occurring in simultaneity with Moroccan independence. However, the ending of the story throws the ultimate meaning of that journey into doubt, because in the trajectory from married to divorced woman, Zahra not only loses her home, ending up in a precarious position, implied by her dream of a ladder falling back from a house (56), but she is reduced to serving the very nation from which independence had been wrested, when she becomes a cleaning lady at the French Cultural Centre in Casablanca. Integrating metaphors of home, homelessness, and journey, Abouzeid paints a moving portrait of female disentitlement.

The first chapter opens with Zahra – still reeling from her husband's unexpected announcement that he is divorcing her – returning to her dead father's home, in which she had never really lived, having been brought up by her grandparents. Describing her own status as 'some store-bought item' being returned to the shop, Zahra rails against a system that can treat a woman as an inanimate object. Underscoring her reduction in spatial identity, we learn that Zahra now has the right to occupy but a single room in this house, since she and her siblings had agreed, upon the father's death, to divide up the home and rent its rooms to tenants. Having nothing to her name but a room and 'whatever the law allows' – the refrain that arises bitterly in her throat each time that Zahra remembers her husband's dismissal, 'Your papers will be sent to you along with whatever the law provides' – she is forced to displace another wretched woman, who had been renting the space, in order to repossess an empty room, at once 'desolate' 'oppressively small,' 'musty,' 'cramped,' and 'dispiriting.' To furnish it, Zahra has only a mattress and a blanket, given to her by a holy man at the shrine where she had spent her first night as a displaced refugee, i.e., a divorced woman. Now an outcast in an impoverished village, stricken seven years earlier by a flood that reduced it to ruins, Zahra wonders, 'What has happened to this town?' concluding, 'They have marginalized it and sentenced it to death, like me' (13). When she walks through the town's market, she feels an oppression of the spirit, as though 'choking iron fingers' (23) were pressing the life from her lungs, a description that prepares us for the spiritual message she will ultimately embrace, that the world is transitory (68), a kind of stopover on the way to one's ultimate spiritual home.

The literal journey that brought Zahra to the stricken village, which in its desperation serves as a mirror of her own despair, had been made by bus, and is the same trip, but in reverse, that she had made ten years earlier when she and her husband moved to Casablanca. In the years of the Resistance, she made many more bus trips on missions for the cause, once travelling from Casablanca to the village of Souk al-Arba, where she was to deliver a male Resistance fighter wanted by the police, and who, disguised as a woman, sat next to her on the bus. She also travelled by bus to visit her husband who was jailed at Al-Adir for organizing a strike, bringing him the traditional basket of food and smuggling in the djellabah and veil that one of his fellow prisoners would wear to escape. She rode a bus to Rabat for the festivities of 18 November to greet the Sultan, Mohammed V, returned from exile, and in the Mechouar (spacious grounds that surround the palace) joined the throngs to exult in freedom. But when the long trek to Independence ends in triumph, she and her husband travel to Rabat by car, a temporary (at least for her) sign of changed status. However, the day she is 'exiled' as a divorced and humiliated woman, rejected by a husband who wants a younger wife more fitting with his new position, Zahra boards a bus in Rabat with only the clothes on her back and a bundle under her arm, headed for her impoverished village and the single room in her dead father's house. When the bus crosses the Bou Regreg River, she feels she is 'returning to some past time, living the past over again, that nothing had changed' (60). She is travelling back to a village she no longer knows, where all her kinsfolk are buried in silent cemeteries. So this is Independence? she asks bitterly. Briefly, she tries to live in her single room and make a livelihood through weaving, but when she realizes that she will never earn enough 'even to buy a shroud,' she decides to leave. There will be one more bus trip back to Casablanca in search of another shabby room and a job in someone else's 'house,' the French Cultural Centre. The same woman who had 'carried out missions for [her] homeland' (24), is virtually 'without a home ... like a passenger in transit' (14), having 'spent [her] life riding from station to station' (60), on a journey, it would seem, without an appropriate end.

By combining metaphors of movement and dislocation, as of home, homeland, and homelessness, Abouzeid would seem to have given her novella an ironic subtitle, were it not for the preposition she chooses – a journey *toward* Independence, not *to* Independence. The journey to independence for women has begun; it is far from over.

Conclusion

In writing women *and*, or *into*, or *left out* of the city, these texts explore the ways that space and place can be used to convey the physical and emotional correspondences between gender and geography. The city may be either real or figurative, used as a parallel discourse, as in Oulehri, a mirrored essence in Nedjma, a microcosm of the body politic in Mernissi, or the mythic mother and spiritual source in Benchemsi. Employing the tools and metaphors of cultural geography, the writer finds in women's journeys and travel a challenge to the tradition of spatial associations that equate women with home and family. As we saw, both Benchekroun and Abouzeid deal with this subject, though with differing effects. Still, the benefit of bringing women's stories to the city and of focusing on women's literal journeys is precisely the potential to reveal female identity as non-static, subject to change. If a major obstacle to women's emancipation in the Arab world is, as K. Safi-Eddine has written, the cultural definition of ideal Arab identity as unchanging, then the theme of the journey to the consciousness of the self as preliminary to social consciousness is a crucial first step.[32]

Today, to speak of women and the city is to recognize new realities in the lives of Moroccan women achieved over the past couple of decades, having to do with changes in both space and *savoir* (or knowledge). While the majority of women in earlier times lived behind walls, never going out into the street except under the protection of the veil and generally with a male chaperon, or, like Scheherazade, travelling only through the power of a story, in recent decades more and more women have attained access to non-domestic spaces. Such displacements were first made possible through women's greater access to school and learning, which a priori means access to the street or public spaces, leading ultimately to their entry into the workforce. Thus, with the extension of education and a greater integration of women into the work world, the spaces of women's lives have begun both to expand and to be transformed. Statistics support Mernissi's claim that Arab women are now challenging the notion of a divided city where one sex manages politics and monopolizes decision making, while the other stays at home.[33] In that sense, the woman writer reflects the story of her society when she explores intersections between the city and woman.

She is also doing more. By telling these stories of woman and the city, she is consciously pursuing a project of cultural decolonization, similar in some ways to the variation proposed by theorists of autobiography in the West who reformulate the traditional identity question, 'Who am I?' to one that asks, 'Where do I belong?' By placing woman in the city or looking at her vis-à-vis the city, Moroccan women writers propose a broader view into 'where woman belongs.' The objective is not so much to argue that the city fulfils a promise of modernity, or that it is either 'good' or 'bad' for the woman, better or worse than the village, but rather to demonstrate the conviction that both men and women are vital to the city understood in its two senses: as a town and as the political nation. By writing woman into the city, women writers challenge old notions of fixity and permanence across time and space, and offer a potentially transformative concept of women's space in the nation.

If, as geographer Doreen Massey has posited, it is possible to spatialize the history of modernity, we might similarly ask whether, when Moroccan women writers move the woman to the city, they are seeking to modernize the question of women's space, just as much as they are representing an actual change in social realities. In fact, it seems to me that we might well speculate that there is a real parallel between the de-Orientalization of the harem and hammam, as studied in the preceding chapter, and the decolonization of the city by bringing women to the urban centres of power. Can we not argue that in the rewriting of women's spaces and the reevaluation of where she 'belongs,' Moroccan women writers are not only 'modernizing' the question of genderized space, but also offering alterative visions of modernity and of the nation?

8 Scheherazade's (Moroccan) Sisters: The Poetics of Identity and Democracy

> Modernity means the emergence of women as citizens, and this emergence suddenly transforms the nature of the state.
> Fatima Mernissi, *Islam and Democracy*, 164

> Any reflection on modernity in the Muslim world today necessarily takes the form of a plea for feminism. Regardless of where you are ... [in the Muslim world] the debate on democracy soon drifts into a debate on women's rights and vice versa.
> Fatima Mernissi, *Scheherazade Goes West*, 51

Gender and Democracy

By the time both chambers of the Moroccan legislature voted changes to the Moudawana, or family code, in January 2004, nearly fifty years had passed since Morocco had won its independence from France, during which time women activists' hopes for a more democratic society had repeatedly been raised, then dashed, as commission after commission bickered and broke faith, revealing deep divisions about what should constitute modernity. Finally, after nearly half a century and much expenditure of the so-called female virtue – patience – the law caught up with the times and offered to women a handful of basic rights previously denied to them as a consequence of 'traditions, a patriarchal and phallocratic society, and retrograde *"foukahas,"*' according to journalist Khalid Jamaï.[1] The new Moudawana, hailed by feminist groups, raised the age of marriage for girls from fifteen to eighteen (the same age as for the right to vote); suppressed the *tutelle* by which women had needed to obtain the consent of a father, brother, or another male before marriage; stipulated equality between spouses in decision making; made polygamy more difficult; and granted women the right to begin divorce procedures, as well as to share the material goods accumulated during marriage.[2] In many ways, the changes bespoke a new willingness on the part of the monarchy to reform society, more in tune with the rhetoric of democracy that since the late twentieth and early twenty-first centuries had literally been on the lips of every citizen of Morocco, from king to shopkeeper. Indeed, as political scientists tell us, in the contemporary world, democracy is assumed to be the global political ideal, and almost every individual and most political regimes, regardless of their nature, claim the mantle of democratic ideals.[3]

For Morocco, the embrace of democracy was a historic change, for as Alison Baker reminds readers in *Voices of Resistance*, real democratic aspirations were not truly a part of the struggle for independence.[4] In fact, in the decades following Independence, she writes, it was problematic in the Maghreb to attempt to frame the argument for women's rights in terms of democracy, because nationalists believed that a new identity for their fledgling nation required the adoption of values that were diametrically opposed to those of their colonizers. Furthermore, there was deep suspicion of modernism and of democratization programs because, as Moroccan sociologist Mohamed Guessous says, these notions were typically associated with imperialism and assumed to serve the interests of the West rather than of the newly liberated nation.[5] Moreover, invasion and occupation by the French colonialists hardly seemed a convincing demonstration of democracy. Accordingly, at the conclusion of the struggle against the French, many nationalists readopted traditional culture, telling women that their services were no longer required by the nation, to return to their homes and domestic tasks, and to seek honour in becoming guardians of tradition. Seen in this light, the post-Independence period seems to reveal, as Baker says, that it was political freedom that interested the nationalists, instead of enhanced freedoms within society, particularly for women. Such a clarification goes a long way toward illuminating why the struggle to bring about significant revisions to the Moudawana would be so long in coming.[6]

Yet, as Fatima Mernissi writes in the preface to the 1998 edition of *Etes-vous vacciné contre le harem*, in the brief span of three years between the first (1995) and second editions of the book, there occurred a veritable sea change in language concerning national goals.[7] Everywhere in the public sphere, the stated goal was now democratization, whether the speaker was from government or business, politics, the media, or education, and regardless of whether their statements were motivated by pressure from the UN or other funding organizations, or by sincere personal adherence to democratic ideals. The message was that Morocco needed to modernize in order to achieve economic development, which in turn meant that it could no longer ignore the contributions that one half of its population were capable of bringing. As Ghita El Khayat wrote, 'Le Maghreb se fera avec les femmes, ou ne se fera pas' (The Maghreb will be built with women, or it will not be built).[8] In joining modernization, economic development, and democratization, the rhetoric positioned women to benefit.

Concurrently, the entire region was engaged in similar deliberations. The first Arab Human Development Report was issued in 1999, and three years later the 2002 Report identified specifically the inadequate status of women as one the three major deficits in the Arab world, the other two being deficits in terms of freedom and knowledge. In her *Le Monde arabe au féminin*, El Khayat had argued that underdevelopment in the Arab world is in direct relationship to the condition of Arab women, saying that as long as females remained locked in tradition, Arab nations would remain crippled and underdeveloped. In 2005, the Arab Human Development Report was entitled 'Towards the Rise of Women in the Arab World,' focusing on the empowerment of Arab women, and arguing that gender inequality was a major impediment for development. To make their point about what had to done, the authors appropriated the image of a bird to envision free women, arguing that to get airborne two wings were needed, one liberated from all forms of discrimination, and the other representing key social reforms. Only by developing the capabilities of women, the Report stipulates, will Arab societies as a whole progress and prosper. Indeed, only by granting women equal opportunity to realize their full potential, El Khayat has said, will Morocco have enough resources to make the plunge into modernity, for the simple reason that any nation that does not include one half of its citizens in its plans for progress cannot be considered modern. Scarcely could there be a clearer argument for the relationship between gender and democratic modernization.

Words and reports, of course, do not speak as loudly as actions. But they do prepare the way.

In Morocco, the rhetoric of democracy, present since the late 1990s, has been a feature of much mainstream print and visual media, whose article of faith is that as the country democratizes, so will the population and the nation modernize and prosper. Not surprisingly, then, when on 16 May 2003 Morocco was struck by three simultaneous terrorist bombs that claimed more than forty lives, the first reaction of the average citizen was to reaffirm the nation's commitment to democratization and to insist that the nation would not be deterred from its goal. In other words, the general population read the attacks as motivated by those who feared the development of democracy and modernity, in the mistaken and unenlightened belief that such values were inimical to the country's traditions. The consensus view of the citizen on the street was that while the terrorists' bombs were intended to send a warning message about further democratization, the people would not be frightened. Interestingly, a decade earlier, Fatima Mernissi had analysed the fear of democracy in *Islam and Democracy*, to which she had appended the subtitle, *Fear of the Modern World*. Now, average citizens, shocked by the violence that had shattered their cherished myth of Moroccan moderation, offered the same reasoning. By the thousands, they took to the streets the day after the attacks to rally to the cause of democracy and to demonstrate solidarity with their Jewish neighbours in Casablanca who had borne the brunt of the terrorists' bombs.[9] Their example convincingly posited the notion that mainstream Moroccan Muslims were united behind the ideals of democracy, underscoring, as have many scholars, that Islam is not the key variable in explaining the lack of democracy in the region.[10]

That average Moroccan citizens were at the forefront of a spontaneous reaction to the terrorist attacks is a positive sign of grassroots sentiment about the national commitment to the goals of democratization, which similarly characterize the numerous non-governmental organizations dedicated to helping the disadvantaged throughout the country. For Moroccan journalist, Aboubakr Jamaï, the hundreds of NGOs active throughout the country in the last decade are evidence of a thriving civil society capable of enacting genuine democracy at the ground level.[11] In Jamaï's view, Morocco needs more democracy, not less, if it is to combat terrorism. But at the same time, he observes, 'Unfortunately, the government's increasing restrictions on the news media ... are stifling this movement toward democracy.'

In terms of freedom of the press and of speech, I would submit that the situation can best be described as 'fluid.' In the last decade, subjects of inquiry and investigation that only years earlier would have been considered 'red lines' over which the press could not step have been discussed, especially on the pages of the weekly press, and addressed openly at other public venues such as the bookstore, Kalila wa Dimna, in Rabat. During the first half of 2003, while living in Morocco, I had many opportunities to see a youthful democracy in action in the interactions between authors and audience at book signings. In particular, I recall a discussion that transpired when the former political dissident, Abraham Serfaty, and his wife, Christine Daure, were presenting their book, *La Mémoire de l'autre*. Asked to comment on his Marxist-Leninist leanings that had landed him in prison for seventeen years, as well as on the form of government he would like to see installed in Morocco and his hopes for the future, Serfaty expressed the wish for a constitutional monarchy along the lines of Britain's. When asked whether he thought that was a real possibility, he said, 'Why not, perhaps in twenty years.' The idea that such a subject could be addressed in a public forum represented a signal example of free (or freer) speech than a Westerner might have expected. On the other hand, in June 2005, when Nadia Yassine, a leading member of the Islamist Justice and Charity political party, stated her belief that the country would be healthier as a republic than as a monarchy, she was summoned before the courts.

Therefore, while government sanctions continue to be feared – perhaps especially because they are applied inconsistently – and self-censorship is frequently practised, other editors and journalists are engaged in pushing the envelope. During the last decade, French-language weeklies such as *Le Journal hebdomadaire*, under the editorship of Aboubakr Jamaï, and *Tel Quel*, with Ahmed R. Benchemsi at its helm, have written about rampant abuses in the system of justice, government corruption and financial scandals, human rights issues, infractions of freedom of the press, the government's handling of the Western Sahara dispute, the impotence of the legislature and many government ministers, the advisability of a constitutional monarchy, women's rights, and laicism versus secularism. These news magazines have featured cover articles on hot-button topics such as prostitution, violence against women, homosexuality, the traffic and sexual abuse of children, racism, prison abuse, and a whole host of social issues and national scandals. Investigations into affairs that formerly had been under wraps, such as the Ben Barka affair, or Hassan II's secret prisons, and even the disappearances of political prisoners have been conducted in the press, sometimes gingerly, other times with strongly unflattering editorial comment.

There have also been repercussions. Hence, while the U.S. Department of State Country Report on Human Rights Practices for 2004 noted the government's general tolerance of 'satirical and often stinging editorials in the opposition parties' dailies,' freedom of speech has been neither constant nor reliable. Crackdowns on free expression still occur and 'errant' journalists have been harassed and even imprisoned, while journals critical of the regime have been suspended indefinitely, or their editors fined so excessively that the magazine's financial viability is jeopardized (see the U.S. Department of State Country Report on Human Rights Practices, 2005, regarding *Tel Quel*). No open debate on the monarchy, Islam, or the country's incorporation of the Western Sahara is officially allowed, although, once again, enforcement against those who do so is inconsistent. In 2005, authorities blocked access to Internet sites advocating independence for the Western Sahara, and government informers monitored campus activities, particularly of Islamist groups. What all this points to is a mixed bag in terms of certain freedoms of speech considered essential to democracy.

Still and all, the NGOs with their commitment to fill the gaps with literacy and healthcare programs, advocacy for women's rights, minority and prisoner rights, plus other progressive concerns, continue their outreach activities, offering examples of bottom-up democracy at its best. Interestingly, in discussing the history of the concept of democracy in the Arab region in general, political scientist Michaelle Browers makes an important observation when she says that with the introduction of the term of 'civil society' in the late 1980s came 'a distinct shift of focus in discussions of democratization from the state to society – that is, from theories that view the state as the locus of political change to theories that see the impetus for change as arising in a non-governmental realm.'[12] This is an important point vis-à-vis both the democratic grassroots efforts of Moroccan women's NGOs and my argument about how Moroccan women writers endeavour to reshape public space and thinking through their fiction. Their writing, I would argue, goes beyond the mere rhetoric of democracy to promote true democratic values and reforms within an Islamic context.

Indeed, the issue of values is paramount. In their book on gender quality throughout the world, Ronald and Pippa Norris argue that the true clash of opinions between Islam and the West is not about democracy but about sex.[13] In support of that conclusion, they point to successive World Value Surveys, taken in more than eighty countries between 1981 and 2001, in which people in Muslim countries revealed themselves as broadly sharing the same views on political participation as people in the West, but disagreeing strongly about gender equality and sexual liberalization.[14] Thus while polling data reveal that populations in the Arab world show a high regard for democratic rule and reject totalitarian rule, at the same time the same polls demonstrate a low tolerance for differences among individuals and groups and place little value on women's civil and political participation. As a consequence, it can be argued that the real 'democracy deficit' within the general population lies in the general lack of tolerance for difference within these societies.

This, too, is particularly pertinent for my discussion of how Moroccan women's fiction promotes democratic reform within an Islamic context, first by revealing the injustices that have marginalized women, then by challenging cultural stereotypes and social rules about gender identity, and, finally, by arguing for a new kind of pluralism. Basically, their novels are about establishing a renegotiated set of values through the double lens of identity and gender for the nation, a society 'in transition,' as political scientists have described contemporary Morocco, or, in Rajae Benchemsi's words, a society *en pleine mutation*.[15] What distinguishes Moroccan women's fiction is that issues of identity in their texts are about more than defining or redefining the female self; they are equally about defining or redefining society. As a consequence, many of their stories are not just texts of self-expression, but initiations into rethinking society. Implicitly, their texts argue for 1) a reassessment of gender identity as key to social reform; 2) a commitment to social justice, compatible with both Islam and democracy; 3) the need for greater diversity and more tolerance in society, consistent with common-good ideals and the positive modernization of the state; 4) the reinvented community, as the ultimate aim.

To explore these relationships, I focus attention on two writers, Leila Abouzeid and Siham Benchekroun. Both are feminist writers, though neither might claim that title for herself; both critique Morocco from the inside, particularly its gender politics, yet both also respect traditional cultural values while arguing for new roles for women in relationship to society and to the community. Abouzeid creates fiction with a strong Qur'anic presence, and her female protagonists in *Year of the Elephant* (1987) and *The Last Chapter* (2000) speak with a quality of voice that is simultaneously modern, outspoken, and sometimes even caustic.[16] As a secular writer, Benchekroun creates a female protagonist in *Oser vivre* (1997) who is more tentative, but the novel itself is just as discerning in identifying the problems within the couple as it is symptomatic of the problems underlying Moroccan society, and points toward a new, more democratic ideal consistent with a modern, Islamic society.

My argument will be that Abouzeid and Benchekroun are not so much involved in a quest for new female identity – a position that I find problematic – but in a process of renegotiating that identity in an Islamic and democratic context. Indeed, I would suggest that the goal of renegotiating female identity has, from the beginning, been central to Moroccan women's writing, corresponding particularly well to their Bildungsroman approach, which follows the life of a single woman, from her early socialization, to the dreams that define her often-romanticized ideals, to her disillusionment with love and marriage relationships, and finally to an understanding of the conditions in society that must be addressed and changed. The stories of their female protagonists are not about a quest for identity – a frequent obsession of Western critics in talking about third-world women as though there were some sort of holy grail of identity – but the processes of identity, similar to the postpositive realist theory of identity posited by certain cultural theorists.[17]

Postpositive realist theory situates itself at a mid-point between the essentialist notion of identity (each person has a 'true' core waiting to be discovered) and the postmodern idea of identity as a social construct and hence completely unstable and constantly changing. In opposition, postpositive realist theory suggests that while cultural and social givens of time and place cannot and must not be forgotten, identity is not wholly fixed by them in a permanent way, but can be moderated or transformed through 'a process that involves learning how to wrestle with actual structures of power.'[18] In terms of Moroccan protagonists in fiction, the 'long work of identity redrafting' often means, as with Benchekroun's Nadia in *Oser vivre*, first, coming, personally and intellectually, to an understanding of how woman's identity has been devised for her, and, second, realizing that female identity is neither fixed nor immutable. For Abouzeid's Zahra in *Year of the Elephant*, identity is a variable associated with the tumultuous events of personal and national history, while for Aisha in *The Last Chapter*, female identity is a continuing struggle with tradition in order to define a new modernity. What particularly allies Benchekroun and Abouzeid with postpositive realists is how their way of talking about gender identity actually reveals a theory about the world. Their stories are not just texts of self-expression, but initiations into rethinking society. Far from being 'simply' the cry of the disadvantaged, their works carry a quality of discourse about female identity that points toward the need for and means of democratic reform at the national level.

It is in the poetics of identity within their texts of fiction that we can locate not only their 'feminist' message to women, but also their arguments for social justice, equality, and pluralism, goals that relate them to the woman of legend, Scheherazade, who, according to Mernissi, emerges as a political hero and a liberator in the Muslim world, a woman whose actions ultimately benefit the entire nation and hence, naturally, other women.[19] In the discourses of identity within Moroccan women's writing, there is an implicit link between the 'I' of the woman and the 'we' of society and the nation, and that link is fully consistent with the ideals of both Islam and democracy. When the 'communal' is of compelling value, as in Islam, then arguments for social justice and women's rights become vital parts of 'a common-good framework,' because simple logic affirms that the strength of the community depends on the strength of its individual members. The discussion below will seek to interweave the poetics of identity in texts by Abouzeid and Benchekroun, with the implicit or explicit discourse of social reform within their texts, best described as the embrace of democratic principles in an Islamic context.

The Poetics of Identity

To study the poetics of identity, we need to scrutinize the choices of these writers in constructing the identity of their female protagonists, whether through images, themes, or structures of time and place, juxtaposition of character types, or the use of dreams to reveal psychic dramas. Through such analysis, we will better see how, on the one hand, the writer deals with conflict and resistance to sclerotic ways of thinking, and on the other, how she makes the case for freedom and movement. To begin with, we might note that because a traditional, conservative society locates female worth in the role of wife and mother, it is striking how often women's stories are about divorced women, or women who are repudiated by a husband, or women who have run away from a husband. In this respect, one has only to think of the novels of Anissa Bellefqih, Chami-Kettani, Oulehri, Trabelsi, Nedjma, and, of course, Abouzeid and Benchekroun. As we know, fiction requires drama and conflict, and the dramatic change in a woman's identity from married to single, separated, divorced, or repudiated is a propitious moment for an author to throw into question identity issues, since the single or newly single or rejected woman is subject to bouts of doubt, introspection, self-criticism or interrogation.[20] At the same time, how a society treats this woman, and more broadly women in general, is profoundly revelatory of both its values and its real commitment to democracy.

Benchekroun: A Woman's Song of Freedom in a Muslim Context

In the writing of many women, there is a propensity for two kinds of recurrent imagery: the prison and the bird of freedom.[21] The first involves spatial signs and structures that either imprison or limit the woman, while the second evokes winged liberation. Benchekroun's novel, *Oser vivre*, about an unhappily married woman who is struggling to assert an individual identity is filled with such images, from the 'veritable coat of mail of obligations and prohibitions' (44) that weighs heavily upon women in Moroccan culture, to general statements describing society as promoting a 'culture of incarceration' (120); to a woman's universe as 'encircled by barbed wire' (71); to the single strongest image of the text, 'the caged woman' (175). The power of this last image, while not original, is wholly fitting, since its opposing complement, deeply rooted in Middle Eastern tradition, is the bird in flight, the open door, the limitless spaces of the terrace located at the top of the house, and modes of movement and travel. Again and again in women's writing, the image of the bird is used, often appearing to accept its gilded cage, but fleeing when it has the chance.[22] In Benchekroun's novel, the description of Nadia as a caged bird was proposed by the painter, Mehdi, with whom she passes an improbably romantic and chaste idyll. That image of herself as in a cage, neither golden nor made of silk, turns out to be key to her own *prise de conscience* about her condition. Subsequently, she incorporates this figure into her creative writing, which prompts her young daughter to object that since her mother is the author, she owes it to the pitiable woman to free her.

Nadia, whose name in Arabic means 'the one who proclaims, the annunciator, the Annunciation,'[23] is representative of all such 'caged' women, and her story serves to chart for them how one woman arrives at a personal understanding of her incarceration and finds the courage to begin the slow work of freeing herself. Toward that end, Benchekroun juxtaposes Nadia with her friend Leïla, who is studying in Paris, and who is her mirror opposite. Leïla is single and independent of family connections, a sensitive and passionate woman, distressed by Nadia's passivity. 'It's your foolishly stoical refusal to live fully that dumbfounds me' (153) she tells her. For Leïla, individual freedom is an important part of democratic justice. She celebrates her own freedom in Paris where she can be 'an anonymous stroller,' subject neither to scorn nor inquisition because she is walking with a man other than brother or husband (155). Tellingly, she continues, 'I feel less foreign in [France] where racism is like a cancer than in my own country where, because I am a woman, others think they have the right to tell me how to act and what to wear' (155). In a sad but pithy phrase, she judges that she is best described as a 'foreigner [when] in a foreign country,' but also 'a foreigner' in her own land (155).

Through Nadia and Leïla, Benchekroun objects to the argument that has been made that cultural identity requires conformity to a set of traditional ideals, for to do otherwise would be unpatriotic or worse yet, 'Western.' Implicitly, this Moroccan woman joins with the thinking of Amy Gutmann who has said that in a modern democracy, 'individuals can think, imagine, and aspire beyond what any single culture determines for them.'[24] Moreover, Gutmann argues, democratic life is necessarily characterized by intermixing and conflicting interpretations more than by the 'constitution of individual identity by a single, coherent cultural group' (195). Free people have multiple and alterable identities (194), she writes, an observation that was at the centre of Nadia's growing feminist consciousness, as analysed on pages 141–4 above, and that Benchekroun further develops in the novel through the character of Leïla, her spokeswoman.

Leïla is a Moroccan patriot, yet she is also a critic of Moroccan society. Leïla would not consider emigrating to France. She loves her homeland, and this love is clear when she evokes visceral memories of Morocco, its colours, smells, tastes, proverbs, popular songs. 'I look fondly on the fabulous tales of our culture,' she tells Nadia, 'our customs, our ways of speaking, not too directly, but by image and symbol ... I've been imprinted by our innocent good humour, the natural and happy kindness of our national character' – or at least, that is, 'before widespread misery taught us violence' (156). This is why she says, 'I will return. Because it's my country ... They will succeed neither in discouraging me, nor making me afraid,' a suggestion that the 'they' are the antidemocrats who attempt comprehensively to determine the identity of individuals rather than leave room for self-shaping. Instead, she declares, 'We must never be silent or submissive; we must not hide our heads in the sand' (157). The real patriot's responsibility, as a woman and as a citizen, is 'never to abandon our country to its wounds,' which would be, she feels, 'complicit with failure.'

This remarkable discourse shows how a Moroccan woman writer challenges cultural stereotypes and social rules about gender identity, and how she reveals and critiques the chasm between official rhetoric and the lack of democratic values. Her interest, like that of other Moroccan women, is not so much focused on bringing about democratic political structures, as it is on forefronting the need for democratic values. Leïla had written Nadia that her desire was to play the role of Antigone, but younger and less innocent than Jean Anouilh's character in his 1944 play (153). What draws her to this character is her heroic, unswerving conviction of justice, the absolute commitment to assert herself, and a refusal to be dissuaded from her principles.

Nadia will eventually draw a similar moral. She will not continue to go along with society's expectations, she will reject conformity, she will argue for pluralism. Her journey – literal, as she travels by train between Fez and Casablanca and back, and figurative and grammatical, from 'her' to 'me' to 'us' – brings her to a new ideal, one that is specifically Moroccan and democratic in spirit. On the second-to-last page, when she announces that her 'chains have been broken,' she offers a veritable credo of the social reformer, saying, 'I will share with others the infinite treasures of tenderness that I formerly reserved for my family ... I will engage in combat over things in which I've always believed, but from which my narrow bourgeois life kept me. I will throw myself wholeheartedly into the struggle against the woes of my society' (269). In other words, her personal liberation will serve others. She will militate for change, and she will confront unflinchingly society's suspicion and violence and scorn. She will not only remake herself, but also strive to remake the social contract expressed in family law in order to form a new understanding both of woman and of her role in the community. Formerly 'she' or 'her' – that is, defined from the outside and imprisoned within society's framework of 'shoulds' and 'should nots' – Nadia will lay claim to the pronouns 'I' and 'me,' moving toward a new definition of 'we' and 'us,' the reinvented *umma*. Importantly, her liberation from the chains of tradition will not be merely for herself, but for the larger community. Her struggle for selfhood, opportunity, and justice will have their fullest expression when she turns her talents to society. 'There is so much misery and loneliness around me,' she says, 'and I am so rich in love, time, patience, and humility' (269). The novel closes in a jubilant ululation as she sings of freedom and bears witness to her friend who had aided her rebirth, 'Oh! Leïla, the boundless joy of freedom, the indescribable pride of being worthy and – at last – whole' (ibid.).

If one combines Nadia's 'song of freedom' with her commitment to serve others, one sees that Benchekroun has sought to resolve an essential dilemma. If it is true, as Ann K.S. Lambton says, that in Islamic thought the 'individual and the state ... are broadly at one in their moral purpose, and so the conception of the individual is not prominent, nor the conception of rights,'[25] then the question is how do Muslim women seek to advance the interests of the individual within the state? What Benchekroun has suggested in her argument for pluralism is that women should have a broader range of choices than what traditional culture has granted them, and that the unity demanded by the *umma* need not imply conformity. Her effort has been to promote individuality while demonstrating that the individual can still be a responsible member of the *umma*. Hence, she preserves Islam's quintessentially communal character while assuring the autonomy of the individual woman.

It is a dilemma that Mernissi had examined creatively with the story of her resourceful character Mina in *Dreams of Trespass* (in chapter 17, 'Mina, la déracinée'). Originally from Sudan, bought and sold on the slave market in Marrakech, Mina is a beloved domestic in the Mernissi household. Every year during the festival of Mouloud, commemorating the birth of the Prophet, Mina dances the *hadra*, a ritual dance of possession, which recalls to her the rhythms of her childhood. As she dances, tossing her hair and getting caught up in the beat of the drum, Mina is described as seeming to hear a kind of private music to which her body reacts. Young Fatima is mesmerized by how beautifully Mina unites two presumably contradictory roles through dance, for she dances in the group, yet follows her own rhythm. This example brings Fatima to say, 'I wanted to dance as she did, with the community, but following my own music at the same time.' For this is the ideal: to be at once a part of the cultural community, in harmony with it, and yet simultaneously an individual, listening to the voice within. Such a position is fully possible, according to Mernissi's Mina, because individual freedom means neither the denial of the community nor complete anarchy.[26]

Mina's example is a striking metaphor for women in Muslim society according to many Moroccan women writers, who reach toward an ideal of mutuality, not separation or exclusion, at the same time as they challenge the basis for authority that characterizes a patriarchal society. They incorporate the theme of *siba* or resistance as key to constructing identity, often by means of a secondary character, such as Leïla in *Oser vivre*. Some writers, like Anissa Bellefqih, believe that the very mission of the writer herself should be located in *siba*. Concerned that women's writing may be becoming too inward-oriented and too focused on the unfulfilled nature of an individual life, she has encouraged women writers to become 'public scribes' and to exercise the power of words for the emancipation of women.[27] The author of *Yasmina et le talisman*, a semi-autobiographical novel – 'C'est moi et ce n'est pas moi' – Bellefqih believes that women need to use their fiction to go beyond personal issues to focus on social issues.[28] Her suggestion is that they make the move from an 'I' to a 'we,' implying that a first-person viewpoint cannot represent a wider perspective. In part, her stance seems to reflect the profoundly communal character of Islam, for she tells women that they must take up the pen 'to say the unsaid in the name of others,' and to find their motivation not in the question of 'Who am I?' but 'What can I do?' Writing must therefore become creatively committed to revealing not only the problems of women, but to finding solutions to their problems. For her, the writer's duty is to become the *passeur* or agent through whom is focused the goal of bringing about a better world.

Bellefqih's charge to women fiction writers to write in an engaged fashion could strike one as located in a somewhat impoverished notion of the literary act, but at the same time it is persuasive evidence that many writers do believe that social reform and literature must be partnered. By publishing works of fiction that challenge the status quo of society and especially its prejudices against women, the woman writer situates herself simultaneously in her society and outside it. Her writing becomes at once a means of possession, an exposé of the realities of a woman's life, and an impassioned brief for change. Writing, therefore, becomes for her, as poet Abdellatif Laâbi has said, a kind of intellectual exorcism that permits her to grapple with present realties while demonstrating her essential humanity and engaging in the struggle for a better world.[29]

Abouzeid's Critique of the Politics and Poetics of Identity

This is precisely the approach of one of Morocco's most distinctive women writers, Leila Abouzeid, who writes in Arabic and whose works are widely available in the United States in English translation. What distinguishes her fiction is a striking combination of politics and poetics, in which she assails colonialism in all its forms, critiques Moroccan society (often very harshly), and offers female protagonists who are in no way silent women. Indeed, they are often not only outspoken, but also armed with decisively sharp tongues, even while caught in the processes of history. Speaking in a highly original voice, both opinionated and tough-minded, Abouzeid writes fictions that are unlike those of any other woman studied in this volume.

What really sets her apart and makes her fiction particularly interesting for Westerners is that Islam and the Qur'an figure so naturally in her writing. Because Abouzeid is a modern, educated, professional Muslim woman, and because religious faith is intrinsic to her own identity, she offers an image of Islam that corrects common misperceptions in the West, presenting the Islamic faith as a positive force for social justice, compatible with democratic ideals. She herself has said that she writes of women and Islam 'not in a quest for any feminist identity or a confrontational crusade to challenge negative stereotypes about Islam,' but simply because she seeks to set down her experiences as a Muslim woman.[30] As a result, she does not politicize Islam or play identity politics of any kind – there are, for instance, no struggles over the veil or between warring factions of Muslims. For Abouzeid's protagonists, Zahra (*Year of the Elephant*) and Aisha (*The Last Chapter*), Islam is simply an important part of daily identity; verses from the Qur'an or the words of the Prophet are referenced naturally, not as didactic intrusions but as sources that heal and calm an unhappy soul, that speak to beauty and truth, and underscore the necessity of social justice and equality.

Abouzeid presents her heroines as real women, involved in the same kinds of dramas with which non-Muslim women can identify. Her female protagonists are definitely not 'goody-two-shoes' types. Aisha, for instance, is a modern woman of strong personal convictions, possessing the acerbic tongue of a 'Moroccan Dorothy Parker.'[31] Yet she also imparts many pithy truths on men and women, society and world affairs, using the Qur'an or the words of the Prophet to support her statements.[32] And even Zahra, the newly literate, suddenly divorced wife in *Year of the Elephant*, uses strong language, calling her ex-husband 'a bastard' when she talks with the holy man at the shrine, and expresses smoldering bitterness at having been so shabbily cast aside after twenty-three years of marriage. But she will ultimately find solace for her battered self-esteem in her faith, understanding that she is not alone in her misfortune, that 'God creates many copies from one mold' (69), and that 'the important thing is ... to remember God and concentrate on [the] idea ... that we are only passing through this life to build a road to the next one' (68).

In choosing to call her novella *Year of the Elephant: A Moroccan Woman's Journey toward Independence*, Abouzeid's poetic reference is

Islam, specifically to chapter 105 in the Qur'an, 'The Elephant,' in which a recalcitrant elephant refuses to advance on Mecca, and Allah sends flocks of birds to rain stones upon the army of foreign invaders; significantly, it is in this same year of the elephant that the Prophet is born. Metaphorically, the year of the elephant represents a struggle or *jihad*, followed by glad tidings. In situating her novella in the 1950s when Morocco fought the French for political independence, and in choosing a female protagonist, Zahra, who participates in the Resistance and is hurtled toward personal independence when her husband divorces her in the early days of national independence, Abouzeid forges a union between the betrayal of trust and loyalty at the personal level and the betrayal of the democratic ideals of the Resistance. Thus the birds sent by Allah are at once all those average Moroccans courageously resisting the French and, specifically, women who assist the cause, like 'Asma who carried food to the Prophet Mohammed and to her own father Abu Bakr, when they were hiding from their enemies in a cave during their flight from Mecca to Medina' (39), or like Zahra whose 'stones' are both her acts of opposition to the occupation and the actual jewels, her emeralds and rubies, that she sells on behalf of the cause. However, there will be no 'glad tidings.'

Toward the end of the novella, Zahra draws a sharp distinction between her own golden 'year of the elephant' in the struggle against the colonizer, when her energies were committed to a national goal, and the falseness of what she calls her 'year of luxury,' when she lived with her husband in a former French villa given to them by the new government. For Zahra, the aftermath of Independence is a bitter disappointment, revealing a tragic gap between the idealism of the movement and its subsequent realities, mirrored equally, on the personal level, in the growing chasm between her and her husband. When he criticizes her for treating the servants as equals and shows his disdain for them, Zahra objects, 'It doesn't please you that I sit with the servants? We fought colonialism in their name and now you think like the colonizers' (54). What is being underscored is what has become a familiar story: the tragic disconnect between the democratic idealism of resistance and independence movements and the subsequent lack of democracy in the newly constituted state, whose detrimental effects impact most upon women.

Moving between the personal and the political, and a temporality that often switches without warning between past and present, between Zahra's emotional devastation of being suddenly divorced and memories of her exploits on behalf of the nation, Abouzeid builds a powerful case for 'all those women and men who put their lives in danger for the sake of Morocco' (as referenced in the epigraph to the novella), and whose dreams of a new society, as both history and the story show, are met by injustice. In the afterword to *The Last Chapter*, the author says that Zahra is 'somewhere between imaginary and real,' since women like her existed, who fought with their husbands in the Resistance movement, only to be later rejected and abandoned.[33] They may not have been numerous, but their contributions were real, and their erasure from history is a reminder of how the ideal of social justice that independence was intended to bring would also be forgotten. As Zahra comments bitterly, 'I, too, entered the struggle and carried out missions for my homeland. But now what does my homeland do for me?' (24).

In a style characterized as a 'fine embroidery of language and emotion,'[34] and that makes use of spatial imagery to chart changes in identity, Abouzeid simultaneously shows the double unravelling of woman and national ideals in the story of her protagonist. From her upbringing by grandparents who replace absent parents, to an arranged marriage to a teacher of French (she, herself, was at the time illiterate), to being a virtual prisoner in the home of her mother-in-law, to the move to Casablanca when her husband is transferred and where they live in prosperity, followed by her role as Resistance fighter on behalf of the nation, and finally to being a 'discarded' – i.e., divorced – woman, Zahra's identity undergoes multiple transformations, consistent with the changes in the structures of power that dominate her life. In the end, as an uprooted and dislocated woman in society, she has to accept a job as a cleaning woman at the French Cultural Centre, an irony that brings her, as she says, 'face to face with the basic fact that we can't do without the French after all' (67). It is a sad commentary both on her own diminution and the betrayal of the ideals of the Resistance. On the last page of the story, she tells the sheikh that she has decided to live by work and faith, and that she is trying 'to believe that life is not full of the wicked alone' (70), despite evidence of the degradation of human dignity in an anti-egalitarian society. By juxtaposing the poetics of identity both at the personal level and at the national level, Abouzeid, the storyteller and social critic, allows Zahra to conclude that Independence could not 'wash away all spite and malice,' and that 'in fact, we loaded Independence down with a burden it could not bear' (67). It is a realistic and honest assessment by a woman who had made an extraordinary journey.

Zahra had not been on a quest for identity, but involved in the circumstances of history that led to her becoming a different person, much as postpositive realists describe. She embraced *siba* (resistance), and clung to a set of principles that made no distinction between men and women, leading a life during the Resistance described by transitive verbs – she *carries* messages from one town to another, *sets ablaze* the shop of a traitor, *delivers* guns, *smuggles* men, *solicits* political donations, *organizes* strikes – all acts that take place outside the common association of woman within the closed walls of the home. In fact, Zahra is no traditional woman, despite what both she and Abouzeid say.[35] Because of the risks she had taken in service to the national cause of liberation, and her pride in having contributed to the coming of a new society, and the fact that she had learned to read and write, Zahra believed she had a right to expect something better with Independence. But, instead, she will be a victim, in the traditional way of the husband dumping an older wife for a newer and younger model. In that sense, it is an old story. But the even larger injustice is at the national level, with laws that support a wife's disenfranchisement – loss of home, standing, and material goods, while asking merely that the husband provide her a basic three-month subsistence allowance. What Abouzeid's text underscores are both the psychological and socio-economic consequences for the woman when there is no safety net, no social justice, no judicial recourse. Zahra learns first-hand that freedom and democracy are not necessarily the same thing. Without rights, her freedom is worth very little. Worse yet, those who had struggled for independence now adopt the roles of the colonialist. Formerly subjected to their French masters, now even a weak Moroccan male becomes the new *sheikh*, *caid*, or *pasha* (36), while the woman is expected to accept a 'return to the shadows' (64), and to erase from her consciousness the ideals intended to define a new identity for the nation. In the past, Independence had been 'the one almighty goal, the key to paradise' (12); now independence is a circular return to old structures of thinking.

As we saw in the preceding chapter, the motif of the journey focuses the text as well as figuring in the subtitle. On Zahra's final bus trip back to Casablanca after a fruitless stay in her native village, she passes through the towns of Fez, Khemisset, and Rabat, and she thinks, 'Three stations, three landmarks. Why has my path passed through them again?' (61). Indeed, what is she to make of a life that has been a journey from station to station, along a route that took her from married woman to guerilla fighter, to citizen, to 'returned package,' to cleaning woman?

Why has the nation let her – and itself – down? What has happened to its democratic aspirations? The intersecting paths of a woman dispossessed and of a society suffering from a deficit of democratic values speak clearly of lost ideals.

A decade and a half later, in another novel, *The Last Chapter*, Abouzeid is once again concerned with a female heroine who is involved not in a struggle to find identity, but to impose it, to be able to leave a personal imprint on a society that she finds disappointingly far from the democratic ideals of the post-Independence euphoria of the 1950s. Aisha is an updated Zahra, a modern, educated woman with a job and a car and a strong sense of herself. Indeed, she is such an outspoken and confrontational woman, so fearless in her truth-telling, that at times she is almost pugnaciously self-confident. 'I believe in self-criticism,' Aisha declares, 'for my own good and for the good of my country' (89). Accordingly, she wears her outspokenness like a badge of honour, in a powerful and indelible demonstration of the anti-silent woman, who believes that criticism is both necessary to, and a sign of, democracy. The novel is ostensibly the story of why she never married, although she holds to the popular saying that 'marriage and death are two afflictions one cannot escape' (44), but in fact, the real interest of *The Last Chapter* lies elsewhere, not in the long line of suitors who are indecisive, smugly incompetent, unable to commit, or ready to betray. As Aisha declares, 'Husbands in our country are born with an instinct for betrayal' (28), and she dismisses a man who leaves his wife and seven children as, 'another man who thinks with his testicles, and blames it on his religion' (30). She accuses men of inconstancy and acting by arbitrary impulse (45), of expounding 'liberated views in panel discussions or newspaper editorials,' while 'in private they're no better than petty dictators' (51). Coming up against paternal arbitrariness, Aisha says, 'My supposed freedom from illiteracy, unemployment, the veil, [was] a joke, an illusion. I still had a chain around my neck' (51). She is the semi-freed woman, occupying an ambiguous place in a society characterized by anti-egalitarianism. Nonetheless, her anti-male, feminist discourse is not, I submit, the real heart of the novel, which is, instead, an examination of the state of the nation.

Like Aisha, a woman caught in an 'in-between,' between modern aspirations and the tenacity of cultural traditions, Morocco straddles two periods in history, unable fully to enter modernity, or to leave behind the conflicts of past history and traditional ways of thinking. In the metaphorical environment of literature, Abouzeid once again blurs the boundaries between her protagonist and the nation to explore the troubled complexities of the postcolonial world. She has averred that national identity is a complex interaction of language, history, and religion, while in *The Last Chapter* she reveals postcolonial female identity as characterized by dislocation and dissonance. Indeed, everything about Aisha speaks of dissonance: her status as a single woman in a society that values marriage and motherhood for women, the feckless suitors who lackadaisically pursue her, the incompetent superior who keeps getting promoted, the clash between rationalism and superstition, leading to her ever sharper criticism of society. The post-Independence disillusionment of Zahra in *Year of the Elephant* becomes the virtual cynicism of Aisha. She is the postcolonial female subject, the decolonized subject who is unable 'to become,' who yearns for Medina, the democratic ideal, when men and women worked together for the good of the community and the good of one another.[36] But she lives in the muddle of contemporary power struggles that have destroyed ideals, while recycling old narratives of betrayal, dishonesty, ineptitude, and her own forced compliance, when not virtual submission.

In an effort to understand the philosophical and political impasse that seems to characterize both the nation and her own life, Aisha takes a trip to Spain (recounted in chapter 5), which becomes an exploration of the relationship between colonialism, postcolonialism, and identity. Her quest, imperfectly articulated to the reader, is at least double: to reconnect with an erstwhile suitor and to reaccess the glories of Arab civilization in Andalusia. The outcome in both instances will be to underscore loss and humiliation. She recounts that, 'to enter Granada is a unique experience, all the more so if you are an Arab. It brings a bitter lump to the throat' (118), for the Alhambra is 'pure Umayyad poetry, untranslatable,' ineluctably lost when the Arabs were pushed back to North Africa in 1492. 'It is like going back to a home you were forced to leave after a divorce,' she says, underscoring the emotional essence. Her visit to Seville, so much like Fez and Rabat, is also a bittersweet experience: 'If you were here, you would cry to see the lovely world your ancestors had to leave behind' (120), she writes, although she also has to admit that colonization 'amounts to the taking of someone else's land, and the imposing by force of an alien language and culture' (121). That political and historical loss is underscored when she shows up, unannounced, at Karim's door, and is shocked to have it opened by his wife and to learn he has a child. She stays just long enough for Karim to arrive back home, and then beats a hasty retreat, in deep humiliation. In a chapter that seems to drift geographically, as Aisha wends her way through Rabat and Tangier toward Andalusia and finally Madrid, Abouzeid underscores the double-sided mirror of disappointment and dishonesty, both personal and political, consistent with her larger themes of dispossession, humbled pride, and perfidy.

What she is trying to explore through Aisha is why the nation has been unable to realize its promise (and promises), and how, or whether, that fact may be related to more than forty years of French colonialism. Mildred Mortimer observes that European colonialism alienated the occupied Maghrebian nations from their traditions and history, as well as from modernity, and that, as a result, the problem for them becomes 'how to negotiate the balance between past and present, personal freedom, and collective good.'[37] This describes precisely the problematic within Abouzeid's writing. To be sure, she does join with other critics of decolonialization to suggest that colonialism alone is not responsible for the woes of the nation,[38] but unlike other writers in this book, she still strikes out against colonialism, as though it were a recent wound. Abouzeid explains in her afterword to *The Last Chapter* that the fact of French colonialism provoked her 'intense aversion' toward the French (154). It was the French who put her father in their jails and tortured him, it was their language that threatened to strip her of her native language and prevented her, until the 1990s, from reconciling herself enough with the former colonist's language to be able to go to France and speak French. She has Aisha express bitterness against the French, exclaiming, 'A curse on colonialism! Phosphates and tangerines weren't enough. It needed our souls as well' (46); and 'All we got from the colonialists in terms of education was a second-rate knowledge of their language' (44). In the character's mind, the colonizer did nothing to develop the country or alleviate its stagnation; indeed, she objects, he turned the country into 'a museum,' dissuading real educators from modernizing, claiming that 'such modernization was not in keeping with Islam ... as if they had any authority in such matters' (33).

Worse yet, is the way Aisha fears that colonialism has impacted national identity, in the long run. 'We're rootless ... The weakest current carries us away,' she judges (30).[39] 'How could just forty years of the French have done so much harm? What if they'd been in Morocco as long as they were in Algeria?' And then, with rare humour, adds, 'Good grief! If a Moroccan spends a night in Cairo, he wakes up speaking fluent Egyptian' (30). Aisha's concern is with what she considers to be the porousness of Moroccan identity and its inconstancy, an argument equally related to the unreliable male characters who are her suitors.

But if Aisha castigates colonialism, she does not spare the nation, criticizing and dissecting its failures, speaking as though she has 'needles in the corners of [her] eyes' (23), a striking image, which I take to mean, 'with painful truthfulness.' On a train passing through the outskirts of Rabat, Aisha describes the landscape as 'a dump sending up strands of noxious smoke,' commenting that the scene is like 'a wasteland flapping with the ubiquitous plastic bags caught like ragged banners on every weed, [while] skinny sheep dusted black as charcoal-vendors grazed on dust' (111). She observes that there is 'a big difference between analyzing a country's problems in a conference room and living with them in front of your nose,' and adds, 'What I saw out of the window was lucky to be designated "third" world. They probably ought to invent new classes' (112).

In the pilgrimage through Andalusian Morocco and across the Strait of Gibraltar, Aisha takes stock of the state of her nation and tries to understand why fifty years of independence have not brought real social and political change, but only a simple transfer of power, together with restricted liberties, and a continuing failure to eradicate poverty and misery, or to eliminate superstition and charlatans. She asserts, 'We talk about our "peaceful society" and delude ourselves that violence is a foreign disease,' because, she says, 'our violence can happen without guns or bloodshed' (54). The 'violence' Aisha experiences is neither physical, nor even so much legal, but rather cultural, the result of the contradictions that seem to define her condition as a citizen and as a woman, permitted to express her opinion more or less freely, but without having any substantive effect on the status quo. Aisha finds herself at an impasse, much as she deems is true for the nation, unable to break from the past and the negative legacy of colonialism in order to enter the era of full modernity and democracy.

In this sense, Abouzeid's fiction functions in terms of what can be called 'the cultural geography of democracy,' a phrase borrowed from Clive Barnett, who studies the interface between democracy and culture.[40] In mapping the social body, she is working within the broader rhetoric of democracy that frames political and social discourse throughout contemporary Moroccan society. Through her concern with issues of choice, justice, freedom, opportunity, and equality – all fully consistent with Islam – her works, initially written in Arabic and hence primarily directed at readers of Arabic, are examples of democratic inquiry by means of fiction. That neither she nor other writers propose solutions to the problems they uncover is merely illustrative of the task of the writer, according to Tahar Ben Jelloun, which is 'always the same – to bear witness, to tell, to denounce, to explore what is imaginary in order to better describe reality.'[41]

Abouzeid's writing, then, becomes the expression of, and for, democratic virtue. She seeks to speak truth to power, to be a witness to incompetence, dishonesty, and superstition, and to emphasize the contradictions between rhetoric and reality. She is the dissenting, though patriotic, voice. A social critic who uses story – the stories of Aisha and Zahra – Abouzeid talks about and to the nation. While the poetics of identity, through which she presents Zahra, is revealed as a trip that circles back on itself, for Aisha, it is a trip that remains unfinished, suspended provisionally, uncertain of its destination. Ultimately, however, while Zahra and Aisha appear superficially to be very different women and do live at different moments in Morocco's history, they share important similarities, especially in that it is through their experience as decolonized yet unfree women that Abouzeid reveals the problems of the nation. With first names beginning with letters from the two parts of the last name of the author – Abou Zeid – Aisha and Zahra are two faces of the same person, presenting the political sentiments and commentary of the author, who chronicles how individual lives are changed, and often broken, by social and political conditions.[42]

Calling her novel *The Last Chapter* is not, however, meant as the last chapter, but rather, more like 'the latest episode.'[43] The last chapter has not yet been written – nor, in the sense of history, will there ever really be a last chapter, but merely successive chapters or episodes in an ever-unfolding story. Consequently, at the end of the novel, Abouzeid breaks with the preceding five chapters narrated by Aisha to terminate with a chapter spoken by a new woman narrator, Hani, who had known Aisha at school. Hani is yet another unhappily married, psychologically abused wife, who suffers at the hands of her husband and mother-in-law, certain that witchcraft is being exercised to keep her subservient. But when she sees Aisha being interviewed on television, answering a question about whether she had remained single in order to devote herself to her career, and replying, 'That's a big question. I could write a book about it,' and hears the interviewer's rejoinder, 'A book, the last chapter of which you will never know' (151), the reader is inclined to speculate that this is Abouzeid's message of the provisional. Neither woman's story, nor the last chapter in the saga of the nation's journey toward democracy has reached its conclusion. In that sense, alone, the future, like the text, remains open, ambiguous, even enigmatic, emphasizing uncertainty and unknowability.

Conclusion

Interestingly, in an address to the First Arab Women's Book Fair in Cairo in late 1995, Abouzeid described the critical reception of *Year of the Elephant* as eliciting completely different emphases depending on whether the critic came from the West or from Morocco. The former, she said 'emphasized the presence of "the voice of women," "the question of identity," "Islam," "language," while the latter stressed "the non-linearity of time," "legend and politics," "catharsis," and issues that might broadly be called "making literature."'[44] In the preceding discussions, I have sought to blend the two approaches, to trace the poetics and politics of personal, as of national identity, and at the same time to reveal how Abouzeid's novels are about more than the story of a single woman, involving, instead, a critique of society, in which she takes issue with the status quo, on behalf of women, but just as much on behalf of the nation. In this respect, her position bears similarities to other North African and West African writers who engage in a robust critique of postcolonial Muslim social orders and cultural practices.[45] Taken together, her two texts reveal how identity, both personal and national, is simultaneously conditioned, fragmented, and sometimes broken not only by radical social and political change, but also by a reluctance to change. Similarly, Siham Benchekroun argues against conformist thinking and for the benefits of diversity, suggesting that it is in the interests of the community for women to fulfil their individual aspirations. By fusing poetics with the call for reform, Abouzeid and Benchekroun give evidence of what Edward Said has said about the social role of literature and its critical role in assessing society.[46] Consistent with the fact that, in Islam, it is society and not the state that is the primary institution, they direct their focus not toward political reform at the level of the nation, but toward the need of the broader populace to recognize that there can be no true progress toward democracy in the absence of a culture of tolerance, mutual respect, and dialogue.

While creative writing is often seen as the constantly renewed quest for a definition of the self, fiction writing for Abouzeid and, to a somewhat lesser extent, for Benchekroun, involves the desire to reshape public space. By holding a mirror up to the problems and disappointments of society, reflecting the cultural structures that exist and the unfinished business of democracy, their fiction represents a bold assertion of a new legitimacy, spoken clearly by the voices of women who are 'still ready' for social change. Sisters of Scheherazade, they have come to the 'palace of literature' to tell stories and to ask questions about justice and power and the future, and to inspire both women and men not just to dream, but to act.

Conclusion

Writing is an act of resistance.

Abdellatif Laâbi

Literature matters because, through its fictionality, it contributes integrally to the dynamism of society. The untruths of the literary imagination enable our imagination to surpass the empirical constraints that surround us. Fictions – and the cultivation of a sensibility enriched by imaginative prowess – can set us free.

Russell A. Berman, 'Why Literature Matters'

In 2002, officials for the sixth annual Salon of the Book in Tangier chose 'Writing and Resistance' as the overarching theme of their book fair which had been designed to focus on prison narratives based on the 'years of lead.' The relevancy of that fact to this book is that the same theme offers an especially appropriate lens through which to study the history and experience of women in Morocco and more particularly the history and experience of the first wave of Moroccan women writers. In her 1998 film, 'Still Ready,' Alison Baker gives a riveting account of three female Resistance fighters, who, like Abouzeid's Zahra, were initially motivated by fathers or husbands or other men to secrete arms and fugitives, plant bombs, pass messages, and carry poison pills for use in case of capture so as to avoid torture. Since most Moroccan women at the time were illiterate, they escaped the notice of the French troops who assumed that all Muslim women were submissive, unaware, and uninvolved in political action. It was a misperception that made these women only all the more effective, as demonstrated by the stories of some 300 female Resistance fighters.

Similarly, there are legions of women in Morocco who have resisted throughout history against the assumptions and prejudices of many within their country and outside its borders who have underestimated them. Among these women, are the writers of this book, who, like the 300 female *résistantes* – a small fraction of the total figure of 300,000 Resistance fighters – may constitute a minority, but whose existence is deeply important in a conservative society that has not traditionally favored women's public expressivity. These are the women writers who have become the voice of many silent voices. They are the scribes for those who cannot speak, as well as the poets searching for sense, unity, knowledge, and beauty through writing. For some, writing is an act of presence, to contest, to affirm, or to impose female difference on the consciousness of the nation, while for others, the creation of text is a mode of intellectual and esthetic exploration. Thus, it would be mistaken to assume that all Moroccan women who write do so for the same reasons, let alone to tell the same story.

Indeed, it is the diversity of their voices that should arrest our attention. If one thing is clear, it is that Moroccan women do not speak with a single voice or compose narratives that resemble one another. Rather, they engage in many types of writing: realistic and surrealistic, experimental and philosophic, engaged and political, romantic and melodramatic, poignant and sociological. They deal with the themes of freedom and mobility, constraints imposed by society, female socialization, fear, love, tenderness, cultural legacy versus modernity, social injustice, and, yes, female vulnerability. But unlike many in the West who tend to see the Muslim woman as oppressed by her history, Moroccan women writers like Rajae Benchemsi show that the past is far more layered and complex than any one categorical statement about freedom can express, and that, moreover, Moroccan women throughout history have found happiness and beauty in coping mechanisms that give them both meaning and pleasure. Aside from a very few authors, women's writing, for the most part, has not been a revolt against male domination, as much as it is an affirmation and promotion of women. Many women writers have therefore written to foster a new collective awareness of women in the nation, as in women, themselves, and to legitimize women's rights as in the interests of the community. It is in this sense, primarily, that we might call their writing 'political,' and that we might approach the inevitable question concerning the relationship between literature and politics in a developing society.

That relationship is all the more complex when we add the category of female gender to the mix, since questions about when women begin to write, what they write, and how their writing is received bear importantly on issues of gendered power, politics, and development. Nonetheless, even while the feminist aspirations present in most Moroccan women's writing can be seen as 'politically' motivated, and even while I have argued that many of these writers are concerned with proposing ways by which society can be made more democratic, particularly for their sex, I certainly do not want to engage in 'reductionist instrumentalization.' Surely, it behooves us to avoid such an automatic route, even when dealing with the literature of a developing country. What this means in terms of Moroccan women's texts, is that while there is always a sociocultural and historical-political context to their writing, there is also a question of art. We have only to recall, I submit, that El Bouih wrote an overtly politically inspired memoir, but did so by the most artistic of means, while Benchemsi combined art and transgression not on behalf of politics but of philosophical inquiry. Obviously, then, a more nuanced approach is called for, one that invites us to be simultaneously *aware* of the socio-political underpinnings of literature, and also *wary* about reading every text produced in a developing society from within a single set of expectations. It may well be that a woman writer in a developing country can never really divorce herself from external political realities, in that she is either consciously or unconsciously a product of those externals, but, nonetheless, her artistic choices are not always and necessarily determined by such realities. To ignore the multiple motivations of textual expression carries the potential risk of overvaluing the political and undervaluing the literary imagination – or vice-versa, as the case may be.

To be sure, I have often suggested throughout this book how Moroccan women's writing has sought to become a dynamic force in social development. Certainly a majority of the authors treated in the preceding chapters make the case either implicitly or explicitly for changing women's diminished status in society – notably, Mernissi, Benchekroun, Nedjma, El Bouih, and Abouzeid. Yet, as I have also stated, not all literature written in a developing society inevitably carries a political agenda, since there are female writers for whom aesthetics and literary imagination are more important, as for instance, with Chami-Kettani, Benchemsi, and El Khayat. What this means, perhaps, is that we should distinguish between politics in the usual sense of the word, and the 'political' with its broader parameters in terms of the processes of creativity. Thus it is not only through opposition politics and/or social messages for change that literature as a cultural field can become 'political,' but also by the introduction of new voices, new viewpoints, and new readers, as we see with Moroccan women writers. In this way, even a text that is not overtly political may still carry a 'political' significance.

Others may go further and ask whether there is perhaps something inherently radical and democratic about the very essence of literature, itself, that validates Russell A. Berman's argument about the 'immanent political predisposition of literature' regardless of the ideological allegiances of the author.[1] For him, *all* literature – as opposed to that written in a developing society, we might suggest – is inherently 'political,' given what he calls the 'emancipatory character of literature,' which cultivates the imagination and nourishes the ability to evaluate, judge, and make choices. For Berman, literature is 'political' and democratic 'because it calls forth a reader as an imaginative and thinking individual, invited into a process of interpretive freedom and reflection' (158) with a writer. Hence there is an important symbiosis between writers and readers, who both, he maintains, enjoy a kind of 'cognitive independence' from real-world limitations. Given that writing and reading are fundamentally involved with individual consciousness and choice, the text becomes the repository of one independent consciousness read by another independent consciousness, and this explains for Berman how literature becomes a dynamic force in social and individual development, and why the very processes of literature and of literary production are always and ineluctably 'political' in a philosophical or ideational sense.

Insisting on the emancipatory impulses within the literary acts of writing and reading, Berman argues that literature becomes political by demonstrating freedom and contributing to the institutionalization of democracy (151). Further, he asserts that the text of literature plays a social and democratic role by proposing alternatives to the current state of affairs, and providing 'an aesthetic experience that contributes to the suppleness of mind of the [reader], while also displaying the inherent tension in democracy between individual integrity and community pressure' (158). Ultimately, Berman concludes, because the written text contributes to society first by 'modelling' the elaboration of individuality through the very processes of creation engaged in by writer and reader, and second by fostering a capacity to project alternatives to any given context, literature can set us free.

It is an argument that is at once supple and intriguing, and when applied to Moroccan women's writing, suggests how we might understand both the political and emancipatory qualities of their texts. Writing as newcomers within an emerging modernity, these women are proposing an alternative to single-sex cultural discourse and demonstrating a kind of independence in keeping with the democratic rhetoric and aspirations of the nation, as proof of the double potential of the written word both to resist and to liberate. In that sense, they are the worthy successors to those earlier *résistantes* who fought to free their nation.

In a mere quarter century, this first wave of Moroccan women writers that we have studied in this book has created a substantial body of work that deserves attention. The challenge for the writers of the future is that it will not be enough to express the self, to break silence, or to speak from a feminist standpoint. Women's works, like men's, will be held to a higher standard. Therefore while women's stories of repudiation, polygamy, and victimization may still be part of the story, they must not be the whole story. The next wave of women writers will need to exercise powerful imagination, rediscover the richness of their history, restrain their romantic élans, avoid melodrama, develop more three-dimensional male characters.

But based on the qualities to be found in the writing of the first wave, we can speculate that they are likely to succeed, leading readers from at home into a greater appreciation for women's work, and readers from the West into a dialogue that will enrich our understanding of the 'other' and fulfill the spirit of the thought expressed in verse 49:12 of the Qur'an, 'You people! We have made you ... into nations and tribes, that you may get to know one another.' It is in that hope that this book is written.

Notes

Introduction

1 Lalami, 'The Missionary Position,' 23.
2 See also Zeidan, *Arab Women Novelists*, which deals with representative writers from the Arab East (Egypt, Lebanon, Syria, and Palestine). A pioneering study of Arab women's fiction is Evelyne Accad's *Veil of Shame: The Role of Women in the Contemporary Fiction of North Africa and the Arab World* (Sherbrooke: Naaman, 1978).
3 Mdarhri Alaoui, 'Approche du roman féminin au Maroc,' 17.
4 Kadiri, 'Entretien,' 39.
5 United Nations Development Programme Country Report, 2005, online. At the same time, the report noted that 80 per cent of urban participants in government-sponsored literacy programs were women, while the figure was 55 per cent for rural areas.
6 In early summer 2006, for instance, *Jeune Afrique*, n. 2368, du 28 mai au 3 juin, 42, reported that for the last trimester of 2005 in urban areas, *diplômés-chômeurs* outnumbered those without diplomas, three to one.
7 United Nations Development Programme Country Report, 2005.
8 See two articles by Mabrouk in *Jeune Afrique*, 'Les Femmes imams arrivent!' and 'La Fatwa des oulémas.' On the same subject, filmmaker Charlotte Magin and director Gini Reticker produced a documentary, 'Class of 2006,' for the American Public Broadcasting System television program, 'Wide Angle,' in 2006.
9 See Brand, *Women, the State, and Political Liberalization*, for her case study of Morocco, 31–91, particularly 46–57 concerning women's NGOs.
10 Aboubakr Jamaï, 'Morocco's Choice.'

11 Fawzia Zouari underscored the point about different kinds of Islamic feminisms in 'La Guerre du hijab aura-t-elle lieu?' While the list of feminist Muslim scholars throughout Islam worldwide is long and growing longer, in Morocco, the outstanding figure is Fatima Mernissi, who in 1987 published *Le Harem politique* (Paris: Albin Michel), translated into English by Mary Jo Lakeland as *The Veil and the Male Elite*.
12 Mdarhri Alaoui says, 'Les préoccupations thématiques et esthétiques des écrits [de femmes] en français et en arabe sont proches, ce qui n'était pas le cas des oeuvres écrites par des hommes dans les années cinquante-soixante, lors de l'avènement du roman maghrébin masculin.' See 'Approche du roman féminin au Maroc,' 10.
13 *Ecritures du Maroc*, 21.
14 In fact, there are more important economic and demographic factors that tend to support the continued use of French by the intellectual elite. According to an article in *Jeune Afrique/L'Intelligent* by Marwane Ben Yahmed, 'Villepin chez lui,' 40 per cent of Moroccans are francophone, meaning, one assumes, that they have some ability to communicate in the language. There are 30,000 French nationals living in Morocco, 45 per cent of whom are binational. In Europe, the Moroccan community in France is composed of nearly 800,000 individuals of which 350,000 are binational. Such figures underscore the likelihood that some quality of bilingualism with French will continue well into the future.
15 Marsaud, 'Un Babel ... oued littéraire.' The Maghreb (also Maghrib) is the Arabic name for northwest Africa, generally including Morocco, Algeria, and Tunisia, and sometimes Libya.
16 Anne Roche, 'La Littérature de langue française,' article reprinted online at http://ottawa.ambafrance.org/ADPF/ecrivfranco.
17 To understand how French in Morocco has been impacted by its contact with other native and non-native languages, see Benzakour, Gaadi, and Queffélec, *Le Français au Maroc*. Common *marocanismes* include words such as *bled* and *douar* to describe rural life; *derb* for street or lane; *medina* (old part of the city), *mellah* (Jewish quarter); *makhzen, mokadem* (references to political and/or civil life); *djellaba, haïk, seroual, tarbouche* (items of clothing specific to Morocco); *joutiya* (flea market); *trabendo* (contraband); *taleb* (student of Islamic theology); *incha all*ah (= God willing); *lalla, sidi* (forms of address); *charaïque* (referring to Muslim law). Nouns in Arabic can be 'Frenchified' to produce new words, such as *hittiste* from the Arabic *hit* or 'mur' + iste, referring to how the unemployed spend their days); or totally new expressions introduced. It is for this reason that it is not uncommon to find a glossary placed at the end of a Moroccan novel published in French. For those who read French, the 200-page lexicon provided in *Le Français au Maroc* is very helpful.

18 Mernissi, *Etes-vous vacciné contre le harem?* 11. First published in 1995.
19 Hervé Vernay, 'Le Prix des cinq continents de la Francophonie,' in *La Langue française vue d'ailleurs, 100 entretiens*, ed. Martin and Drevet, 11.
20 This is the view of Danièle Latin, who is the coordinator of the research project, 'The Study of French in Francophonie,' as she writes in the preface to Benzakour, Gaadi, and Queffélec, *Le Français au Maroc*, 9.
21 Martin and Drevet, *La Langue française vue d'ailleurs, 100 entretiens*, 51.
22 Ibid., 38.
23 In discussing the ten years she lived in France where she received a doctorate in literature, Benchemsi is quoted as saying, 'Ma vie à Paris, au lieu de m'arracher à mes racines, au lieu de m'en éloigner, m'a peu à peu transformée en une sorte de carrefour entre la culture française et la culture marocaine et arabo-musulmane. Aujourd'hui, je ne conçois l'écriture que dans la fusion de ces deux espaces. Je peux penser ma culture dans une langue qui n'est pas ma langue maternelle. C'est une liberté extraordinaire.' *Le Magazine littéraire*, avril 1999, quoted online, BiblioMonde.
24 Huff-Rousselle, 'Fatima Mernissi.'
25 Ibid.
26 Talk given at the First Arab Women's Book Fair, Cairo, November 1995, and reprinted at the end of her novel, *The Last Chapter*, 154.
27 Professor Fatima Sadiqi of the University of Fez believes that English will increasingly replace French as the foreign language of choice for university students, because for them English signifies modernity as well as access to global markets, mass pop culture, and scientific writing. 'The Spread of English in Morocco.'
28 Marsaud, 'Un Babel ... oued littéraire,' 82.
29 Benchemsi is quoted as saying, 'La francophonie est un concept politique, qui est, je pense, le résultat d'une grosse défaillance politique de la gestion de la langue française. Les vrais enjeux ne sont pas dans le fait d'utiliser cette langue, mais plutôt dans celui d'arriver à dire avec force qui l'on est.' See Glaiman et al., 'Interview de Rajae Benchemsi.'
30 Çinar and Bender, Introduction, *Urban Imaginaries*, xi–xxvi.
31 Mdarhri Alaoui, *Ecritures féminines au Maroc*, 20.

1 Morocco's New Voices

1 Déjeux, *La Littérature féminine de la langue française au Maghreb*, 45, cites Elissa Chimenti's *Au Coeur du harem* (1958) as the first novel by a Moroccan woman, although he acknowledges that her work owes much to French women's texts from North Africa written during the colonial period. In addition, he identifies these other early Moroccan female novelists: Halima

Ben Haddou *Aïcha la rebelle* (1982); Leila Houari (*Zeïda de nulle part*, 1985, and *Quand tu verras la mer*, 1988, observing, however, that Houari was soon to leave Morocco for Belgium); Badia Hadj Nasser (*Le Voile mis à nu*, 1985); Farida Elhani Mourad (*La Fille aux pieds nus*, 1985); Noufissa Sbaï (*L'Enfant endormi*, 1987); Yamina Chehab, *L'Eau de mon puits* (n.d.); Antoinette Ben Kerroum-Covlet, *Gardien du seuil* (1989); Nouzha Fassi, *Le Ressac* (1990); and Fatiha Boucetta, *Anissa captive* (1991). In addition, he cites several poets: Saïda Menebhi, *Poèmes, lettres et écrits de prison* (1978, posthumous); Rachida Madani, *Femme, je suis* (1991); and Fatema Chahid Baroudi, *Imago* (1983), *Songes de hautes terres* (1988); and Selma El Melih, *Vie trahie* (1985) and *A L'Ombre du papyrus* (1990). In passing, he mentions Fatima Alaoui, a journalist, Fatima Mernissi, and Leila Abu Zeïd. Since his subject is all women writers of the Maghreb who publish in French, he includes a section on Algeria (21–44) and another on Tunisia (51–6), observing that the first novel in French by an Algerian woman was written in 1935 and published in 1947, while the first Tunisian women began publishing novels in the mid-1970s.
2 Abdelmajid Ben Youssef of the Ministry of Culture, whom I interviewed in his Agdal (suburb of Rabat) offices in spring 2003.
3 Mdarhri Alaoui et al., *Ecritures féminines au Maroc*. See especially Mdarhri Alaoui's two articles, 'Présentation: Ecritures féminines au Maroc,' 4–9, and 'Approche du roman féminin au Maroc: Historique, dénomination et réception de la littérature féminine,' 16–23.
4 Mdarhri Alaoui, 'Approche du roman féminin au Maroc,' 17.
5 The first edition of *Opening the Gates* was published in 1990 by Indiana University Press, as was the second edition in 2004. The anthology, which is organized according to what the editors call stages, or levels, of feminism, from 'awareness' to 'rejection' to 'activism,' contains excerpts from women's written texts, poems, and interviews. The excerpt from Farida Benlyazid (1948–) is from her film, 'The Gate of Heaven is Open' (variously translated as 'A Door to the Sky' and 'Une Porte sur le ciel'). The text for Fatima Mernissi (1940–), 'Who's Cleverer, Man or Woman?' is a folktale from Marrakech (analysed in chapter 3), while the text entitled 'My Life' on the third Moroccan woman, the artist Chaibia (1929–2004), is a transcribed interview conducted by Fatima Mernissi. Married at thirteen, widowed at fifteen, Chaibia was an illiterate mother who came to art because she needed to provide for her son. She subsequently became Morocco's most famous woman artist and from the age of forty had at least one show a year in France.
6 Mdarhri Alaoui, 'Approche du roman féminin au Maroc,' 19.

7 For an illustrated synopsis of Moroccan literature, see the richly illustrated exhibition booklet, *Ecritures du Maroc*, published by the Institut du Monde Arabe in Paris, April 2001.
8 Memmes, 'Littérature d'expression française.'
9 Fernea, introduction to Leila Abouzeid, *Year of the Elephant*, and her article, 'The Challenges for Middle Eastern Women in the 21st Century,' 188–9.
10 Grotti and Ksikes, 'Interview-vérité: Fatéma Mernissi,' 32.
11 Christine Daure, the daughter of a French *résistant* during the Second World War, first came to Morocco in 1962 with a personal commitment to right the wrongs of French colonialism. She taught in Tangier for five years, and then in 1967 was transferred to Mohammed V Lycée. In 1972 she was asked to harbour a political dissident, Abraham Serfaty, who because of his views was forced to live clandestinely. (See also page 220, note 7.) Later, in 1986, during Serfaty's seventeen-year prison term, they married. See Chadwane Bensalmaia, 'Et Dieu créa la femme.'
12 Mernissi says in *Islam and Democracy*, 'The lot of a woman in an Arab society that is at peace is precarious enough. But that lot is shaky indeed in an Arab society put to fire and sword by foreign forces' (3). Similarly, in the introduction to the second edition of *Opening the Gates*, the editors reflect on how world events in the 1990s and early twenty-first century have adversely affected Arab women.
13 See, for instance, Denoeux and Maghraoui, 'King Hassan's Strategy of Political Dualism.'
14 In using anthologies of Middle Eastern and North African women's writing, the reader often needs to pay attention to the criteria of inclusion, specifically concerning writers who, because they have lived abroad for years, may no longer have the pulse of the region or of their peers' concerns at home.
15 This view was expressed to me by academician, Moufti Barkat, who felt that women's writing had benefited, alongside other kinds of verbal expression – notably the literature of immigration and children's literature – from special encouragement by public authorities. I met Professor Barkat at a conference, 'Littérature de Jeunesse et Apport des Technologies de l'Information,' in Rabat, 7–8 March 2003.
16 I spoke with author and playwright Marie Redonnet, who was in spring 2003 the director of the Service du Livre, a cultural arm of the French Embassy. She described the criteria used in selecting books by Moroccan authors whose publication would receive partial subventions from France as being exclusively determined by merit and not by sex.
17 Mdarhri Alaoui, 'Approche du roman féminin au Maroc,' 16–17.

18 An associated issue for the West is the decline of reading. In the United States, for instance, Chaudhry, 'In These Times,' cites the report, *Reading at Risk: A Survey of Literary Reading in America*, published by the National Endowment for the Arts in June 2004, showing a substantial decline in the role of reading in the nation's culture, with the percentage of American adults reading literature dropping from 56.9 per cent in 1982 to 46.7 per cent in 2002.

19 Unemployment figures have varied between 7.7 per cent and 19 per cent (averaging 14 per cent) for the past five years, and a particularly worrisome problem has been the large number of university-educated but unemployed young adults. In Rabat, groups of the unemployed with university certificates have been regular features of daily demonstrations in front of the gates of Parliament, on Avenue Mohammed V, just below the train station.

20 The writer Salim Jay, who published the *Dictionnaire de la littérature marocaine* in 2006, ratifies that statement: 'Beaucoup de Marocains manifestent toujours une espèce de dédain pour l'écrit,' he states, 'qu'ils négligent au profit de la télévision et d'Internet.' Ghorbal, 'Casablanca tourne la page,' 97.

21 Mouaatarif, 'Le Grand Chantier de l'alphabétisation.' The Moroccan minister who carries the portfolio concerned with literacy and informal education said that in 1956–7, more than 80 per cent of the population was illiterate, whereas by 2004, that figure was cut to 43 per cent. Two and a half years later, the Ministry in charge of literacy announced that nationally the rate of illiteracy had fallen by 4.5 per cent in two and a half years – from 43 per cent to 38.5 per cent in 2007. Report of the Secrétariat de l'Etat à l'Alphabétisation, reported in 'Maroc, j'écrirai ton nom,' *Jeune Afrique*, n. 2415, du 22 au 28 avril 2007, 6.

22 Figures vary widely, but the United Nations Development Programme report on Morocco for 2005 declared that female adult illiteracy was 64 per cent, compared to 38 per cent for males. In rural areas, the rate of female illiteracy was thought to be as high as 90 per cent, while figures for primary school enrolment show girls at a disadvantage, with 86 per cent of boys enrolled, against 67 per cent for girls. The report cites a judgment by the World Bank that economic status is at least as much of a factor as gender in determining who goes to school.

23 In his book, *Literacy, Culture, and Development*, Wagner asks, 'Is literacy cause or consequence of economic growth, or simply unrelated?' (5–6). Lind and Johnston write in *Adult Literacy in the Third World*, 'Illiteracy is a symptom, not a cause of underdevelopment, injustice, and poverty … The

simple provision of literacy training will [not] transform the lives and social and economic relations of the illiterate population. Without literacy being integrated into a general process of social change, or into a social movement dedicated to creating social change, it is clear that it will have little chance of changing fundamental parameters of life' (19).

24 Sedjari, 'Quand la jalousie ou la roublardise dominent, le développement est compromis.'

25 One of the most prolific of Moroccan women writers, who refuses to be pigeonholed either as a feminist or a woman writer, as opposed simply to a writer, El Khayat is especially known for her essays on Arab women, including *Le Maghreb des femmes*. The phrase cited in the text comes from an article she wrote, 'Rentrée littéraire,' for the monthly women's magazine, *Femmes du Maroc*.

26 Wagner, *Literacy, Culture, and Development*; Goody, *Literacy in Traditional Societies*; and Friere, *Pedagogy of the Oppressed*.

27 The short story is from her collection, *Femmes inachevées*.

28 Of course, normal relationships of power can also be reversed when it is the children who know how to read, or to read a language foreign to the parents. In Tahar Ben Jelloun's novel, *Les Yeux baissés*, the young *narratrice*, who goes to school in France, reads all kinds of signs and documents and letters for her parents. She says, 'J'étais, pour eux, l'espoir et la clé d'un monde extérieur. Je leur lisais les lettres, je remplissais les formulaires, je leur expliquais le journal, je leur servais d'interprète, j'étais devenue indispensable, je ne dépendais plus d'eux, mais eux dépendaient de moi. Ma grand-mère aurait dit: "'C'est le monde à l'envers."'

29 Fatima Sadiqi, who is a professor of linguistics and gender studies at the University of Fez, suggests that Darija is often considered to be woman's language because it has no official place in public speech. See her 'Gender and Language in Morocco.' We should note that there have been a number of initiatives since 2005 to develop Darija as a written language. See Miadi, 'La Revanche de la darija'; and Mouaatarif, 'En "darija" dans le texte.'

30 Ben Yahmed, 'Villepin chez lui,' observes that trade relations between Morocco and France have long been strong. France supplies nearly one third of all technical and scientific aid received by Morocco, and the two countries have entered into multiple partnerships on the economy, infrastructure, health, and culture. At the same time, Spain, another former colonial power, whose flag flies over two cities on the Moroccan mainland, Ceuta and Melilla, is becoming increasingly competitive.

31 Benzakour, Gaadi, and Queffélec, *Le Français au Maroc*, 115. I observed this phenomenon once on a train ride between Rabat and Casablanca. A young

Moroccan mother was holding a baby on her lap and talking to her in French about images in a French-language periodical. Two young men, who had been speaking Darija, addressed the mother whom they did not know. One was obviously very taken with the baby, who soon ended up on his lap, as the three Moroccans became engaged in animated and friendly discussion. To a foreigner's ear, their conversation was most extraordinary, moving between Arabic and French, yet privileging neither language.

32 Great Britain, Germany, Russia, Spain, and the United States have also established cultural centres in the big cities. (Based on personal observation in 2003, I would note that the American cultural centre in Rabat was comparatively poorly endowed, with a collection of outdated books and relatively few current periodicals.) Furthermore, the French language is well represented at newsstands in the major cities and train stations, undoubtedly due to the large number of French nationals residing in Morocco or married to Moroccans, as indicated in the preceding footnote.

33 El Oufir, 'La Société civile s'investit dans la diffusion du savoir,' 64.

34 El Yazami, Enquête sur la lecture au Maroc.

35 In response to this problem, Fennec-Poche announced in 2004 that it would reissue Mernissi's Rêves de femmes for the very modest sum of 20 dirhams, about two dollars. Religious literature, on the other hand, is subventioned by Gulf countries, which makes it consistently less expensive and therefore well within most budgets. Ghorbal, 'Casablanca tourne la page,' 97.

36 In her doctoral dissertation, 'Enquêtes sur les textes destinés à l'enfance et à la jeunesse marocaine,' Latifa El Hadrati presents research on grade-school children in Rabat-area schools to demonstrate that while they exhibit the potential for learning to love reading, the scarcity of reading materials at their disposal, plus the often unsupportive attitudes of parents, teachers, and even librarians counteract their interests. It may be these reasons that led Yomad Editions in Rabat to address this void, by asking well-known writers such as Driss Chraïbi and Abdelhak Serhane each to write an illustrated book for children. Chraïbi produced L'Ane K'hal maître d'école (1999) for the very young, and Serhane wrote Pommes de grossesse (1999) for ages eight to eleven. Yomad has even published a few dual language (French and Arabic) books for children, including the charmingly illustrated Salem et le sorcier (2003). The availability of popular literature for somewhat older children depends on being able to read French. I was told by an 11-year-old girl who attends an elite private school that she and all her friends loved to read, but that they mostly read in French because they did not enjoy books in Arabic since it is not a

language they speak or use in daily life. She indicated that while she especially liked reading about heroines her age, she and her friends have read all the Harry Potter books available in French.
37 Draoui, 'Le Livre dans un piteux état.'
38 While oral culture is inarguably rich, it remains inadequate and ultimately uncommunicative in the global world. As Cameroonian filmmaker Jean-Marie Teno said in his 1992 film, 'Afrique je te plumerai,' the existence of a strong oral culture should not be used to justify the lack of a reading public, since it is by the written word of journalism, literary creation, and publication that the fundamental social contradictions of the present are revealed. In an article entitled 'Twilight of the Books,' Caleb Crain discusses the qualities of mind and behaviour of people constrained by illiteracy versus 'literates' according to research done by psychologists. These scholars describe how those who are literate can deal with concepts in their minds abstractly, whereas those of an oral tradition need to embed knowledge by stories. Further, they tend to value cliché and stereotype and redundancy as aids in following complex arguments while those who are literate can use reading to help account for 'the past's inconsistencies ... [through] a process that encourages skepticism and forces history to diverge from myth' (138).
39 Ben Jelloun, *L'Islam expliqué aux enfants*, 91.
40 Sebti, a specialist in Moroccan law as it applies to women, maintains a website that deals with more than sixty specific issues from abortion to prostitution to dowries and marriage law, etc. See http://www.techno.net.ma/femmes/e-guide.htm.
41 'Initiatives du Ministère de la Culture pour encourager la lecture: un acte impératif,' *Maroc Hebdo International*, 557, du 9 au 15 mai 2003, 28.
42 This is the same official that was cited in note 2 above.
43 Personal interview, April 2003, at the Center for Cross Cultural Learning in Rabat. The point is reiterated by Leila Chaouni of Le Fennec who is quoted as saying, 'Nous n'avons aucun contact avec les autres éditeurs arabes. Les livres en arabe soutenus par la France et vendus en Egytpe n'entrent même pas au Maroc.' See Merckx, 'Traduction et coédition,' 7.
44 According to Ghorbal, 'Casablanca tourne la page,' although in Morocco, there are roughly 100 publishing houses, which in 2006 published about 1500 titles, relatively few of them are interested in publishing fiction.
45 Kéfi, 'Le Blues des écrivains arabes,' 67.
46 It is interesting that in Tunisia with its 9 million inhabitants, press-runs rarely exceed 2000, much like Morocco. However, Morocco has a population nearly three times as large as Tunisia's (ibid.).

47 In the article referred to in note 25 above, 'Rentrée littéraire,' El Khayat excoriates the lackluster book scene in Morocco, where there is no such thing as France's *rentrée littéraire*, or 'new literary season' to celebrate. While, to be sure, a comparison between book publishing in France and Morocco is not fair, it does give a sense of the great disparity between developed and developing countries to learn that for *la rentrée littéraire* 2004, France counted 660 new novels, of which there were 440 from French writers and 220 from non-French writers; almost no Maghrebian or Arab writers figured on the list.
48 Gaasch, 'Entretien avec Nadia Chafik,' in *Anthologie de la nouvelle maghrébine*, 45.
49 Mdarhri Alaoui, 'Approche du roman féminin au Maroc,' 19.
50 Fouad Laroui, in *Jeune Afrique/L'Intelligent*, du 3 au 9 juillet 2001.

2 Mernissi and Scheherazade in Dialogue

1 Husain Haddawy, in the introduction to his English language translation of *The Thousand and One Nights*, based on the text edited by Muhsin Maâdi (New York: Norton, 1990) and referred to by Fatima Mernissi, in *Scheherazade Goes West*, 47; and Malti-Douglas, *Woman's Body, Woman's World*, 21.
2 *Scheherazade Goes West*, 54. For more on Cheddadi's reading of Scheherazade and his notion of the triumph of imagination or fiction represented by Scheherazade, over 'truth' represented by Shahriyar, see 53–5.
3 Sallis, *Sheherazade Through the Looking Glass*, says that the original Arabic printed editions (Bulaq I, Breslau, Macnaghten, and Leidan), and following them, Lane, Payne, Burton, and Haddaway do not describe Scheherazade physically at all in the frame story. Instead, all emphasis is on her intelligence and wisdom (101).
4 Abdelfattah Kilito, *L'Oeil et l'aiguille* (Casablanca: Le Fennec, 1992), excerpted in Jean-Louis Joubert, ed., *Littératures francophones du monde arabe*, 97.
5 Sallis, *Sheherazade Through the Looking Glass*, 96.
6 May, *'Les Mille et une nuits' d'Antoine Galland, ou Le Chef d'oeuvre invisible* (Paris: Presses Universitaires, 1986). The twelve volumes of tales, adapted by Antoine Galland (1646–1715) were published between 1704 and 1717. In his analysis of Galland's translated adaptation, eighteenth-century French literature specialist, Georges May (1920–2003), reveals how Galland transformed an Eastern oral tradition into a text for eighteenth-century French society.
7 Kilito, *L'Oeil et l'aiguille*, excerpted in *Littératures francophones du monde arabe*, 97.

8 A dispute that has consumed much ink is whether to read the function of Scheherazade's stories as a 'time-gaining' device or as 'healing narrative.' Did she temporize and thus save herself by her storytelling, as Mia Gerhardt argued in *The Art of Storytelling: A Literary Study of The Thousand and One Nights* (Leiden: E.J. Brill, 1963), 397–8, a view to which others, including Todorov and Khatibi, have assented (see Maurice Olender and Jacques Sojcher, eds, *La Séduction* [Paris: Aubier Montaigne, 1980], 131–47), or did she survive by curing the king of his madness through her narratives, as Jerome Clinton suggests in 'Madness and Cure in *The Thousand and One Nights*' (*Studia Islamica* 61 [1985], 107–25)? See Malti-Douglas, *Woman's Body, Woman's Word*, chapter 4, 'Narration and Desire: Shahrazad,' 11–28. As for Mernissi, she finds no discord in uniting the two arguments, both of which support her position of Scheherazade's feminist self-affirmation through powerful and result-producing speech.
9 See M. Lahy-Hollebecque, *Le Féminisme de Schéhérazade*, 81.
10 Robert Scholes, *The Protocols of Reading*, and *The Crafty Reader*.
11 Proust, *A La Recherche du temps perdu*, 911, 'En réalité, chaque lecteur est, quand il lit, le propre lecteur de soi-même.' He continues, 'L'ouvrage de l'écrivain n'est qu'une espèce d'instrument optique qu'il offre au lecteur afin de lui permettre de discerner ce que, sans ce livre, il n'eût pas vu en soi-même. La reconnaissance en soi-même par le lecteur, de ce que dit le livre, est la preuve de la vérité de celui-ci, et *vice versa*, au moins dans une certaine mesure, la différence entre les deux textes pouvant être souvent imputée non à l'auteur mais au lecteur.' Matei Calinescu, a Romanian-born literary critic and professor of comparative literature, is primarily known for his modernist and post-modernist criticism. See his *Rereading*.
12 Calinescu, *Rereading*, 145–6.
13 Quoted in Calinescu, *Rereading*, 146.
14 Ibid., 18.
15 Most scholars concur that it is common for translations and adaptations to have their own idiosyncrasies that twist interpretation in one direction or another. Antoine Galland, for instance, who brought *The Thousand and One Nights* to Europe in the eighteenth century, is noted for cleaning up the sexier aspects of the text, with the result that versions derived from him tend to reveal Victorian colouring. Another translator, Richard Burton, is often charged with incorporating both racist and racy material, which leads to readings focusing on homo-eroticism. See Sallis, *Sheherazade Through the Looking Glass*, 100 and 106.
16 For the English reader, Sallis recommends the version by Husain Haddawy, calling it not only the most readable, but also an accurate and

impersonal translation, showing no evidence of rewriting in his own image. *Sheherazade Through the Looking Glass*, 47. Haddawy's English language translation (New York: Norton, 1990) is based on the Arabic version by Harvard University professor, Muhsin Mahdi (Leyden: Brill, 1984), which Mernissi lauds in *Dreams of Trespass*, chapter 2, note 1.
17 Sallis, *Sheherazade Through the Looking Glass*, 104.
18 Calinescu, *Rereading*, 19.
19 Beaumont, *Slave of Desire*, 61.
20 Irwin, *The Arabian Nights*, 160.
21 Malti-Douglas, *Woman's Body, Woman's World*, 11–28.
22 Hasna Lebbady, 'There is No Such Thing as a Mere Story:A Poststructuralist Reading of Aïcha Bent Ennejar,' in *Women's Spaces*, ed. Fouzia Rhissassi et al., 181–8. For further on Lebbady, see 'The Myth of the Silent Woman,' chapter 3.
23 Malti-Douglas, *Woman's Body, Woman's World*, 13.
24 Mernissi, *Chahrazad n'est pas marocaine*, was originally written in French. Her playful title is intended to indicate that Moroccan women have much to learn from the assertive model of Scheherazade, who would never have accommodated herself to be as economically oppressed as her Moroccan sisters. See the opening pages of *Chahrazad n'est pas marocaine*. Malti-Douglas's reference is to page 9.
25 Ibid., 16, citing the Mardrus translation of *Les Mille et une nuits* (Paris: Laffont, 1980), 11.
26 The article 'The Satellite, the Prince and Sheherazade: The Rise of Women as Communicators in Digital Islam,' for the catalogue to the show at the Centre de Cultura Contemporania de Barcelona, also exists in a longer English-language manuscript, dated Rabat, January 2003. The first was accessed on Fatema Mernissi's Internet site.
27 With regard to *Scheherazade Goes West: Different Cultures, Different Harems*, Mernissi reprises a favourite theme: even women in the West are confined as much as any harem women when they buy society's notions about the 'ideal body' and its proportions.
28 Mernissi, *Dreams of Trespass*, chapter 2, 'Schéhérazade, le calife et les mots,' note 2.
29 Huff-Rousselle, 'Fatema Mernissi: A Contemporary Scheherazade's Tales of a Borderless World.' The original article appeared in *Cairo Times* in May 2003. A shortened version can be found online.
30 Mernissi, *Chahrazad n'est pas marocaine*, 5.
31 See Gauch, *Liberating Shahrazad*, 37, 51.
32 Ruth Viktoria Ward is a German-born mixed media artist and photographer who lives in the United States where she has pursued both

German literature and visual arts. She has worked and taught abroad in Europe, Pakistan, and Morocco, and collaborated with Mernissi on projects and exhibitions supporting women.

33 Lejeune defines autobiography in *Le Pacte autobiographique*, 14, as a 'Récit rétrospectif en prose qu'une personne réelle fait de sa propre existence, lorsqu'elle met l'accent sur sa vie individuelle, en particulier sur l'histoire de sa personnalité.' For discussions of Lejeune's criteria, explored in his first chapter, see Malti-Davis, *Woman's Body, Woman's World*, 114, and Gauch, *Liberating Shahrazad*, 43–4.

34 The English translation is *Doing Daily Battle: Interviews with Moroccan Women*. For the pages on Batul Binjalluna, see 21–30.

35 Nancy K. Miller, 'The Unfolding Dilemmas of Identity Politics,' B7.

36 See also the discussion by Gauch, *Liberating Shahrazad*, 49–50.

37 This definition comes from Lee Gutkind, the founder and editor of the journal, *Creative Nonfiction*. See especially the Internet home page for the journal and his articles, 'The 5 Rs of Creative Nonfiction,' and 'The Creative Nonfiction Approach,' online. In addition, Aaron Pope's online article from 2002, 'Lines in the Mud: Exploring Creative Non-Fiction,' is also useful. The non-fiction novel is, of course, based on real events and real people told with the techniques of the fiction writer.

38 Mernissi, *Scheherazade Goes West*, 44.

39 Calinescu, *Rereading*, 158–9.

40 Ibid., 176.

41 Caillois, *Man, Play, and Games*, 33.

42 Malti-Douglas, *Woman's Body, Woman's World*, 6.

43 It is also an example that justifies the phrase of two interviewers who characterize Mernissi as 'a feminist attached to her artifices,' Grotti et Ksikes, 'Interview-vérité: Fatéma Mernissi,' 33.

44 Gauch, *Liberating Shahrazad*, 38.

45 Something similar transpires in chapter 13 of *Scheherazade Goes West*, when Mernissi both humorously and self-deprecatingly relates her unsuccessful attempt in an American department store to find a skirt that fits. Having been told by a snobbish sales clerk that the cause is her 'particularly generous hips,' Mernissi recalls, to her chagrin, that those same hips had elicited 'flattering remarks from men on Moroccan streets,' leading her 'to believe that the entire planet shared their convictions.' The real objective of her story is not the size of her hips, but a critique of America, in which, in spite of feminism, she believes that American women are policed by the dictates of the elusive 'size six.' Making fun of herself is a way to relate to her reader.

46 Typically, Mernissi moves from the personal and particular to the general, drawing in her reader by a striking juxtaposition and a leading question, focusing on the immediate or the contemporary as a hook or point of departure, and then joining it with the historical. For instance, in opening *Sultanes oubliées*, she begins with a chapter entitled 'Benazir Bhutto est-elle la première?' thereby intriguing the reader by suggesting a connection between past and present. Similarly, she begins *Chahrazad n'est pas marocaine* by recounting an anecdote in which she herself plays a role and is accused of sullying the reputation of Moroccan women by equating them with Scheherazade. And, as we have already seen, in *The Veil and the Male Elite*, Mernissi recounts a scene in which male customers are horrified when she asks the grocer a supposedly 'innocent' question about whether women could govern.

Mernissi opens *Etes-vous vacciné contre le harem?* with a first sentence that delights the reader with its mock seriousness, plays on words, and winks to cultural insiders: 'Je ne veux pas alarmer notre ministre de la santé qui a déjà beaucoup de chats et de chattes à fouetter, mais il paraît, d'après des rumeurs persistantes de Radio Medina que toutes les paraboles de Derb Ghallaf n'arrivent pas à faire taire, que l'épidémie du 'Harem' fait des ravages à Casablanca.' The author suggests that there is a threat to 'public health' and that a 'vaccination' against the 'epidemic' (of harem-like thinking or rampant sexism in society) is a matter that the Minister of Health (responsible public officials) should address. As always, Mernissi's first concern is to connect with her reader, to hook and to reel in her 'fish,' even that person who casually picks up the book. By piquing the reader's interest with an arresting or categorical statement, amusing him, making the story personal, creating a bond of sympathy and friendship at the outset, Mernissi's intention is to emulate Scheherazade: change minds and teach, through narrative.

47 Azar Nafisi, whose *Reading Lolita in Tehran* figured on the bestseller lists from 2003 to 2005 in the United States, and whose politics made her the darling of conservatives, makes precisely that point in describing why she asked her informal reading group in Iran to study the frame story of *The Thousand and One Nights*. By introducing her class to the theme of the trapped woman in a literary classic, Professor Nafisi sought to draw attention to how the artistic element of confining space can be changed into a site of liberation (19).

3 The Myth of the Silent Woman

1 El Bouih, *Une Femme nommée Rachid*, 22. In a striking image, El Bouih speaks of their 'doigts devenus plumes, flancs devenus pages.'

2 Mernissi, *Doing Daily Battle*, 1.
3 Ghazali, 'Sur Le Gril.' El Bouih cited the proverb in her interview with Susan Slyomovics, online.
4 Grotti, 'Mémoire(s) de femme.'
5 El Khayat, 'Marocaines soumises.'
6 Mernissi, *Sultanes oubliées: Femmes chefs d'Etat en Islam*. In typical fashion, Mernissi opens her book with a catchy introduction, asking 'Benazir Bhutto est-elle la première?' before going on to tell her reader about all the early and extraordinary female heads of state.
7 For more on women's history in Morocco, see Brand, *Women, the State, and Political Liberalization*, chapter 2, 'In The Shadow of the Mudawwanah,' 46–91. See also *Féminisme et politique au Maghreb* by French-born journalist Zakya Daoud, who has lived in Morocco since the mid-twentieth century.
8 Even nearly forty years ago, Waterbury in *The Commander of the Faithful*, 124–5, wrote with nuance about the influence of women. While stating that women had no overt role in the political elite, he nonetheless underscores women's social role not only in the instruction and socialization of children, but also in mediating disputes between families, selecting marriage partners, advising husbands (some actively seek their wife's counsel), and even serving the political elite as contacts or negotiators, sources of intelligence and information, and 'respected counsel on policy.'
9 This is the argument advanced by Lebbady in 'There is No Such Thing as a Mere Story.' Her point is that a folktale often thought to carry a feminist message, in fact, sustains the hierarchical structure of power that keeps women in an inferior position. See further on Lebbady's thesis in my discussion of Farida Benlyazid's film, 'Women's Wiles,' on page 64.
10 Heinze, *Jews and the American Soul*, 1.
11 Mdarhri Alaoui, in *Ecritures féminines au Maroc*, ed. Mdarhri Alaoui et al., 17. Taking an opposite position, Malti-Douglas, *Woman's Body, Woman's World*, insists that these women were exceptions, saying that Arabic literature, whether medieval or modern, is a masculine tradition, particularly in terms of prose writing (128). I would suggest that much the same could be said about the literature of the West, if only because for most of history, the sheer number of male writers has typically outweighed that of females.
12 Power, 'A Secret History,' 22, 24.
13 Lalami, 'The Missionary Position,' 28.
14 For a brief, general article on oral literature in Morocco, see El-Moujahid, 'La Littérature orale.'
15 Fatima Mernissi has also retold the story, giving it the title, 'Who's Cleverer, Man or Woman?' in the anthology edited by Badran and Cooke, *Opening the Gates*, 318–27.

16 Lebaddy, 'There is No Such Thing as a Mere Story,' 183.
17 For instance, Karen E. Rowe, 'Feminism and Fairy Tales,' in *Don't Bet on the Prince; Contemporary Feminist Fairy Tales in North America and England*, ed. Jack Zipes (New York: Routledge, 1986).
18 Mernissi, *Scheherazade Goes West*, 9.
19 Warner, *From the Beast to the Blonde*, xxiii.
20 In chapter 4, 'The Storyteller's Craft,' 103–19, of his *The Arabian Nights: A Companion*. Robert Irwin traces the early history of storytellers in Arab lands, observing that in medieval Fez, they would gather at the gates of the city, along with other types of street performers, including snake charmers, jugglers, fortune-tellers, and peddlers of herbs and quack medicines. Later, when coffee drinking gained popularity, the storytellers moved from the street to the coffee houses of Cairo and Damascus, where they entertained for tips and a small weekly fee. Today in Morocco, the only storytellers who continue to ply their trade outdoors are those of Djemma el-Fna, who perform not only for tourists, many of whom do not understand Arabic, but also for the locals. An eighteen-minute film, 'The Past and Present of Djemma-el-Fna,' presented by a young Moroccan male nicely presents the significance of this famous square and its storytellers (Filmmakers Library, 1995).
21 Déjeux, *La Littérature féminine de langue française au Maghreb*, 115. Déjeux is working with a quote on autobiography from Gusdorf, *Les Ecritures du moi*, 15.
22 Video recording, 'The Thousand and One Nights,' conceived and written by Mahmoud Hussein, produced by P. Calderon, FIT Production, La Cinquième, Canal Sur Télévision, 1999. Princeton, NJ: Films for the Humanities & Sciences, 2001.
23 The phrase is Messud's, 'Fairy Tale in Reverse,' 36.
24 Bacholle, Review of *Cérémonie*; *emarrakech.info*, online, 22 February 2003; Larrivée, 'La Crypte et la vie'; De Graincourt, 'La Variante Ecriture de Yasmine Chami Kettani'; Ben Jelloun, 'Déchirures marocaines.'
25 The apple as a sign of fertility and/or eroticism comes from *The Thousand and One Nights*, and continues to function in modern literature by North African writers. Abdelhak Serhane, for instance, uses the apple in his tale for children, *Pommes de grossesse* (Rabat: Yomad and Paris: Méditerranée, 1999), as symbolic of the unequal division between girls and boys, set forth in Islamic thinking. A woman who eats an entire apple will have a boy child; only a half is needed for a girl. In Algerian Assia Djebar's 'La Femme coupée en morceaux' in *Oran, langue morte* (Paris: Actes Sud, 1997, 163–215), the wife, who does not want to become pregnant, tells her husband

that before she will agree to sexual relations, she must have an apple, even though the fruit is not in season. After a great search, the husband returns with three magnificent fruits, but one apple soon disappears and leads to all manner of misunderstandings and the murder of his wife, whom he unjustly suspects of having an affair with a black slave.

26 The story of unjust murder in 'Le Conte des trois pommes,' which is recounted in *Les Mille et une nuits* between Nights 19 and 20, concerns both the death of the innocent woman, who had been cut to pieces, and the death sentence confronting the caliph's vizier if he is unable to deliver the woman's murderer to the caliph. This tale of falsehood, cruelty, and injustice, which inspired Djebar's story (see note 28), replays the dynamic by which the innocent are sacrificed and the guilty go free, while the death of a woman is never paid off.

27 Riding, 'A Muslim Woman, A Story of Sex.'

28 Najat Chatr, 'Le Choix du libraire,' *Le Journal hebdomadaire*, du 26 juin au 2 juillet 2004), 59.

29 Fouzia Rhissassi, 'Moroccan Women Writers and the Violence of Family Spaces.'

30 However, Amina Wadud reads the verse contextually and culturally to argue that it simply means that two women must be present, in support of one another, so as to prevent any male coercion of the evidence (only one, however, would give the actual testimony), and that, moreover, both the stipulation and the verse concern only certain kinds of financial contracts. *Qur'an and Woman*, 85–6.

4 Transgressive Narratives

1 In *Woman's Body, Woman's World*, 9, Fedwa Malti-Douglas writes that only in the last decades of the twentieth century has Arabic literature in general and Arabic women's literature in particular achieved a level of relative frankness on questions of corporality and sexuality, citing in particular Egyptian writer, Nawal al-Sadawi's *Memoirs of a Woman Doctor* (1969) and *The Hidden Face of Eve* (1977), which speak of female sexuality and women's position in the Middle East. In this regard, then, Moroccan women who came to writing later than their female counterparts in other Arab countries have caught up very quickly.

2 For an exploration into these invisible but powerful cultural constraints, see Grotti and Daïf, 'Hchouma.' They quote anthropologist Lahcen Haddad, who says that *hchouma* is a system of values that underlies all social and familial expectations in Morocco, and is derived from patriarchal attitudes

that ascribe to women the primary responsibility for upholding traditional values (28).
3 Referred to in Rajae Benchemsi, 'Kira et Slima,' in *Fracture du désir*, 29.
4 Mohamed Choukri, one of Morocco's literary giants, was illiterate until age twenty-one, living a hand-to-mouth existence on the streets and engaging in petty crime. At age thirty-seven he wrote *For Bread Alone* (not published in Arabic until 1982, as *Al-Khobz al-hafi*; two years earlier it had been published in French as *Le Pain nu*), a powerful text of realistic, often vulgar language frequently dealing with sex rather than with love. As Youssef Rakha says about Choukri's subjects, 'Genitalia take up as much space as cheap restaurants and are treated with the same open, precise and shameless interest' ('Madman of the Roses').
5 Sanaa Elaji, who published her first short story at age seventeen in the Arabic-language daily, *Al Itihad al Ichtiraki*, came out with a novel, *Majnounatou Youssef* (*Folle de Youssef*), published by Argana in 2003, featuring an independent female who revels in carnal passion and an adulterous affair. Elaji's vitriolic critique of the hypocrisies of Moroccan society, in which women can do everything but must not say it, is a well-aimed blow against *hchouma*. See Mouaatarif, 'Haro sur les tabous.'
6 As mentioned in the previous chapter, there has been some controversy about whether the author of this text could possibly be a woman, given its often vulgar and scorching prose. However, since Moroccans themselves tend to accept the anonymous author as a woman, and since the American journalist Alan Riding met an actual Moroccan woman laying claim to authorship of *The Almond* (see page 77 and 215n27), I am inclined to accept the prima facie evidence that supports that claim.
7 Nedjma spoke of violence against the body in her interview with Alan Riding, 'A Muslim Woman, A Story of Sex.' As the dust jacket of the Grove Press U.S. edition reveals, *The Almond* received ecstatic critical reviews in the West, being called 'bold,' 'fearless,' 'heartrending,' 'important and unforgettable,' while the author was acclaimed as 'a literary guerrilla warrior,' whose book of 'political resistance' portrays 'the provocative rebellion of a Muslim woman who recaptures her senses, her body, her lust and her language' (*Der Spiegel*). On the other hand, Laila Lalami, a Moroccan author who lives in the United States and writes the Web log, *moorishgirl.com*, took a critical view, accusing Nedjma of weak characterization, lack of accuracy in certain realistic descriptions, and of reinforcing negative views of Arab Muslims in the West, while flattering Europeans by means of Driss's literary recommendations to Badra. See Lalami's Web blog for 27 July 2005. In Morocco, Najat Chatr, the manager of a bookstore

in Marrakech, calls the novel 'un cri de liberté' in a review for *Le Journal hebdomadaire* du 26 juin au 2 juillet, 59, and enthusiastically recommends the novel for its message of liberation to women.

8 Definitions of pornography are notoriously subjective and politically charged, as Walter Kendrick argues in *The Secret Museum*, while Lucienne Frappier-Mazur in an essay in Lynn Hunt, *The Invention of Pornography*, 206, says that the pornographic effect is a function of context. Disagreement about the differences between erotica and pornography is also substantial, with Angela Carter observing that erotica is merely the pornography of the elite in *The Sadeian Woman and the Ideology of Pornography*, 17, and Susanne Kappeler declaring that neither 'obscene sex' nor 'violent sex' is indicative of the pornographic, since pornography is not a special case of sexuality, but rather a form of representation in *The Pornography of Representation*, 2.

9 By entitling her text *L'Amande*, which suggests at once the shape and elegance of the young and fragile skin of the nut plucked from the tree, as well as the tradition whereby almonds are thrown in welcome, Nedjma makes both an ironic statement about the sexual awakening of a Muslim woman and a clever cultural one.

10 The Tunisian writer and historian Abdulwahab Bouhdiba argues in *Sexuality in Islam* that Islam takes a strongly positive view of sexuality, a view seconded by Moroccan sociologist Soumaya Naamane-Guessous in *Au-delà de toute pudeur*, though much less so by Malise Ruthven in *Islam: A Very Short Introduction*, perhaps because she gives greater attention to patriarchal orthodoxy. See esp. Ruthven's chapter 5, 'Women and the Family,' 89–112, for a useful and balanced approach about Islam and women. For a fuller view of sexuality in Islam interpreted by a feminist, see Barlas, *'Believing Women' in Islam*, chapter 5, 'The Qur'an, Sex/Gender, and Sexuality: Sameness, Difference, Equality' (129–66), in which the author argues that the Qur'an recognizes the importance of sexual desire equally in men and women and views sex as fulfilling and wholesome, even aside from its procreative role.

11 Benguigui's film, produced in 2000, promises to be an exploration of the myths and realities of sensuality and sexuality in North African society, but is criticized by reviewers Ghechoua and Miadi in their article, 'Fragments d'un discours amoureux,' for its pedestrian view of 'the sexual misery of Arab women in general and Maghrebian women in particular.' I would agree that had Benguigui consulted more expert witnesses, notably Moroccan sociologist, Soumaya Naamane-Guessous, she might have been led to interview more articulate and insightful subjects than those from the public who figure in the film.

12 Cited in Mernissi, *Beyond the Veil*, 29.
13 See discussion in Naamane-Guessous, *Au-delà de toute pudeur*, 205, for a discussion of *nikah*. El Bokhari, or Muhammad b. Isma'il al-Bukhari (810–70), is responsible for the collection entitled the *Sahih*, meaning *Sound, True or Authentic*, often considered by Muslims as second only to the Qur'an, according to Netton, *A Popular Dictionary of Islam*, 59.
14 Laila Lalami, 'Nedjma's *The Almond*,' Web blog, moorishgirl.com. Lalami is the author of a collection of short stories in English, *Hope and Other Dangerous Pursuits*, and often writes on North African literature for *The Nation*.
15 The problem of violence against women has received substantial notice in Morocco, especially in the weekly and monthly press such as *Tel Quel* and women's magazines, *Citadine*, *Femmes du Maroc*, and *Ousra*, as well as in film – particularly Farida Benlyazid's *Porte sur le ciel* (1988) in which the female protagonist opens a refuge for abused women, and Saïd Chraibi's *Femmes ... et femmes* (1997) with its cast of misogynist men, wife-beaters, two-timing and self-centred lovers, all of whom are turned into literal and moral dwarfs in one dream sequence. More recently, a film by Narjiss Nejjar, 'Les Yeux secs' (2003), about the existence of a virtual 'harem of prostitutes' in a rural village of Berber Morocco caused a national scandal for its multiple violences against women – those perpetrated by society, by an ostensibly sympathetic woman director, and by the government. Although Nejjar, who told the story through the sympathetic eyes of a man, intended to demonstrate that the women had been marginalized in a society that left them no option but to sell their bodies, the actual prostitutes, who had roles alongside actors, later were to claim, with the help of unscrupulous lawyers, that they had been manipulated into thinking that Nejjar was making a documentary. The government was called upon to censure the film but refused, claiming its support for artistic freedom. Members of the press were then quick to point out that typically officialdom had no such compunctions about censoring the country's printed press.
16 It is interesting to note that the United Nations defines violence against women as not only physical – sex-selective abortions, infanticide, rape, the commercial sex market, female genital mutilation, honour killings, murder, domestic violence and battering – but also economic, pointing out that of the 1.3 billion people living under the poverty line, 70 per cent are women.
17 Neil L. Whitehead, ed., *Violence* (Santa Fe and Oxford: School of American Research Press and James Currey, 2004), 9.

18 Barrière, *Des nouvelles du Maroc*, 17–25.
19 Rhissassi, 'Moroccan Women Writers and the Violence of Family Spaces,' in *Women's Spaces*, 139–55.
20 Neil L. Whitehead, who studies 'the poetics of violence,' or what he calls the 'discursive amplification of violent practice in society,' says that art may be a better or more shocking, more 'true' way of engaging intellectually with violent acts. See *Violence*, 6. See also his chapter entitled 'On the Poetics of Violence.'
21 For references to violence against women in Morocco, see note 15, above.
22 Moroccans will often say that when sex is the subject of discussion, people tend to fall quickly into French, because the use of the foreign language has the advantage of psychologically and linguistically distancing them from a subject that would otherwise be considered *hchouma*. We should not, however, buy into the myth that transgressive writing can be done only in French. See note 5, above.
23 *L'Opinion*, 18 janvier 2003, 8.

5 A Prison Narrative

1 El Bouih quotes the guard as snarling at her, 'As of this moment, your name is Rachid. You are not to move or to speak unless you hear your name. Rachid.' *Une Femme nommée Rachid*, 16. Other women prisoners were likewise given male names. Widad was known as 'Hamid,' while another woman, Latifa Ajbabdi, was called 'Saïd' or 'Tawil' or 'Doukkali,' and Maria Zouini became Abdel Mounaïm. The women held in Derb Moulay Cherif, along with Fatna, were Widad Bouab, Latifa Ajbabdi, Maria Zouini, Khadija Boukhari, and Bouda Nguia. Later, they would be joined by Fatima Oukacha and Rabia Fetouh.
2 Renaming and in essence 'disappearing' the prisoner also makes it impossible for Fatna's family to know anything about the whereabouts of their daughter.
3 The *hâj* is the trip to Mecca; *el hâj* is the title of the pilgrim who has made that trip. Hence, the torturer's demand to be called by that title represents a kind of twisted irony.
4 Fatna El Bouih affixes to her memoir two powerful first-hand accounts of prison (*Autres Témoignages*) by women, one by Latifa Ajbabdi, and the second by Widad Bouab. Both had originally been published in the Arabic language newspaper, *Al Ittihad al-Ichtiraki*. Later, at the Ghbila prison in Casablanca, Latifa and Fatna shared a cell of about 6 1/2 by 6 feet, so tiny

that the toilet took up two-thirds of the space, which meant that the two women had to sleep huddled together on the floor, their feet in the toilet hole. Ajbabdi, one of Morocco's pioneer feminists, became in 1983 the founder of the feminist journal, *Le 8 Mars*, named for International Women's Day, and of the women's action group, Union de l'Action Féminine in 1987. In 2003 she was asked to be one of the sixteen members of the truth commission, Instance Equité et Reconciliation, established to uncover the truth about 'the years of lead' and to reconcile Morocco with its past.

5 The victim was Khadija Boukhari. Later, Khadija became an educator, as did Fatna, Maria, Widad, and Latifa; Bouda a journalist; Fatima an engineer; Rabia, an executive secretary. In other words, they are all modern and professional women. See Fatema Mernissi's website devoted to Ouvrage des ateliers d'écriture Synergie Civique.

6 See, for instance, Mdidech, *La Chambre noire*. Mdidech was twenty-three when he was arrested because of earlier Marxist-Leninist activities. In 1975, he was held for eight months at Derb Moulay Cherif, then tried along with 178 others at a single trial, and sentenced to twenty-two years in prison. In 1989, after serving fourteen years and four months, he was pardoned by Hassan II.

7 For decades Hassan II denied the existence of Tazmamart, the prison of death that Abraham Serfaty, a Moroccan Jew and one of the country's most famous political prisoners, compares to Auschwitz because of its inhumane conditions and horrendous death toll. Serfaty, himself, was imprisoned in Kenitra for seventeen years of a life sentence that ended in 1991, when he was freed on condition that he live in exile. For eight years, he and his wife, Christine, resided in France, where Serfaty published *Dans Les Prisons du roi*, and *Le Maroc, du gris au noir*. It was through Christine Daure-Serfaty's book, *Tazmamart: Une Prison de la mort au Maroc*, that the world finally learned about the existence of the secret prison. In September 1999, following Hassan II's death, Serfaty was given permission by Mohammed VI to return to Morocco. In 2002, the Serfatys published a joint account of their years of separation, entitled *La Mémoire de l'autre*.

8 Kadiri, 'Entretien: Laâbi, passionnément,' 36–9.

9 The fictionalization of events while they are still very contemporary raises interesting questions. While it can be argued that real events made into fiction have the greatest chance of being kept alive by ever-new generations of readers, others may object that there should be 'a statute of limitations' before fiction writers write about events still fresh and painful to those who lived them. For his part, Russell A. Berman writes that what is great about literature is that it has the ability to survive its initial historical

context and ultimately to surpass it. See his *Fiction Sets You Free*, xiv. Some critics believe that Ben Jelloun's 2004 novel, *Le Dernier Ami*, about the breakdown of a friendship in the latter years of life, is an effort to both re-conceptualize the multiple uncertainties of betrayal, and, indirectly, to address accusations of betrayal made against him.

10 Ben Jelloun himself spent one and a half years in an army disciplinary camp in Morocco from July 1966 to January 1968, along with ninety-four other students suspected of having organized widespread student demonstrations in March 1965. His first published piece, a poem, 'L'Aube des dalles,' written in secret in prison, was published in *Souffles*, the famous journal of culture and intellectual opposition under the editorship of Abdellatif Laâbi. Subsequently, in 1971 Ben Jelloun left Morocco for France when it was decreed that henceforth Arabic was to be the only language of instruction for philosophy, a subject Ben Jelloun had been teaching in French at lycées in Tetouan and Casablanca.

11 Michèle Fitoussi collaborated with Malika Oufkir on *La Prisonnière*. In 2006 Oufkir published *L'Etrangère* (Paris: Grasset & Fasquelle), in which she recounts her life in France since 26 February 1991, when she was freed from prison and fled to Europe.

12 Rabea Bennouna was married to the director of the military school of Ahermoumou, Abdelatif Belkbir, who claimed that his forces were called to Skhirat to protect Hassan II.

13 Hassan II, the son of 'the father of the country,' Mohammed V, came to the throne in March 1961 following his father's premature death, and faced numerous challenges, including political and economic crises and the necessity to outmanoeuvre rival power centres and opposing factions. Less progressive and liberal than his father, according to Pierre Vermeren, *Histoire du Maroc depuis l'indépendance*, 31, Hassan II spent the first two decades of his thirty-eight-year reign (1961–99) struggling to save the monarchy and to solidify the state, often choosing brutal and repressive means to accomplish his ends. Today, Hassan II's reputation is decidedly mixed, with some applauding his real successes in modernizing the nation, and others focusing on the 'disappearances' and lack of human rights that characterized the 'years of lead.' The differing views are represented by John Waterbury's largely positive *The Commander of the Faithful* and Gilles Perrault's negative portrait in *Notre Ami le roi*.

14 See the interview conducted with Fatna El Bouih in the monthly woman's magazine, *Citadine*, in March 2001, pp. 33–6, 'Fatna El Bouih, de l'ombre à la lumière.' El Bouih was also profiled in a series on noteworthy figures in the battle for human rights in Morocco in a 2003 article, 'Mémoire(s) de femme,'

by Laetitia Grotti, in the weekly newsmagazine *Tel Quel*. Despite this coverage, until the 2003–4 truth commission, very few educated Moroccans, including young women, had heard of Fatna El Bouih.
15 In 2001 women prisoners in Morocco constituted about 4 per cent of the total prison population of 58,000. See the special issue of *Tel Quel*, entitled *Telles Quelles*, devoted to a study of 'Femmes du Maroc,' including an essay on 'Les Oubliées du 8 mars,' 30–1.
16 Grotti, 'Mémoire(s) de femme,' 18.
17 Ghazali, 'Sur le gril: Fatna El Bouih, de l'ombre à la lumière,' 34.
18 For further information, see Vermeren, *Histoire du Maroc depuis l'indépendance*, 46, who says that militants claimed that 1500 had been killed in Casablanca, as opposed to the official estimate of 70 dead. Casablanca has always been fertile ground for political opposition and labour unrest, according to John Waterbury, because as a busy port and the country's primary industrial producer, it is home to thousands of unionized workers. Hence, Waterbury says, 'the political climate of the entire country is to no small extent determined by that of Casablanca.' *The Commander of the Faithful*, 156.
19 This is the time of the Ben Barka affair, his threat to the monarchy and probable secret murder in France. Mehdi Ben Barka (1920–65?) was a leading politician in the opposition, who is thought to have been assassinated in France, with the secret cooperation of the French government, and whose remains may or may not have been returned to Morocco. In 2003 and 2004, formerly secret documents were released that, while not providing final answers, point to the complicity of France, Israel, and the United States in the disappearance of Ben Barka. With Ben Barka gone, Hassan II solidified the power of the monarchy. See, for example, *Jeune Afrique / L'Intelligent* 2294–5, du 26 déc. 2004 au 8 janv. 2005, 36–41.
20 Vermeren, *Histoire du Maroc depuis l'indépendance*, 52. For further views on the concept of Makhzen, see Ellyas and Stora, *Les 100 Portes du Maghreb*, 218–20. Waterbury describes the political processes of *mahkzan* in a chapter entitled, 'The Makhzan: A Stable System of Violence,' in *The Commander of the Faithful*, 15–32.
21 The first is known as the attempted coup d'état de Skhirat and took place on 10 July 1971, and the second failed attempt, which ended in the death (probable assassination) of General Oufkir, occurred the following year on 16 August 1972.
22 Of Hassan II, Perrault wrote, 'He reigns as master of each and every person, breaking any hint of opposition through repression, corrupting

[the body politic] by corruption, deceiving by fraud, and bending [the people to his will] by fear.' *Notre Ami le roi*, 356.
23 Slyomovics, Interview with Fatna El Bouih.
24 She told journalist Laetitia Grotti, 'Ecrire est pour moi une invitation à penser autrement la mémoire officielle et la mémoire collective,' 'Mémoire(s) de femme,' 18. Furthermore, 'Si la mémoire des femmes constitue une source inépuisable de récits et de témoignages, sa transmission constitue pourtant un geste subversif qui soulève de nouvelles interrogations sur la place accordée aux femmes dans le discours officiel, dans la réalité.'
25 In order, the titles translated are: 'A Special Visit,' 'The Minaret Has Fallen: Hang the Barber' (a play on the title of a well-known folktale), 'Moments in the Life of a Prisoner,' 'Autumn of a Life without a Spring,' 'The Journal of a Hunger Striker,' 'In Prison is Born a Free Man.' Several of these artfully named chapters will be dealt with in the text. 'En Prison naît un homme libre' concerns the birth of a baby who, because his mother is a prisoner, is, through no crime of his own, sentenced to a jail term. The actual birth occurs in the toilets where the young mother had withdrawn, so as not to be heard moaning in pain. She is a double victim, in El Bouih's view, first of a sexual assault, and then of a sluggish justice system that did not take up the case against her assailant until she was already in her ninth month of pregnancy. Another female victim appears in 'Automne d'une vie sans printemps,' a woman in her sixties who has spent seventeen years in prison, and, on the night before her liberation, is petrified because of her upcoming freedom. In the 'evening of her life' (92), how will she navigate in a world she no longer knows and in which all former ties had been broken? Is her release from prison deliverance or a new sentence to a dead end? Her desperation reveals why El Bouih has devoted her post-prison activities to the plight of female prisoners.
26 Mouride, *On affame bien les rats!* is an illustrated book that shows with full visual horror the kinds of torture to which prisoners at Derb Moulay Cherif were subjected. In an interview in the woman's magazine, *Citadine*, entitled 'Dessiner contre l'oubli,' Mouride describes how he made his designs at night in his cell by candlelight, hiding them in cracks in the wall – 'like a piece of gruyere cheese,' he says – and then secreting the drawings to family or friends in the visitor's parlour. Born in 1949, Abdelaziz Mouride was a founding member of the 23 Mars movement of the extreme left toward the end of the 1960s. He was arrested in 1974 and sentenced to twenty-two years in prison for political activity. He was

released from prison in 1984, after serving ten years. Today he is a journalist in Casablanca.
27 Certain of the strategies developed in prison have remained with El Bouih in real life. Fatima Mernissi, who visited the young woman in prison ('Une Visite exceptionnelle') and later interviewed her in May 2003, recalls her as a beautiful woman with an unsettling gaze. Fatna explains that after Derb Moulay Cherif, where she never saw her jailers, she developed the unblinking gaze, which still characterizes her today, as a mode of resistance and a refusal to be subjugated. For Mernissi's interview published online, see http://www.mernissi.net/civil_society/portraits/fatnaelbouih.
28 This observation about the lack of contextualization could likewise be made about any number of the non-fiction prison memoirs by Moroccan male writers, suggesting a different culture of expectation on the part of both writer and reader.
29 Grotti, 'Mémoire(s) de femme.' The role of sexual humiliation, when not actually sexual sadism, has a long tradition in the torture of prisoners, as Susan Sontag has written in 'Regarding the Torture of Others,' observing that 'rape and pain inflected on the genitals are among the most common form of torture,' whether in Nazi concentration camps or at Abu Ghraib (28), or, as we have seen, in a Moroccan torture centre in the 1970s.
30 Women's experience in prison further differs from men's in that while both dread hearing the same threatening footfalls of guards approaching, the screams of comrades being tortured, followed by their moans or the silence that intimates death (30), women prisoners also hear the retching of pregnant women, the muffled cries of a woman in the throes of childbirth in the toilet staff ('En Prison naît un homme libre,' 73–5), the wails of a child who lives in a cell with its mother who had been charged with having killed two other children and deprives this one of maternal love ('Ilham, cri étouffé de désespoir,' 77–8).
31 Fatna remembers her torturers at Derb Moulay Cherif as 'enraged dogs,' but she feels perhaps even greater bitterness toward the matrons, whom she describes as 'dominatrices' and 'rapacious,' like birds of prey, hiding behind vague orders and meting out arbitrary punishments. They are, she feels, particularly repellent because of their double betrayal, as members of the human race and of the female sex.
32 Schachter, *Searching for Memory*.
33 Latifa Ajbabdi remembers those journeys between prisons as a veritable circus of overreaction on the part of prison officials, who commanded a bevy of armed police to accompany the women's van, escorted by a police car with siren screaming and helicopters overhead. She says she hardly knew

whether to laugh or to be offended as a feminist when some of the policemen complained about all that 'grotesque mobilization' for mere women ('Témoignage de Latifa Ajbabdi,' affixed to *Une Femme nommée Rachid*, 117).
34 El Bouih pays tribute to Mernissi, saying that she teaches not to make disciples, but to produce free human beings. 'This woman whose image in my memory is synonymous with freedom, incites us to dream,' writes the memoirist (56).
35 Berrada's reference is to the massive March 2000 street marches in Rabat and Casablanca whose purpose was to demonstrate in favour (Rabat) and against (Casablanca) the proposed changes to modernize the Moudawana (7). For more on the modernizing the Moudawana, see the opening pages of chapter 8.

6 The Female Body and the Body Politic

1 Fatima Mernissi observes that the last actual harem disappeared in 1909 when young Turks forbad the harem, and the sultan of Turkey was obliged to liberate his slaves. In 1921 Kernal Atatyrk gave Turkish women the right to vote, and five years later the Turkish Civil Code abolished polygamy, granting both husband and wife the right to ask for a divorce and equal rights regarding their children. 'Fantaisies du harem et nouvelles Schéhérazade,' exposition temporaire au Muséum d'Histoire Naturelle, Rhône, du 23 septembre 2003 au 4 janvier 2004, online.
2 Malti-Douglas, *Woman's Body, Woman's World*, 10. Malti-Douglas's approach, however, differs from my own, given her focus on *écriture féminine*. In *Arab Women Novelists,* Joseph T. Zeidan emphasizes how Arab women writers of the first generation of the 1950s often rejected the female body precisely because they felt that typically it had been reduced by men to its sexual parts. As Zeidan observes, women's early female protagonists might cut off their hair or refuse to wear high heels; one even wished to cut off her breasts (140).
3 Mernissi, *Le Harem politique*, has been translated into eight languages. Its English translation by Mary Jo Lakeland is known as *The Veil and the Male Elite*. One can speculate that the fairly substantial change in the title from the French to English was made to emphasize for an American audience the hot-button topics of veil and feminism, and to steer clear of the metaphor of the political harem, since joined with the Prophet, the concept could be considered disrespectful.
4 In an interview with *Tel Quel* in 2003 (13–19 septembre 2003, 34), Mernissi said, 'I quickly understood that to censor something in the Muslim world

is to make publicity for it.' In this respect, she humorously recounts how an Egyptian publisher who had published a translation of *Le Harem politique* without sending her any royalties defended himself by saying that he had, in essence, already paid her by the fact of publishing a book that had been censored. As for that censure, in fact, large numbers of Islamic scholars have taken and continue to take issue with her interpretation of Islam and the Qur'an. In the English edition, Mernissi defends *Le Harem Politique* by acknowledging her considerable debt to Alem Moulay Ahmed al-Khamlichi, who teaches Muslim law at the University Mohammed V in Rabat, and who is both a religious scholar and a specialist on women in Islam. Hearing him expound on 'the initiative of the believer with regard to religious texts,' Mernissi says, convinced her to make such a new interpretation in her book.

5 Among the contemporary women artists from North Africa and the Near East that she names are Jananne Al-Ani, Ghada Amer, Samta Benyahia, Shadi Ghadirian, Susan Hefuna, Malekeh Nayiny, and Nadine Tourna.

6 Amina Wadud came to the task from the standpoint of having first converted to Islam and then becoming a committed feminist, determined that if honest scholarly research revealed that the sexes were not equal in the Qur'an, she would abandon her faith, according to her preface in *Qur'an and Woman*. Bringing to her research deep scholarship and a thorough knowledge of Arabic, she concluded that 'primordially, cosmologically, eschatologically, spiritually, and morally,' woman in the Qur'an is a full human being, sharing full equality with men. One proof is in the Creation story of the Qur'an (4:1). In most Qur'anic versions, woman is created from Adam's rib, as in the Christian Bible. But Wadud offers a completely different reading, working with four key words: *ayah* (pl. *ayat*: 'sign,' that which indicates something beyond itself); *min* ('from,' either extracted from or drawn out; from or of the same nature); *nafs* (self, soul, person, cell); and *zawj* (mate, spouse, one part of a pair). Her translation reads: 'And *min* His *ayat* (is this:) that He created You (humankind) *min* a single *nafs*, and created *min* (that *nafs*) its *zawj*, and from these two He spread (through the earth) countless men and women' (*Qur'an and Woman*, 17). As a basis of comparison, N.J. Dawood's translation reads: 'Have fear of your Lord, who created you from a single soul. From that soul He created its spouse and through them He bestrewed the earth with countless men and women' (*The Koran, with Parallel Arabic Text*). But in Wadud's translation, man is not created first; nor was woman created from man and after him. When the key word, '*nafs*,' is translated as 'cell,' a whole different ungendered significance emerges.

7 See also Mattson, *The Story of the Quran*. Another, Laleh Bakhtiar, is the first American woman to translate the Qur'an from Arabic into English.
8 The English translation of 33.53 that Mernissi uses is that of Marmaduke Pickthall, *The Meaning of the Glorious Koran* (New York: Dorset Press, n.d.), 305, which reads, 'O ye who believe! Enter not the dwellings of the Prophet for a meal without waiting for the proper time, unless permission be granted you. But if ye are invited, enter, and, when your meal is ended, then disperse. Linger not for conversation. Lo! That would cause annoyance to the Prophet, and he would be shy of (asking) you (to go); but Allah is not shy of the truth. And when ye ask of them (the wives of the Prophet) anything, ask it of them from behind a curtain. That is purer for your hearts and for their hearts' (Mernissi, *The Veil and the Male Elite*, 85).
9 Majid, *Unveiling Traditions*, 106. See also pp. 107–9 for Majid's continued critique of Mernissi.
10 Huff-Rousselle, 'Fatema Mernissi.'
11 Mernissi, 'Au sein du harem, c'[est] la révolte permanente,' she is quoted as saying in *Tel Quel*, 13–19 septembre 2003, 32.
12 For instance, in the last story, 'Saadia,' the title character is a maid who marries outside her class, and when the inevitable happens and the husband becomes disinterested in her, the story's narrator makes an interesting sex-class comparison to explain why the forsaken wife is about to undertake an adulterous affair: 'She still felt capable of seducing men. But her husband no longer slept with her, which meant she was still a domestic. And a domestic is not the same thing as a woman' (135).
13 Similar themes are taken up in Benchemsi's 2006 novel, *La Controverse des temps*, in which her female protagonist, Houda, returns to Morocco after completing a doctoral dissertation on Hegel in Paris, and meets Ilyas, a Soufi master. Though they are mutually attracted, everything from spiritual commitment to laicized emancipation separates them, making their love virtually impossible.
14 On the other hand, it should be pointed out that Mernissi joins with Benchemsi's criticism of a certain kind of feminism when, in chapter 14, 'Les Féministes égyptiennes visitent la terrasse,' of *Rêves de femmes*, she has the Fez women lament that 'the lives of the feminists did not include enough singing and dancing' (169). While they applauded the independence of the *radiates* – early twentieth-century feminists, such as the Egyptians Aisha Taymour and Huda Sha'raoui, and the Lebanese Zaynab Fawwaz – the women on the terrace in Fez felt there was something missing in a feminism that spoke only of 'struggles and unhappy marriages, and never of happiness, or of magnificent nights of pleasure, and of lovers transported by

passion.' This brought young Fatima to conclude, 'If I were one day to engage in the struggle for the liberation of women, I certainly would not forget about the pleasures of being alive.' And Aunt Habiba adds, 'A feminist revolution must plunge both men and women in a hammam of tenderness' (169).

15 For a brief reading of this film and how Boughédir thwarts conventional impulses in depicting the hammam, see Brahimi, *Cinémas d'Afrique francophone et du Maghreb*, 103–6.
16 Segarra, *Leur Pesant de poudre*, 124.
17 Malti-Douglas, *Woman's Body, Woman's World*, 129.
18 See Mehta, *Rituals of Memory in Contemporary Arab Women's Writing*, esp. 121–4, for a discussion of the deep spiritual and cultural significance of water in Arab-Islamic religion and society.
19 Naamane-Guessous, *Au-delà de la pudeur*, 213.
20 Segarra, *Leur Pesant de poudre*, 76–7.
21 Chebel, *Le Corps dans la tradition au Maghreb*, 23.
22 Naamane-Guessous discusses both the beauty rites and routines and the visits to the hammam that mark various stages in a woman's life, 213–19. Also, see Mehta, *Rituals of Memory in Contemporary Arab Women's Writing*, 'Hammams and the Culture of Beauty,' 141–51.
23 For more on the olfactory essences of Moroccan culture, and the amalgamation of spices and culture-specific beauty products, see Sijelmassi, 'Arômes,' in *La Civilisation marocaine, arts et culture*, ed. Sijelmassi et al., 292–301, including material on the hammam.
24 Glaiman et al., 'Interview de Rajae Benchemsi.'
25 Grotti and Daïf, 'Hchouma,' 28.
26 It would be interesting comparative work for feminist scholars to study whether women writers from other North African and Middle Eastern cultures have similarly revalorized the harem and positively encoded the hammam, as Moroccan women writers have done.
27 Canto, 'The Politics of Women's Bodies,' 339–40.

7 Women and the City

1 In the last two decades, the number of studies on women and the city has grown significantly, in tandem, it appears, with a broad swath of disciplines that have actively developed research into issues of space. Doreen Massey in *For Space* (London: Sage Publications, 2005) argues that both the social sciences and the humanities have taken 'a spatial turn,' and Edward Soja agrees, saying in *Postmodern Geographies* (London: Verso, 1989) that as

early as 1980, Foucault had objected to conventional thinking about the time-space dichotomy in which Space was treated as 'dead,' 'fixed,' 'undialectical,' 'immobile,' while Time was considered 'richness, fecundity, life, dialectic.' For a useful critical review of the literature of gender and space, see McDowell, *Gender, Identity, and Place*. In terms of specific studies on women and the city, Janet Levarie Smarr, *Italian Women and the City: Essays* (Teaneck, NJ: Fairleigh Dickinson University Press, 2003), cites Katherina Von Ankum, ed., *Women in the Metropolis: Gender and Modernity in Weimar Culture* (Berkeley: University of California Press, 1997); Deborah Epstein Nord, *Walking the Victorian Streets: Women, Representations, and the City* (Ithaca: Cornell University Press, 1995); and Alison Blunt and Gillian Rose, eds, *Writing Women and Space: Colonial and Postcolonial Geographies* (New York: Guilford Press, 1994).
2 Ward, 'Espaces symboliques de femmes.'
3 Fatima Zahid studies women's spatial networks in rural areas in Morocco and reports that such networks are considerably broader and richer than normally thought, since an individual women's personal and social contacts encompass her nuclear family, the extended family, the small holding, the *souk, douar*, and the tribe, 'Relations et gestion de l'espace par les femmes rurales au Maroc.' This article and several others in *Women's Spaces* usefully remind us not to generalize about 'Arab women,' let alone Moroccan women.
4 Smarr, introduction to *Italian Women and the City*, 11.
5 Çinar and Bender, *Urban Imaginaries*, xi–xii. Kevin Lynch, *The Image of the City* (Cambridge, MA: MIT Press, 1960).
6 For the growth of urban Morocco, see Troin, *Maroc: Régions, pays, territoires*, 'L'Urbanisation au Maroc,' 102–3. Today more than half the population lives in one of the 220 urban areas, of which there are 24 cities of more than 100,000 inhabitants, 19 with a population of between 50,000 to 100,000, 38 cities whose population ranges from 20,000 to 50,000, and 139 towns claiming between 5,000 and 20,000 inhabitants. In the twentieth century, the number of cities increased eightfold: in 1900, there were 27 cities, whereas in 1960 there were 100, and by 2000, the figure reached 220. Greater Casablanca is the largest area with a population of 3,300,000; Greater Rabat includes a population of 1,600,000; Fez has 940,000; Marrakech, 800,000; Greater Agadir, 700,000; Greater Tangier, 625,000.
7 Mehrez, 'The Subversive Poetics of Radical Bilingualism,' 258.
8 Amahan-Cambazard and Métalsi, 'La Maison traditionnelle,' 171.
9 This is not to imply, however, that the woman may not see the city through the lens of paradox, as, for instance, when Benchekroun's Nadia says,

'Casablanca, ma cité chérie et abhorrée, le coeur immense et tiraillé du Maroc, sa seule vraie ville miroir, exhibant dans un même corps pustules et grains de beauté, la misère puante et le lustre insolent, les rancoeurs du passé et les fantasmes de l'avenir' (*Oser vivre*, 163). Clearly, for her, the city in its extremes carries a double potential for good and for ill.
10 Florida, *Cities and the Creative Class*, 1. Although Florida is talking about the role of great cities as incubators of creative ideas in terms of science and engineering, research and development, and the arts and aesthetic design, and knowledge-based professions (health-care, finance, and law), his general comments are equally applicable to the large cities in developing countries.
11 As proof of these more dynamic borders, today the Moroccan city offers the middle-class woman a variety of changing socio-economic possibilities. She may even find that gender relationships in the contemporary urban world are neither as patriarchal nor male-dominated as they formerly had been. Given both the number of divorced women and the high rates of male unemployment, we are told, women often emerge as the real breadwinners in urban milieus. See, for instance, Clare, 'Sisters and Brothers.'
12 Momsen and Kinnaird, *Different Places, Different Voices*, 4.
13 McDowell, *Gender, Identity, and Place*, 228.
14 Mdarhri Alaoui, 'Approche du roman féminin au Maroc,' 20.
15 Laâbi, *Le Fond de la jarre*. Author presentation at Kalila wa Dimna bookstore in Rabat, 7 January 2003.
16 Mernissi, *Scheherazade Goes West*, 211.
17 In *The Politics of Design in French Colonial Urbanism*, Gwendolyn Wright explores the ways in which French colonial architecture in Morocco, Indochina, and Madagascar sought to accept and encourage cultural difference, while simultaneously promoting modern urban improvements intended to foster economic development for Western investors. She argues that by asserting modernist and universalist cultural aspirations – often considered 'red flags' of imperialist intentions – in fact, colonialist policy resulted not only in destabilizing traditional forms, but ultimately and ironically, in subverting the goals of European imperial domination by causing the indigenous population to rebel against the invader.
18 The knowledge that locals – both men and women – have of the labyrinthine passageways of the medina serves them well during the struggle for independence. In her documentary film 'Still Ready: Three Women from the Moroccan Resistance' (1998), Alison Baker talks with Moroccan female independence fighters who had moved freely in the medina, carrying arms in their market baskets or under their robes to pass to males. While the participation of Algerian women, immortalized in Gillo Portecorvo's 1966

film, 'Battle for Algiers,' is well known, the role of the 300 Moroccan women resistance fighters among the full 300,000 men thought to have participated in the independence movement, is less recognized. Mernissi's purpose, however, is not to trace that story, but to present a charming tale, and by means of its very charm, to uncover the similarities between gendered and colonial space.

It is generally thought that the construction of these new cities, or 'les villes européennes,' was done so that Europeans could separate themselves from the 'foreignness' of the indigenous population. Not all urban historians, however, share that view. Some, in fact, credit General Lyautey with the desire to preserve intact the indigenous character of existing cities, most notably the medina, arguing that his objective was not to destroy local culture and traditions, but to find a way for both the traditional and the modern European to exist side by side. In Lyautey's *Paroles d'action*, he had written, '… notre conception initiale [était de] toucher le moins possible aux villes indigènes,' quoted in Mazières, 'Héritage colonial en urbanisme et en architecture' (180).

19 Today, Agadir is a regional capital and a city of 200,000, a tourist mecca for Europeans because of the sea and sand, variously known as 'the Nice of Morocco' or 'the Las Vegas of the South.' It is, of course, short of the 'real' south, that great expanse of barren and rocky desert, leading down to the contested area of Western Sahara.
20 Displacement is a theme related to the larger notion of travel that feminist geographers analyse for the theoretical, psychological, and political implications. See especially Kaplan, *Questions of Travel*, 144.
21 Some of these same questions are taken up in Oulehri's second work of long fiction, *La Chambre des nuits blanches* (2002), a rather more mannered novel, with a heroine who leaves her husband and children for a vacation on her own, 'to find herself.' Showing Oulehri's erudition and her attraction to European literature, this novel offers a heroine whose search for herself, given the social context of Moroccan society, seems as unlikely as the novel, which, while very rich in multiple discourses, is ultimately unsuccessful.
22 Tangier, from *Tanjah* in Arabic and *Tanger* in French, is often incorrectly referred to in English as Tangiers. Located on the northern coast of Morocco, across the Strait of Gibraltar to Europe and hence an important point of embarkation for travellers between the two continents, it is today a city of roughly one half million.
23 As Smarr observes, there is a long tradition of representation that associates the city with a woman, reflected in many European languages through

gender – in French, *la ville, la cité, la femme* – and in allegorical and political painting when a ruler is crowned or blessed by the female city he administers. Introduction to *Italian Women and the City*, 10. Further, the city is often portrayed as the enclosing maternal space of protection and familiarity, although of course it can also become like a stifling womb that destroys rather than giving birth (15).

24 Jacques Majorelle (1886–1962) is the French-born painter who created the Majorelle Gardens in Marrakech over a forty-year period and after whom is named the vivid cobalt hue known as 'Bleu Majorelle.' Kees Van Dongen (1877–1968) was a Dutch-born French artist, one of the precursors of Fauvism, who visited Morocco in 1910, where he painted one of his best-known works entitled *Moroccan Women at Cap Spartel*, showing two figures of women in white haïks against a background of rectilinear Moorish structures in pink, white, and gold, by the sea. Another twentieth-century painter whose name is associated with Morocco is Henri Matisse (1869–1954), who in 1912 painted a work known as *View of the Bay of Tangier*. American writer Paul Bowles (1910–99) lived in Tangier from 1947 until his death and attracted to his circle many other writers, including Tennessee Williams (1911–83) as well as French playwright Jean Genet (1910–86), whom he befriended. Paul Morand (1888–1976) is a French writer and traveller who left behind sceptical and vivid depictions of the modern world.

25 Benchemsi, *Marrakech, lumière d'exil*, 13. Moroccan writer Khireddine Mourad makes a similar observation, saying that Marrakech, founded by nomads, carries inscribed on its walls and in its monuments 'the indelible marks of human passage.' See Gaasch, *Anthologie de la nouvelle maghrébine*, interview with Mourad, 139–43.

26 McDowell, *Gender, Identity, and Place*, 227.

27 Saddiki, 'Place Jamaâ al-Fna.' An article by Marlise Simons in *Jeune Afrique*, n. 2357, du 12 au 18 mars 2006, 'Le Dernier Conteur,' suggests that before long the storytellers, who have been present on the square since the construction of the city in the Middle Ages, will likely disappear. Today they are only eight in number, including seventy-one-year-old Mohamed Jabiri, who can scarcely read and write, and who learned his trade by listening (61).

28 McDowell, *Gender, Identity, and Place*, 203. She cites, in particular, studies by James Clifford, *Routes: Travel and Translation in the Late Twentieth Century*, (Cambridge: Harvard University Press, 1997) and Kaplan, *Questions of Travel*.

29 Daoud, *Casablanca en mouvement*.

30 Interview in Gaasch, *Anthologie de la nouvelle maghrébine*, 208.
31 This is how McDowell describes how metaphors of travel, movement, and boundaries are used by feminist geographers in *Gender, Identity, and Place*, 215.
32 Safi-Eddine, 'Crossing Boundaries,' 96.
33 Mernissi, *Islam and Democracy*, 156.

8 Scheherazade's (Moroccan) Sisters

1 Khalid Jamäi, 'Et s'il n'y avait pas un problème de femme mais un problème d'homme marocain,' 6.
2 In the early months after the Moudawana was revised, the changes continued to be lauded as a great advance for Moroccan women, but within a short time their sometimes lax enforcement led to expressions of disappointment concerning numerous loopholes and the discretionary power of judges in the family courts who too often interpreted articles of law in favour of men. See, for instance, Grotti, 'La Moudawana à l'épreuve du terrain.'
3 Browers, *Democracy and Civil Society in Arab Political Thought*, 4.
4 Baker, *Voices of Resistance*, 273.
5 Guessous, 'Le Maroc ne sera jamais un Etat laïc.'
6 For the complete history of feminist activity in Morocco, see Daoud, *Féminisme et politique au Maghreb*. A French journalist, married to a Moroccan, Zakya (from her first name, Jacqueline, or Jackie) arrived in Rabat in 1958 and became a Moroccan citizen the following year. She recounts how, as early as 1962, female workers throughout Morocco met in Casablanca to create the Union Progressiste des Femmes Marocaines, which called for women's rights, democracy, justice, fair division of wealth, and changes to the Moudawana. Daoud describes the importance of the periodical, *Lamalif*, founded in 1965 and continuing to publish until 1988; and the short-lived but important, *Le 8 Mars*, begun by Latifa Ajbabdi in 1985 to create a new feminine consciousness, and later to reappear in 1990, continuing its demands that the Moudawana be changed. Both journals owed their existence to disappointments associated with Independence, when it appeared that the democratic agenda would not be realized. Following the protest strikes and riots in Casablanca in March 1965, brought about principally by economic stagnation (see Waterbury, *The Commander of the Faithful*, 299–315) and the clampdown by the regime, plus the politically unsettled years of the 1970s, the women's movement was silenced largely until the mid-1980s with the birth of numerous women's associations and NGOs. The story that Daoud tells is remarkable in that it

reveals how early in the nation's history clear-sighted women were calling for justice and equality of women, and how their voices did not bring about the desired end until early in the twenty-first century.

7 In preparing a new preface to the 1998 edition, Mernissi says that she consciously decided against updating the text of her book, precisely because she wanted to give proof of how far and how fast Morocco had come. Of course, it could also be argued that, as with *Scheherazade Goes West* (2001), her real target was to skewer those in the West who seemed to enjoy keeping Morocco imprisoned in a time warp in order to prove their own cultural and intellectual superiority.

8 El Khayat, *Le Maghreb des femmes*, 11.

9 I was in Morocco at the time on a semester-long research grant and was able to observe this phenomenon first-hand in the media and in discussions with local people.

10 Michaelle Browers is only the latest scholar of Middle Eastern studies to observe that Islam is not the key variable as to why democracy has not taken hold in Muslim Arab countries. See *Democracy and Civil Society in Arab Political Thought*, 190.

The question of the compatibility of Islam and democracy has given rise to arguments on both sides of the issue. Mernissi suggested that because the word for democracy – *Dimuqdratiyya* from Greek – is of foreign origin, some people have assumed that the concept is foreign to Arab understanding. In reply, she says that since other words of similar foreign origin, like those for telephone, electricity, and automobile, pose no such problem, the same should be true for 'democracy.' It is only when Islam loses touch with the real essence of its origins, she argues, that it becomes anti-democratic (*Islam and Democracy*, 51–4).

Taking the contrarian's side, an Iranian, Mohsen Rezvani, stipulates that Islam is 'anthropologically, theologically, and epistemologically incompatible with democracy' (quoted by Ash, 'Soldiers of the Hidden Imam,' 6). This is so, he says, because liberal democracy, based on reason and not faith, requires liberal individualism, and the exclusion of God from the public sphere.

For French scholar and a leading expert on Islam, Olivier Roy, the very framing of the argument in terms of Islam versus democracy is highly problematic ('Islam et démocratie'). In his view, the words 'Islam' and 'Arab' are too frequently made synonymous, whereas in fact the Arab world is only a small part of the entire Islamic world. Three fourths of the world's Muslim population lives outside the Middle East, in countries such as Bangladesh, Turkey, and Indonesia, which are arguably more democratic than their non-Muslim neighbours, writes Pakaj Mishra in 'The Misunderstood Muslims.' For Roy, the real stickler is not religion, but the governments of Arab countries, which, with the exception of the monarchies, he says, are modelled on the European dictatorships of the 1920s, like Mussolini's Italy. Roy concludes that while there is a lack of democracy in Arab countries, the problem lies in political sociology rather than in Islam. Mishra agrees, referencing other contemporary Muslim thinkers like Tarik Ramadan, Reza Aslan, and Anouar Majid, who believe that ideals of social justice, public service, and equality, often identified in modern times as Western, are equally found in the Qur'an and the traditions or Hadiths of the Prophet.

Aslan, for instance, in *No god but God*, argues that democracy can be built in Muslim states based on Islamic traditions and values, including respect for other religions, egalitarian laws, and pluralism. He says that if Judaeo-Christian values lie at the base of Western nations, and if religion can be the basis of their constitution, laws, and customs, even as church and state are kept apart, then an Islamic democracy could be founded upon an Islamic moral framework, while the state would not have to be ruled by clerics. Moreover, he believes, Islam, with its emphasis on the good of the community would seem to offer ideal conditions for a communitarian form of democracy. It is precisely this latter point that I see functioning in Moroccan women's writing.

11 Aboubakr Jamaï, 'Morocco's Choice.'
12 Browers, *Democracy and Civil Society in Arab Political Thought*, 19.
13 Norris and Norris, *Rising Tide*.
14 In demonstration of how fast the rhetoric can change, however, a recent Gallup global survey, 'The State of Global Well-Being 2007,' released in the fall of 2007, revealed that Muslim men believe that Muslim women should have more civil rights (Greve, 'Firm Surveys Worldwide Well-Being').
15 Glaiman et al., 'Interview de Rajae Benchemsi.' Abraham Serfaty is quoted as saying, 'Logically, ever since the Constitution of 1996, we've been in a period of transition. We're not living in a democracy, but under an enlightened despotism.' See Boukhari, 'Les Epoux Serfaty font part de leur mémoire,' 19.
16 Abouzeid, *Year of the Elephant*, was first published in Morocco as a novella in 1987, three years after having appeared in serial form in the newspaper *Al Mithaq*. I am using the 1989 edition published by the Center for Middle Eastern Studies at The University of Texas. *The Last Chapter* was published by The American University in Cairo Press in 2000, with the first paperback edition in 2003. The original was first published in Arabic in 2000 as *al-Fasl al-akhir*. It has appeared in French as *Le Dernier Episode*.

17 See, for instance, Moya and Hames-Garcia, *Reclaiming Identity*.
18 Quoting Paula M.L. Moya, in McLemee, 'Think Postpositive, A14.
19 Mernissi, *Scheherazade Goes West*, 46–9.
20 In a 2003 interview, Tahar Ben Jelloun made a related observation about a significant change in Moroccan society, saying, 'Today we are witnessing the difficult emergence of the individual ... together with the recognition of that individual as a person rather than a mere member of the clan.' Such a heightened sense of one's own individuality and subjectivity, Ben Jelloun asserts, is related to the increase of breakups within the couple. Interview with Ben Jelloun by Yasmine Belmahi, 'La Distance, pour mieux voir,' *Citadine*, juillet–août 2003, 8–11. As for woman's other traditional role, motherhood, it is interesting that Moroccan women writers do not adopt the position of 'maternal feminism,' such as it has been advanced by Egyptian political scientist, Heba Raouf Ezzat (see Browers, *Democracy and Civil Society in Arab Political Thought*, 197–202), and may even, like Abouzeid and Benchekroun, consider that the bourgeois family in its traditional configuration promotes society's conservative agenda for women and hence has a negative impact on the individual woman.
21 Malti-Douglas, in *Woman's Body, Woman's World*, 172, observes that the use of the prison to depict the Arab woman's existence is familiar imagery, and that often the family, as well, is portrayed in fiction as a prison from which the female character wishes to flee.
22 Mernissi in chapter 10, 'Women's Song: Destination Freedom,' in *Islam and Democracy*, 151, gives an early example of the bird as symbol of female flight, drawing on Muhammad al-Fasi, *Chants anciens des femmes de Fès* (pirated edition published in Morocco, n.d.), page 38, quatrain 43: 'Birdie! Birdie! / To keep it I built a cage of silk / And never thought it would fly away / After letting itself be tamed.' It is also reminiscent of 'The Tale of the Lady with the Feather Dress,' Grandmother Yasmina's favourite tale from *The Thousand and One Nights*, actually called 'The Tale of Hassan al Basri,' which Mernissi uses to open *Scheherazade Goes West*, 1–10. The tale concerns the man's sighting on a beach of a graceful bird that to his amazement steps out of its feather dress, revealing a beautiful naked woman who runs into the waves to swim. Enamoured, he steals her feather dress and hides it, and subsequently she becomes his treasured captive. But in Yasmina's delightfully subversive feminist distortion, the woman never stops looking for her dress, until one day she finds it and flies away to freedom with her children.
23 El Khayat, *Le Livre des prénoms du monde arabe*, 91.
24 Gutmann, *Identity in Democracy*, 195.

25 Quoted in Browers, *Democracy and Civil Society in Arab Political Thought*, 2.
26 This idea of individual freedom within the group is also very much a part of the philosophy of Mernissi, who defines freedom as related to the collective and not to individualism (Grotti and Ksikes, 'Interview-vérité, Fatéma Mernissi,' 35). Such is precisely the spirit of her annual Caravane Civique, in which she brings together European NGO activists and funding organizations with Moroccan villagers or other groups with identified needs.
27 Bellefqih, 'L'Ecriture féminine au Maroc.'
28 Bellefqih, *Yasmina et le talisman*. See also 'Point de vue d'une écrivaine,' 13.
29 Kadiri, 'Entretien: Laâbi, passionnément,' 37. Laâbi describes the act of writing as an extraordinary act of resistance against despair and inaction, even while acknowledging that the writer alone will not be able to change very much. ('Ce qui est miraculeux c'est que l'écriture est un exorcisme qui permet de mieux maîtriser intellectuellement ce qui se passe aujourd'hui et d'attester qu'on peut rester profondément humain et continuer le combat pour un monde meilleur et une humanité plus fraternelle.')
30 See the afterword to *The Last Chapter*, 160–1.
31 According to the description in the *Cairo Times*, cited on the back cover of the paperback edition of *The Last Chapter*, Aisha is 'an intellectual with the tongue of a Moroccan Dorothy Parker.'
32 For instance, in decrying the embrace of sorcery and charms by certain elements of the population, she quotes the Qur'an, saying, 'Whoso traffics in magic, has no portion in the Hereafter' (61). Or in derogating an incompetent male boss, she declares, 'Our Prophet was right: "When responsibility is entrusted to those who cannot bear it, expect the apocalypse"' (74).
33 This was the case with Abouzeid's own mother as she recounts in the first chapter of her autobiographical, *Return to Childhood*.
34 This characterization of her writing comes from the critical reaction in Morocco to her book. Abouzeid writes this in the afterword, *The Last Chapter*, 156.
35 Ostensibly, it is because she is too 'traditional' that her husband divorces her. In any event, this is how she tries to explain the divorce to the *faqih*: 'I don't eat with a fork. I don't speak French. I don't sit with men. I don't go out to fancy dinners' (8). But the argument is shorthand for something else – she, Zahra, has remained true, while the husband has been false, betraying her much in the same way that the goals of national liberation have been betrayed.

36 Aslan, *No god but God*, 53, argues that for all Muslims, regardless of their politics, Medina is the ideal, 'what Islam was meant to be.' For feminists, that would be the city in which the Prophet Mohamed instituted legal reforms to their benefit.

37 Mortimer, introduction to *Maghrebian Mosaic*, 6.

38 It is also the position taken by Memmi, *Portrait du décolonisé arabe musulman et de quelques autres* (2004), published in English translation in 2006 as *Decolonization and the Decolonized*. In a substantial departure from the sympathies of his highly influential and groundbreaking work, *The Colonizer and the Colonist* (1957), Memmi, the secular humanist, argues that decolonization has been largely disastrous, resulting in more violence and the continued oppression of women. Furthermore, Arab-Muslim society, he says, 'suffers from a serious depressive syndrome that prevents it from seeing any way out of the current situation' (65). Hence, he writes, a depressed, resentful North Africa continues to blame French colonialism, adopting the attitude of 'dolorism,' a tendency to exaggerate one's pain, as a kind of modus vivendi.

39 The question of national identity is much on the mind of Abouzeid, as she takes the pulse of the nation. In view of Morocco's geographical situation, with a double maritime exposure of more than 1000 kilometers on both the Mediterranean Sea and the Atlantic Ocean, the country has historically been open to invaders by the sea – Berbers, Carthaginians, Romans, Vandals, and Byzantine Greek, all before Islam was installed in the kingdom in 788. (For a brief exposé of early Moroccan history, see the opening pages of Lugan, *Histoire du Maroc, des origines à nos jours*.) Moreover, because Morocco is a mere fifteen kilometres across the Strait of Gibraltar from Spain, it has been the natural crossroads between Sub-Sahara Africa and Europe. As a result, the country has had a complex relationship with outsiders, including colonialists, who left their imprint, sometimes even linguistically, as witnessed by the influence of both French and Spanish on Moroccan Arabic. While this many-layered mixture makes for a rich legacy, it has led Moroccans themselves sometimes to ask, 'Just who are Moroccans, anyway?'

40 Barnett, *Culture and Democracy*. Barnett suggests that democracy is a boundary concept in which one can study the formation of the spaces of autonomy, sociability, and decision making through which democracy as a politics is made and unmade. His interest is in analysing the theory and practice of what he calls the cultural geography of democracy in terms of patterns of mediation rather than the media per se. I am suggesting that women's fiction may be studied both for such patterns and as the literal medium.

41 Roger Celestin, 'Interview with Tahar Ben Jelloun,' *Sites* 3.2 (fall 1999), online.
42 In respect to the two female characters representing two faces of the same person, readers of Tahar Ben Jelloun's *L'Enfant de sable* and *La Nuit sacrée* will be reminded of his character, Ahmed-Zahra, together with themes of repression of the female voice and subsequent liberation.
43 In French, the title is *Le Dernier Episode*, which carries the ambiguity I am suggesting.
44 'Afterword,' *The Last Chapter*, 161.
45 Wehrs, *Islam, Ethics, Revolt*. In essays on Camara Laye, Cheikh Hamidou Kane, Mariama Bâ, Assia Djebar, Rachid Boudjedra, and Yambo Ouologuem, Wehrs probes 'the cultural, psychological, social and religious stakes involved in fashioning patterns of modern Islamic selfhood that neither reflect Western modernity uncritically nor repudiate it by lapsing into self-isolating traditionalism or some rejuvenated, radical Islam that equates piety with political and intellectual terrorism' (1).
46 Damrosch, 'Secular Criticism Meets the World,' the first Edward W. Said Memorial Lecture, at the American University in Cairo. Damrosch declares that Said's essay, 'Secular Criticism,' initially published as the introduction to *The World, the Text, and the Critic* in 1983, and in which 'secular' really means 'worldly,' is Said's manifesto for the social role of literature and the crucial role of the critical intellectual in assessing literature and society alike.

Conclusion

1 Berman, 'Why Literature Matters,' in *Fiction Sets You Free: Literature, Liberty and Western Culture*, xx. Berman is writing out of a passionate concern for what he sees as the growing crisis in the humanities and the dwindling importance given to literature in the broader academy in the United States – hence, the word 'Western' in the book's title. But I find that much of what he says is applicable to the importance of writing and the literary imagination throughout the world, even in the non-Western world and for undeveloped societies.

Bibliography

Abouzeid, Leila. *The Director and Other Stories from Morocco.* Introduction by Elizabeth Warnock Fernea. Austin: Center for Middle Eastern Studies at the University of Texas, 2005.
– *The Last Chapter.* Trans. by Leila Abouzeid and John Liechety. Cairo and New York: The American University in Cairo Press, 2000.
– *Return to Childhood: The Memoir of a Modern Moroccan Woman.* Trans. from the Arabic, *Ruju 'Ila Tufula* (1993), by the author, with Heather Logan Taylor. Austin: Center for Middle Eastern Studies at the University of Texas, 1989.
– *Year of the Elephant: A Moroccan Woman's Journey toward Independence, and Other Stories.* Trans. by Barbara Parmenter. Introduction by Elizabeth Fernea. Austin: Center for Middle Eastern Studies at the University of Texas, 1989.
Ahmed, Leila. *Women and Gender in Islam: Historical Roots of a Modern Debate.* New Haven: Yale University Press, 1992.
Ait Sabbah, Fatna, pseud. *La Femme dans l'inconscient musulman.* New ed. Paris: Albin Michel, 1986.
Ajbabdi, Laṭifa. 'Témoignage.' In *Une Femme nommée Rachid*, by El Bouih, 102–17.
Alloula, Malek. *The Colonial Harem.* Trans. by Myrna Godzich and Wlad Godzich. Introduction by Barbara Harlow. Minneapolis: University of Minnesota Press, 1986.
Amahan-Cambazard, Catherine, and Mohamed Métalsi. 'La Maison traditionnelle.' In *Civilisation marocaine, arts et culture*, ed. Mohamed Sijelmassi et al., 168–73. Casablanca: Oum, 1996.
Amine, Khalid. *Moroccan Theater: Between East and West.* Tetouan: Faculté des Lettres et des Sciences Humaines, Le Club du Livre, 2000.

Ash, Timothy Garton. 'Soldiers of the Hidden Imam.' *New York Review of Books*, 3 November 2005.
Aslan, Reza. *No god but God: The Origins, Evolution, and Future of Islam.* New York: Random House, 2005.
Bacholle, Michèle. Review of *Cérémonie*. *French Review* 75.1 (2001), 185.
Badran, Margot, and Myriam Cooke. *Opening the Gates: An Anthology of Arab-Feminist Writing.* 2nd ed. Bloomington and Indianapolis: Indiana University Press, 2004.
Bahéchar, Souad. *Ni Fleurs ni couronnes*. Casablanca: Le Fennec, 2000.
Baker, Alison. 'Still Ready: Three Women from the Moroccan Resistance.' Film, 1998.
– *Voices of Resistance: Oral Histories of Moroccan Women.* Albany: State University Press of New York, 1998.
Barlas, Asma. *'Believing Women' in Islam: Unreading Patriarchal Interpretations of the Qur'an.* Austin: University of Texas Press, 2002.
Barnett, Clive. *Culture and Democracy: Media, Space, and Representation.* Tuscaloosa: University of Alabama Press, 2003.
Barrada, Hamid. 'Les Vertus de la transparence.' *Jeune Afrique*, n. 2436, du 16 au 22 septembre 2007, 56–9.
Barrière, Loïc, ed. *Des Nouvelles du Maroc*. Paris: Méditerranée, and Casablanca: Eddif, 1999.
Beaumont, Daniel. *Slave of Desire: Sex, Love, and Death in 'The 1001 Nights.'* Madison, NJ: Fairleigh Dickinson University Press, and London: Associated UniversityPresses, 2002.
Belarbi, Aïcha, et al., eds. *Femmes et Islam*. Casablanca: Le Fennec, 1997.
Bellefqih, Anissa. 'L'Ecriture féminine au Maroc.' *Le Matin*, 14 mars 2003, 5.
– 'Point de vue d'une écrivaine: motivation, problématique, vision, interrogations, perspectives.' In *Ecritures féminines au Maroc: Etudes et bibliographie*, ed. Abdallah Mdarhri Alaoui et al., 10–15. Rabat: Coordination des Chercheurs sur les littératures maghrébines et comparées, 2001.
– *Yasmina et le talisman*. Paris: L'Harmattan, 1999.
Benchekroun, Siham. *Les Jours d'ici*. Casablanca: Empreintes, 2003.
– *Oser vivre*. 3rd ed. Casablanca: Eddif, 2002.
– *A Toi* (poems). Casablanca: Empreintes, 2000.
Benchemsi, Rajae. *La Controverse des temps*. Paris: Sabine Wespieser, 2006.
– *Fracture du désir*. Arles: Actes Sud, 1999.
– *Marrakech, lumière d'exil*. Paris: Sabine Wespieser, 2002.
– *Paroles de nuit* (poems). Rabat: Marsam, 1997.
Benguigui, Yasmina. 'The Perfumed Garden.' Film, 2000.
Ben Jelloun, Tahar. *Cette Aveuglante Absence de lumière*. Paris: Seuil, 2001.
– 'Déchirures marocaines.' *Le Monde*, Littératures, 4 juin 1999.

- *Le Dernier Ami*. Paris: Seuil, 2004.
- *L'Enfant de sable*. Paris: Seuil, 1985.
- *L'Islam expliqué aux enfants*. Paris: Seuil, 2002.
- *La Nuit sacrée*. Paris: Seuil, 1987.
- *Les Yeux baissés*. Paris: Seuil, 1991.

Benlyazid, Farida. 'Une Porte au ciel' (A Door on the Sky). Film, 1988.
- 'Keid Ensa' (Women's Wiles, Ruses de femmes). Film, 1996.

Bennouna, Mehdi. *Héros sans gloire: échec d'une révolution, 1963–1973*. Paris: Méditerranée, and Casablanca: Tarik, 2002.

Bennouna, Rabea. *Tazmamart: Côté femme*. Casablanc: Addar Al Alamia Lil Kitab, 2003.

Bensalmaia, Chadwane. 'Et Dieu créa la femme.' *Le Journal*, du 14 au 20 avril 2001, 47.

Ben Yahmed, Marwane. 'Villepin chez lui.' *Jeune Afrique/L'Intelligent*, n. 2334, du 2 au 8 octobre 2005, 30–1.

Benzakour, Fouzia, Driss Gaadi, and Ambroise Queffélec. *Le Français au Maroc: Lexique et contacts de langues*. Preface by Danièle Latin. Brussels: De Boeck & Larcier, 2000.

Berman, Russell A. *Fiction Sets You Free: Literature, Liberty, and Western Culture*. Iowa City: University of Iowa Press, 2007.

Bogue, Ronald, and Marcel Cornis-Pope. *Violence and Mediation in Contemporary Culture*. Albany, NY: State University of New York Press, 1996.

Bouhdiba, Abdulwahab. *La Sexualité en Islam*. In English, *Sexuality in Islam*. Trans. by Alan Sheridan. London: Al Saqi, 1985.

Boukhari, Karim. 'Les Epoux Serfaty font part de leur mémoire.' *Le Journal*, du 21 au 27 septembre 2002, 18–19.

Bourequat, Ali-Auguste. *Tazmamart: Dix-huit ans de solitude*. Paris: M. Lafon, 1993.

Boussejra, Houria. *Le Corps dérobé*. Casablanca: Afrique Orient, 1999.
- *Femmes inachevées*. Rabat: Marsam, 2000.
- *Les Impunis, ou Les Obsessions interdites*. Rabat: Marsam, 2004.

Brahimi, Denise. *Cinémas d'Afrique française et du Maghreb*. Paris: Nathan, 1997.

Brand, Laurie A. *Women, the State, and Political Liberalization: Middle Eastern and North African Experiences*. New York: Columbia University Press, 1998.

Brooks, Peter. 'Stories Abounding.' In *Chronicle of Higher Education*, 23 March 2001, B11.

Browers, Michaelle L. *Democracy and Civil Society in Arab Political Thought: Transcultural Possibilities*. Syracuse, NY: Syracuse University Press, 2006.

Caillois, Roger. *Men, Play, and Games*. Trans. by M. Barash. New York: Schocken Books, 1979.

Calinescu, Matei. *Rereading*. New Haven and London: Yale University Press, 1993.

Canto, Monique. 'The Politics of Women's Bodies: Reflections on Plato.' In *The Female Body in Western Culture: Contemporary Perspectives*, ed. Susan Rubin Suleiman, 339–53. Cambridge, MA: Harvard University Press, 1986.
Carter, Angela. *The Sadeian Woman and the Ideology of Pornography*. New York: Harper and Row, 1980.
Chafik, Nadia. *Filles du vent*. Paris: L'Harmattan, 1995.
– *A l'ombre de Jugurtha*. Casablanca: Eddif, 2000.
– *Le Secret des djinns*. Casablanca: Eddif, 1998.
– 'Le Tatouage bleu.' In *Des Nouvelles du Maroc*, ed. Loïc Barrière, 17–25. Paris: Méditerranée, and Casablanca: Eddif, 1999.
Chami-Kettani, Yasmina. *Cérémonie*. Paris: Actes Sud, 1999.
Chaudry, Lakshimi. 'In These Times.' *Chronicle of Higher Education*, 13 October 2006, B2.
Chebel, Malek. *Le Corps dans la tradition du Maghreb*. Paris: Presses Universitaires, 1984.
Chikhaoui, Naïma. 'Et si on ôtait le voile sans se dénuder.' In *Femmes et Islam*, ed. Aïcha Belarbi et al., 35–48. Casablanca: Le Fennec, 1997.
Chraïbi, Saïd. 'Femmes ... et femmes.' Film, 1997.
Çinar, Alev, and Thomas Bender, eds. *Urban Imaginaries: Locating the Modern City*. Minneapolis and London: University of Minnesota Press, 2007.
Clare, Horatio. 'Sisters and Brothers.' In *Meetings with Remarkable Muslims*, ed. Barnaby Rogerson and Rose Baring. London: Eland, 2005.
Cooke, Miriam. 'Telling Their Lives: A Hundred Years of Arab Women's Writings.' *World Literature Today* 60 (spring 1986): 212–16.
Crain, Caleb. 'Twilight of the Books.' *The New Yorker*, 24 & 27 December 2007, 134–9.
Damrosch, David. 'Secular Criticism Meets the World.' *Cairo Review of Books, Al-Ahram*, November 2005, 3–6.
Daoud, Zakya. *Casablanca en mouvement*. [n.p.]: Autrement, 2005.
– *Féminisme et politique au Maghreb: Sept Décennies de lutte*. Casablanca: Eddif, 1993.
Daure-Serfaty, Christine. *Tazmamart: Une Prison de la mort au Maroc*. Paris Stock, 1992.
Dawood, N.J. *The Koran, with Parallel Arabic Text*. Reprinted with revisions and notes. London: Penguin Books, 1998.
De Graincourt, Mehdi. 'La Variante Ecriture de Yasmine Chami-Kettani.' *Citadine*, janvier 2000, 14–15.
Déjeux, Jean. *La Littérature féminine de la langue française au Maghreb*. Paris: Karthala, 1994.
Denoeux, Guilain, and Abdeslam Maghraoui. 'King Hassan's Strategy of Political Dualism.' *Middle East Policy* 4.4 (January 1998): 104–30.

Draoui, Oumama. 'Le Livre dans un piteux état.' *Journal hebdomadaire*, du 3 au 9 mai 2003, 28.

Ech-Channa, Aïcha. *Miseria: témoignages*. 3rd ed. Casablanca: Le Fennec, 2000.

Ecritures du Maroc. Album de l'exposition. Paris: Institut du Monde Arabe, 2001.

Edmundson, Mark. 'The Risk of Reading: Why Books are Meant to be Dangerous.' *New York Times Magazine*, 1 August 2004, 11–12.

– *Why Read?* New York: Bloomsbury, 2004.

Edwards, Brian T. *Morocco Bound: Disorienting America's Maghreb, from Casablanca to the Marrakech Express*. Durham, NC: Duke University Press, 2005.

Eickelman, Dale. *Knowledge and Power in Morocco: The Education of a Twentieth-Century Notable*. Princeton: Princeton University Press, 1985.

– 'Redefining Muslim Publics.' In *New Media in the Muslim World: The Emerging Public Sphere*, ed. Dale Eickelman and Jon W. Anderson, 1–18. Bloomington: Indiana University Press, 1999.

Elaji, Sanaa. *Folle de Youssouf (Majnounatou Youssef)*. N.p.: Argana, 2003.

El Bouih, Fatna. *Une Femme nommée Rachid*. Trans. from Arabic *Hadit al atama* by Francis Gouin. Casablanca: Le Fennec, 2002.

El Hadrati, Latifa. 'Enquêtes sur les textes destinés à l'enfance et à la jeunesse Marocaine.' Doctoral dissertation, Université Mohammed V, Rabat, 2002.

El-Moujahid, El-Houssain. 'La Littérature orale.' In *Civilisation marocaine, arts et culture*, ed. Mohamed Sijelmassi et al., 118–24. Casablanca: Oum 1996.

El Khayat, Ghita (Rita). *Les Femmes arabes*. 3rd ed. Paris: L'Harmattan, 1988.

– *Le Livre des prénoms du monde arabe*. Casablanca: Eddif, 1991.

– *Le Maghreb des femmes: Les Défis du XXIème siècle*. 2nd ed. Rabat: Marsam, 2001.

– 'Marocaines soumises: mythe ou réalité.' *Civilisation marocaine, arts et cultures*, ed. Mohamed Sijelmassi et al., 78–87. Casablanca: Oum, 1996.

– *Le Monde arabe au féminin*. Paris: L'Harmattan, 1988.

– 'Rentrée littéraire: "cette gifle va bien à cette joue" selon notre proverbe populaire.' *Femmes du Maroc*, octobre 2000, 24.

– *Le Sein*. Casablanca: Aïni Bennaï, 2002.

– *Les Sept Jardins*. Paris: L'Harmattan, 1995.

El Oufir, Saloua. 'La Société civile s'investit dans la diffusion du savoir.' *Citadine*, février 2003, 62–5.

El Yazami, Abdelali. *Enquête sur la lecture au Maroc*. Rabat: Association Marocaine des Professionnels du Livre and Bureau du Livre, Ambassade de France, 1998.

Ellyas, Akram, and Benjamin Stora. *Les 100 Portes du Maghreb*. Paris: Editions de L'Atelier / Editions Ouvrières, 1999.

Emarrakech.info. Review of *Cérémonie*, online, 22 février 2003.

Erickson, John. *Islam and Postcolonial Narrative*. Cambridge: Cambridge University Press,1998.

Fernea, Elizabeth. 'The Challenges for Middle Eastern Women in the 21st Century.' *Middle Eastern Journal* 54.2 (spring 2000): 188–93.

— Introduction to Leïla Abouzeid, *The Year of the Elephant: A Moroccan Woman's Journey toward Independence and Other Stories*. Trans. by Barbara Parmenter. Austin: Center for Middle Eastern Studies at the University of Texas, 1989.

— 'Islamic Feminism Finds a Different Voice.' online, May 2000. www.afsa.org/may00/fernea.cfm.

Florida, Richard. *Cities and the Creative Class*. New York and London: Routledge, 2005.

Friere, Paulo. *Pedagogy of the Oppressed*. Trans. by Myra Bergman Ramos. New York: Continuum, 1970.

Gaasch, James. *Anthologie de la nouvelle maghrébine*. Casablanca: Eddif, 1996.

Gauch, Suzanne. *Liberating Shahrazad: Feminism, Postcolonialism and Islam*. Minneapolis: University of Minnesota Press, 2007.

Ghazali, Keltoum. 'Sur le gril: Fatna El Bouih, de l'ombre à la lumière.' *Citadine*, mars 2001, 33–6.

Ghechoua, Afafe, and Fadwa Miadi. 'Fragments d'un discours amoureux.' *Jeune Afrique/L'Intelligent*, n. 2064, du 1er au 7 août 2000, 49.

Ghorbal, Samy. 'Casablanca tourne la page.' *Jeune Afrique*, n. 2407, du 25 février au 3 mars 2007, 96–7.

— 'Les Déçus de la démocratie.' *Jeune Afrique*, n. 2438, du 30 septembre au 6 octobre 2007, 48–9.

Glaiman, Dorothy, et al. 'Interview de Rajae Benchemsi.' Evene.fr, Actualité Livres, online, March 2006. http://www.evene.fr/livres/actualité/interview-rajae-benchemsi-controverse-temps-285.php.

Goody, Jack. *Literacy in Traditional Societies*. Cambridge: Cambridge University Press, 1968.

Gregory, Derek. *Geographical Imaginations*. Oxford: Blackwell, 1994.

Greve, Frank, 'Firm Surveys Worldwide Well-being.' *The New Mexican*, 5 October 2007, A4.

Grotti, Laetitia. 'Mémoire(s) de femme.' *Tel Quel*, 25–31 janvier 2003, 18–22.

— 'La Moudawana à l'épreuve du terrain.' *Jeune Afrique*, n. 2320, du 26 juin au 2 juillet 2005, 52–4.

Grotti, Laetitia, and Maria Daïf. 'Etre homosexuel au Maroc.' *Tel Quel*, 27 mars au 2 avril 2004, 24–31.

— 'Hchouma.' *Tel Quel*, 8–14 mai 2004, 24–30.

Grotti, Laetitia, and Driss Ksikes, 'Interview-vérité: Fatéma Mernissi.' *Tel Quel* 13–19 septembre 2003, 32–5.

Guessous, Mohamed. 'Le Maroc ne sera jamais un Etat laïc.' *Le Journal Hebdomadaire*, 19 mai 2005, online.

Gusdorf, Georges. *Les Ecritures du moi*. Paris: Odile Jacob, 1991.

Gutmann, Amy. *Identity in Democracy*. Princeton: Princeton University Press, 2003.

Hadraoui, Touria. *Une Enfance marocaine*. Casablanca: Le Fennec, 1998.

Hassan, Fayza. 'A Lesson in Logic.' *Cairo Review of Books*, October 2005, 8–9.

Heinze, Andrew R. *Jews and the American Soul: Human Nature in the Twentieth Century*. Princeton: Princeton University Press, 2005.

Hessini, Leila. 'Signification du voile au Maroc: Tradition, protestation, ou libération.' In *Femmes, culture et société au Maghreb*, ed. R. Bourqia, M. Charrad, and N. Gallagher, 1:91–104. Casablanca: Afrique-Orient, 1996.

Huff-Rousselle, Maggie. 'Fatima Mernissi: A Contemporary Scheherazade's Tales of a Borderless World.' *Cairo Times*, May 2003; shortened version, on Mernissi's website, http://www.mernissi.net/civil_society/portraits/fatimamernissi.html.

Hunt, Lynn, ed. *The Invention of Pornography: Obscenity and the Origins of Modernity, 1500–1800*. New York: Zone Books, 1993.

Inglehart, Ronald, and Pippa Norris. *Rising Tide: Gender Equality and Cultural Change Around the World*. Cambridge: Cambridge University Press, 2003.

Irwin, Robert. *The Arabian Nights: A Companion*. London: Tauris Parke, 2004.

Jamaï, Aboubakr. 'Morocco's Choice: Openness or Terror.' *The New York Times*, 31 May 2003, A25.

Jamaï, Khalid. 'Et s'il n'y avait pas un problème de femme mais un problème d'homme marocain.' *Le Journal hebdomadaire*, 18–24 octobre 2003, 6.

Jay, Salim. *Dictionnaire de la littérature marocaine*. Casablanca: Eddif, and Paris: Méditerranée, 2005.

Jayne, Susan. 'The Effects of Education on Health.' In *Literacy: An International Handbook*, ed. Daniel A. Wagner et al. Boulder: Westview, 1999.

Jeune Afrique and Financial Times. 'Pourquoi les electeurs n'y croient plus.' *Jeune Afrique*, n. 2436, du 16 au 22 septembre 2007, 58–9.

Joubert, Jean-Louis, ed. *Littératures francophones du monde arabe*. Paris: Nathan, 1999.

Kadiri, Abdeslam. 'Entretien: Laâbi, passionnément.' *Tel Quel*, 22–8 février 2003, 36–9.

Kapchan, Deborah. *Gender on the Market: Moroccan Women and the Revoicing of Tradition*. Philadelphia: University of Pennsylvania Press, 1996.

Kaplan, Caren. *Questions of Travel: Postmodern Discourses of Displacement*. Durham, NC: Duke University Press, 1996.

Kappeler, Susanne. *The Pornography of Representation*. Minneapolis: University of Minnesota Press, 1986.
Kéfi, Ridha. 'Le Blues des écrivains arabes.' *Jeune Afrique/L'Intelligent*, n. 2089, du 23 au 29 janvier 2001, 67–70.
Kendrick, Walter. *The Secret Museum: Pornography in Modern Culture*. New York: Viking, 1987.
Kilito, Abdelfattah. *L'Oeil et l'aiguille*. Casablanca: Le Fennec, 1992.
Kristof, Nicolas D. 'Looking for Islam's Luthers.' *The New York Times*, 15 October 2006, Week in Review, 13.
Ksikes, Driss. 'L'Essai maghrébin disséqué: Le Statut de la femme écrivain.' *Tel Quel*, 15–21 mars 2003, 45.
Laâbi, Abdellatif. *Chroniques de la citadelle: Lettres de prison (1972–1980)*. Paris: Denoël, 1983.
– *Le Fond de la jarre*. Paris: Gallimard, 2002.
Lahy-Hollebecque, M. *Le Féminisme de Schéhérazade*. Paris: Radot, 1927.
Lalami, Laila. *Hope and Other Dangerous Pursuits*. Orlando: Harcourt, 2005.
– 'The Missionary Position.' *The Nation*, 19 June 2006, 23–33.
– Web blog, moorishgirl.com, 27 July 2005.
Larrivée, Isabelle. 'La Crypte et la vie: Etude de *Cérémonie* de Yasmina Chami-Kettani.' 'Frontières.' Online review from Presses de l'Université du Québec.
Lebbady, Hasna. 'There is No Such Thing as a Mere Story: A Poststructuralist Reading of Aïcha Bent Ennejar.' In *Women's Spaces*, ed. Fouzia Rhissassi et al., 181–8. Conferences and Colloquia 97. Rabat: Mohammed V University, Publications of the Faculty of Letters and Human Sciences, 2001.
Lejeune, Philippe. *Le Pacte autobiographique*. Paris: Seuil, 1975.
Lind, Agneta, and Anton Johnston. *Adult Literacy in the Third World: A Review of Objectives and Strategies*. Stockholm: Swedish International Development Authority, 1990.
Lugan, Bernard. *Histoire du Maroc, des origines à nos jour*. Paris: Perrin/Criterion, 2001.
Lyons, Martyn. *The Triumph of the Book*. Trans. from French. Paris: Promodis, 1987.
Mabrouk, Sonia. 'La Fatwa des oulémas.' *Jeune Afrique*, n. 2374, du 9 au 15 juillet 2006, 58.
– 'Les Femmes imams arrivent!' *Jeune Afrique*, n. 2364, du 30 avril au 6 mai 2006, 37.
Majid, Anouar. *Unveiling Traditions: Postcolonial Islam in a Polycentric World*. Durham, NC: Duke University Press, 2000.
Malti-Douglas, Fedwa. *Woman's Body, Woman's Word: Gender and Discourse in Arabo-Islamic Writing*. Princeton: Princeton University Press, 1991.

Marsaud, Olivia. 'Un Babel ... oued littéraire.' *Jeune Afrique*, n. 2404, du 7 au 10 février 2007, 80–2.
Martin, Patrice, and Christophe Drevel. *La Langue française d'ailleurs, 100 entretiens*. Casablanca: Tarik, 2001.
Marzouki, Ahmed. *Tazmamart: Cellule 10*. Casablanca: Tarik, 2000.
Massey, Doreen. 'Politics and Space/Time.' *New Left Review* 196 (1992): 65–84.
Mattson, Ingrid. *The Story of the Quran: Its History and Place in Muslim Life*. New York: Wiley, 2008.
May, Georges. *'Les Mille et une nuits' d'Antoine Galland*. Paris: Presses Universitaires de France, 1986.
Mazières, Nathalie de. 'Héritage colonial en urbanisme et en architecture.' In *Civilisation marocaine, arts et culture*, ed. Mohamed Sijelmassi et al., 180–6. Casablanca: Oum, 1996.
McDowell, Linda. *Gender, Identity, and Place: Understanding Feminist Geographers*. Minneapolis: University of Minnesota Press, 1999.
McLemee, Scott. 'Think Postpositive: A Latina Cultural Theorist Wrestles with Notions of Identity and Experience.' *The Chronicle of Higher Education*, 13 February 2004, A13–14.
Mdarhri Alaoui, Abdallah. 'Approche du roman féminin au Maroc: Historique, dénomination et réception de la littérature féminine.' In *Ecritures féminines au Maroc: Etudes et bibliographie*, 16–23. Rabat: Université Mohammed V, Coordination des Chercheurs sur les littératures maghrébines et comparées, 2001.
– .'Désir d'identité, désir de l'autre.' In *Désir d'identité, désir de l'autre*, ed. Mustapha Bencheikh, 237–47. Meknès: Université de Meknès, Faculté de Lettres, 2002.
Mdarhi Alaoui, Abdallah, Samira Douider, and Abdelfettah Lahjomri, eds. *Ecritures féminines au Maroc: Etudes et bibliographie*. Rabat: Université Mohammed V, Coordination des Chercheurs sur les littératures maghrébines et comparées, 2001.
Mdidech, Jaouad. *La Chambre noire, ou Derb Moulay Chérif*. Préface by Abraham Serfaty. Casablanca: Eddif, 2000.
Mehrez, Samia. 'The Subversive Poetics of Radical Bilingualism: Postcolonial Francophone North African Literature.' In *The Bounds of Race: Perspectives on Hegemony and Resistance*, ed. Dominique La Capra, 255-75. Ithaca, NY: Cornell University Press, 1991.
Mehta, Brinda. *Rituals of Memory in Contemporary Arab Women's Writing*. New York: Syracuse University Press, 2007.
Memmes, Abdellah. 'Littérature d'expression française.' In *Civilisation marocaine, arts et culture*, ed. Mohamed Sijelmassi et al., 136–41. Casablanca: Oum, 1996.

Memmi, Albert. *Portrait du décolonisé arabe musulman et de quelques autres*. Paris: Gallimard, 2004. Trans. into English by Robert Bononno as *Decolonization and the Decolonized*. Minneapolis: University of Minnesota, 2006.

Menebhi, Saïda. *Poèmes, écrits, lettres de prison*. 2nd ed. Rabat: Editions Feed-Back, 2000.

Merckx, Ingrid. 'Traduction et coédition: deux remèdes à la crise du livre au Maroc.' *Le Matin*, 27 janvier 2003, 7.

Mernissi, Fatima. *Beyond the Veil*. Rev. ed. London: Al Saqi, 1985.

– *Chahrazad n'est pas marocaine, autrement, elle serait salariée!* Casablanca: Le Fennec, 1988.

– *Doing Daily Battle: Interviews with Moroccan Women*. Trans. by Mary Jo Lakeland. New Brunswick, NJ: Rutgers University Press, 1989. In French, *Le Maroc raconté par ses femmes*. Rabat: Smer, 1983.

– *Etes-vous vacciné contre le harem?* Casablanca: Le Fennec, 1998.

– *Islam and Democracy: Fear of the Modern World*. Trans. by Mary Jo Lakeland. Cambridge, MA: Perseus Books, 1992.

– *Rêves de femmes: Contes d'enfance au harem*. Casablanca: Le Fennec, 1997. In English, *Dreams of Trespass: Tales of a Harem Girlhood*. Trans. into English by Claudine Richetin, reviewed and adapted by the author. Reading, MA: Addison-Wesley, 1994.

– 'The Satellite, the Prince and Sheherazade: The Rise of Women as Communictors in Digital Islam.' Article for the catalogue, 'Harem Fantasies.' Centre de Cultura Contemporania de Barcelona, 2003, excerpts online at http://www.mernissi.net/books/articles/Rise-of-women.html.

– *Scheherazade Goes West: Different Cultures, Different Harems*. New York: Washington Square Press, 2001.

– *Sultanes oubliées: Femmes chefs d'Etat en Islam*. Paris: Albin Michel, and Casablanca: Le Fennec, 1990.

– *The Veil and the Male Elite: A Feminist Interpretation of Women's Rights in Islam*. Trans. by Mary Jo Lakeland. New York: Basic Books, 1991. In French, *Le Harem politique: Le Prophète et ses femmes*. Paris: Albin Michel, 1987.

– Web site: http://www.mernissi.net/civil_society/portraits/fatnaelbouih.

Messud, Claire. 'Fairy Tale in Reverse.' Review of Malika Oufkir, *Stolen Lives: Twenty Years in a Desert Jail*. *New York Review of Books*, 9 May 2002, 35–7.

Miadi, Fadwa. 'La Revanche de la darija.' *Jeune Afrique/L'Intelligent*, n. 2336, du 16 au 22 octobre 2005, 34–5.

Miller, Laura. 'How Many Books Are Too Many?' *New York Times Book Review*, 18 July 2004, 23.

Miller, Nancy K. 'The Unfolding Dilemmas of Identity Politics.' *The Chronicle of Higher Education*. 9 August 1996, B7.

Mishra, Pakaj. 'The Misunderstood Muslims.' *New York Review of Books*, 17 November 2005, 15–18.
Momsen, Janet H., and Vivian Kinnaird, eds. *Different Places, Different Voices: Gender and Development in Africa, Asia and Latin America*. London and New York: Routledge, 1993.
Morocco. New York: Knopf, 1994.
Mortimer, Mildred, ed. Introduction to *Maghrebian Mosaic: A Literature in Transition*. Boulder, CO: Lynne Rienner, 2001.
– 'Re-presenting the Orient: A New Instructional Approach.' *French Review* 79.2 (December 2005): 296–312.
Mouaatarif, Yasrine. 'En "darija"dans le texte.' *Jeune Afrique/L'Intelligent*, n. 2353, du 12 au 18 février 2006, 72.
– 'Le Grand Chantier de l'alphabétisation.' *Jeune Afrique*, n. 2367, du 21 au 27 mai 2006, 70–1.
– 'Haro sur les tabous.' *Jeune Afrique*, n. 2365, du 7 au 13 mai 2006, 76.
Mouride, Abdelaziz. 'Dessiner contre l'oubli.' *Citadine*, septembre 2004, 34–6.
– *On affame bien les rats!* Tarik, Paris Méditerranée, 2000.
Moya, Paula M.L., and Michael R. Hames-Garcia, eds. *Reclaiming Identity: Realist Theory and the Predicament of Postmodernism*. Berkeley and Los Angeles: University of California, 2000.
Mustafa, Hala. 'On the Discourse of Reform.' *Al-Ahram*, 15-21 April 2004.
Naamane-Guessous, Soumaya. *Au-delà de toute pudeur: La Sexualité féminine au Maroc*. 10th ed. Casablanca: Eddif, 1997.
Nafisi, Azar. *Reading Lolita in Tehran: A Memoir in Books*. New York: Random House, 2003.
National Endowment for the Arts. *Reading at Risk: A Survey of Literary Reading in America*. June 2004.
National Storytelling Association. 'What Storytelling Is: An attempt at defining the art form.' http://www.eldrbarry.net/roos/st_defn.htm.
Nedjma, pseud. *The Almond*. Trans. by C. Jane Hunter. New York: Grove, 2005. In French, *L'Amande*. Paris: Plon, 2004.
Nejjar, Narjiss. 'Les Yeux secs.' Film, 2003.
Netton, Ian Richard. *A Popular Dictionary of Islam*. London: Curzon Press, 1992.
Nkrumah, Gamal. 'The Myriad Faces of Islam.' Review of Barnaby Rogerson and Rose Baring, eds, *Meetings with Remarkable Muslims*. *Cairo Review of Books*, October 2005, 10–11.
Nochlin, Linda. 'The Imaginary Orient.' In *The Politics of Vision: Essays on Art and Society*, 31–59. New York: Harper & Row, 1989.
Norris, Ronald, and Pippa Norris. *Rising Tide: Gender Equality and Cultural Change Around the World*. Cambridge: Cambridge University Press, 2003.

Oufkir, Malika, with Michèle Fitoussi. *La Prisonnière*. Paris: Grasset & Fasquelle, 1999. In English, *Stolen Lives: Twenty Years in a Desert Jail*. Trans. by Ros Schwarz. New York: Hyperion, 2001.
Oulehri, Touria. *La Chambre des nuits blanches*. Rabat: Marsam, 2002.
– *Les Conspirateurs sont parmi nous*. Rabat: Marsam, 2006.
– *La Répudiée*. Casablanca: Afrique Orient, 2001.
Oumassine, Damia. *L'Arganier des femmes égarées*. Casablanca: Le Fennec, 1998.
'The Past and Present of Djemma-el-Fna'. Film. Filmmakers Library, 1995.
Perrault, Gilles. *Notre Ami le roi*. Paris: Gallimard, 1990 and 1992.
Pijpers, Harmke. 'Morocco: The Rights of Women.' Film. Filmmakers Library, 1996.
Power, Carla. 'A Secret History.' *New York Times Magazine*, 25 February 2007, 22–4.
Prakash, Gyan, and Kevin M. Kruse. *The Spaces of the Modern City: Imaginaries, Politics, and Everyday Life*. Princeton: Princeton University Press, 2008.
Proust, Marcel. *A La Recherche du temps perdu*. Vol. 3. Paris: Gallimard, Bibliothèque de la Pléïade, 1954.
Radi, Ahmed. '"Visual Representation" and "Cultural Geography": Constructing Linkages – a Reading of Fatima Quazzani's *At My Mother's House*, posted at 'The Literature and Culture of Morocco in the Postcolonial Web,' online. www.postcolonialweb.org/morocco/arts/radi3nl.html.
Rakha, Youssef. 'Madman of the Roses.' *Al-Ahram*, 20–6 November 2003, 17.
Rhissassi, Fouzia. 'Moroccan Women Writers and the Violence of Family Spaces.' In *Women's Spaces*, Fouzia Rhissassi et al., eds, 139–55. Publications of the Faculty of Letters and Human Sciences, Conferences and Colloquia, n. 97. Rabat: Mohammed V University, 2001.
Rhissassi, Fouzia et al., eds. *Women's Spaces*. Publications of the Faculty of Letters and Human Sciences, Conferences and Colloquia, n. 97. Rabat: Mohammed V University, 2001.
Riding, Alan. 'A Muslim Woman, A Story of Sex.' *New York Times*, 20 June 2005, B1 and cont.
Rodriguez, Pablo. 'Il était une fois … l'islam.' *Jeune Afrique / L'Intelligent*, n. 2335, 9–5 oct. 2005, 70.
Rogerson, Barnaby, and Rose Baring, eds. *Meetings with Remarkable Muslims*. London: Eland, 2005.
Romano, Carlin. 'Who Killed Literary Reading?' *Chronicle of Higher Education*, 23 July 2004, B13.
Rothstein, Edward. 'The Harem is the Exotic Dancer in a Historical Peep Show.' *New York Times*, 16 June 2001.

Roy, Olivier. 'Islam et démocratie: un faux problème.' Originally in *Le Figaro Magazine*. Reprinted in *Jeune Afrique/L'Intelligent*, n. 2232, du 19 au 25 octobre 2003, 34.
Ruthven, Malise. *Islam: A Very Short Introduction*. Oxford: Oxford University Press, 1997.
Saddiki, Tayeb. 'Place Jamaâ al-Fna.' In *Civilisation marocaine, arts et culture*, ed. Mohamed Sijelmassi et al., 164–7. Casablanca: Oum, 1996.
Sadiqi, Fatima. 'The Spread of English in Morocco.' *International Journal of Languages* 87 (1991): 99–114.
– *Women, Gender and Language in Morocco*. Leiden: Brill, 2002.
Safi-Eddine, K. 'Crossing Boundaries: Arab Women's Empowerment from the Private to the Public Sphere.' In *Women's Spaces*, ed. Fouzia Rhissassi et al., 91–104. Publications of the Faculty of Letters and Human Sciences, n. 97. Rabat: Mohammed V University, 2001.
Safire, William. 'Narrative: The New Story of Story.' *New York Times Magazine*, 5 December 2004, 34.
Said, Edward W. *Culture and Imperialism*. New York: Random House, 1993; Vintage Books, 1994.
– *Orientalism*. New York: Random House, 1978; Vintage Books, 1979.
Sallis, Eva. *Sheherazade Through the Looking Glass: The Metamorphosis of 'The Thousand and One Nights.'* Surrey, Great Britain: Curzon, 1999.
Scarpetta, Guy. 'La Littérature, miroir de l'histoire? Ce que seuls les romans peuvent dire.' *Le Monde diplomatique*, mars 2003, 30.
Schachter, Daniel. *Searching for Memory: The Brain, the Mind, and the Past*. New York: Basic Books, 1996.
Scholes, Robert. *The Crafty Reader*. New Haven: Yale University Press, 2001.
– *The Protocols of Reading*. New Haven: Yale University Press, 1988.
Sebti, Fadela. *Moi, Mireille, lorsque j'étais Yasmina*. Casablanca: Le Fennec, 1995.
Sedjari, Ali. 'Quand la jalousie ou la roublardise dominent, le développement est compromis.' *L'Economiste*, 18 mars 2003, 24.
Segarra, Marta. *Leur Pesant de poudre: Romancières francophones du Maghreb*. Paris: L'Harmattan, 1997.
Serfaty, Abraham. *Dans Les Prisons du roi; Ecrits de Kénitra sur le Maroc*. Paris: Messidor, 1992.
– *Le Maroc, du gris au noir*. Paris: Syllepse, 1998.
Serfaty, Abraham, and Christine Daure-Serfaty. *La Mémoire de l'autre*. Paris: Stock,1993; Casablanca: Tarik, 2002.

Serhane, Abdelhak. *Kabazal: Les Emmurés de Tazmamart; Mémoires de Salah et Aïda Hadad.* Casablanca: Tarik, 2004.
Sijelmassi, Mohamed, et al., eds. *La Civilisation marocaine, arts et culture.* Casablanca: Oum, 1996.
Slyomovics, Susan. Interview with Fatna El Bouih. *Middle East Report* 218, spring 2001, online. http://www.merip.org/mer/mer218/218_bouih.html.
Sontag, Susan. 'Regarding the Torture of Others.' *New York Times Magazine,* 23 May 2004, 23–7, cont. on 42.
Stora, Benjamin, and Akram Ellyas. *Les 100 Portes du Maghreb.* Paris: L'Atelier, 1999.
Telles Quelles. 'Femmes du Maroc.' Édition spéciale, du 8 au 14 mars 2003.
Tessler, Mark. 'Do Islamic Orientations Influence Attitudes toward Democracy in The Arab World? Evidence from Egypt, Jordan, Morocco, and Algeria.' *International Journal of Comparative Sociology* 43.3–5 (2002): 229–49.
'The Thousand and One Nights.' Film conceived and written by Mahmoud Hussein, produced by Philippe Calderon; a coproduction FIT Production, La Cinquième, Canal Sur Télévision; Princeton, NJ: Films for the Humanities & Sciences, c. 2001.
Trabelsi, Bahaa. *Une Femme tout simplement.* Casablanca: Eddif, 1995.
– *Une Vie à trois.* Casablanca: Eddif, 2000.
Troin, Jean-François. *Maroc: Régions, pays, territoires.* Paris: Maisonneuve, & Larose: Tarik Urbama, 2002.
United Nations Development Programme Country Report, 2005.
U.S. Department of State Country Report on Human Rights Practices, Morocco, 2005.
Vermeren, Pierre. *Histoire du Maroc depuis l'indépendance.* Paris: La Découverte, 2002.
– *Maghreb: La Démocratie impossible?* Paris: Fayard, 2004.
Wadud, Amina. *Inside the Gender Jihad: Women's Reform in Islam.* Oxford: Oneworld Publications, 2006.
– *Qur'an and Woman: Rereading the Sacred Text from a Woman's Perspective.* New York and Oxford: Oxford University Press, 1999.
Wagner, Daniel A. *Literacy, Culture, and Development: Becoming Literate in Morocco.* Cambridge University Press, 1993.
Ward, Nicole Jouve. 'Espaces symboliques de femmes: La Jeune Fille sans mains.' In *Women's Spaces,* ed. Fouzia Rhissassi, et al., 157–61. Publications of the Faculty of Letters and Human Sciences, n. 97. Rabat: Mohammed V University, 2001.
Warner, Marina. *From the Beast to the Blonde: On Fairy Tales and Their Tellers.* New York: Farrar, Straus & Giroux, 1994.

Waterbury, John. *The Commander of the Faithful: The Moroccan Political Elite, A Study in Segmented Politics*. New York: Columbia University Press, 1970.
Wehrs, Donald R. *Islam, Ethics, Revolt: Politics and Piety in Francophone West Africa and Maghreb Narrative*. Leham, MD: Lexington Books, 2008.
Whitehead, Neil L. 'On the Poetics of Violence.' In *Violence*, ed. Neil L. Whitehead, 55–77. Santa Fe: School of American Research Press, and Oxford: James Currey, 2004.
Woodhull, Winifred. *Transfigurations of the Maghreb: Feminism, Decolonization, and Literatures*. Minneapolis: University of Minnesota, 1993.
Wright, Gwendolyn. *The Politics of Design in French Colonial Urbanism*. Chicago: University of Chicago Press, 1991.
Yacoubi, Rachida. *Je Dénonce*. Paris: Paris-Méditerranée, 2001.
– *Ma Vie, mon cri*. Casablanca: Eddif, 1996.
Yeazell, Ruth Bernard. *Harems of the Mind: Passages of Western Art and Literature*. New Haven: Yale University Press, 2000.
Zahid, Fatima. 'Relations et gestion de l'espace par les femmes rurales au Maroc.' In *Women's Spaces*, ed. Fouzia Rhissassi et al., 77–89. Publications of the Faculty of Letters and Human Sciences, n.97. Rabat: Mohammed V University, 2001.
Zeidan, Joseph T. *Arab Women Novelists: The Formative Years and Beyond*. Albany, NY: State University Press of New York, 1995.
Zouari, Fawzia. 'La Guerre du hijab aura-t-elle lieu?' *Jeune Afrique*, n. 2397, du 17 au 23 décembre 2006, 46–8.

Index

Abouzeid, Leila, 7, 16, 36, 177, 196; and aversion for French language, 9, 11, 189; bourgeois family, 236n20; female identity and postpositive theory, 176–7; Islam, 175, 183–4; national identity, 238n39; social role of literature, 192
– works:
   Last Chapter, The (*Le Dernier Episode*), 175, 187–92; identity issues, 175, 176, 177, 189–90; social critique, 182, 187, 190, 191, 192; women's speech, 187, 190
   Return to Childhood, 237n33
   Year of the Elephant, 16, 154, 175, 183–7; aftermath of Independence as double betrayal of personal and national ideals, 184, 186–7; critical reception, 192; journey as poetic trope of self-discovery, 163, 165, 167; themes of home, homelessness, homeland, 165, 166, 167
Abu Hamid al-Ghazali: on sexual desire, 86
Agadir, 16, 229n6; description, 231n19; earthquake, 157–8; parallel discourses, 153, 156, 159

Ahmed, Leila, 129, 141
Ajbabdi, Latifa, 60, 106, 109, 117, 219nn1, 4, 233n6; founder of *Le 8 Mars*, 220n4; member of IER, 220n4; on police overreaction, 224n33
Algeria, 9, 200n15; Algerian women writers, 24, 202n1; 'The Battle for Algiers,' 231n18
Ali, Kecia, 129
Arab Human Development Report 2005, 'Towards the Rise of Women in the Arab World,' 171
Arab women: early feminists, 60
Arab women writers (non-Moroccan), 3, 24, 215n1; the body, 225n2; early women's voices, 62, 213n11; prison imagery, 236n21; symbol of bird, 171, 178
Arab identity: cultural definition, 167
Aslan, Reza, 235n10, 238n36

Bacholle, Michèle, 73
Badran, Margot, 3, 19
Bahéchar, Souad, 81; *hchouma*, 103; *Ni Fleurs, ni couronnes*, 32, 91, 92–3, 103; rape-mutilation, 92
Baker, Alison: 'Still Ready,' 60, 194, 230n18; *Voices of Resistance*, 170

Balafrej, Souad, 31
Barlas, Asma, 129, 217n10
Barnett, Clive: 'cultural geography of democracy,' 190, 238n40
Bataille, Georges, 82; on eroticism, 88; poetry and violence, 94
Beaumont, Daniel, 42
Belarbi, Aïcha, 61
Bellefqih, Anissa, 177, 181–2; *Yasmina et le talisman*, 182
Ben Barka, Mehdi, 21; Ben Barka affair, 173, 222n19; UNFP (Union Nationale des Forces Populaires), 112
Benchekroun, Siham, 7, 15, 16, 27, 91, 153, 154, 177, 196; bourgeois family, 236n20; and *hchouma*, 103
– work: *Oser vivre*, 27, 91, 163, 164, 175, 178–81; feminist discourse, 143–4, 175, 179–81; hammam, 141–3, 144; harem, 132; issues of identity, 165, 176, 178, 179; marital rape, 92, 103–4; poetics of reform, 192; social role of literature, 192; traditional female socialization and socially sanctioned misogyny, 142–3; journey as poetic trope, 16, 154, 163, 164–7, 180. *See also* hammam; harem
Benchemsi, Ahmed R., editor of *Tel Quel*, 173
Benchemsi, Rajae, 7, 14, 15, 16, 81, 93, 141, 153, 196; complexity of the past, 195; critique of feminism dependent on laws, 135–6; on francophonie, 12, 201n29; literary violence, 93; philosophical-literary objectives, 100–1; relationship to French language, 11, 201n23; tradition and modernity, 135, 136, 138, 147; transgressive poetry, 94, 96

– works:
La Controverse des temps, 227n13
Fracture du désir, 15, 22, 81, 82; 94–101; 'Au Bord de la mémoire,' 101; 'La Boutique russe,' 98–100; 'Elle,' 101; 'Foire des Zaërs,' 97–8, 100; 'L'Homme qui ne mourut pas,' 101; 'Kira et Slima,' 91, 94–6, 100
Marrakech, lumière d'exil, 135–9; feminist quest and memory, 137; femininity and feminism, 137; hammam, 147–8; rewriting of harem theme, 132, 135–9, 149; Jemaa-el-Fna, 136, 162, 163; Marrakech as palimpsest, 161–3; rape, 92; theme of freedom 137, 139. *See also* hammam; harem
Bender, Thomas: *Urban Imaginaries*, 151
Benguigui, Yasmina: 'The Perfumed Garden,' film, 86, 217n11
Ben Haddou, Halima: *Aïcha la rebelle*, 18, 23
Ben Jelloun, Tahar, 22, 23, 27; Ahmed-Zahra (character), 239n42; departure from Morocco, 221n10; disciplinary camp, 221n10; emergence of individual, 236n20; his Fez, 154; relationship to French language, 12; role of writer, 191; *Souffles*, 21, 221n10; on women's literature, 35, 73

– works:
Cette Aveuglante Absence de lumière, 108–9
Le Dernier Ami, 221n9
L'Enfant sable, 239n42
L'Islam expliqué aux enfants, 32
La Nuit sacrée, 239n42

Les Yeux baissés, 205n28
Benlyazid, Farida, 14, 19, 63
- films: 'A Door to the Sky,' 202n5, 218n15; 'Women's Wiles' (*Ruses de femmes*), 63–5, 77, 213n9
Bennouna, Mehdi: *Heures sans gloire, échec d'une révolution*, 108
Bennouna, Rabea: *Tazmamart: Côté femme*, 109, 221n12
Berman, Russell A.: literature and history, 220n9; literature and society, 194, 239n1; political and emancipatory predisposition of literature, 197
Blanchot, Maurice, 82, 94, 100
Boughédir, Férid: 'Halfaouine,' film, 140, 145, 228n15
Bourequat, Ali-Auguste: *Tazmamart: Dix-huit ans de solitude*, 108, 109
Boussejra, Houria, 15, 29, 81, 125; class divisions, 92–3, 134, 135; principle of harem as class warfare, 132, 133–5, 149; rape, 92; violence and oppression, 93, 134; women's violence, 91. See also harem
- works:
Femmes inachevées, 125, 205n27
'Saadia,' 29, 227n12
'Tamou,' 93, 132–5
Bowles, Paul, 160, 232n24
Browers, Michaelle, 174; Islam and democracy, 234n10; 'maternal feminism,' 236n20

Caillois, Roger, 53, 99
Calinescu, Matei, 209n11; artistic play, 52–3; kinds of reading and rereading, 39, 40, 41, 42; ludic, 39
Canto, Monique, 149
Casablanca: character of, 152; described by Daoud and Trabelsi, 163; described by Waterbury, 222n18; in *Oser vivre*, 163–7, 229–30n9; political events, 222n18, 233n6; population, 229n6; prisons and trials of leftists, 106, 112, 113; in *La Répudiée*, 156, 157, 158; terrorist attacks of 2003, 172; in *Une Vie à trois*, 104; Waterbury on 1965 strikes and riots, 233n6; women and the city, 151; in *Year of the Elephant*, 165, 166, 167
Chafik, Nadia: advice to women writers, 35; relationship to French language, 9–10; 'Le Tatouage bleu,' 101–2
Chaibia, 19, 202n5
Chami-Kettani, Yasmina, 7, 14, 22, 101, 177, 196; challenge to Orientalism, 144, 147
- work: *Cérémonie*, 22, 63, 72–6; art and power of storytelling, 71–2; body as text, 147; family legends as ceremonies, 74–5; function of ceremonies, 73, 76; hammam, 145, 146–7. See also hammam
Chatr, Najat, 77, 216n7
Chatt, Abdelkader: *Mosaïques ternies*, 18, 20
Chaouni, Leila, 31, 34, 61, 207n43
Chebel, Malek, 145
Choukri, Mohamed: Choukri compared to Nedjma, 160; life and work, 81, 216n4
Chraïbi, Driss: *L'Ane maître d'école*, 206n36; *Passé simple*, importance of, 21
Çinar, Alev: *Urban Imaginaries*, 151
Citadine, 6, 31, 36, 104, 218n15, 221n14, 223n26
cities: associated with the female, 232n23; and cultural geography,

152; identities in transition, both city and women, 151, 153, 230n11; mediators of female condition, 153; in national development, 153, 230n10; relationship to gender and history, 150; similarities between colonial space and gendered space, 153; studied by social scientists and humanists, 150; urban cities of Morocco, 229n6
colonialism, 111, 124, 189; in Abouzeid, 189; colonial Fez in Ben Jelloun, Laabi, Mernissi, 154; colonial space, 153, 155, 156; in *Dreams*, 128; failure to educate native population and effects, 23; French Protectorate, 8, 111, 154, 159; French colonial architecture and colonialist policy, 230n17; in *The Last Chapter*, 188, 189, 190; Memmi on, 238n38; in *Year of the Elephant*, 183–7
Cooke, Myriam, 3, 19

Daoud, Zakya: on Casablanca, 163; on history of women's movement, 213n7, 233–4n6
Daure-Serfaty, Christine, 23, 203n11; *La Mémoire de l'autre*, 173, 220n7; *Tazmamart*, 109
decolonization: of the city, 149, 168; figurative, 3, 152, 168; in *The Last Chapter*, 189, 191; Memmi on, 238n38
Déjeux, Jean: autobiography vs autobiographical, 70–1; early novels by North African women, 201–2n1
democracy: in action, 173; common-good framework, 177, 235n10; 'cultural geography of,' 190, 238n40; 'democracy deficit,' 234–5n10; feminism and, 13, 17; fiction and democracy, 197; global ideal, 170; and Islam, 169, 172, 234n10; *Islam and Democracy*, 172, 203n12, 234n10; in *The Last Chapter*, 187, 190, 191–2; literature and, 82, 190, 197; Moroccan women's fiction and democracy, 175, 177, 192, 193, 198, 234–5n10; Nedjma and, 82; NGO activities, 16, 172, 174; political structures vs values, 180; and print culture, 29; relationship of gender and democracy, 169, 171, 178; rhetoric of, 3, 170, 171, 190; role of reading in democratization, 31; student demands of 1970s, 112; suspicion of modernism and democratization, 170; terrorist attacks of 2003, 172; women's rights, 169, 233n6; in *Year of the Elephant*, 186
Derb Moulay Cherif, prison, 106, 108, 112, 113, 121, 123, 219, 220, 223n26, 224nn27, 31
developing societies and literature, 13, 27–8, 196, 208n47. See also *under* reading
Djebar, Assia: 'La Pomme coupée en morceaux,' 214n25, 215n26
Djemma-el-Fna, 162, 214n20; in *Marrakech, lumière d'exil*, 136, 138, 162, 163, 214n20; 'The Past and Present of Djemma-el-Fna,' film, 214n20; storytellers, 65, 101, 232n27

Eddif, publishing house, 34
Elaji, Sanaa, 81; *Folle de Youssef*, 216n5
El Bouih, Fatna, 7, 15, 71, 196, 222n14; arrests, 105–6, 112; breaking silence,

107; on memory, 110; memory and memoir in the modern nation, 124; personal history, 111–14; post-prison activities, 113, 223n25; trial and charges, 112–13, 118
– work:
Une Femme nommée Rachid, 34, 59, 114–23; body memories, 121–3; hunger strike, 115–16, 122; journeys, 120; memory, 110, 114, 119, 122; memory and art, 114–23; multiple objectives, 108; time, space, and perspective, 115–19; prison space, 116, 121; style and imagery, 119–21, 132; torture in prison, 106–7; water imagery, 120
El Hadrati, Latifa, on children and reading, 206n36
El Khayat, Ghita, 60, 196, 205n25, 208n47; Aïni Bennaï, editions, 34; on high rate of illiteracy, 29, 35; women and the modernization of Morocco, 171
El Yazami, Abdelali, reading practices in Morocco, 31

feminism: critique of feminism of laws, 135–6; female identity as unfixed, 4; femininity and feminism, 15, 137–8, 227–8n14; feminism and democracy, 13, 17, 169; feminist Muslim scholars, 7, 200n11; Islamic feminisms, 6–7, 200n11; 'maternal feminism,' 236n20; Moroccan women's feminisms, 6–7, 16, 141–4, 233n6; relationship to Western feminism, 13, 138, 211n46
Femmes du Maroc, 36, 104, 205n25, 218n15

'Femmes ... et femmes,' film, 218n15
Fez, 152, 229n6; Ben Jelloun's, 154; colonial space and gendered space, 153, 154–6; Laâbi's, 154; Mernissi's, 154
Foucault, Michel, space and time, 229n1
Friere, Paulo, 29; *Pedagogy of the Oppressed*, 31–2

Genet, Jean, 160, 232n24
Goody, Jack, 29
Guessous, Mohamed, 170
Gutmann, Amy, on democracy and identity, 179

Haddad, Lahcen, 148
Haddawy, Husain, 37; translation of *The Thousand and One Nights*, 209n15
Hadraoui, Touria, 14; *Une Enfance marocaine*, 67; child's awakening to sex, 90–1; similarities with *Dreams*, 67, 70; story making, 69–70; storytelling, 63, 65, 67–70
'Halfaouine,' film, 140, 145, 228n15
hâjs, 106, 121
hammam, 15; circumscribing and signifying the body, 126, 149; defined, 125; 'Halfaouine,' 140, 145, 228n15; illustrative of body politic, 149; new values attributed to by women, 141, 149; Orientalist, 139, 140, 145, 149; painters of, 125–6; as refuge in women's works, 140–1, 145; Segarra on, 140; viewed differently by men and women, 126, 140–1; *Une Femme nommée Rachid*, 120; use of for critique of society, 144; water, 148, 228n22. *See also*

Benchekroun, Siham; Benchemsi, Ahmed R.; Chami-Kettani, Yasmina; Mernissi, Fatima
harem, 15; circumscribing and signifying the body, 126; defined, 125; *Une Femme nommée Rachid*, 121; historically, 127, 128; metaphors of, 132; as multivalent concept, 127–8; Orientalism, 125, 139; painters of, 125, 127; spatial relations, power, and powerlessness, 128, 131, 139; symbolics of, 149; theatre of body politic for women, 149. *See also* Benchekroun, Siham; Benchemsi, Ahmed R.; Boussejra Houria, *under* 'Tamou'; Mernissi, Fatima
Hassan II, King, 15, 21, 22, 24, 71, 107, 109, 110, 112, 113, 173, 220nn6, 7, 221n12; ascension to throne and subsequent actions, 221n13; assassination and coup attempts against him, 71, 109; Perrault on, 222–3n22; reputation, 221n13; secret prisons and torture centre, 109, 173; solidification of power, 222n19
hchouma, 63, 80, 91, 103–4; definition, 80, 215n2, 216n5, 219n22
Huff-Rousselle, Maggie, on Mernissi, 45-6

IER (Instance Equité et Réconciliation), truth commission, 110, 220n4, 222n14
illiteracy, national, 8, 34; change over decades, 204n21; figures for sexes compared, 5, 204n22; in *The Last Chapter*, 187; about national history, 110; oral literature, 62; qualities of mind in oral vs reading cultures, 207n38; rates of, 28; in relation to women's books, 25; in rural areas, 28; sociolinguistic factors, 29
Irwin, Robert: appraisal of feminism in *Nights*, 43; early Arab storytellers, 214n20
Islam: Arab world constitutes small part of, 234n10; communal character, 182; and democratic values, 174, 234n10; feminist interpretations, 129, 215n30, 226n6; Medina as ideal, 188, 238n36; *morchidates* and literacy lessons, 6; opposing views on democracy, 234–5n10; relations between individual and community, 181; spiritual and cultural significance of water, 228n18; subversive rereadings of the Qur'an, 131; women and sex in, 217n10; various views, 217n10

Jamaï, Aboubakr: editor of *Le Journal hebdomadaire*, 173; women's NGOs and democracy, 6, 172
Jamaï, Khalid, 169
Jbabdi, Latifa. *See* Ajbabdi, Latifa
Jemma-el-Fna (Djemma-el-Fna, Jamaa-el-Fna). *See* Djemma-el-Fna.
Journal hebdomadaire, Le, 6, 36, 77, 173

Kalila wa Dimna, 27, 28, 31, 172, 230n15
Khair-Eddine, Mohammed, 21, 22
Khatibi, Abdelkébir, 22–3; immateriality of language chosen by writer, 9; on Scheherazade, 209n8; *Souffles*, 21, 22; on women writers, 36
Kilito, Abdelfettah, 22, 36; on Scheherazade's strategy, 38; on storytelling, 71
Kinnaird, Vivian, 154

Laâbi, Abdellatif, 4, 21, 22, 27; *Chroniques de la citadelle*, 108, 109; colonial Fez in *Au Fond de la jarre*, 154; imprisonment, 108: on literature, 108; *L'Oeil et la nuit*, 22; *Souffles*, 21, 22, 112, 221n10; on women's works, 35; writing and resistance, 4, 182, 194, 237n29

Lahy-Hollebecque, M., 42

Lalami, Laila, 218n14; on *The Almond*, 88, 216n7; speaking women throughout history, 62; women as pawns in both East and West, 3

Lamalif, 233n6

Lambton, Ann K.S., relations between individual and community in Islam, 181

languages in Morocco: dual-language literary environment, 9; issues of cultural and linguistic identity, 8, 29; orality of languages, 33; plurilingualism, 9
- Arabic: Arab conquest, 20; *Fus'ha* (Modern Standard Arabic), 8; official language, 29–30
- Berber languages, 8, 10; original language, 20; spoken by percentage of population, 20, 29
- Classical Arabic, 8, 10, 30
- Darija (Dialectical Moroccan Arabic), 8, 10, 29, 30, 205–6n31; borrowings, 20, 238n39; initiatives to make it written, 205n29; mixture with French in social interaction, 205n31; sometimes considered woman's language, 30, 206n29
- English, 12, 201n27
- French: acceptance by writers today, 8–9; by-product of colonialism, 8, 30; continuing importance, 11, 30, 200n30; in education, 30; enrichment of by non-native writers, 10; francophonie, 12, 201n29; French libraries and cultural centres, 30; future role of, 8, 12–13; importance in trade relations, 12; language that communicates with outside world, 30; number of French citizens living in Morocco, 200n14; percentage of francophone Moroccans, 200n14; use in discussions of sexuality, 219n22. *See also* Moroccan French

Laroui, Fouad, 36

Lebaddy, Hasna: 'Aïcha Bent Ennejar,' 43, 63–4, 213n9

Le Fennec, Editions, 6, 31, 34, 47, 61, 207

Le 8 Mars, 60, 61, 220n4, 233n6

Lejeune, Philippe, 48, 211n33

literacy: criteria for determining, 28; cultural centres, 30; in developing countries, 13, 27–8; and economic development, 29, 204n22, 204–5n23; empowerment through, 29; functional literacy defined, 28; libraries, 26, 30–1, 33; literacy programs and women's participation, 199n5; reading in Morocco, 25–36. *See also* illiteracy, national; Morocco, *under* reading; sociology of literature in Morocco

Lugan, Bernard, 238n39

Lyautey, Louis-Hubert, General: urban planners and architects, 163, 231n18

Lynch, Kevin: 'city as a field of experience,' 151

Maghreb (Magrib): definition, 200n15

Majid, Anouar, 131, 235n10
Majorelle, Jacques, 160, 232n24
Makhzen, 112, 200n17; Ellyas and Stora, and Waterbury on, 222n20
Malti-Douglas, Fedwa: on Arab women writers, 213n11, 215n1; on *Chahrazad n'est pas marocaine*, 43–4; *écriture féminine*, 43, 225n2; on the female body, 140; on feminism, 43, 141; on qualities of Scheherazade, 37, 43, 209n8; on woman's voice and body in Arabo-Islamic discourse, 126, 225n2
marocaineté: definition of, 4; in literature, 21; in terms of Moroccan French, 9
Maroub, Fadoua, 31
Marrakech, 152, 229n6: as palimpsest, 153, 161–3
Marzouki, Ahmed: *Tazmamart: Cellule 10*, 35, 108, 109
Massey, Doreen, 168, 228n1
Matisse, Henri, 160, 232n24
Mattson, Ingrid, 129
May, Georges, 38, 208n6
McDowell, Linda, 154, 162, 233n31
Mdarhri Alaoui, Abdallah, 4, 16, 154; assessment of women's works, 35; factors leading to emergence of women's writing, 24; long history of speaking women, 62; women's texts compared to men's, 20; women's texts in French compared with those in Arabic, 8, 19, 200n12
Mdidech, Jaouad: imprisonment, 220n6; *La Chambre noire*, 108
Mehrez, Samia: on decolonization, 152
Memmi, Albert: colonization and decolonization in Arab-Muslim society, 238n38

Menebhi, Saïda, 15, 108, 116, 124; *Poèmes, écrits, lettres de prison*, 34, 109, 201–2n1
mères célibataires, 5
Mernissi, Fatima, 7, 15, 16, 19, 26, 36, 61, 153, 196; bird symbolic of female flight to freedom, 236n22; critique of Western feminism, 45, 49, 210n27, 211n45; cross-cultural communication, 45, 50; education, 23; feminist subversiveness, 39, 40, 57; harem as lynchpin of her thinking, 127–8; imperial harems, 225n1; language usage, 10–11; relations between reader and writer, 39, 47, 52, 55, 56, 57; rhetorical devices, 54–5, 212n46; and Scheherazade, 7, 32, 39–40, 42, 44, 45, 46, 57, 177; on sexual desire, 86; theme of freedom, 156, 225n34, 237n26. *See also* hammam; harem
– works:
  Aït-Débrouille, Les, 11
  Chahrazad n'est pas marocaine, 43–4, 55, 210n24, 212n46
  Dreams of Trespass, 7, 11, 14, 46–57, 127, 131, 138, 154, 231n18; colonialism as revealing harem-like relations, 128, 155; domestic and invisible harems, 127, 156; game theory, 53; hammam scene, 140, 144; hybridity, 14, 58; narrative pleasure, 56–7; poetics of trespass, 14, 48; storytelling in, 64, 65–6; subversiveness, 40, 46–54, 56–7
  Etes-vous vacciné contre le harem? 10, 56, 127, 131, 170–1, 212n46, 234n7
  'Fantaisies du harem et nouvelles Schéhérazade,' art show, 44, 127

Le Harem européen, 131
Islam and Democracy, 168, 172, 203n12, 234n10, 236n22
Le Maroc raconté par ses femmes, 49
Scheherazade Goes West, 44, 45, 54, 56, 127, 131, 169, 210n27, 234n7; 'The Tale of the Lady with the Feather Dress,' 64, 236n22
Les Sultanes oubliées, 60, 212n46, 213n6
The Veil and the Male Elite (*Le Harem politique*), 54, 56, 126–32, 212n46, 227n8
'Who's Cleverer, Man or Woman?' 202n5, 213n15
Miller, Henry: *Tropic of Cancer*, 161
Miller, Nancy K., 49
Mohammed V, King, 21, 49, 71, 221n13; return from exile, 166
Mohammed VI, King, 6, 21, 110, 220n7
Momsen, Janet H., 154
Morand, Paul, 160, 232n24
morchidates, 6
Moroccan French, 9–10; *marocanismes*, 200n17
Morocco:
- architecture, traditional and urban, 153
- freedom of press and speech, 78–9, 172
- geography, 20, 238n39
- history: attempted coups and repressions, 21–2, 107, 222n21; colonialism, 8, 23, 124, 189, 203n11, 238n38; early history, 238n39; freedom of press and speech, 78–9, 172; geography, 20, 238n39; IER, truth commission, 110, 220n4; Marxism-Leninism, 60, 81, 108, 112, 173, 220n6; mass political trials, 22, 107, 112; modernity and tradition, 169, 171, 187, 189; the plots of 1971 and 1972 against regime, 109, 112; poverty, 5; strikes and protests, 22, 111–12, 222n18, 233n6; terrorist attacks of 2003, 172; unemployment, 5, 27, 204n19, 230n11; 'years of lead,' 15, 23, 107, 108, 124, 194, 220n4, 221n13 (*see also* Ben Barka, Mehdi; Hassan II, King; Mohammed V, King; Mohammed VI, King)
- languages (*see* languages in Morocco)
- literary history, 20–5; women's history of writing, 24–5
- population, 5; Moroccan community in France, 200n14; native French in Morocco, 200n14, 205n30; urban, 152, 229n6
- press: freedom of expression, 172, 173–4; censorship, and self-censorship, 173; hot-button subjects, 173
- reading: absence of reading culture, 13, 28, 31, 36; books reviewed in media, 36; challenges faced by women's texts, 25; children and their literature, 206n36; and citizenship, 29, 32; and educational system, 13, 26, 31; as empowering, 29, 205n28; factors contributing to absence of culture of reading, 18–19, 26–8, 31, 204n20; government initiatives, 32–3; *ijtihad*, 32; preferred reading of young girls, 206–7n36; as promoted in Islam, 32; qualities of mind developed through reading, 31, 207n38; relationship of school libraries and democratization, 31;

status of fiction reading in West, 25, 204n18; status of novel-reading in Morocco, 25, 27; validation of reader in women's texts, 32 (*see also* illiteracy; literacy)
- women: colonialism and its effects, 23; decolonization of the city, 149; divorce, 5, 170; employment and unemployment, 5–6, 168, 230n11; history of women's activism, 60–1, 169; in law, 207n40; literacy and illiteracy, 5, 204n22; membership in parliament, 6; *mères célibataires*, 5; *morchidates*, 6; nationalists' attitude toward women at Independence, 170; NGOs, 28, 172, 174, 233n6; passing of citizenship to a child, 5; *petites bonnes*, 5; polygamy, 170; postcolonial identity, 188; primary wage earners, 6, 230–1n11; in prison population, 222n15, 224n30; relationship to modernization of nation, 5, 171; repudiation, 5, 156–9; resistance fighters, 60, 194–5, 230n18; right to vote, 6; spatial networks in rural areas, 229n3; traditional marginalization, 5; violence against, 80, 91, 103, 113, 172, 173, 218nn15, 16; vis-à-vis national history, 124; women's speech, 78–9 (*see also* Moudawana)

Mortimer, Mildred, 189
Moudawana, 5, 61, 169, 170, 225n35; loopholes in 2004 revision, 233n2
Moudden, Abdelhay, 33
Mouride, Abdellaziz, 223n26; *On affame bien les rats*, 108, 109, 116, 124, 223n26

Naamane-Guessous, Soumaya, 104, 141, 217n11, 218n13; on hammam, 144, 228n22; Islam's view of sexuality, 217nn10, 11
Nedjma (pseud.), 7, 14, 81, 153, 177, 196; and *hchouma*, 63, 103; identification of author, 216n6; interview with Riding, 77
- work: *The Almond*, 63, 82–90; eroticism and pornography, 217n8; interpretations, 88–90; issues of feminism, 89; narrative techniques, 83–6; pornography, considerations of, 76, 81, 82, 85, 88, 89, 90, 217n8; reception, 77, 85, 88, 216n7; relationship between Tangier and woman, 159; sex and religion, 86–8; violating speech codes, 76–8

Nefzaoui, Cheikh, 83
NGOs, women's, 174, 199n9, 233–4n6; literacy programs, 61; sign of hope for democracy, 16, 172
Nissaboury, Mostafa, 21
Norris, Ronald and Pippa: views on sex and democracy in Islam and West, 174

Opening the Gates, 3, 19, 24, 202n5, 203n12
L'Opinion, 6, 104
Orientalism, 125–6, 139; challenges to, 126, 144–8; de-Orientalization, 149, 168; Orientalist stereotypes, 140
Oufkir, Malika, 113; *L'Etrangère*, 221n11; *La Prisonnière (Stolen Lives)*, 35, 63, 109; as a storyteller like Scheherazade, 71–2
Oufkir, Mohamed, General, 22, 35, 71, 109; death of, 222n21
Oulehri, Touria, 16, 177; Agadir, 153, 156–9, 167, 229n6; *La Chambre des nuits blanches*, 32, 231n21; earthquake,

157–8; Fez and Casablanca, 156; *La Répudiée*, 16, 153, 156–9
Oumassine, Damia: rape in *L'Arganier des femmes égarées*, 92
Ousra, 104, 218n15

Perrault, Gilles: criticism of France's role, 113, 222n19; Hassan II, 113, 221n13, 222n22; *Notre ami le roi*, 113
petites bonnes, 5
postpositive theory, 16, 186; defining the self and society, 175; and identity, 176
prison literature, 15, 122, 194; lack of contextualization, 224n28; of Morocco, 108–14; space, 116; time, 115. See also Ajbabdi, Latifa; Ben Jelloun, Tahar; Bennouna, Mehdi; Bennouna, Rabea; Bourequat, Ali-Auguste; Daure-Serfaty, Christine; El Bouih Fatna; Laâbi, Abdellatif; Marzouki, Ahmed; Mdidech, Jaouad; Menebhi, Saïda; Mouride, Abdellaziz; Oufkir, Malika; Raiss, Mohammed; Serfaty, Abraham; Serhane, Abdelhak
Prologues, literary review, 36
Proust, 148; on reader, 39, 57, 209n11
publishing in Morocco: children's literature, 206n36; comparison with France, 208n47; crisis in, 31, 33–4; criteria of selection, 203nn15, 16; difficulties of, 34–5; number of books published annually, 207n44; publishing houses, 6, 33, 34, 207n44; translation, 33; typical press-run, 35

Rabat, 12, 26, 27, 152, 173, 204n19, 225n35, 229n6; in Abouzeid, 166, 188, 189, 190; cultural centres, 206n32; in El Bouih, 105, 113

Raiss, Mohammed: *De Skhirat à Tazmamart*, 108, 109
Ramadan, Tarik, 235n10
Redonnet, Marie, 34, 35, 203n16
Renan, Ernest: collective memory and forgetting, 110
Rêves de femmes. See under Mernissi, Fatima, *Dreams of Trespass*
Rhissassi, Fouzia, 103
Riding, Alan: interview with Nedjma, 77, 82, 216nn6, 7
Roche, Anne, 9, 10
Rouse, Carolyn Moxley, 129
ruse, use of in literature: in folklore, 54; in Mernissi, 40, 53, 54; in 'Ruses de femmes,' 54, 63–5; in Scheherazade, 53–4
'Ruses de femmes' (Women's Wiles), film. See under Benlyazid, Farida

Safi-Eddine, K., cultural definition of ideal Arab identity, 167
Said, Edward: 'silence of the native,' 79; social role of literature, 192, 239n46
Sallis, Eva, 38, 41, 42, 208n3, 209n15, 216n16
Scheherazade, 7, 14, 16, 17, 167, 193; feminism of, 42; function of her stories, 209n8; ideological readings of character, 41; narrative cure, 39, 209n8; narrative strategies, 40; political hero and liberator, 177; qualities of mind, 32, 37, 208n3; reading metaphors, 37–8; the ruse, 53–4; subversion, 39, 56; trapped woman and resistance, 57
Scholes, Robert, 39
Sebti, Fadela: *Moi, Mireille lorsque j'étais Yasmina*, 32; women in law, 207n40

Sedjari, Ali, on illiteracy and economic development, 29
Segarra, Marta: 'le regard subi,' 145; women's view of hammam, 140
Serfaty, Abraham, 109, 112, 113, 173, 203n11, 220n7; on democracy, 235n15; imprisonment, 220n7
Serfaty, Christine Daure-. *See* Daure-Serfaty, Christine
Serhane, Abdelhak, 22, 23, 108; *Kabazal*, 109; *Pommes de grossesse*, 206n36, 214n5
siba, resistance, 181, 186
silent woman, myth, 4, 17, 25, 58, 60, 61–2; challenging the myth, 14, 15, 63, 78, 79, 103, 107, 124; history of women's speech, 60, 62, 78; pernicious myth, 79; *le silence féminin*, 59; women challenge myth, 15, 79, 103
Slyomovics, Susan, interview with El Bouih, 113
Smarr, Janet Levarie, on urban space, 151
sociology of literature in Morocco, 12–13, 25–36; bookselling, 18; cultural centres, 30; 'cultural geography' of literary production and consumption, 18–19; in developing society, 13, 27–8, 196, 208n47; libraries 9, 12, 28, 30, 31–2 (school), 33 (city). *See also* languages in Morocco; literacy; publishing in Morocco
Souffles, 221n10; founding of, 21; principles, 22
space, as used in literature: colonial space, 153, 155, 156; decolonization of spaces, 149; emotional correspondence between gender and geography, 167; exploring women's role in the body politic, 149; identity and metaphors of itinerancy, 154; mediator of women's consciousness, 16; poetic trope of journey, 16, 120–1, 154, 164, 165, 167, 180, 191; public and private, 151; rewriting where women 'belong,' 150–1; similarities between colonial and gendered space, 153; studied by social scientists and humanists, 150, 228n1; symbolics of harem, 149; women's writing contests reconstruct boundaries through space, 151. *See also* cities; hammam; harem
'Still Ready: Three Women from the Moroccan Resistance,' film, 60, 194, 230n18
storytelling: Djemma-el-Fna storytellers, 65, 101, 232n27; early Arab storytellers, 214n20; functions and empowerment through, 65–6; Moroccan women's, 62–3; reform through, 38, 40; tradition of oral literature, 62; women's storytellers, 65–70

Tangier, 12, 67, 152, 229n6, 232n24; in *The Almond*, 82, 83, 89, 152, 159–61, 164; Book Fair, 194; Daure-Serfaty, 203n11; in *The Last Chapter*, 189; name, 231n22
Tazmamart, prison, 108, 109, 112, 113, 220n7
Tel Quel, news weekly, 36, 173, 174, 218n15, 222nn14, 15, 225n4, 227n11
Thousand and One Nights, The (*Les Mille et une nuits*), 37, 38, 39, 44, 46–8, 236n22; apple symbolism, 214n25; appraisals, 209n8; El Bouih, 105, 132; 'Le Conte des trois pommes,' 215n26; enduring

relevance, 71; feminism, 42–3; film, 214n20; Galland's translation, 208n6, 209n15; Haddawy, 208n1; Irwin, 214n20; Lebaddy, 64; Mernissi, 50, 51, 52, 65, 236n22; murder of a woman, 75, 214n25, 215n26; Nafisi's use of trapped woman theme, 212n47; Oulehri, 158; source for women storytellers, 65

Trabelsi, Bahaa, 81, 177; on Casablanca, 163; and *hchouma*, 104; sexuality in *Une Femme tout simplement* and *Une Vie à trois*, 91

transgression: challenge to myth of silent woman, 15; concentration on flesh, gender, sex, 14; narrative transgressions in Benchemsi and Chafik, 94–102; role and function of, 82, 102–4; social, sexual, and moral transgression in Nedjma, 82–90; transgressive writing, 80, 81, 82; violent sexual transgressions in women's writing, 91–3

Tunisia, 9, 49, 136, 200n15; Bouhida, 217n10; Prix Didon, 35; Tunisian women writers, 24, 202n1; typical press-run, 207n46

UN Conference on Women, Beijing, 24
UNEM (Union Nationale des Etudiants Marocains), 106, 112

Van Dongen, Kees, 160, 232n24
Vermeren, Pierre: on Casablanca strikes, 222n18; on Hassan II, 221n13; on Makhzen, 112
violence, 14; against women, 80, 91, 103, 113, 173, 218nn15, 16; *L'Amande*, 81, 84, 144, 216n7; *Une Enfance marocaine* and family

violence, 70; and eroticism, 80, 81, 82; function in women's writing, 91–2; *The Last Chapter*, 190; Memmi on violence, 238n38; in Moroccan society, 172, 218n16; *Ni Fleurs, ni couronnes*, 93; *Oser vivre*, 179; 'poetics of violence,' 93, 94–102, 219n20; *The Thousand and One Nights*, 38, 57; UN definition of violence against women, 218n16; in women's writing, 91–2

Wadud, Amina, 129; woman's equality in Islam, 226n6; women's speech and Qur'an, 215n30
Wagner, Daniel A., 29
Ward, Nicole Jouve, 151
Ward, Ruth V., 47, 210–11n32
Waterbury, John, 233n6; Casablanca as bellwether of national political climate, 222n18; on Makhzan, 222n20; view of Hassan II, 221n13; on women's influence, 213n8
Williams, Tennessee, 160, 232n24
women's speech: censorship and self-censorship, 78–9; in fairy tale, 64; long tradition, 62, 78; political protest, 60; power of, 104, 110, 160; Wadud on women's speech in Qur'an, 78, 215n30; in 'Women's Wiles,' 63–5

Yacine, Kateb: *Nedjma*, 111
Yacoubi, Rachida, 27–8
Yassine, Nadia, 7, 173
'years of lead.' *See under* Morocco, history
'Yeux secs, Les,' film, 218n15
Yomad, Editions, 34, 206n36

Zeidan, Joseph T., 225n2